P9-DXL-270

CALGARY PUBLIC LIBRARY
APRIL 2014

What is English?

for my mother
Rita Machan Elliott

WHAT IS ENGLISH?

AND WHY SHOULD WE CARE?

TIM WILLIAM MACHAN

OXFORD

UNIVERSITY PRESS

OXFORD

UNIVERSITY PRESS

Great Clarendon Street, Oxford, OX2 6DP,
United Kingdom

Oxford University Press is a department of the University of Oxford.
It furthers the University's objective of excellence in research, scholarship,
and education by publishing worldwide. Oxford is a registered trade mark of
Oxford University Press in the UK and in certain other countries

© Tim William Machan 2013

The moral rights of the author have been asserted

First Edition published in 2013
Impression: 1

All rights reserved. No part of this publication may be reproduced, stored in
a retrieval system, or transmitted, in any form or by any means, without the
prior permission in writing of Oxford University Press, or as expressly permitted
by law, by licence, or under terms agreed with the appropriate reprographics
rights organization. Enquiries concerning reproduction outside the scope of the
above should be sent to the Rights Department, Oxford University Press, at the
address above

You must not circulate this work in any other form
and you must impose this same condition on any acquirer

British Library Cataloguing in Publication Data

Data available

ISBN 978–0–19–960125–7

Printed in Great Britain by
CPI Group (UK) Ltd, Croydon, CR0 4YY

Contents

Acknowledgments

Working on this book, I have had the good fortune to benefit from the assistance of friends, colleagues, and students. I begin with John Davey, my editor, who once more envisioned a better book than the one I originally imagined and who helped me write that book. And I thank the anonymous readers at OUP, and also Julie Coleman, Anne Curzan, Timothy McMahon, and Jeremy Smith for reading all or part of the manuscript in draft. This is a much-improved book for their efforts. Milton Bates, Ardis Butterfield, Camilia Cenek, Helen Cooper, Siân Echard, Irene Guenther, Simon Horobin, Michael Keller, James Martin, David Matthews, Alastair Minnis, Krista Ratcliffe, Herbert Schendel, Sarah Wadsworth, Larry Watson, and Nicholas Watson provided various kinds of assistance and encouragement. And my students in a graduate seminar in the fall of 2010 offered stimulating discussions on much of what appears here. No one but I, however, am responsible for any errors of fact or judgment, including all foreign-language translations, which, unless otherwise stated, are my own.

I thank the Marquette Committee on Research for a Summer Faculty Fellowship in 2009 and for a later travel grant that allowed me to consult archival materials at the Cumberland County Historical Society (where the records of the Carlisle Indian Industrial School are kept), the United States Army Heritage and Education Center, and the Benson Ford Research Center. I'm grateful to the librarians and staffs at all these institutions, and also at Marquette University, for their assistance.

And I thank once more my family—most immediately Christine, Charlie, and Tim, for indulging my passion for languages, ancient, medieval, and modern. For a long time I have been working with words, and my family has had no choice but to work along with me; that they have done so willingly and happily has made all the difference. And also, more distantly, I thank my immigrant Bohemian and Polish grandparents.

Writing this book gave me a sense of what linguistic life must have been like for them in the early days of the twentieth century, and so of what linguistic life must be like for all those who come newly to English. As glad as I am to read Greek, Latin, and Icelandic, I'm gladder still that my grandparents took the trouble to learn English, so that I could speak it, too.

T. W. M.

PART ONE

The Consequences of Definition

CHAPTER ONE

The River of English

The questions considered in this book, put simply, are: What is English? How do we know? And why should we care? These are partly historical questions, addressing the language's past and future as well as its present; questions whose answers might begin with something as simple as 'English is what I speak', as complex as 'English is a sociological argument that appropriates structural data', or as evasive as 'English is what the grammars and dictionaries say it is'. And they are questions that have become increasingly difficult to answer at the beginning of the twenty-first century, when speakers of English—both those who learned the language from birth and those who acquired it later—together account for perhaps one and one-half billion of the Earth's nearly 7 billion people.

Both the *what* and the *why* of the title run through the following chapters, but for the moment I want to lay aside the *what* in order to concentrate on the *why*, since in doing so I also address the reason for this book's existence. A good place to begin is the ways in which English, and a definition of English, plays a gate-keeping role in some of the most powerful domains in any Anglophone society. Access to employment, eligibility to participate in lucrative international markets, citizenship, social status—these are all affected by knowledge of some agreed-upon version of the language. For a great many English-dominant universities (such as Monash in Australia) regulations stipulate that foreign nationals must demonstrate competence in English to gain admission, and even schools in English-dominant areas (such as the prestigious English boarding school Harrow) explicitly use the language in this gate-keeping fashion. Harrow's web page advises only the overseas applicants, "We cannot accept pupils whose English is not good enough."[1]

Once enrolled in any Anglophone school, students encounter English both as the means for education and as a subject itself. In places where English is expanding as a first and second language, universities like the National University of Singapore specify English as the language of instruction, while most universities in English-dominant areas and even in some non-Anglophonic countries (such as Sweden and the Netherlands) simply, though not always easily, take this as a given. At the University of Washington, an increase of Chinese students paying non-resident tuition has supplemented the university's operating funds but also has created challenges in the classroom that hinge on the definition of English. According to the director of writing in the College of Arts and Sciences, "We recognize that people from other countries often speak with an accent. If we're truly going to be a global university...we have to recognize that they may write with an accent as well."[2] The need for schools and universities to confirm students' English proficiency, increasingly in the form of standardized tests and assessment, dominates curricula, just as the students themselves face the need to score high marks in order to advance through education and into well-paying careers. Partly to meet such requirements, programs for teaching English as a Second Language (ESL) to non-native speakers have proliferated. By preparing speakers for jobs as well as university instruction, the industry of instruction in second-language acquisition uses a definition of English not only to open financial opportunities for its students but also to generate a significant financial return for itself.

Outside the business of second-language acquisition, senses of English may be less rigorous but still financially and professionally consequential. Perhaps improbably, the notion that there's money to be made in the meaning of English in fact has a long history predating modern ESL programs. When Dr Johnson produced his massive and ground-breaking two-volume *Dictionary of the English Language* in 1755, he did so via the common eighteenth-century process of subscription, which may not have made him wealthy, but did make the book possible, and the book in turn eventually led to his getting a pension from King George III. Joseph Priestley's 1761 *Rudiments of*

English Grammar, which appeared in nine issues before 1800, was widely used by subsequent grammarians and at least in part led to a job offer at the Warrington Academy in Cheshire. More remunerative still was Bishop Robert Lowth's 1762 *Short Introduction to English Grammar*. This went through 45 editions by the end of the century, making money for someone if not necessarily Lowth himself, who died in 1787. Lindley Murray's 1795 *English Grammar* may be among the most lucrative grammars of all (though again not for the author, who died in 1826): in the nineteenth century, the book's three versions were issued over 300 times.[3]

Potential financial gain may in fact, as much as anything else, account for the proliferation of grammatical materials in the eighteenth and nineteenth (as well as the twentieth and twenty-first) centuries.[4] Beyond all manner of frequently reprinted academic books (such as John Earle's *The Philology of the English Tongue* or William McGuffey's various *Eclectic Readers*) the nineteenth century witnessed publications like *Poor Letter H*, which promised users the accent modification (in this case elimination of 'dropped h') that would lead to personal and professional success. It's the same promise made today by print and online programs like *Lose Your Accent in 28 Days*, *American English Pronunciation: It's No Good Unless You're Understood*, and *English Grammar for Dummies*. To attract paying customers, such programs target stigmatized regional varieties like 'New Yawkese' and speakers whose first language is not English. With red ink, scattered upper-case graphs, and a bold font, one web program claims, "We *GUARANTEE* that people will begin COMPLIMENTING you in only 7 days, or we will REFUND your $9.95 during the first week! Try it NOW! You've got ABSOLUTELY NOTHING to LOSE but your Accent!"[5] Since speakers' enrollment indicates that they already believe their success is tied to language, and not to any other personal characteristics they might have or to the prejudices of those doing the hiring, those whose lives do not improve after the course may attribute their failure to not having worked hard enough. And so the programs' definitions of English generate revenue from new participants as well from those whose failures make them try harder.

It may be that speakers respond only to a perception of English or an accent (the *what* of my title), but the consequences of their response (the *why*) are no less for this. A 2006 survey of 9,000 individuals from nine different countries thus found that American customers "balk more at customer service agents with hard-to-understand accents than with those who don't understand the problem they are calling about." "Even if the level of customer service is exceptional," the survey showed, "the extent to which poorly-understood accents trump quality of service speaks to English-speaking customers' growing intolerance of non-native speech, more so than in other countries." With "86% of respondents . . . likely or very likely [to] move to a competitor following a poor experience," companies and their clients have a great deal invested in the definition of English. Or, as another study assesses the role of English from within an American business model, "English language skills have been put on equal standing with formal schooling and on-the-job-training, and viewed as a form of human capital that has been acquired at current cost in the expectation of future returns."[6]

The assessment is well justified. As the language of international business and some of the largest multinational companies, English has been called "the language of capitalism . . . either the modernizing panacea or the ruthless oppressor, depending on your place in the world."[7] While recognition of English's impact may be uniform, it's clear that what matters (and varies) is not simply English in general but a specific definition of the language, with some kinds of English in effect being more English than others. In 2000, Singapore's Prime Minister, Goh Chok Tung, thus said, "If we speak a corrupted form of English that is not understood by others, we will lose a key competitive advantage. My concern is that if we continue to speak Singlish, it will over time become Singapore's common language."[8] One study suggests that "where an alien from Mexico can read and speak English, earnings are nine percent higher than for those who possess only one or neither of these language skills," and another that speakers "with poor fluency face a 25.5% wage penalty."[9] Mexican Americans or immigrants who speak English with an accent readily identifiable as Mexican, that is, earn less than Mexican Americans who cannot be so identified. They also earn less than individuals who speak with the regionally characteristic accents of earlier generations of immigrants, such as German or Italian. Speakers with characteristically French accents, in turn, enjoy better hiring rates in the United States than do those with characteristically Japanese accents.[10]

English, then, is often understood to be something that second-language speakers do or do not approximate, depending on non-linguistic issues of ethnicity and with significant economic results. In 2008, the United States Ladies Professional Golf Association went so far as to issue a directive that, by the following year, all of its members (many of whom speak Korean or Japanese as their first language) had to be conversant in English or run the risk of suspension from the golf tour. The rationale for the directive may have been arguable, but it at least was easily stated: given the tour's dependence on corporate sponsorship, the ability to speak English is a crucial marketing tool. In the words of Libba Galloway, the Association's deputy commissioner, "The suspension demonstrates the importance we are placing on effective communication in English, something that is vital to the success of our business and to the success of our membership."[11] By targeting Asians who already spoke English with non-native accents and grammars, the directive presumed a specifically American definition of the language. Golfers could not get by speaking just any variety of English with any accent; they had to speak a particular kind of English.

National identity depends just as significantly on definitions of English. The official requirements for United States citizenship specify, for example, that applicants "must be able to read, write, speak, and understand words in ordinary usage in the English language."[12] At present, hundreds of communities have enacted laws requiring English for advertisements, business transactions, social services, and so forth, while 31 individual states legally identify English as their official language. One of these states (Arizona) has a provision in its state constitution that "the ability to read, write, speak, and understand the English language sufficiently well to conduct the duties of the office without the aid of an interpreter, shall be a necessary qualification for all state officers and members of the state legislature."[13] Law courts have heard cases about employers' rights to require English in the workplace, and legislatures have made laws that mandate the circumstances under which Anglophone translators or non-English voting materials must be used, as well as (by implication) those for which English alone is necessary.

Underlying these legal (and economic) consequences, are the cultural ramifications of English, however it's defined. To speak a variety judged as Standard English, as opposed to one judged as non-standard or as an interlanguage (such as an intermediate language that occurs when a new language is partially learned) is to gain access both to the language's historical literary patrimony and to its current status as the world's first truly global language. This is the variety that allows one to say one shares a language with the Bill of Rights, Shakespeare's plays, and the King James Bible, however unintelligible these writings might be today to some English-speakers. English serves as the password to a kind of cross-cultural, transhistorical club that one might or might not want to join, and it's precisely this reason that can generate controversy for the language and its speakers. Agitation on behalf of official language laws, for example, arises in part from convictions over what a city or nation is or should be, and requiring English is a way to enforce views about society or ethnicity through language. Outside English-dominant areas, the language's cultural ramifications can be just as volatile. In Rwanda, government efforts to foster broadly national identity have done much to unify indigenous ethnic groups. But one current way for Rwandans to distinguish between the Hutu and Tutsi groups is to refer to the former as "French speakers" and the latter as "English speakers," based on the fact that many of the latter fled to Uganda after the 1994 genocide.[14] English, then, is something that evokes the horrors of the past and encodes the tensions of the present. More broadly, among the harshest critics of the modern expansion of English at the expense of indigenous languages, knowledge of the language can reflect complicity in an insidious plan to repress local populations and establish Anglo-American ideology around the world. In Robert Phillipson's view, English is "a kind of linguistic cuckoo, taking over where other breeds of language have historically nested and acquired territorial rights, and obliging non-native speakers of English to acquire the behavioural habits and linguistic forms of English."[15]

DEFINING ENGLISH: PRAGMATICS AND GRAMMAR

In circumstances like these, the definition of English (the *what*) falls within the realm of what's called pragmatics, or, roughly stated, language in action. From this perspective, whether in business or government, speakers produce a definition through actions that depend on that definition. So the hiring (or not) of job candidates on the basis of their command of English, the pronouncement of English as an official language, and the assertion that English is replacing the world's languages all necessarily imply some sense of the language's definition. Only rarely do such pragmatic approaches define what they mean by English, and they don't do so particularly well. One accent-reduction book states that it will teach "the standard American accent. Some people also call it 'broadcaster English'. It's the kind of standard, neutral speech that you hear on CNN and in educated circles."[16] But there's nothing here about particular linguistic structures, and "neutral," of course, is a loaded term that points to the pipe dream of an accentless variety. The American 'no child left behind' law of 2001 does little better with its definition of Limited English Proficiency, or the threshold for entering mainstream classrooms. Here again the definition is formed not structurally but as a function of age, place of birth, native language, and other unspecified difficulties that prevent students from achieving in the classroom or participating fully in society. The state of South Carolina defines students with limited proficiency more narrowly and less precisely as "students for whom English is a second language."[17] We might disregard the conceptual problems with these educational definitions, which could mark a fluent bilingual as limited and a native illiterate 16-year-old as proficient, but we are still left with explanations that are mostly pragmatic in the way they focus on where or how English is used. And even these definitions are rarities. More typical, especially in legislation, is a simple statement like the following, which appears in a proposed English Language Unity Act of 2009: "The official language of the United States is English."[18] Such legislation may go on to detail how this proposition affects education, naturalization, and the posting of laws, but no bills that I've seen define just what they mean by 'English'. Which pronunciations? Which words? Which syntax? Which varieties? How good enough (to return to Harrow) is good enough English?

These kinds of questions might better be described as grammatical—as having to do especially with the formal codification of language in dictionaries and grammar books. Codification, or the prescription of correct usage, may be the most popular sense of just what 'grammar' means, and, by extension, of what English is. Indeed, in leaving unstated just how they understand English to be defined, many of the pragmatic senses that I've considered seem to appeal tacitly to grammar in this sense. When the Language Unity Act states that English will be an official language, it's likely that it intends not Singlish, or African American Vernacular English, or even 'New Yawkese', but whatever structures that can be located in works of codification and that appear in so-called mainstream domains, including schoolrooms. Another sense of grammar should also be mentioned, however. And this is a descriptive sense used particularly by linguists. It seeks only to characterize what typical speakers of the language typically do with it, whether the characterization is a traditional account such as the one found in Randolph Quirk's *Comprehensive Grammar*, a generative account such as that in Noam Chomsky's landmark *Aspects of the Theory of Syntax*, or the recent analyses of individual varieties of global English, such as *The Handbook of World Englishes*.

Yet if all these conceptions of English seem categorically different from pragmatic senses—fixed descriptions as opposed to variable interpretations—it's important to recall three things. Firstly, any speaker always draws on both kinds of definition. Teachers of English or contestants on a quiz show might invoke the grammatical senses, but when even they meet people on the street or in a restaurant, it's the pragmatic senses that matter most. If we are fluent in English, we don't carry on conversations by consulting grammar books and asking ourselves whether what is said qualifies as English, but by the simple criterion of whether we can—and perhaps want to— understand the person with whom we're speaking. Secondly, creating, citing, or presuming grammatical definitions are themselves examples of language in use, or pragmatics. Language is not defined in the abstract, that is, but in particular circumstances by particular speakers, whether they be Dr Johnson, Noam Chomsky, or the author of *Lose Your Accent in 28 Days*. And thirdly, to accommodate the historical change and contemporary variation of English, any work of codification has to operate at a fairly abstract level. This means such a work must bracket off from discussion a good deal of what might be called the structural laxity that speakers tolerate in order to communicate and see themselves as part of a broad Anglophone community. In fact, much (maybe most) of what is simply called English—by pragmatic or grammatical criteria—is incomprehensible to many speakers who otherwise regard themselves as Anglophones.

Such difficulty in comprehension is particularly apparent when we look at the earliest stages of the language. If we open the tenth-century Old English epic *Beowulf*, we read (or maybe just see):

> Hwæt! We Gardena   in geardagum,
> þeodcyninga,   þrym gefrunon,
> hu ða æþelingas   ellen fremedon.[19]

But even though written much closer to the present—postdating major linguistic changes in syntax and vocabulary—the language of Milton's *Paradise Lost* can be just as impenetrable, as in the following passage, where Satan gazes on Eve in her unfallen condition. Having taught this poem many times, I know that modern readers are sometimes baffled how the "goodness" evident in Eve's appearance and character should seem unpleasant and terrible ("awful") to a character as committed to evil as the devil:

...Abasht the Devil stood,
And felt how awful goodness is, and saw
Virtue in her shape how lovely; saw, and pin'd
His loss...[20]

Even English uttered within the past century can prove obscure, as in the classic 1946 holiday film *It's a Wonderful Life*. There, Nick the bartender enigmatically tells a transformed George Bailey, experiencing life as it would have been if he'd never been born, "I don't know you from Adam's off ox." This is the case as well in James Kelman's novel *How Late It Was, How Late*, published in 1994, in which a fairly typical passage of narration reads, "And there were shoppers roundabout; women and weans, a couple of prams with wee yins, all big-eyed staring at him; then a sodjer was here and trying not to but it looked like it was too much of an effort and he couldnay stop himself, he stuck the boot right in, into Sammy's belly, then another."[21] And if, for the time being, we include Hawaiian Pidgin English as a variety of English, we encounter language still more detached from whatever the drafters of the Language Unity Act had in mind and from whatever many Anglophones find normal or intelligible: "You speak you want one good Japanese man for make cook."[22]

Examples like these could of course be multiplied many times over, but all to the same effect. And the fact that we can construct convincing, empirical explanations for such obscurities does little to diminish just how much linguistic variation and change any definition of English must accommodate or disregard. Knowing that Milton evokes the literal sense of 'awful' ('full of awe', and so 'awe-inspiring') underscores the painful irony of Satan's contemplation of Eve: he is at once fully aware of her noble virtue and miserably unable to accept "goodness" as anything positive. And if we had the knowledge of a 1940s audience, which was more familiar with rural life than we are, we'd know that the 'off ox' was the animal on the right in a team of two. The driver walked beside the left-hand one, and as a result could become far more familiar with that one than with the off ox. When this ox was Adam's, himself already a measure of the unknown ("I don't know you from Adam"), a kind of double distancing took effect.[23]

But understanding the flux of linguistic change and variation goes only a very small way towards creating unity for such structurally diverse examples. If we are going to refer to them all by one name—English—lots of questions remain. Why and how, we might ask, have 1,500 years of recorded linguistic variation been designated 'English'? If the poet of *Beowulf* could meaningfully say "Hwæt! We Gardena in geardagum"; if Milton could use 'awful' as he did and if the script writer of *It's a Wonderful Life* could presume an audience that would know what an 'off ox' was, and if not only contemporary Anglophones can fail to understand them all but also these writers themselves would likely have failed to understand one another, how is it that we call what all of us have spoken and written by the same name? How can we use a single label for the language, even though some changes can affect only some varieties, much as the Celtic languages initially affected the English used today in Ireland and Wales?[24] Inasmuch as what we call English does not evolve everywhere (or for all people in a given area) in the same way or at the same rate, on what basis, material or theoretical, can we say that they all speak the same language? For what reasons do we believe that English describes both what I speak and what Kelman writes? Or Milton and the *Beowulf* poet but, perhaps, not speakers of Tok Pisin, Mobilian Jargon, or Afrikaans? Would it matter whether Hawaiian Pidgin English were categorized as a regional variety of English or as a distinct linguistic code? For that matter, for what reasons is English *not* categorized as a regional variety of German or Norwegian? Even if we designate each of the examples I've given as a sub-variety, so that *Beowulf* is written in Old English and Kelman writes Scots English, English remains the underlying continuity in all these varieties. And that continuity implies some sameness, something essential shared among all the varieties that qualify as English, something that motivates histories of the language and its literature, and justifies claims for shared traditions. Again: what is English? And how do we know?

Clearly, the simple criterion of intelligibility isn't an exclusive consideration in the language's identity, since *Beowulf* remains unintelligible to most modern Anglophones, while if *Paradise Lost* initially seems intelligible—as in the account of Satan's gaze—it often really isn't. From the opposite perspective, an utterance like the following may fail to meet several kinds of grammatical criteria for English but nonetheless makes sense: "Store go wants me." Moreover, as I'll suggest in Chapter Five, intelligibility can be as much a matter of attitude as linguistic fact. English-speakers who express their view on language in a similar way to that sometimes expressed about art—saying they might not know English but they know what they speak—are often also saying something about those to whom they want to speak. When we want to understand someone, for whatever social or practical reason, we are far more likely to accept that person as an Anglophone than we might otherwise be.

Equally limited as a determination of what is and is not English would be speakers' geographic location, a criterion present since the Anglo-Saxon days of the Venerable Bede. There certainly are countries in which English is either a declared official language or functions as a de facto national language, used by the majority of speakers, in the majority of domains, for the majority of the countries' histories. But even so, not every speaker in (for example) the United Kingdom, Canada, or the United States speaks or spoke English. By the same token, Anglophones speak and reside throughout the globe in areas where English is not predominant and where other languages may in fact be official, as in Belgium and Switzerland. The vast majority of those who speak English today speak it as a second language and inhabit areas where English has not been the historically dominant language, at least in terms of the numbers of speakers.

Definitions that rely on an ideal rooted in matters of structure, such as phonology, morphology, and syntax, have their own problems. For one thing, as the excerpts from *Beowulf* and *Paradise Lost* demonstrate, these may change across time and vary at any given moment, complicating the transhistorical way in which English is understood to exist. We call it the same language, that is, even though its form can and has changed radically. And for another, even if we can demonstrate historical continuities and connections, doing so offers little by way of a stable sense of just what English is. So, *geardagum* doesn't look or sound ('yaredahguhm', approximately) like anything any contemporary Anglophone would utter, but the first element has 'year' as its reflex and the second 'day'. The –*um* ending marks a dative plural. Like most of English's original inflectional endings, this one atrophied in exactly the same way throughout the language when word order became increasingly important in the eleventh and twelfth centuries. The ending left no trace behind, and it is because of analogy with the historical nominative plural ending that nearly all modern English nouns show –*s* everywhere in the plural. All of which means that *geardagum* is, in some sense, the same as 'year-days'. But however explicable this history is, and even if the meaning of *geardagum* is at least largely transparent, the word still fails to qualify in shape or meaning (or sound, for that matter) as anything acceptable within any sense of English today. And the real problem with using morphological continuity as justification for the *what* of English is that it relates so poorly—maybe not at all—to the *why*. Everything I've said about *geardagum* is true, but none of it explains the gate-keeping role of English, or the fact that some accents can be considered closer to English than others, or the reason that anyone would want to make English an official language.

It's worth pausing here, as we survey the difficulty of defining English, to consider how today it's not just the language but its speakers who differ from those of the past. As recently as 1950, when the world's population would have been about 2.3 billion, fewer than 400 million people spoke English.[25] The fourfold growth of this population in the intervening years is unprecedented; indeed, there's nothing remotely like it in any period of any language's recorded history. But just as radical—more so, in fact—have been the changes in the demographics of English speakers. In 1950, well over half of the world's Anglophones resided in the English-dominant areas that Braj Kachru has described as the Inner Circle: the United Kingdom, the United States, Australia, New Zealand, and Canada. The populations of these regions certainly have increased since the Second World War. In the United States, where the population grew from 123 million to 132 million between 1930 and 1940, the 2010 census records 309 million people, over 80% of whom speak only English and an additional 10% of whom speak English along with another language. During the same period, the United Kingdom's population has grown by about 15 million to almost 63 million in 2013, nearly all of whom likewise can speak English, mostly as a first language. The remarkable thing is that, together, these and other areas of first-language use now account for only about 25–30% of the world's Anglophones. In other words, even as the total number of Anglophones has quadrupled and English has expanded in domains unknown (such as the Internet) or barely known (such as international business) before the Second World War, the percentage of Inner Circle speakers among the world's Anglophones has dropped significantly. The number of individuals who speak English as a first language has similarly declined in comparison to those who speak all other languages. In 1950, such speakers accounted for 8% of the global population; by 2050, this percentage is predicted to be under 5%.[26]

Because of changes like these, it's become commonplace to talk about the current state of English as not simply unprecedented but perilous in various ways. Speakers in Kachru's Inner Circle can worry that the language is deteriorating as it slips from their control, with a popular writer like Lynn Truss imagining that with the deterioration of formal, schoolbook grammar, specifically of punctuation, will come nothing less than the loss of communication and even civilization. But serious scholars worry as well. John McWhorter, for instance, equates the loss of cultivated language in the United States with the impoverishment of political discourse.[27] For their part, speakers outside Kachru's Inner Circle, such as Phillipson, can express anxiety over the fact that the global spread of English has led to the loss of indigenous languages and cultural individuality. According to such arguments, where English goes, Anglophone business and social values follow, erasing indigenous cultures and languages in their path.

As linguistic science has progressed in the past century, it's also become commonplace to speak about varieties of English in increasingly nuanced ways. Subtle classifications thus become ways to recognize linguistic differences even as they assert some overall integrity. Besides his Inner Circle, for example, Kachru refers to an Outer Circle (where English has been transplanted and become indigenous) and an Expanding Circle (where

English serves primarily as a second language).[28] Other critics distinguish English as a Native Language from ESL and English as a Foreign Language. Or they distinguish all three from the creole and pidgin varieties that language contact can produce. Or they speak about an ethnic and intellectual particularity for individual languages that is reflected in how words are used and that serves as the main framework among varieties of a language: if it looks like English at this abstract level, it must be English.[29]

But one thing about English today is that as much as it has changed from English of the past, many qualities, both pragmatic and grammatical, have remained constant. We should say of many contemporary forms and uses of the language, I think, that they are unprecedented but not uncharacteristic. As unparalleled as the recent expansion of speakers and domains has been, for example, it builds on patterns present from the language's beginning. In the two centuries prior to the Second World War, English was already spreading across the globe, just as the population of Anglophones was already climbing. Between 1820 and 1932, perhaps 56 million people emigrated from Europe. Some 75% of these, whatever their homeland, ended up in English-speaking areas. And speakers from Anglophone areas were themselves just as given to traveling and taking their language abroad. While about one-half million emigrants left Great Britain in the eighteenth century, in the following century (broadly understood as 1815–1924) that number climbed to 25 million. This same pattern occurred but on a smaller scale in the United States, where eastern seaboard colonists gradually but insistently crossed the Appalachian mountains and spread throughout the West. Between 1790 and 1810 the population west of the mountains grew (by birth but mostly by immigration) from only about 100,000 to 1 million settlers. But in just the next half century, in what are now Midwest states like Illinois, Wisconsin, and Minnesota, the settler population increased from perhaps 650,000 to 7 million. In this same period the number of settlers increased from 150,000 to 4.6 million individuals in current southern and southwest states like Alabama, Louisiana, and Texas, while the immigrant population of Australia rose to 1.2 million (from 12,000) and to 1.4 million in Canada.[30] If one wanted to go far enough back (as I will in other chapters) one could find similar patterns of demographic expansion accompanying linguistic growth and change in early modern colonization efforts, in the settling of Britain by continental Angles and Saxons, and, indeed, in the westward movement of Germanic peoples from their Indo-European homeland. Anglophones, in short, have always been moving, their demographics have always been shifting, their numbers have always been increasing, and the characteristics of their language have always been changing.

Another thing about English today is that the various ways in which the language can be defined have their own histories. These, too, might be described as unprecedented but not uncharacteristic. All such critical positions—pragmatic, grammatical, historical, and theoretical—are ultimately acts of imagination. They are ways of first conceptualizing facts like languages and their elements, and then identifying how these facts vary and change. There's nothing insidious in this—it's simply how cognition in the social sciences (as opposed to the natural sciences) works, and a feedback loop always makes it possible to redefine the facts. But as imaginative acts, any one of these positions cannot by itself refute another, categorically different way of defining English. In a sense, as different kinds of definition, mutual intelligibility and geography largely talk *past* one another. And this means that the *what* of English has always had and always will have as many answers as the *why* can invite.

HERACLITUS, HISTORY, AND HERITAGE

So far, I have approached this *why* in a fairly limited way: I've suggested English is important because we connect educational, financial, and political issues to it. But why do we do that? How is it that English—more so than other forms of social performance, such as clothing, hair color, or athleticism—should bear significance beyond anything to do with its apparently primary purpose, the simple act of communication? And for that matter, the *what* remains in doubt as well, since any definition ought to be able to accommodate the fact that a variety of sometimes conflicting definitions already exists. To get at these points, as well as at the argument of this book, I want to take a metaphor from antiquity.

The Greek thinker Heraclitus, who wrote and lectured in Ephesus around 500 BCE, might be called the philosopher of flux. To Heraclitus, the world is not the stable product of stable phenomena but rather an ongoing process in which conceptual opposites and the continual change of experience are inevitable and necessary. More than this, whatever stability there is in the world arises from these very discontinuities. However discrete and even contradictory individual moments might be, says Heraclitus, they nonetheless produce a coherence that renders the moments and their continuity meaningful. One of the central beliefs of Heraclitus's philosophy is thus a paradox: life's discontinuities fabricate the unity that holds all life together.

What we know of Heraclitus comes from a series of fragments and from quotations in others' works, and so we might well consider the present condition of his writings to be an apt metaphor of the flux and continuity he explained. But a river provides a metaphor that is just as fitting. On one hand, in some intuitive sense, since a river's course and momentum may remain essentially unchanged for many years, the river has a unity and integrity that enable us to speak of the same river at various moments and at various locations up and down stream. It is the same River Thames, whether we see it upon Westminster Bridge or from Oxford, and likewise the same whether we view it from Hammersmith on a Monday or a Friday. On the other hand, since water keeps moving, streaming away and being replenished by still more water, fluctuating with the movements of the tide, the river's identity constantly changes. It can never contain precisely the same waters flowing in precisely the same way. The paradox of a river is that for it to retain its unity as a river, it must always be changing. Because of this Heraclitus once said, "For those who step into the same rivers, other and still other waters flow."[31]

As a philosopher, Heraclitus thus shares more with Kant and his emphasis on perception than with Locke and his emphasis on empirical experience. In Heraclitus's philosophy, as the flowing of the river prevents us from stepping a second time into precisely the same water—but not the same river—so the flowing of time prevents us from visiting the same place twice, or hearing the same piece of music twice, or eating the same meal twice. Bœuf bourguignon may always be bœuf bourguignon, but having eaten one serving, we can never eat that very same serving again. For rivers and meals alike we nonetheless perceive unity and transhistorical identity in these sometimes discontinuous experiences, and we do so in largely similar ways. Partly this happens through repeated structural components—bœuf bourguignon must always have beef and the Thames must always follow what we tautologically define as the Thames riverbed. And partly it happens through an imaginative act, rooted in a set of facts and theoretical propositions that enable us to accept differing iterations of meals and rivers as the same. It is through this act that we can posit and recognize unity in what are inescapably disparate phenomena.

Simple as it is, Heraclitus's river has much to commend it as a metaphor for thinking about language and the complex questions of this book. To take a straightforward example, while we can repeat words and phrases, the flowing of time prevents us from speaking the same utterance twice. We might believe ourselves to do so, just as we might imagine ourselves to continue to speak the same language. But even if we use identical words and expressions in similar circumstances, they will never be exactly the same and our language will never be static. For one thing, our intonation and articulation will necessarily differ, since that kind of variation is inevitable in human speech, with its sensitivity to environment, a speaker's physical and emotional well-being, and the nature of what's being talked about. We might pronounce the same word very differently, depending on whether the temperature is hot or cold, whether we're climbing a flight of stairs or sitting on a chair, and whether it figures in a mundane request for the correct time or an emotional appeal for assistance from a bystander. For another, even very similar circumstances are not absolutely identical. We may twice say the same thing to the same person in the same setting—like a frustrated parent or teacher—but the mere fact that the second occasion repeats the first can mean that it has a pragmatic emphasis that was initially absent.[32]

As the second or third utterance of the same form can differ from the first, so too can the overarching grammatical and discursive system composed of such particular utterances—a speaker's linguistic competence. When reflecting on our personal linguistic histories, whether those histories are six or 60 years in length, we all confront numerous examples not only of the situational variation I have described but also of how our language itself has changed. For some individuals, the English they speak today might be a secondary language, acquired in school or adulthood as a supplement to (and maybe replacement of) a birth language. But even those who understand themselves to have spoken only one language all their lives know, upon reflection, how much that language has changed for them—how today they might use some words and expressions only in certain circumstances, how the slang of their youth has diminished, and, if they have particularly good memories, how they mastered new vocabulary and even difficult pronunciations as they matured. They might have always spoken the same language, but they never twice spoke it in precisely the same way.

What provides obvious confirmation of the continuity behind such flux and what allows us to say we have spoken just English since birth are our lives. Our speech may differ as we age or move about, but to the extent that we recognize our own integrity (despite inevitable changes in personality, circumstance, and so forth) we are ourselves corroborations of the fact that we still speak the same language. Speakers' recollections of awkward moments when they first realized that they had been regularly mispronouncing or misusing a particular word also remind them of the discontinuities and transitions in their speech habits over time, as does the occasional realization, which seems to increase with age, that one once knew a word (or its meaning) that's now faded away. In this sense, every Anglophone might be regarded as living proof of the discontinuous continuity of English for him- or herself.

If we multiply any individual speaker by the number of Anglophones today—conservatively, 1.5 billion, including those who know English as a second language—and then by the number of those who have known it since the days of *Beowulf* (perhaps another billion and a half?) we arrive at a fantastically large population, all of whom have some historical, grammatical, or social claim to speak the same language, however much any one individual's language may have varied from another's or diverged from that of an earlier speaker. Simply by designating the collective utterances of this enormous population as English, we necessarily invoke Heraclitus's paradoxical notion of a continuity that builds from (and transcends) the discrete, changing moments of spoken language in time. Like Heraclitus's river, English is indeed a paradox. Like a river, the language contains basic structural elements (phonology, syntax, and morphology) that swell, contract, and change through different periods in time and different places, never apparently acting the same way twice. And as with a river, we nonetheless manage to find unity in this undulating linguistic record, accumulated from billions of speakers from across the entire globe.

All this is certainly not to say that English cannot be and has not been defined among the changing forms and varieties of its histories. Quite the contrary. There are lots of definitions, explicit and implicit in speakers' conversational practices and world views, in histories and grammars of English, in commercial hiring practices, in pedagogical objectives, and in government policies on voting, immigration, and citizenship. Using Heraclitus's metaphor, we might say that these definitions are maps that, like maps of a river, both point to certain empirical features but also depend for their integrity on an observer's judgment. And the diversity of maps of English points to the diversity of those who would define the language and of those whom they would include in their definition.

Every English-speaking person achieves that designation by meeting some arguable (if not always expressed) criteria for defining the language. We might say that Anglophones are those understood to have stepped into the same linguistic river, even as that river constantly varies and changes through fluctuations in its forms, speakers, registers, dialects, domains, grammars, cognate languages, historical stages, creoles, pidgins, and co-existent languages. To identify any main channel for the river of English, whether individually or in groups, speakers need also to locate the tributaries, distributaries, estuaries, watershed, and the bodies of water that are unconnected to it.

Less metaphorically, they need to exercise an imaginative act by which they can identify, discriminate among, and respond to both variation at a particular moment and change across time. Any grammar or history of the language thus runs the perhaps inescapable risk of becoming an exercise in question-begging. It must at the outset presume the category English in order to exclude non-English utterances and to select and assemble evidence of the language's nature and development for whatever breadth of identity or length of lifespan that one attributes to the language. And the lifespan of English, of course, is question-begging as well.

In a fundamental way, by extension, any map (or grammar) that distinguishes English from not-English is neither self-evident nor value-free. Indeed, as in part an act of imagination, by pointing to different histories such definitions point as well to different beliefs about the character of the language and the culture it enables. The standard-based conception of the language that prevailed into the twentieth century restricts the river of English only to the channels that flow through literate, primarily British English. A more expansive conception would include the large Anglophone nations in Kachru's Inner Circle but still exclude all areas of second-language acquisition. A still more expansive conception would accept the channels occupied by regional and non-standard varieties in these areas of native speakers. Kachru and others would broaden the watershed of English even more, to include some or all global varieties that are often considered non-standard, such as Black South African English and Chinese English. And perhaps the most expansive conception of the river of English would include interlanguages like Kriol (spoken in Belize), Spanglish (a mixture of Spanish and English), and a historical variety like the blend of Latin, French, and English used in some fifteenth-century business records. Each of these conceptions of English in some way has to precede the evidence, to pre-determine what English is, in order to allow for adjudication between, say, pronunciations or words that are non-standard, regional, or non-English. And in doing so, each conception affects how the history of English is written, what's taught in grammar and preparatory schools, how powerful domains of business and government are conceptualized, and how command of English relates to the dynamics of Anglophone societies.

The most influential of these maps of the nature and history of English have rendered much of the language's diversity as streams and offshoots whose interest lies primarily in the way they have sustained or clarified an abstract main channel of the sort imagined from the days of the Anglo-Saxons to those of Chomsky's ideal speaker-listener. In 1905, the great Victorian philologist Joseph Wright suggested that, once these branches had fulfilled their purpose of producing a standard, they would dry up and vanish:

There can be no doubt that pure dialect speech is rapidly disappearing even in country districts, owing to the spread of education, and to modern facilities for intercommunication. The writing of this grammar was begun none too soon, for had it been delayed another twenty years I believe it would by then be quite impossible to get together sufficient pure dialect material to enable any one to give even a mere outline of the phonology of our dialects as they existed at the close of the nineteenth century.[33]

Wright, of course, was wrong: certain dialect forms have disappeared, but dialects themselves remain, simply because regional variation is inherent in any language that's spoken across a broad expanse of land. Further, even if some British dialects are less distinctive than they were in Wright's day, new ones, involving West Indian contact for example, have come into existence. But Wright's views do provide a gloss on all definitions of English. Even empirically based definitions, much less pragmatic ones, can be more intuitive than factual, resting on a Platonic ideal of English that emerges particularly clearly in the early modern period. They chart the main channel of the language in the development of Standard English from the written variety preferred by early modern printers and late-medieval court officials. And on this chart regional forms and varieties not in this channel (along with their speakers) may be historically useful and interesting but remain fundamentally lesser and finally ephemeral, only peripherally connected to English, and the cultures and traditions it embodies. In our own minority–majority linguistic era, an era when second- and third-language speakers outnumber native born Anglophones three to one, this Platonic ideal remains a powerful frame for defining English.[34]

If Heraclitus helps us to conceptualize the *what* of a language that forever changes and yet retains some kind of stability for its speakers and their activities, he also provides a way to think about the *why*. And here I want to draw a distinction between history and heritage. By the former we typically understand an enterprise concerned above all with proof, with finding what is known and testable, with identifying the absolute truth. The nineteenth-century German historian Leopold von Ranke established this emphasis on showing the past "exactly as it happened" as the basis of modern historiography,[35] but the notion of an objective truth, of course, has a long history of its own. It is even perhaps embedded within Western literate culture as a kind of epistemological constant—as a necessity in how we imagine and think about the world. For there to be interpretations judged either right or wrong, that is, we seem to need a sense that there really is, or was, a reality. Otherwise, there can be no competing versions of history. And by extension, presumed objectivity would cognitively seem to require an invested, interpretive gesture like heritage.

While history looks for what's known and testable, heritage looks for a past that will enhance and provide meaning to the present. Like history, heritage seeks truth, though it defines truth more impressionistically than factually. And like legend, it identifies a heroic age that can fashion unity, community, and cultural and political memory. We might thus think of history as the supposedly disinterested search for what happened, and heritage as the avowed impulse that gives us a reason to search in the first place. It is the product of creatively working with and thinking about the past, and in this regard heritage can use events, land, and language as malleable ways to construct not just any past but a meaningful one. Libraries, literary canons, and historical series like the Early English Text Society have all served this purpose. Dictionaries, grammars, and conceptions of who speaks a particular language have as well. Like eighteenth-century philology as understood by a Friedrich Wolf or Johann Eichhorn, heritage is what produces a memorable past against which a modern era can measure itself. Put simply, history might identify the details of a battle, while heritage would marshal a parade in its honor.[36]

In the abstract, a distinction between history and heritage makes a good deal of sense. In the sometimes messy realm of human experience things are less clear. Is English, for instance, history or heritage? Grammar books of all kinds, infused as they are with a Platonic ideal of the language, seem to regard the language as an objective truth, but when it's an impressionistic criterion for employment or citizenship, English clearly serves social agenda. Even if one were to retreat in time to a moment when the limits of English effectively overlapped with the limits of England—say, any moment between the sixth and sixteenth centuries—distinctions between history and heritage are sometimes no clearer. Partially this is so because during this millennium there is a relative scarcity of metalinguistic discussion of English—of comments specifically about the language. There are therefore certain things that we don't know and that we probably can't know. But mostly it's because it's we, and not medieval Anglophones, who are viewing in retrospect what happened and deciding what it means.

Phonological change and lexical borrowing seem objective enough, for example, and in many ways they are, but how they figure in the shape of a language, its variation, or its development have more to do with what we consider heritage because they depend on someone looking back at them for some reason. We use these phenomena to draw a map for the river of English: a shape of what the language is, of what its legitimate variants are, of which changes occurred in its history, and of where it's spoken. This same map distinguishes those who speak English from those who do not and, therefore, also those who can from those who cannot participate in the history, traditions, and privileges of Anglophone culture. Whether drawn by native Anglophones or second-language learners, maps like these are as much sociolinguistic exercises in heritage as they are historical witnesses. They depict how speakers imagine their relationships not just with the languages around them but with other speakers and the world as well. They image how the world appears or how someone might like it to be. And they are in this sense as forever unstable, changing, and partisan as are the grammatical and pragmatic impulses to which they respond.

Heritage, then, is the *why* behind the various kinds of *why* I examined at the outset of this chapter. Why should so much importance be invested in a standard version of English? At least in part because doing so maintains certain institutions, traditions, and worldviews. Why would anyone want an official language? Because at least in the United States doing so furthers a particular vision of what it means to be an American. What's the *why* behind this *why*? Why would an official language relate to what it means to be an American? Here as at every other level of inquiry there are alternative answers. Perhaps an official language defines American identity because it responds to the propositions of the *Declaration of Independence* by creating a level of equal opportunity for all individuals. Or perhaps it does so because it provides specific advantages for some and disadvantages for others by furthering a sense that the country is fundamentally European and white, and that it is the responsibility of immigrants to conform through the idea of a melting pot.[37] And why would speakers believe that language can affect social reality in this way? Is it because there's something inherent in language that invites uses like this, or simply because there's precedent, a history of doing so? Like old-fashioned barbershop mirrors, heritage continues to reflect itself.

In the following chapters I explore various locales on the river of English, as it were. Even though I've questioned any neat distinction between grammatical and pragmatic definitions of the language, I have organized the chapters around this distinction because I think it makes the argument clearer. The first four thus focus on grammar, the next six, arranged chronologically, on pragmatics. Obviously, my approach is selective—a series of case studies—but it has two important arguments in its favor. Firstly, its selectivity mirrors the impermanence and changeability of English itself. There can be no one definition of English, I will argue, and so by extension all definitions can be only examples. And secondly, the moments I've selected prove to be among the most consequential in the language's history. Each in a very different way, these case studies consider why and how—whether from a popular or an academic perspective—the unity of English has been identified in the changing, shifting forms of its use. And collectively they point to the conclusion that all definitions of English are situational. But they point beyond that, too. Building on Roger Lass's notion that a language is "a population of variants moving through time, and subject to selection," I will argue that one of the things subject to selection is the selection process itself—the methods and materials for writing definitions.[38] A definition may take into account the variability inherent in language, as Lass in fact does. Or it can ignore the variability or pronounce it wrong in order to posit a definition of language as something stable and abstract, as do critics as disparate as Chomsky and Bishop Lowth. But in either case, the methods are as subject to a kind of social natural selection as are the data they describe. I also will argue, then, that by nature the *what* and the *why* of English—the language's history and heritage—have a kind of symbiotic relationship, each nurturing and giving rise to the other.

In one sense, my focus in this book is largely retrospective, since I look at how the mainstream of English has been drawn by grammarians, historical linguists, commentators, and speakers in general. In another, it's contemporary, involving consideration of the current policies and attitudes that follow from this constructed history. And both views lead me to consider the future as well. Once we know what the river of English has been to this point, can we know where it will lead from here? Or better, where we want it to lead? In these ways, my intention is not to champion one definition to the exclusion of others, nor to resist the inevitable changes English has experienced as a natural language. It is rather to lay open both the necessity of imaginative choice over heritage in something as apparently categorical and historical as the definition of English as well as the inevitability of the social consequences rooted in that choice. How we define English goes a long way towards how we define the world in which it is spoken. And we care what English is because to a large extent defining the language amounts to saying who we are.

A WORD ABOUT 'WE'

In his short story "Xing a Paragrab," Edgar Allan Poe narrates the curious tale of a small-town printer who writes a stylistic tour de force in which the graph *o* appears at least once in nearly every word, only to have his compositor discover that all the *o*s have disappeared mysteriously from the box of type font. Rather than rewrite the paragraph or print the newspaper with a blank space wherever the fourth most common letter in English ought to occur, the resourceful compositor substitutes an *x*, so that "told you so, you know" becomes "txld yxu sx, yxu knxw," "do be cool, you fool" becomes "dx be cxxl, yxu fxxl," and so forth. It is possible, as readers and the compositor discover, to tell a story without an important graph, but it's not easy to do so.[39]

Writing a book about English that has at its heart questions about just what English means, I think I have a sense of the compositor's dilemma. I really should refrain from using the word 'English' or 'we', 'Anglophone', 'history of English', and 'indigenous'—all of which I've already used several times— because every time I do so I find myself engaging in question-begging, in presuming the very thing I'm trying to understand or prove. It's not the idea of distinctions between English and non-English or between Anglophones and non-Anglophones that's the problem. These are the distinctions that grammar books and pragmatic practices are designed to make and always have made, and what I do here is critique them.

Nor is there a problem in the fact that every example I study contains disagreements over and transformations of what English is or who we are, often with material consequences. Consider 'indigenous'. In the fourth century an indigenous Anglophone would have to have been born in northwest Europe, where the English-speaking ancestors of the Angles and Saxons lived prior to emigrating; in the tenth century in England; in the nineteenth century somewhere in Kachru's Inner Circle. Where do indigenous Anglophones live today, who decides, and why does it matter? (All I'll say here is that it certainly does matter.) Or we might think about two scenarios involving individuals who speak different language varieties. If a speaker from France and one from England sit down to dinner, calling one a Francophone and the other an Anglophone would be uncontroversial. And having nothing invested in the label, the French-speaker would probably express small resistance to not being called an Anglophone. The speaker might even be flattered. But if a speaker of Singlish, a speaker of Standard American English, a speaker of African American English, a Chicano who speaks with a strong Mexican accent, and a speaker of Hawaiian Pidgin English apply for a job requiring fluency in English, calling one or more an Anglophone matters a great deal. Each of these speakers invests employment prospects, personal identity, or both in how we define and use words like 'English', 'broken English', 'accented English', and 'ungrammatical English'.

One could say that these are words whose meanings get negotiated by speakers in what they say and do and that, inevitably, these negotiations result from conflicts of one kind or another. Moreover, their meanings are tantamount to a map of the river of English, and as such not only are these meanings variable at any one time and place but they change across time. What also emerges from the following case studies, then, is the unsurprising fact that some Anglophones are more equal than others. Some get to propagate definitions that have greater impact, whether in classrooms or in hiring practices, than others' definitions. Some get to define a 'we' of the English speakers that includes them but excludes others who nonetheless regard themselves as Anglophones.

The problem I face, then, is that I have to use 'English', 'we', and the other words even as I try to define just what they mean in particular contexts. And I never found a way around these lexical dilemmas. Not by qualifying each use of 'we' with something obscure and ungainly like "socially dominant people who can enforce their own self-styled normativity through social institutions and ideology." Nor by hedging each use of 'English' with "what is widely considered." Nor by putting scare quotes around every occurrence of 'history of English', 'indigenous', and the rest. Not even by following Poe's compositor and substituting x whenever one of these words otherwise would appear. On occasion I address the issue directly, but much of the time I simply let the words pass without comment.

If this disclaimer is a little unsatisfying, I think it can be justified in three ways. Firstly, one of the points of this book is that the meanings of words like these are situational, constructed by individuals to fit individual circumstances. Their meanings in any one situation—or any one case study—are therefore, in the first instance, limited to that situation and ought to emerge from what I say about that situation. Secondly, in every domain of English, as I have said, some speakers have more influence in deciding who we are and what English is. They are the speakers—nearly but not always native-born Anglophones rather than those who came to English as a second language—whose meanings have the greatest influence on linguistic usage and social practice, and most need examination. And thirdly—the one constant—everywhere in this book 'we' must refer as well to anyone who can read what I've written, since that reader is necessarily an Anglophone. That everyone who is part of this 'we' might not agree on just who we are, or on what English is, is another of the points I hope to make.

PART TWO

English by the Books

CHAPTER TWO

Words in the Shape of English

For many of us, words are the first thing we notice about language. Excited young parents talk about when babies utter 'mom' or 'dad', not when they produce voiced fricatives, relative clauses, or tag questions. Travelers concentrate on memorizing greetings and basic vocabulary like numbers rather than learning inflectional morphology (i.e. the endings we put on words to make nouns plural or to change a verb tense). And when adult Anglophones confront gaps in their knowledge of English, the gaps come in the form of words, not syntactic structures or phonemes.

Linguists would disagree about this priority. They would describe words (and pronunciation) as relatively low order, compared to syntax, in the sense that while words and pronunciations come and go, syntax tends to remain stable. Syntax is also what generates (to use a common language model) utterances in which individual words are essentially placeholders, and for this reason it's typically judged to be the more foundational, more distinctive quality of any language. All that's very true. But syntax does not give rise to decency laws or make films R-rated, nor does it drive readers to reference books to find the meaning of something they don't understand.

Words do that because they are in some ways the most accessible part of a language. We can learn new words to expand our vocabulary, avoid words that are considered insensitive, measure intellectual growth by the breadth of the words we use, identify one language's equivalent for another language's word, and resist slang words or variations in the meanings of words. We can (and need to) add new words more easily than we can add syntax or pronunciation. Perhaps for all these reasons, most speakers can talk about words (and pronunciations) in ways that they cannot talk about verb phrases, fronting, and cleft sentences. They can use words, quite simply and sometimes with great conviction, to define the shape of a language. When we hear someone speak a word we don't recognize, we in fact might respond by saying that it is "not English." We allow dictionaries to make the same judgment for us when we consult them to see whether they include the word. In these ways, the vocabulary of English (its lexicon), as well as its syntax, can seem to function as almost an agency in its own right, and the language, in turn, can seem to exist apart from the words its speakers use. An Anglophone might use a word, but if we can't find the word in a dictionary, we might not accept it as English.

In this chapter and Chapter Three I am concerned with these foundational roles of lexicon in any definition of English. While we might like to concede the shape of English's lexicon to dictionaries, the relationships between speakers and words turn out to be complex, dynamic, and situational. Here I suggest that even with the help of a dictionary, the lexicon of English has inherently fuzzy contours that can be focused only through arguments that take account of who uses the lexicon and why. And I argue that the lexicographical principles that sustain these arguments are arguments themselves. Chapter Three explores ways in which speakers can manipulate lexis and hence the definition of English. Together, these two chapters maintain that the vocabulary of English always takes it shape from the usages of those who are accepted as Anglophones and that Anglophones give it this shape in specific social contexts with specific social implications.

A CENTER WITHOUT A DISCERNIBLE CIRCUMFERENCE

A reasonable place to begin my discussion is with the question, "How many words are there in the English language?" to which a reasonable answer would be, "It's hard to say." The pre-eminent dictionary for English, the *Oxford English Dictionary* (OED), records approximately 600,000 words, though many of these are obsolete. It also omits a great deal of slang, regionalisms, and expressions found in the interlanguages that result from contact between English and other languages. And while some literary coinages have found their way into the OED (Lewis Carroll's 'slithy' and 'tove', for instance) numerous others (including many of the words in *Finnegans Wake*) have not.

For the time being we might classify slang and literary expressions as ephemeral and outside the limits of lexicography, but uncertainties about the size of the English lexicon would remain. Should proper nouns be counted if Anglophones utter them? Are 'Paris' and 'Berlin', listed in many American English dictionaries with the exact same spelling they have in (respectively) French and German, really English words? Should the same form be counted more than once if it can exist as two or more distinct parts of speech (e.g., 'present' as noun, adjective, and verb)? Should compound words (e.g., 'greengrocers') be counted for their individual elements as well as for the compounds themselves? In the continuous flow of spoken language ('wanna' for 'want to' or 'gonna' for 'going to') and in light of derivations like the participles we form by adding *ing* to verbs, even the apparently simple notion of a distinct word is sometimes difficult to maintain.[1]

Having sorted through such complexities, one reputable authority has estimated that a million lexemes—a million base words, irrespective of inflectional endings—are used currently by some Anglophone somewhere on some occasions, and I certainly have no reason to disagree.[2] I also know of no way to verify the accuracy of that estimate. A precise measure of even one individual's vocabulary cannot be done, or at least cannot be done easily. A speaker who had the time and patience to read methodically through a stack of general and specialized dictionaries, marking each familiar word and then tallying the total of marked words, might well arrive at a relatively accurate number of his or her vocabulary. Needless to say, such a speaker (and therefore such a number) is difficult to imagine. Using a version of this kind of analysis to survey a small group of educated Anglophones, David Crystal recorded an average active vocabulary (words actually used in speech or writing) of about 50,000 words and an average passive vocabulary (words known but not used) of an additional 63,000.[3] Some individuals, the ones who read English indefatigably or just have good memories, undoubtedly would exceed these numbers, and others would fall short.

What might be called the Englishness of English words can be just as ill-defined as the size of the language's lexicon. If contemporary English does indeed have one million words, well over half began their lexical lives as words in some other language. French or Latin account for many of these borrowings, but Bantu, Punjabi, Cantonese, and Hawaiian have all contributed as well. Already in the mid-fifteenth century (it's been asserted), half of the words in use were not Germanic, and half of those that were originated in Old Norse, the language of the Vikings.[4] As James Murray, the main editor of the first OED, understandably said, "The circle of the English language has a well-defined centre but no discernible circumference."[5] We know that words like 'dog' and 'cat' are certainly English, that 'wallies' and 'hula' probably are, and that 'mipela' and 'chumpy' probably are not. How to draw distinctions among the certain and probable words, and where to put particular words, are other matters.

The more we stare at the English lexicon, in fact, the more it can seem like an optical illusion, dependent on individual speakers and the context of their speech. If an individual has never used or even seen a word like 'chthonic', does it really exist simply because a dictionary says it does or because some other Anglophone uses it? What of nonce formations that were created for particular circumstances and used in the expectation that they aren't real words and will *not* become common? Forms like 'slithy' and 'tove' largely derive their significance in just this way. Shakespeare places the verb 'incarnadine' in Macbeth's mouth, I think, for essentially the same reason, although ironically it has become one of the best-known words in all his plays. In fact, while Shakespeare's vocabulary is often praised as one of the largest and most creative in English literary history, the demise of 31% of his neologisms (by one estimate) could undermine any claims that they were words in the first place.[6] And the uncertain status of all such forms doesn't change from the fact that some well-read and affected speakers might use them today, since they do so in recognition of the words' status as non-words. Everyone who utters "frabjuous day" does so with a wink.

These kinds of fleeting nonce formations are of course not exclusively literary. They're also common in advertising or social commentary, where their wit or phonology might underscore their immediacy. A moribund word like 'Bushlips', for an insincere promise, played on the first President Bush's 1988 challenge to read his lips when he said "no new taxes" and later raised taxes anyway. And 'teledildonics' whimsically used phonemes evocative of technology to deny any seriousness to its referent: the field of computer-controlled sex toys.[7] The playfulness and historical specificity of both creations marks them as lexically atypical (like 'slithy') and therefore neither intended for general currency nor likely ever to find it. And the same is true of well-known slips of the tongue, like 'misunderestimate' or 'refudiate'. If a word is created (or at least functioning) as a linguistic mayfly, can it be said ever to have been part of the English lexicon?

Virtually the same conundrum arises from ghost words, or words that occur only because of an error in reading or printing. On one hand, some source (a dictionary, edition, whatever) cites the word and therefore makes it alive at least for anyone who consults that source; on the other, the citation is to something that doesn't in fact exist. As documentation, ghost words are the lexical equivalents of griffin sightings. Throughout all its initial printings, thus, Sir Walter Scott's novel *The Monastery* contained the following sentence, "Hardened wretch (said father Eustace) art thou but this instant delivered from death, and dost thou so soon morse thoughts of slaughter?" Variously explained as Lowland Scots, a reflex of Latin *mordere* ('to bite'), and a derivative of Old French *amorce* ('powder', and so here in the sense of 'to prime', as a musket), the verb *morse* in fact represents a compositor's misreading of Scott's manuscript, which has the perfectly ordinary 'nurse'. "This is a most instructive instance," observes Walter Skeat, "as proving that a false form, if once introduced, can maintain itself through countless editions without detection, or at any rate without correction."[8]

A particularly convoluted example of a ghost word involves the *Boece*, Chaucer's late-fourteenth-century translation of *De consolatione philosophiae.* All three editions of the OED cite the *Boece* for the only two instances of a verb *forline* ('to degenerate'), as in "thei ne schulde nat owtrayen or forlynen fro the vertus of hir noble kynrede" ('they should not stray or degenerate from the virtues of their noble ancestors'). And all three cite Frederick Furnivall's 1886 edition of the translation as their source. Yet in both instances, Furnivall's edition actually reads not *forlynen* but *forlyuen* (another rare word that the OED cites separately, meaning 'to outlive one's strength'), though it does so in error. In the manuscript he transcribed (Cambridge, University Library MS Ii.3.21), the graphs *n* and *u* are interchangeable, but the French intermediary that Chaucer here follows quite closely (Jean de Meung's own translation of the *Consolatio*) uses forms of *forlignier*, and so *forlynen*, with an *n*, must in fact be what Chaucer wrote. Technically, the citations in the OED are to ghost words—words that, to Skeat, "we may seem to see...or may fancy that they exist; but they have no real entity"—since they misread what Furnivall wrote. But since Furnivall himself miswrote what his source read, the ghost words turn out to be material (if just as rare) after all. Which words qualify as medieval English words is not easy to say.[9]

This all might be idle lexical speculation—something like a crossword puzzle or word jumble and akin to questions about the sound of a tree falling with no one around, though in the case of *forlinen* it's as if the tree recorded itself on the way down. But the fact of the matter is that we evidently care a great deal about the contours of English. For one thing, beginning with Richard Trench's 1851 *On the Study of Words* and running through Owen Barfield's *History in English Words* (1926) and C. S. Lewis's *Studies in Words* (1960) to the present day, the topic has inspired all manner of books whose very titles suggest something of the whimsy, excitement, and even joie de vivre that seem to be associated with the size and shape of the English lexicon. Titles like *The Reverend Guppy's Aquarium, Blooming English, The Dord, the Diglot, and an Avocado or Two,* or *The Secret Life of Words.*[10] In books like these, the expansion of English's lexicon—sometimes pointedly labeled 'promiscuous'—supports an argument that the language is unique, fascinating, irreverent, semantically nuanced, and (nonetheless) reflective of the ingenuity and aspiration of those who speak it. These same qualities in these same books frame changes in vocabulary over time as a quirky rise to the respectability of a global language, something that made English, to paraphrase the title of another such book, a bawdy language that slept its way to the top.[11]

And because we tie vocabulary to the identity of those who use the language, the issue of which words make it into a dictionary has real-life consequences for what vocabulary those speakers might use, for how their speech might be evaluated, for what social status and economic utility might accrue to particular varieties of English, and, indeed, for how the language is defined. Skeat himself, who first coined the expression 'ghost word' in an 1886 address to the Philological Association, urges that his audience "jealously guard against all chances of giving any undeserved record of words which had never any real existence, being mere coinages due to the blunders of printers or scribes, or to the perfervid imaginations of ignorant or blundering editors."[12] Ours may be a quirky language, but it's also a respectable one that needs to be protected from the errors of its speakers.

DICTIONARIES, LEXICOGRAPHY, SELECTION

Whenever Anglophones say "look it up in the dictionary," they say it with the conviction that the covers of a dictionary demarcate what is in the language from what is not. They haven't always said this, however, nor have they always believed that a book might define English. Indeed, dictionaries are a relatively recent development in the language's history, whether we date its beginning to the Anglo-Saxon invasions of the fifth century or to some pre-migration moment. Bilingual Latin-English wordlists like the *Medulla Grammatice* and the *Promptorium Parvulorum* first survive from the late Middle Ages, but, lacking semantic thoroughness and even alphabetical consistency, these really aren't dictionaries in a modern sense. By the sixteenth century, this limited bilingual pattern was extended to works dedicated to specific kinds of vocabulary, such as John Rastell's 1523 *Exposiciones terminorum legum Anglorum* and John Skene's 1597 *De Verborum significatione*, both of which focused on legal terminology and both of which also lack the systematic thoroughness of their modern counterparts. The first real dictionary of English, Robert Cawdry's *A Table Alphabeticall,* did not in fact appear until 1604, over halfway through the language's recorded history.

In the apparently straightforward act of choosing what words to include in his *Table,* Cawdry gave shape to English, and identifying this shape was in fact a primary objective of the broader seventeenth- and eighteenth-century codification enterprise—the writing of grammars and histories of the language that I consider in other chapters. Depending on whether a dictionary is understood to provide a mirror of language, something for it to aspire to, or an aid to readers, this shape changes considerably. Like most seventeenth-century lexicographers, Cawdry went with the principal of aiding readers, even subtitling his book (in the long-winded style characteristic of the time):

contayning and teaching the true writing and vnderstanding of hard vsuall English words, borrowed from the Hebrevv, Greeke, Latine, or French, &c. With the interpretation thereof by plaine English words, gathered for the benefit and help of all vnskilfull persons. Whereby they may the more easily and better vnderstand many hard English words, vvhich they shall heare or read in scriptures, sermons, or else vvhere, and also be made able to vse the same aptly themselues.

Cawdry's subtitle suggests just how useful his approach can be, but it also defines English only for the literate and already well-read (the illiterate, after all, couldn't read his book, much less recognize borrowings from Latin and Greek), even as it leaves the broad contours of the language undefined, since we all use more than hard words. Of the great many words that are not difficult, we might ask Cawdry, which ones still qualify as English? And more generally: must a dictionary's sense of English be a function of the book's intended audience and purpose? These are questions that can be asked and answered not by the language but only by its speakers (including lexicographers), and the history of English dictionaries is largely the history of this inquiry. As the answers have changed, so too has the lexical and conceptual shape of the language.

Edward Phillips's 1658 *New World of English Words* offers a lexicon that recalls the alive-yet-dead literary coinages already discussed. On one hand, Phillips's book depicts an almost three-fold expansion of English since Cawdry's work; on the other, by using a dagger to mark words that Phillips thought inappropriate, the work establishes degrees of acceptability. Some English words are indeed more English than others. John Ray's 1674 *Collection of English Words not Generally Used* takes this principle one step further. As the language's first dialect dictionary, the *Collection* recognizes regional words only by quarantining them from the broader (unspecified) vocabulary of English. Because they depend on users' attitudes, however, boundaries among regionalisms, hard words, inappropriate words, slang words, and just plain English have never been written in stone. The boundaries (and therefore the words that fall within them) are inevitably situational, with the result that so, too, is the sense of English conveyed by any one dictionary. Thus, in his expansive 1676 *An English Dictionary*, the schoolteacher Elisha Coles became the first English lexicographer to bring together slang and what might be called aspirational vocabulary. And the shape of the language changed yet again in the 1702 *New English Dictionary*, which established the practice of including ordinary words along with the 'hard words' that still predominated in English lexicography.[13] A half century later, Dr Johnson expanded the shape of the language's lexicon with literary excellence, for although he desired to make a book useful to contemporary speakers of English, he nonetheless defined the language by selecting particular words in part based on their beauty or on the prominence of the authors who used them. And another century later, in his 1857 Philological Society lectures surveying the state of dictionaries, Trench championed lexical objectivity over Johnson's aesthetics, "It is no task of the maker of [a dictionary] to select the *good* words of a language." With the detachment of a modern descriptive linguist, Trench continues, "The business which [the lexicographer] has undertaken is to collect and arrange all the words, whether good or bad, whether they do or do not commend themselves to his judgment."[14]

Murray once observed of the OED that "the perfection of the dictionary is in its data," and that's certainly correct.[15] But however accurate they might be, the data themselves are the fundamental lexicographical complication, even problem. From a popular perspective, dictionaries offer a picture of the language, a reflection of something external to them. Words would then be in the dictionary because they already are English words. But from another perspective, it is dictionaries that in fact regulate what does and does not qualify as English. They don't so much select the English words that are out there as determine, despite all the complications I have cited, which words these are. In effect, the shape of the language must precede the dictionary, even as the dictionary defines that shape, and so the data inevitably affirm the accuracy of the dictionary's presentation.

As far as the lexicon is concerned, this shape in many ways has emerged from a retrospective, even nostalgic, view. The frequent ordering of senses in a chronological pattern and a record of their etymology emphasize the origins of individual words as crucial to their essence, something that conceptually precedes (and perhaps supersedes) any current usage practices. The same retrospection governs English orthography. Simple words like 'knight' and 'white' are spelled this way because they have had those now counterintuitive spellings since the fifteenth century, when letters and pronunciation matched each other much more closely. Spellings that reproduce those of the language from which a word has been borrowed, again without necessarily involving a close sound–graph correspondence, reflect this same historical orientation. Dr Johnson thus spells 'enchant' and 'enchantment' as he does "after the *French*," and 'incantation' "after the *Latin*."[16] A word like 'doubt' shows just how powerful the pull of history can be in defining English. Borrowed from French in the thirteenth century, the word's earliest form was *dute*, matching the French and reflecting the fact that in French the *b* in Latin *dubito* (the French source) had long-since ceased to be pronounced. In recognition of the ultimately Latinate source, English forms of *doubt* with "restored" *b* began to appear in the fifteenth century, even though probably no one has ever articulated the sound. By the seventeenth century lexicographers had come to spell the

English word with a historical form that reflected the classical heritage underlying much English codification, although the form itself had no history.

As even popular desk dictionaries present it, the lexicon of English thus has a fundamentally transhistorical quality: English is what it was. It's for this reason that Murray argued a good deal about etymologies, pronunciations, and the permissible number of illustrative quotations with the directors of Oxford University Press, who, anxious to shorten the gargantuan OED in any way they could, thought that such material might be expendable. And it's for this reason that word origins can serve as a way to validate the Englishness of modern English words. Beginning with antiquarians in early modern England, who used them to establish the origins of the English nation, etymology and lexical history have been ways to discriminate among words and to appeal to history in order to justify a heritage that privileges some languages, users, and nations over others. William Camden, for example, ridicules popular etymologies such as 'money' from 'my honey' or 'maid' from 'my aid', even as he proposes to derive 'call' from $\kappa\alpha\lambda\acute{\epsilon}\omega$ and 'path' from $\pi\acute{\alpha}\tau\text{os}$.[17] The latter etymologies are as absurd as the former, but by connecting English words to Greek words, rather than simply other English words, they claim for England some of the glory that was Greece (if not the grandeur that was Rome). Irrespective of Camden's fancy, words deriving from the Germanic languages, French, and Latin as well as Greek are necessarily likely to have greater antiquity in English, and a mere record of their history becomes an argument that they have a greater claim to being English than do those that come from Maori, Hindi, or Algonquian. So lexicographical methods render the shape of English fundamentally old European rather than modern and global, even if a relatively recent Chinese derivative like 'ketchup' seems far more familiar in form and sense than an original Anglo-Saxon word like 'hurds' (meaning 'coarse flax').

We might leave Camden entirely out of the discussion, and etymology still would provide fairly slippery evidence for the definition of English. Since the beginning of English is more an argument than an empirically fixed moment, borrowings and word origins can be identified only in accordance with some otherwise defined genealogy, rooted in non-linguistic issues like geography and ethnicity. If English began on the Continent as a dialect of the other so-called Ingvaeonic languages (Old Saxon and Old Frisian), 'wine' and 'angel', though they respectively occur earlier in Latin *vinum* and Greek ἄγγελos, ought not to be considered borrowings since they entered the Germanic languages prior to the Anglo-Saxon migrations. English had them, in other words, when it began. If English is to be distinguished as a twelfth-century development from Saxon, as the nineteenth-century scholar John Earle preferred, then 'seraphim', which derives from Latin and ultimately Greek and Hebrew and which is first recorded in about the year 900, is likewise not borrowed, as it would have been in the language when it began. Should the beginning of English be dated otherwise, of course, or should varieties like Hawaiian Pidgin English be excluded from the river of English, then the point of reference—and thus the evidence—of word origins will change as well.

Because of its polemical nature, etymology can contribute to language definition in conflicting ways. On one hand, etymology would seem largely irrelevant to ordinary language use. Words like 'wine' and 'angel' do not take their sense strictly on an etymological basis, nor do they resonate as foreign to the language. And this is true as well for a good many more recent borrowings such as 'plaza' and 'café', the first of which is a Spanish borrowing initially recorded in 1673, the second a French borrowing of 1789. The pronouns 'they', 'them', and 'their' likewise seem entirely English, though they were in fact borrowed from Old Norse and survive abundantly in documents only from the fifteenth century. A word like 'fakir' might seem to declare an obviously borrowed status, yet it is first recorded over four centuries ago, while 'frameup', 'kindheartedly', and 'sidestep' (the verb), all apparently pure Germanic forms, date only to around 1900. The origin of a word in fact often has little to with the word's naturalness or status in the everyday usage of speakers.

On the other hand, perhaps because of the significance vocabulary in general has for definitions of English, word origins have played their own significant role in sustaining ideas of the language. We care about them because we care what English is.

Since word origins are in fact obscure for many speakers, it is perhaps better to say that it is the *idea* of word origins that has been significant. A recent morphology textbook, for instance, maintains that, though the core vocabulary has been passed down for centuries, over 80% of the current lexis represents borrowings.[18] A figure like this would suggest two things: firstly, that most of the words most people use are in some sense foreign; and secondly, the facts of word origins can be incidental to definitions of English, since it's possible for some Anglophones to separate the language from its overwhelmingly borrowed vocabulary. By demonstrating antiquity, etymology can validate the character and integrity of English even when many English words are arguably not of English origins.

The English language may be without circumference (as Murray noted), but the same cannot be said of dictionaries. Even the ones that seem infinitely expandable (online publications like OED3 or the *Urban Dictionary*) have limits at any one moment in time. And since limits are predicated on principles— since what English is depends in part on why lexicographers and speakers care—so they produce different pictures of English. Cawdry drew a circumference around hard words, which Coles expanded to include slang. Johnson drew the circumference still wider, to incorporate literary language, and in doing so established a lexicographical reliance on written language, specifically learned or belletristic written language, that remains influential to this day.

The OED, thus, has always defined the language largely not through spoken usages or ephemeral written ones, which account for the overwhelming majority of English utterances, but through the words of someone like Chaucer, who was responsible for 11,000 quotations in the dictionary's first edition.[19] In OED3, the top most cited sources are the *Times* of London, Shakespeare, Walter Scott, the *Philosophical Transactions* of the Royal Society of London, the *Encyclopedia Britannica*, Chaucer, and Milton. Even when barely half of the original OED had appeared, George Krapp expressed his view that language, in the first instance, is always spoken and that "past literary use is only one of many tests that must be applied in determining present use."[20] But despite this early view and despite the emphasis modern linguistics places on specialist corpora (collections of unedited, ordinary speech or writing) of spoken language,[21] the common, influential desk-works to which Anglophones turn when they want to look something up in the dictionary (such as *Webster's New World Dictionary of the American Language*) continue to rely on the principles of a writing-based understanding of English vocabulary. *Chambers Twentieth-Century Dictionary* follows this same OED model by featuring literary words recorded since the sixteenth century, whatever their current usage.

Like etymology, these principles shape the language with implications beyond language alone. Since literacy and education are to a significant extent functions of class—especially so in Johnson's day but still today—any definition that emphasizes written language, particularly literary language, necessarily incorporates social criteria beside linguistic ones. The entire notion of a dictionary as a measure of language—even of a dictionary alone—depends on a literate population, not all of whose members in fact will be literate in the same way or to the same degree. If dictionaries can treat some words as more English than others, they also thus can foster the same sense about some varieties of the language and about the speakers who utter those varieties and the uses to which they put them.

Other principles can have just as much social (even political) significance. Like many lexicographers, Trench puzzled over how to map foreign and obsolete words—how to decide when the former have become naturalized and which of the latter merit inclusion in English's lexicon. As always, any representation of this lexicon depends in part on the size limits allowed by a publisher, and in order to keep dictionaries manageable Trench advocated jettisoning "a whole army of purely technical words; such as, indeed, are not for the most part, except by an abuse of language, words at all, but signs." With the elimination of such "rubbish," dictionaries would have room to include regionalisms, even those passing from usage, which deserve a place not "in right [sic] of what they now are, but of what they once have been."[22] Of course, the argument that historical regionalisms were more English than modern scientific language extends the historical orientation of dictionaries in general, and this, too, is an argument with implications for heritage, since above all it ties the lexicon of English to usage in England, where the language has been spoken for the longest time. To Trench, the English past is worth remembering, but not the advances of modern technology.

Murray's own circumference reflects a Victorian sensibility. Given the scope and status of the OED, he tried to be lexically tolerant, far more so, in fact, than many of his critics then or now have acknowledged. But in doing so, and in conjunction with his frequent appeals to readers to produce the quotations that form the basis of the OED, Murray ended up amplifying and complicating the selection that is inherent in all lexicography. The more words he sought and got, the more the vocabulary of English grew. And the larger it became, the more selective he had to be and the more difficult (and longer) his task became. In the event, the principles of the OED allowed for a good many regionalisms and antiquated forms but excluded most words relating vulgarly to excrement, sex, or race, along with (more benignly and following British lexicographic practice) county names, street names, person names, place names, and many kinds of nonsense words. Like Trench, Murray wrestled over which foreign or regional words ought to be accepted as English. To resolve such selection difficulties, he went so far as to mark some headwords with parallel lines to indicate that the words were "non-naturalized or partially-naturalized."[23] Like the improper words Phillips had marked with a dagger, these words were and were not English. And like Trench, Murray considered English to be more an extension of the past than a creation of the present.

If lexicography today embraces a broader social spectrum of words than it did in Murray's day, it still must exercise principled selectivity, by which some speakers (lexicographers) designate as English only some of the words Anglophones use. The four-volume OED supplement published between 1972 and 1986 sometimes made its designations based on "matchability." If a word was already in the dictionary, that is, that word justified the inclusion of morphologically similar ones, and in this way, 'Minorcan' allowed for 'Ibicenan', but morphologically unprecedented words had a tougher going.[24] And today's principles sometimes still echo not only the historical orientation of earlier lexicography but its social views as well. The OED thus continues to designate some words as Americanisms, Australianisms, Canadianisms, and New Zealandisms, but only with the online OED3 has begun designating as specifically British words like 'chav' (a loutish youth) and senses like 'residential boarding school' for 'house'. It likewise defines certain words—such as 'French fried potatoes' for 'chip'—in ways that will make sense to British Anglophones but not to anyone who learned English in the United States or from American speakers.[25] In its history and current form, the OED thereby continues to grant to English's oldest varieties and their heritage a centrality in the language's definition.

One approach to these complex issues of selection has been, in essence, to try to avoid them by making each dictionary larger than its predecessor. The first *Webster's International Dictionary* (1890) thus had 175,000 entries, the *Century Dictionary* (1889–91) 215,000, and *Funk and Wagnalls Standard Dictionary* (1893–94) 304,000. *Webster's Third International Dictionary* appeared in 1961 with 2,662 pages and 450,000 entries. To reach 600,000 words, OED3 includes all manner of words previously judged regional, vulgar, or slang. It's as if size alone might silence unease about how a dictionary defines English, even as it serves as a promotional feature for new volumes in a competitive market. Or in Sidney Landau's assessment of the printed volumes predating the virtual OED3, "The prestige of owning an immense unabridged dictionary, representing in its solid, blocklike weight the stability and power of the whole of the English language, as the Bible represented faith in God, was a powerful argument for purchase."[26] Such prestige persisted into the not-too-distant past, when any bright American heading off to a university brought along a collegiate dictionary and a typewriter. For keyboarding students of today, the former seems to be as quaint as the latter, even if the OED remains a few keystrokes away.

Another, specifically modern response to the challenge of circumscribing what Murray characterized as uncircumscribable has been the proliferation of kinds of dictionaries. In this way, lexicographers can avoid some of the messy issues I have considered by focusing on the vocabulary of a specific field. The past century in particular has thus witnessed terrific growth in the publication of thesauri, place-name dictionaries, pronunciation dictionaries, phraseological dictionaries, dialect dictionaries, collegiate dictionaries, etymological dictionaries, and so forth. While examples of these types of dictionaries predate the modern era (e.g., Rastell's 1523 *Exposiciones terminorum legum Anglorum*), their current popularity reflects a modern response to the theoretical difficulties involved in defining the limits of a language: the difficulties are simply evaded through a focus on what is (or might be) circumscribable—parts of the language. Since the 1960s, the argument of limited comprehensiveness also has made possible dictionaries devoted to the regional varieties of Australia, New Zealand, South Africa, the United States, Canada, and so forth.

In dismissing attempts to write rigid definitions of English, Murray once said that "the question, whether a particular word or construction is 'English', is constantly settled by each man according to his own feeling and usage, as if *his* English were all of English."[27] But like all dictionaries, the OED was (and is) in precisely the same position as the speaker Murray imagined: it had to define the language in accordance with its own feeling (regionalisms qualified as English but vulgarity did not) and usage, which came in the form of submitted quotations. If certain words and usages were strictly oral, were confined to unprinted and unread manuscripts, or simply were overlooked by readers, the OED obviously could not include them, however much they might have been used at some point. Any dictionary's command of English may be privileged among Anglophones, but, like any Anglophone in Murray's analysis, it is also inherently conjectural, sometimes in ways to which it (like any speaker) can be blind.

Whether large or small, dictionaries ultimately construct arguments: about what's in a language and what's not, about the social status of the words they include, about their meanings. As the arbiters of lexicon, they are also the arbiters of English, and in both cases they make what can seem to be absolute decisions on tenuous evidence. Even if we consult dictionaries only to find the spellings or meanings of words—which is in fact the overwhelming reason most people ever use them, if they ever use them—we will not and cannot agree that words mean *only* what the dictionaries say they do or that the *only* real words are those listed in dictionaries. Pretty clearly words change meaning through usage (with which prescriptive as well as descriptive grammarians would agree), and as much English as there is today, and as many people as there are speaking it, no one dictionary can ever define all the usages. Nor (I think) can any single user find all the uses, whether in dictionaries, corpora, or the ephemerality of speech.

THE EVANESCENT IMAGE

When dictionaries argue with each other, over spellings, etymologies, and so forth, they do so with the kinds of social implications I have described. By granting that some words are more English than others, they privilege the language of the speakers (and the speakers themselves) who have the best access to this English, whether through education, birth, or social standing. Other kinds of lexical argument are even more explicit in this regard. Sixteenth- and seventeenth-century quarrels thus focused on whether English vocabulary should be limited to a simple, pure, and largely Anglo-Saxon core, or should become elegant and copious (in the rhetoric of the day) through the addition of learned borrowings from Latin and Greek in particular. In his 1605 *A Restitution of Decayed Intelligence*, Richard Verstegan put the argument this way. Some critics, he says, "think our toung thereby much bettred" through borrowing, but others say "that it is of it self no language at all, but the scum of many languages" and still others "that it is most barren, and that wee are dayly faine to borrow woords for it . . . out of other languages to patche it vp withall."[28] With a 33-page alphabetized list of "our moste ancient English woords" and their modern synonyms and orthographic equivalents, Verstegan's *Restitution* sided with those who thought lexical stability should come internally, from English's native word stock. But contemporaries such as Richard Carew, in his "Excellency of the English Tongue," advocated that an infusion of learned borrowings— derisively labeled inkhorn terms by their opponents—was the best way for English to achieve lexical balance. And still other critics, like Thomas Wilson, saw inkhorn terms as a problem not because they were Latinate but because they represented variance from whatever constancy English already had: "Among al other lessons, this should first be learned, that we neuer affect any straunge ynkehorne termes, but so speake as is commonly received: neither sekyng to be ouer fine, nor yet liuyng ouer carelesse, vsyng our speache as most men do, & ordryng our wittes, as the fewest haue doen."[29]

What makes the inkhorn controversy more than a trivial academic debate is the way it allowed participants to discuss social issues through the shape of English. Latin and Greek (or rather Rome and Greece) provided more than linguistic targets. To a country beginning to establish colonies and trade around the globe, early empires offered a model for national identification and a select club (as it were) that Britain hoped to join. To speak with Latin and Greek words could be seen as evidence of imperial status. Closer to home, lexicon interacted with early modern social changes in the expansion not simply of literacy but of a moneyed economy. Already in the late-medieval period, the legend of Dick Whittington and his cat (which became a popular early modern stage play) expressed a sense that through hard work and initiative, any individual might achieve success. By the time of the inkhorn controversy a few centuries later, economic expansion had produced a social hierarchy (extending from peasant to noble) that in fact was less fixed than it had been in the Middle Ages. It could be difficult to distinguish a yeoman (maybe even a gentleman) from a rustic on the basis of income, housing, occupation, or clothing—the latter despite sumptuary laws that regulated the kinds of clothing individual estates (or social ranks) might wear. In these circumstances, speakers' words could be used to confirm either their social rank or their pretense to be something other than they were. Like much attention to language, whether trivial concerns about punctuation or larger ones about new varieties of English, such views had an inherently conservative effect. Proper command of Latin, French, and any specialized words that derived from them was the sort of linguistic skill accessible primarily to an educated elite, whose social status thus was maintained in part by the way dictionaries defined English.[30]

A comparable social impetus, variously nationalistic and moralizing, underwrote the creation of the OED. As much as Trench stressed the historical value of the then-proposed work, frequently describing it as an "inventory" of words, he also saw "honour" in its production through the contributions of individuals joined "hand in hand" across Britain like, rather disconcertingly, Persian soldiers as they cleared an island of its inhabitants (in Herodotus's account).[31] And Trench's day job, it's worth noting, was as Dean of Christ Church in Dublin. In the event, the unprecedented size and scope of the dictionary made their own arguments for its cultural significance. It may not have been Murray's intention to do so, but he necessarily contributed to the formation of an emergent Victorian Britain as world leader and paragon of civilization that might be witnessed in colonial activities, political reformation, and cultural achievements like the National Portrait Gallery and the OED.[32]

This is the sociolinguistic status, with its triumphant implications for what English and its vocabulary are, that forms part of the context for the scathing reaction to the 1961 publication of *Webster's Third New International Dictionary*. Declining to impose a traditional designation like 'colloquialism', and expanding the English vocabulary to include vulgarities and slang like 'ain't', *Webster's Third* became (for some critics) a symbol of social permissiveness and national apathy. Indeed, its swift, hostile reception focused less on the accuracy of any definitions or etymologies and more on the social implications of the shape the dictionary gave to English. According to an editorial in the *New York Times*, "Webster's has, it is apparent, surrendered to the permissive school that has been busily extending its beachhead on English instruction in the schools. This development is disastrous because, intentionally or unintentionally, it serves to reinforce the notion that good English is whatever is popular."[33]

By way of a conclusion to this discussion, it's useful to remember that dictionaries alone are in no position to enforce their own arguments about the shape of English's vocabulary. Neither OED3 nor *Webster's Third* can compel Anglophones to use certain words in certain ways. Rather, the dictionaries' authority and schools' power to enforce this authority are qualities that readers invest in them. In effect, as much as lexicographers might have to know upfront what English is in order to record it, so Anglophones have to know upfront (or upon reflection) whether or not they agree with the dictionary. When it appeared, the OED clearly happened to tell a good many speakers, including those whose varieties the dictionary excluded or marginalized, what they already believed or were prepared to believe about English; *Webster's Third* did not.

It is because dictionaries offer arguments that are subject to their users that such disagreements over the shape of English are inevitable and, at least sometimes, irresolvable. In the contemporary era, when speakers outside of Kachru's Inner Circle have become numerically dominant in the ranks of Anglophones, nationalism and ethnic identity (rather than antique roots, beauty, scientific objectivity, or structural consistency) offer heritages that can motivate the expansion of dictionaries and lexicography to include specific regional varieties. And the fault lines between English and non-English accordingly can take shape less on the issues of social class and education that animated the inkhorn controversy and more on the identity of speakers. "It is a natural sociolinguistic development," according to Jeannette Allsopp, "that where a recognized language exists there should be a dictionary to ensure that the variety selected by the speech community concerned is codified, and that this dictionary should be generally recognized as the authority in matters of usage."[34] For any dictionary, this authority always relies not on self-evident data but on lexicographical claims about English with which readers may (or may not) agree. Those who accept the arguments implicit in grammars and dictionaries of Asian, Black South African, or Singaporean English have already accepted the social implications of such speech communities and of an English that includes such varieties. Those who reject such arguments—and some do so vehemently—have not.[35] By themselves, dictionaries can do very little to settle such disagreements.

In describing what he saw as a lexicon with a center and no circumference, Murray maintained that "the vocabulary of English-speaking men ... may be compared to one of those natural groups of the zoologist or botanist, wherein typical species forming the characteristic nucleus of the order, are linked on every side to other species, in which the typical character is less and less apparent."[36] Given Murray's training as a philologist and philology's own debts to nineteenth-century scientific methods, the metaphor is very much of its time. But it also overlooks the dynamics between Anglophones and the words they use. Murray imagines English as an independent organism, something that, like a plant or animal, reproduces on its own and survives by means of its adaptability to a changing environment. In times of drought or famine, the hardier organisms pass on their DNA, while the others die off, with the result that the species in its entirety exists and is changed by the viability of its members. But at least so long as English is a living language, a metaphor like this fails to capture the fundamental duality of vocabulary. In order to exist, words require speakers, agents who are external to them and who control their pronunciation, sense, and frequency. It is speakers who reproduce words, not the words themselves, and much as dictionary users might want dictionaries to image their language, they themselves are the ones who do so. The organic world has no parallel to such an arrangement. Despite a popular (and occasionally professional) belief that a language and its dictionary are synonymous, lexicographers can attempt to record only the outlines of something—a language—that either has no fixed limits or, to the extent that it has at least virtual limits, embodies those limits only in dictionaries themselves.

A better metaphor for the lexical shape of English, then, might come from photography. Like photographers, lexicographers try to capture the image of something that doesn't have a specific shape until they frame or pose it in that way and take the picture—i.e., until, having decided what English is, they produce a book that supports their belief. It's a belief that other lexicographers and Anglophones are free to reject. And it's an image of a lexicon that, once photographed, immediately changes through the addition and obsolescence of words and the transformations of their meanings.

CHAPTER THREE

When Words Die

As much as we like to think about vocabulary from historical perspectives—as something that exists independently of speakers—heritage creeps in. It does so when we judge some words as more English than others, or when we invest vocabulary with a measure of national dignity and identity, and even when we cede to dictionaries the power to define the language we speak. We may look to dictionaries for the stability of spellings and usage, but we find as well arguments about the nature of language, the relations between grammar and usage, the role of history in definitions of a language, and the relative status of regional varieties and sociolects (language varieties that correlate with a social feature such as education, race, ethnicity, or sex, rather than geography). Anglophones are not so much subject to the authority of dictionaries for deciding what is and is not English, I have suggested, as they are the authorities who enable dictionaries to shape English, whether directly as lexicographers or indirectly as those for whom dictionaries are marketed. In Chapter Two I discussed how Anglophones distinguish English words from non-English ones. Here I consider how they separate the living vocabulary from the dead. Once we decide a word qualifies as English, however we decide this, how do we know if it's current?

In the abstract, the fact that words die should occasion no surprise. Long ago in his *Poetics* the Latin poet Horace thought this to be as natural as the falling of autumn leaves:

> As forests in each advancing year exchange their leaves—
> the first ones to fall—so an old generation of words perishes,
> and words new in usage and form flourish and thrive.[1]

Word death might even be considered healthy, affirming that a language and its speakers are alive, crafting what is said in relation to what is experienced. For as Murray said in the OED, "The 'origin of language' is not to be sought merely in far-off Indo-European antiquity, or in a still earlier pre-Aryan yore-time; it is still in perennial process around us."[2] Only dead languages, disengaged from this "perennial process," have words that cannot die. Of course, neither can a language like ancient Greek create any new words: nearly all the genuinely ancient Greek words that ever were or will be written can be located in Liddell and Scott's *Greek-English Lexicon*.

Like words' quirks and creations, their deaths nonetheless can prompt a kind of cultural soul-searching. Charles Mackay's 1874 *Lost Beauties of the English Language* thus acknowledges that great languages like Sanskrit, Greek, and Latin have all experienced some diminishment on their way to "apotheosis." And it regards English as in its "vigorous youth" without any "symptoms of decay." Nonetheless, Mackay worries over the vocabulary English has lost, particularly from among the language of peasants, and he accordingly offers an alphabetized list of words that might be revived, illustrated with copious quotations from Spenser, Shakespeare, Pope, Burns, and the like.[3] While Mackay's argument is thus ultimately aesthetic and cultural, modern accounts of word death share the amused irony of their counterpart discussions of word creation. Entries for the *Word Museum* were selected on their "eccentric phonic essence" and "to spotlight endearing, rough-hewn, and humorous aspects of Old World life"; and so it includes *giggle-trot* (an 'older woman who marries'), *lant* ('stale urine'), and the like.[4] Titles such as *Gallimaufry: A Hodgepodge of our Vanishing Vocabulary* and *Dewdroppers, Waldos, and Slackers: A Decade-by-decade Guide to the Vanishing Vocabulary of the Twentieth Century* reflect a similar sensibility about the whimsy of vocabulary, the novelties of its history, and the ironic detachment of observers who see in dead words confirmation that they speak a superior form of the language. Lexical demise thereby satisfies the same curiosity as does lexical creation—which seems to be the curiosity one might have while marveling at a preposterous clockwork toy.

Pleasing as this toy might be, the fundamental distinction between a word's life and death is itself not easy to make, partly because it's a distinction often based as much on the judgment of the toymaker (as it were) as on any empirical test, and partly because it is embedded in the heritage that language perpetuates. And here I offer some of my own linguistic history and heritage—a personal anecdote about my grandfather, who was born in 1889 and raised on farms in Nebraska and Wisconsin, and who always seemed ancient and slightly exotic to me. He'd ridden on a covered wagon, was trained as a blacksmith, and could still shoe a horse well into his 70s; had seen former heavyweight champions John L. Sullivan and 'Gentleman' Jim Corbett stage an exhibition boxing match; and had attended a performance of Buffalo Bill's Wild West, featuring the Congress of the Rough Riders. It was as if he'd emerged from a black-and-white photograph or maybe even a daguerreotype, at least once I knew what daguerreotypes were. And he had odd ways of speaking that I noticed already as a child. He pronounced 'accept' as if it were spelled 'assept', sometimes spoke so quickly I could hardly understand him, and frequently used the word 'dasn't'.

I'd never heard that word from anyone else. In fact, I've still never heard anyone else use it as a part of ordinary conversation. Neither the OED nor *Webster's New World Dictionary* records 'dasn't', though the word does appear in the *Dictionary of American Regional English* (DARE), where it's listed as a contraction of 'dare not'. The earliest quotation, from Benjamin Dearborn's 1795 *Columbian Grammar*, cites "Dazzent for Dare not" among a "List of Improprieties, commonly called Vulgarisms, which should never be used in *Speaking, Reading*, or *Writing*."[5] This may be an inauspicious way for a word to come into existence, but 'dasn't' does seem to have enjoyed a hearty if brief life from the beginning of the nineteenth century to the middle part of the twentieth. Examples of the word range across a broad swath of the country, primarily east of the Mississippi river: much of the Midwest and upper South, as well as New England and the Atlantic seaboard. Most of the citations are to linguistic discussions, however, suggesting that even if 'dasn't' wasn't always regarded as improper, there was always something odd about it. A 1907 piece in *Dialect Notes* goes so far as to "conjugate" the word: "I dassent, you dassent, he dassent, we dassent, you dassent, they dassent."[6] The word's most distinguished occurrence may be in Mark Twain's *Adventures of Huckleberry Finn*, though even here it's a little discredited by the company it keeps. "She was afraid to go to bed," Huck says of Aunt Sally, whom he and Tom Sawyer have been tormenting with vague and unnecessary warnings as a part of Tom's cruel plot to free the already freed slave Jim; "but she 'dasn't' set up."[7] Like an ornithologist in search of an ivory-billed woodpecker, a DARE fieldworker turned up a live specimen in a 1968 interview: "He goes everywhere up here but down there he dasn't." And in parts of the country the word still seems to be known (though rarely used), chiefly among elderly speakers. For the most part, 'dasn't' has died a quiet death, periodically displayed by linguists in a kind of taxidermied form, as I have here.[8]

That 'dasn't' should have been vital and anything but mummified for my grandfather makes complete sense. He lived his entire life in the Midwest (a nesting ground of 'dasn't' usage), his lifetime spanned the latter half of the word's own lifetime, and he'd attended formal school only through the eighth grade, with the result that his speech habits were never colored by the regionally non-specific vocabulary and forms of standard language. He'd used 'dasn't' the way most speakers use most words: without affectation and without any metalinguistic sense of how individual words might relate to the larger, structured patterns of dialects and languages. All that is clear.

What's less clear is why 'dasn't' should have, in effect, died out at virtually the same time my grandfather passed away. Though restricted to the United States, the word's geographical habitat was essentially the eastern half of the country, which in 1900, when 'dasn't' was middle-aged, had about 76 million people. Since the majority of the population lived east of the Mississippi river, perhaps 40–50 million people had the opportunity to hear and use 'dasn't'. So the number of speakers shouldn't have presented difficulties. Given my grandfather's background and the predominance of citations in DARE to wordlists and the like, it's certainly possible that throughout its lifetime 'dasn't' bore the social marking Dearborn ascribed to it—a low-class word that people of quality avoided, even if they knew what it meant. The DARE citations do not provide much evidence of this, however, outside of a comment in Elmer Atwood's 1953 *A Survey of Verb Forms in the Eastern United States*: "Most cultured informants lack a negative contraction of this verb [*dare*], and about half the noncultured in s[outhern] N[ew] Eng[land] fail to give such a form." This would mean, of course, that 'dasn't' tokens come entirely from the other half of the "noncultured" speakers. The distribution of usage in *The Adventures of Tom Sawyer* as well as *Adventures of Huckleberry Finn* points in a similar, if similarly inconclusive, direction. The word is used three times in the former, twice by Tom Sawyer and once by the slave Jim; and 11 times in the latter, eight times by Huck (including the passage I quoted above), once by Jim, once by Aunt Sally, and once by an "old doctor." Of the 14 occurrences, then, only one (the doctor's) is spoken by someone who is not clearly lower class and uneducated.

The form of the word may have presented problems as well, since abstracting 'dares not' from 'dasn't' seems less straightforward than, say, 'cannot' from 'can't'. Comparably obscure, 'won't' for 'will not' at least has history on its side; it's been around since the fifteenth century. Speakers outside of the most productive age brackets and dialects for 'dasn't' thus may have shared my own genuinely confused reaction. And their incomprehension could have stigmatized the form and led many of those who said 'dasn't' to restrict their usage for fear of giving away their age and provincialism—the way singing along to an outdated song can.

These are all hypotheses that could be empirically supported in only limited ways. Research of old newspapers and books might turn up some significant examples—significant because they might clarify the demographics of the word's most frequent users, or because they might directly comment (like Atwood) on the word's social status. And we might follow in the footsteps of the DARE fieldworker by going in search of 'dasn't', beginning with elderly informants in remote places where it was last heard. Oddly enough, this would be an eclectic group of locales: New Mexico, Utah, Georgia, Mississippi, Pennsylvania, and

New York. We could in this way build up a biography of 'dasn't' that would identify just who did use it, how, where, and for what purposes, and with this biography we could offer a postmortem judgment that death was due to specific natural causes—such as that 'dasn't' had in fact become associated with the elderly or uneducated—or to causes unknown.

What interests me in this example (beyond the fact, I confess, of a secret hope to revive 'dasn't') is how it epitomizes word death, speakers' roles in it, and the limitations of our knowledge. Some of the word's history reads like a dispassionate autopsy: who used the word, where and when they did so, and how its form may have affected usage. Some of the history reads more like social critique, suggesting not only that Anglophones may have been the ones to kill off 'dasn't' but that they did so in ways that reflected their social status: lower-class speakers, that is, may have been complicit in upper-class speakers' stigmatization of the word. Some of the history reads like science fiction, since it's not really clear whether 'dasn't' is in fact dead. It's living in this book, of course, just as all the words found in OED3, however infrequently some of them might be used, remain forever alive in a kind of cryogenic state. And some of what I've traced reads like a mystery novel. We might never formulate an exact theory of just why 'dasn't' died (if it is in fact dead) or whether something killed it. Even if we did, we'd have no way to test the theory. We can't very well replicate entire speech communities for any length of time by fashioning controlled environments and, in the spirit of the *Twilight Zone*, maintaining model populations within them in order to evaluate the performance of words like 'dasn't'. As important as the death of words is to the shape of English, and as important as the shape of English is to Anglophones, there's just a lot we don't know.

CAUSES OF DEATH—NATURAL AND OTHERWISE

We do know, in very general terms, that word death has been attributed to both mechanical and social factors. By 'mechanical' I mean reasons rooted in claims about the structural viability of words or about the psycholinguistics of their production, use, and retention. As comparative and historical linguistics developed in the nineteenth century, such mechanical analyses prevailed, particularly in approaches imbued with the principles of the day's most celebrated scientific theory, evolution. The nineteenth-century linguists Max Müller and August Schleicher, for example, drew on natural selection in order to argue that languages (and by extensions words) that die out do so because they are less fit, less adapted to their linguistic environment, than are the ones that survive. Schleicher, indeed, thought that the retreat of North American Indian languages before the advance of European ones served as proof that linguistically, as well as biologically and culturally, only the fittest were able to survive.[9]

At roughly the same time, the zoologist Charles Lyell wondered if the same natural laws governed both languages and species. Believing that a divine force instigated the evolutionary principles that Darwin described, Lyell understood these principles to have defined the broadest characteristics of the descent and development of species, including the kinds and numbers of species that might come into being. And if the natural world adhered to such constraints, why not human language?[10] This was how Darwin himself had imagined language in *The Descent of Man*. "We see variability in every tongue," he said, "and new words are continually cropping up; but as there is a limit to the powers of the memory, single words, like whole languages, gradually become extinct."[11] For Lyell, Darwin, and many of their contemporaries, such arguments amounted to reasoning from language to the natural world, since they began with language change and development and used them to explain by analogy the transmutation of species. These are arguments reflecting the neo-grammarians' conviction not only in language change as an exceptionless process but also in universal constants that define an ordered, harmonious universe governed at all levels by forces that mimic and mirror one another. Such theories have little popularity today, since modern linguists, for all their interest in universal grammar, tend to be skeptical about explanations rooted in universal human experience. At the same time, Lyell and Darwin do raise an interesting point for word death and the shape of English.

In Chapter Two, I suggested that a fluent Anglophone may well have an active vocabulary that represents less than a tenth of the words recorded in the OED. One implication of this ratio is that all speakers, even the very well read and educated, necessarily encounter words that are recorded in dictionaries but that they've never seen or heard before—whether the words are learned (*kapha*, one of the humors in Ayurvedic medicine) or colloquial (*rutchie*, a Pennsylvanian word for a sledding-slope). But another, less obvious implication may be what ties together biology and the definition of English.

Might the ratio between an individual's lexicon and that of the language in its entirety owe not simply to the specific experiences of that individual but to the capacity of the human language faculty to store, remember, and use words? Darwin suggested, indeed, that there may be an upper limit of the number of words (active or passive) that speakers can control. As active as Anglophones are in creating new words to describe new phenomena and experiences, some words may thus have to die (or at least get moved to the attic of our passive vocabulary) because in order to acquire new words, we have to clear some metaphorical space in our mental lexicons. And so we as individuals forget the slang of our youth or the lexicon of a foreign language we are struggling to learn. By this argument perhaps languages in their totality, in order to allow for lexical growth, *have* to phase out unused or little-used words—sort of a biolexical imperative that keeps the river of English below flood stage.

But analyses like these only shift the focus of discussion, of course. My argument throughout this book is that languages are not self-contained, volitional organisms; they are what speakers make of them. And if speakers (or languages) in some sense need to let certain words die, what determines what these words will be and whether speakers will regard them as dead? What would it mean to be an unfit word or language? An unfit organism is easy enough to identify: it's the one that cannot survive and reproduce in its environment. But what would an unfit word (or language) be? Pronunciation alone is not determinative, since words that might be regarded as phonologically complex, containing several different kinds of sounds, can be as resilient as the phonologically simple; 'a' and 'is' have been around for nearly a millennium, but so have 'tomorrow' and 'smothering'. And when pronunciation adjustments like assimilation and naturalization are taken into account, there seems to be no reason why a word's phonology could ever by itself make it unfit for survival. If it's difficult for Anglophones facing 'psychology' to muster up something like the Greek pronunciation 'psoochologeea', 'saikahlojee' has considerably simplified the matter. A word's survival is similarly not tied to the complexity of its sense. The semantically and phonologically straightforward 'milk' and 'cat' have been used for centuries, but so too have the morphologically complex 'resemblance' and 'delicious'. The building-blocks of words, their morphemes, may themselves be subject to atrophy and death but likewise offer few insights into lexical fitness. A morpheme may become less productive, or die, as has perhaps the adjectival suffix *–ic*, deriving ultimately, via French *–ique* and Latin *–icus*, from Greek *–ικός*. But if the morpheme occurs in familiar words, it cannot be the cause of its own death. And this is precisely the case with the *–ic* that remains in common words like 'grammatical', 'acidic', and 'chaotic'.

The cognitive linguist Stephen Pinker offers one way to approach the concept of fitness among words. Pursuing an analysis of the elements of meaning in words (a semantic component analysis), he stresses the relevance of universal conceptual categories that various languages combine in various ways. Irrespective of individual words' history, then, the fit ones would be the ones that best channel these categories for a particular group of speakers.[12] Other critics fold usage into their mechanical approach to word death. Frequency in particular, it is sometimes argued, may figure in survivability: the more common a word is, the more likely it is to survive. For one thing, words that occur commonly seem to be more immediately comprehensible—and thus less likely to go unused—than are scientific, regional, or technical words that occur infrequently and in limited contexts.[13] And for another, the more common a word is, the more likely it is to be polysemous and thus viable in different contexts.[14] The OED records 27 distinct senses for the common verb 'suffer', for example, and one for 'polysemous': 'that has a multiplicity of meanings'.

But like fitness, word frequency by itself cannot explain why some words survive and others don't. In fact, frequency is a virtual synonym for survival, since a word that occurs frequently is of necessity also a word that's not dead yet. By Pinker's semantic analysis, frequency would be a function of how well a word fits universal conceptual categories. Other psycholinguists attribute the creation and retention of new words not only to their frequency but also to the diversity of contexts of usage, semantic transparency, and potential for being understood as representations of some larger semantic category.[15] By extension, a word that violated all these criteria would not be likely to survive, so that their absence could be considered a cause of death. But this analysis still leaves unanswered the question of why some words are polysemous and others are not.

It is because of questions like this that social causes have also been used to explain why words die. By this I mean causes that are rooted in how, when, why, and by whom a word is used. Their focus is less on the structure of language or its relations with cognition and more on the pragmatics of individual users and usages, including the users' attitudes about whether particular words are alive or dead. A word might die simply because it was never very much alive—never used by a socially or numerically viable group of speakers. Such can be the case with slang, cant (thieves' slang), teenage vernacular, and regionalisms, including, perhaps, 'dasn't'. Other kinds of ephemeral or arch language, such as the obscure vocabulary of cults and learned cliques, can also be mentioned here. The whole point of such vocabulary is that it be both group-defining and incomprehensible to anyone outside the group. Once they do gain currency, such words might pass into general usage but, often enough, their currency leads to their rejection, both by those who initiated the vocabulary and by those who would emulate it. The former reject the words because they are no longer restricted to their group, and the latter because once the original speakers reject them, their purchase on those speakers becomes obsolete. Indeed, as quickly as the lexicon associated with specific groups or experiences comes to life and expands, it often disappears, or at least much of it does, into oblivion. American university students at the end of the nineteenth century defined themselves with any number of now long-defunct words and usages (*flam, frivol,* and *pape*), while the Second World War produced *moaning minnie* for an 'air-raid siren', and that phrase, too, has fallen mostly silent along with the sirens.[16]

Oddly enough, such word histories mean that teenagers, criminals, and academics can have much in common. Words like 'cheddar' ('money') and 'noob' (an 'ignorant person') pass into and out of usage with the lifespan of adolescence precisely because they are one of the ways—along with clothing, music, or hairstyles—that can help define any stage of life.[17] As in the case of slang like the thieves' slang of early Australia (known as flash), such lexical self-definition also facilitates illicit activity against speakers who do not know the meaning of particular words. Once a prospective nineteenth-century target realized that 'mazzard' meant 'face' and 'beans' 'five-dollar gold pieces', a burglar who hoped to be successful would need to discard the words and move on to other neologisms (newly coined words).[18] And this same motivation to use obscure language for self-definition and exclusion animates the inkhorn controversy that I discussed in Chapter Two. On one hand, critics like Thomas Blount in his 1656 *Glossographia* accepted words such as *advigilate* (to 'watch diligently') and *adoxy* ('ignominy') as part of a variety of English accessible only to those trained in the classical languages. On the other, in his posthumously published translation of the New Testament John Cheke (1514–57) responded to ephemeral Latinate language and its socially stratifying impact by coining equally peculiar group-defining words from native Anglo-Saxon roots: *mooned* for 'lunatic', *tollers* for 'publicans', *hundreder* for 'centurion', and *crossed* for 'crucified'.[19] Cheke's coinages defined a popular rather than a learned audience but in the end proved no more durable than *advigilate* or *adoxy.*

From another social perspective, English words sometimes seem to die because they have become colored by those who use them, or because a particular word's reference has become sacred, obscene, vulgar, or otherwise compromised. From the Old English period through the eighteenth century, for instance,

English had two words similar in form but distinct in sense and, for much of this period, pronunciation: *queen,* meaning a 'female monarch', and *quean,* meaning an 'impudent woman', 'hussy', and even 'prostitute'. By the eighteenth century, the two words, which are closely related in etymology anyway, had become identical in pronunciation, and *quean* (the argument goes) largely dropped from the vocabulary (or merged with *queen*), presumably to avoid embarrassments of homophonic confusion. In this case, one might say the word was intentionally killed, but a quiet fading away, in the presence of a new alternative, is also possible. Such a word first becomes rare, then obsolete, then antiquated, and finally extinct. Even more benignly, words might die because the object they referred to did. We don't use swords much anymore, and neither do we have the range of Anglo-Saxon words used to describe them, including *bil, handseax,* and, with a poetic twist, *irena cyst* ('best of irons'). (We do, however, still 'dial' phones, even though most of those using them today have never done anything but push buttons to connect.)

As these example suggest, while we may have difficulty predicting word death, we sometimes still might be able to offer retrospective explanations for a particular word's demise. But even these explanations ill justify conclusions about whether words in general, in similar situations, also might die and (by extension) about what might be the essence of English. In scientific vocabulary, for instance, a good many Anglo-Saxon words have been replaced by Hellenic or Latinate equivalents: *tungolcræft* by 'astronomy', *læcedóm* by 'medicine', *rímcræft* by 'mathematics'. But while such substitutions certainly make sense, the existence of Greek or Latin equivalents doesn't guarantee word death in learned professions, since probably more individuals go to ear, nose, and throat doctors than to otolaryngologists. Likewise the native *þrínes* has disappeared before the Latinate 'trinity', as might be expected given the early connections between Latin and religion in England. But the Anglo-Saxon 'God' holds its own in competition with Latin 'deity', and in 'cross' English has adopted a Norse-derived form (*kross*) rather than something more closely related to its Latin source *crux* or the native *ród*.

Lacking predictive power, social and mechanistic explanations cannot so much determine word death as affirm it. And in doing so, they affirm as well the malleable relations between speakers and their language, for as much as words can seem part of a historical record, their presence in that record owes to the choices made by speakers. What we think English is, from this perspective, depends on why we care. And for this reason alone, the apparently simple distinction between living and dead words, a distinction fundamental to any definition of English, is itself sometimes difficult to make.

A death certificate seems easy enough to write for a word like *lið*, which is as dead as a doornail, or, as Dickens would have it, a coffin-nail. Meaning 'ship' or 'fleet', *lið* has not been in currency for perhaps 800 years, replaced by other native forms (like 'ship' or 'fleet', in fact), as well as by tonier borrowings like 'vessel', 'yacht', and 'armada'. It has a graph—*ð*, or *eth*—that disappeared from English in the thirteenth century (replaced everywhere by *th*), and it even represents a lexical category that no longer exists: it's a neuter noun, from a time when English had grammatical gender, as it has not had since about the time *lið* sank out of use. And there's a host of other words, some of them once very common indeed, that has not been used in any meaningful way for some time and are thus likewise easily pronounced dead: *fæhð* ('feud'), *hende* ('convenient'), *rebato* (a type of collar). These are all old words, but the lexical reaper can work quickly, too. Not even two centuries old, Dickens's *Life and Adventures of Martin Chuzzlewit* alone yields now unfathomable words like *biffins* (baked Norfolk apples), *fellows* (a type of pistol), *lummy* ('first-rate'), *loco-foco* (a wooden match), and *swipey* ('intoxicated'). Granted, Dickens was particularly interested in language, especially the language of speakers at the margins of society, yet the exuberance of his linguistic play only exaggerates what's already there: the ephemerality of the English lexicon as it continually glides by. The same is true of Christian names like Hygelac, Wealhþeow, and Ingeld from *Beowulf*, none of which has a modern counterpart. Much more recently, while growing up I had aunts with the imposing names of Lorraine, Florence, and Gertrude; the next-door neighbor's name was Blanche. These names for women may survive, in a way that Wealhþeow has not, but the ebbing of their popularity suggests that they, too, may someday be as dead as *lið*.[20]

Only marginally less straightforward would be a class of words like *forsooth* and *quoth*. These may be alive in the sense that anyone with an educated vocabulary knows them very well, but remain as dead as *lið* in the sense that no one produces them, except perhaps playfully or when staging early drama. And the same would be true of words that refer to defunct objects but that nonetheless remain part of many speakers' passive vocabularies. Except when speaking about the past, no one has occasion to use 'guinea', 'six-pence', or 'half-crown', even though they remain familiar at least to many British Anglophones. If all of its words had morbidity (or vitality) this clear, the shape of English would be perfectly clear. They don't, and it's not.

Regionalisms in particular present challenges for any definition of English. Throughout the historical Danelaw, Norse reflexes, at least until relatively recently, replaced (if not exactly killed) many Anglo-Saxon words that remained in use elsewhere: *stithy* for 'anvil', *lake* for 'play', *stee* for 'ladder', *mun* for 'must', and so on.[21] Meanwhile, there are other regionalisms that everywhere overtook and eliminated the historical forms, such as 'die' (from Norse *deyja*) for *steorfan*, 'give' for *yive*, or, perhaps most remarkably of all, the third person personal pronouns 'they', 'them', and 'their' (from Norse *þeir, þeim, þeirra*) for the historical *hie, him,* and *hiera*. They all began life as borrowings from Viking immigrants in the old Danelaw; they all competed for a time with native forms; they all replaced these forms at different times in different locales; and they all have become naturalized, even as any number of other Norse-derived regionalisms, such as *skift* ('to change') or *graith* ('ready'), have disappeared. And then there are the regionalisms that have passed away in speech but that, even when unspoken, remain widely recognized linguistic markers of a region. In my own dialect, the tag question *ainna*, as in "nice day, ainna," is a case in point: no one, so far as I can tell, uses the word anymore, even as dialect studies solemnly record it as a regionally distinctive form. Regional forms like these complicate what it means to be a dead word but also what it means to be a native English one.

This vampire-like survival of dead words has become all the more noticeable as English has spread around the globe. Both the OED and Merriam-Webster record 'billabong' ('lake') and 'pakeha' ('European'), for instance, but though many Anglophones in the United Kingdom or the United States might recognize them, the words are likely to be parts of speakers' productive vocabulary only in, respectively, Australia and New Zealand. Also moribund and somehow alive in the context of global English might be 'bunyip' ('a monster') and 'tinnie' ('can of beer'), which only the OED records but which, again, are unlikely to be used actively by many Anglophones outside of Australia. Merriam-Webster alone lists 'bubbler' ('drinking fountain'), and its area of usage is even more restricted than that of 'dasn't'—essentially, the eastern half of Wisconsin. In every case, a word's vitality is tied to the fact that it's used by only some speakers, who know the word's alive and have no reason to think about it. For the vast majority of Anglophones, nearly all of whom will never meet each other face-to-face, regional words like these can exist only on the odd chance that they encounter them, and then only if they are identified in a dictionary as English words. Almost like Schrödinger's cat, they're both alive and dead until someone looks at them.

Reducing the complexity of a word to its parts—orthography, sense, and morphemes—only further obscures word death and the shape of English. Both *shew* and *show* were listed in dictionaries for years, even though they have the same source word. The former is now obsolete, but is it dead? What about a common word that is unquestionably alive but that has changed its meaning? In Anglo-Saxon times 'meat' meant one's dinner, and it now refers only to the animal flesh eaten at that dinner. And 'deer' then meant any four-footed beast but now describes a particular kind of beast: a ruminant with deciduous antlers, like a reindeer or a whitetail deer. For Chaucer, a 'lewd' person was an ignorant one, while today it's one with an over-stimulated and tawdry libido. Then there's 'swell'. As a noun and verb 'swell' may be very much alive, but the sense 'pompous person' or 'rake', evoking the worlds of Dickens and Lord Peter Whimsey, is not. For that matter, neither is 'rake' in the sense 'a swell'.

Morphology complicates the distinction of living from dead words in other ways. We might consider, for instance, *–kin* and *–ling*. Once productive affixes for indicating familiarity or diminution, both have long passed from currency; not only are *lambkin* and *frogling* essentially dead, then, but so too are the derivational morphemes by which such forms could be made. We may use 'fledgling', but we cannot create 'blogling' or 'cellphonekin'. The suffix *–ette* does survive for the derivation of diminutives (as in 'kitchenette'), but not, for the most part, for the derivation of specifically feminine forms; 'majorette', 'usherette', and 'bachelorette' are all at the very least stylistically marked, and I can't imagine any Anglophone creating 'scholarette'. Similar complexities appear in inflectional morphology. 'Oxen', a historically 'weak' noun, may live, but as the plural of 'toe', *toon* is certainly dead, as are most weak nouns that have, through analogy, acquired *–s* as their plural inflection. But if the words are dead, so too is the morphological potential to mark plurality with *–n*, since new words (e.g., 'tweet') inevitably adopt the dominant *–s* inflection. *Toon* still can be found, of course, if one reads the works of Chaucer and other medieval writers. The same might be said of the Old English *dwelland, wǽron, speakeþ*, and *góða*, which changes in inflectional morphology have transformed into the now ordinary 'dwelling', 'were', 'speaks', and 'good'. As a prefix for perfective verb forms (e.g., 'seen' in "I have seen"), the departed *ge-* has left behind no modern reflex at all, though it might be imagined as a phantom haunting the front of past participles.[22]

In most of these examples—including the regional words that I have discussed—the words and forms are and are not dead: dead in one version (chronological or regional), very much alive in another. More importantly, the disappearance of words' spellings, meanings, and morphology can be used in two very different ways to define English and the heritage it projects. When changes in a word's morphology, meaning, and usage are treated as evidence of a category English that transcends individual moments and uses, then the language is a trans-historical code spoken by Winston Churchill as well as King Alfred. In this case, *góða* has not so much disappeared as become 'good', while 'rake' retains the sense 'swell' because, even if that sense now occurs only rarely in Anglophone speech, it does figure in canonical English literature. By this analysis, English exists apart from its speakers, retaining a core identity amid sometimes radical variation and change that therefore must be considered superficial: 'good' is the same as *góða*, despite differences in their spelling, pronunciation, and morphology. But the lexical changes I have discussed might also be taken as evidence of morphological and lexical discontinuity in the category we traditionally call English. Read this way, historical evidence situates identity less in the language than in its speakers, their usages, and their domains, and it thereby undermines the notion that English transcends chronology and geography. The choice between these two ways of approaching word death is not so much structural as conceptual, resting on whether speech communities desire a lot or a little linguistic continuity with the past.

In either case, the shape of English's vocabulary is determined as much by argument as by empirical data. Depending on where we draw the boundaries of contemporary English, for instance, certain words, morphemes, spellings, and senses will or will not be dead. The OED contains an 1889 quotation for *lambkin*, while Wright's 1905 *Dialect Grammar* records [ð] (i.e., *-eth*) as a third person singular verbal inflection "among the older generation of dialect speakers" in Somerset and Devon.[23] In light of this, should I revise my claim that these forms are dead? Or should we redraw the boundaries of modern English, which is often said to begin grammatically no later than the eighteenth century, so that its origins postdate the demise of now unused morphemes? Whether or not we want to identify with Wright's dialect speakers is a question that cannot be answered by the data alone: it must draw on arguments about speakers, ethnicity, and culture.

Such variability is one of the things that makes predictions about the future of the river of English difficult and that, in turn, might seem to reduce lexical history to lists of words.[24] This variability also foregrounds the conscious and unconscious choices made by speakers in particular speech communities at particular times, and the effects these choices have not simply on the language they use but on their sense of what constitutes English. Speakers choose to assign social significance to certain words or certain kinds of words, to perceive them as inherently foreign and others as potentially English, to accept some lexical changes as traits of the language and others as artificial features imposed on it, and to include some words in a dictionary but to exclude others. More generally, they choose to use language as a way to mirror and further change cultural practices; or to manage social reality through language; or to allow language to develop with minimal supervision by its speakers, whatever the consequences for particular morphemes, words, and pronunciations. These are the choices that produce the heritage witnessed in the history of English.

LEXICIDE

Nearly a century ago in his classic study of English vocabulary, Owen Barfield argued that words, in their origin and development, both reflect the history of culture and define its character. English has a lot of Greek words to represent our thoughts and inner world, and a lot of Latin words for the physical world, precisely because (he maintained) it was from Greece that England derived its philosophical outlook and from Rome its view of civic activity. Similarly, it is in the eighteenth-century Age of Enlightenment that English first cultivated semantic changes to old words—like 'temper', 'conscience', and 'disposition'—that suggest the 'internalization' in English culture underway at that time.[25]

If the creation of words reflects new cultural influences, features and changes, then their demise suggests a loss, rejection, suppression, or adaptation of these same influences. We see these very impulses in all the causes of natural word death that I have already discussed; since we don't use swords or the old British currency, we have little need to preserve an extensive vocabulary for them. And since English no longer competes with Latin for cultural prestige, its speakers have no reason (except in science and technology) to supplement their vocabulary with Latinate borrowings. Where an earlier generation of Anglophones might have fashioned 'decogitation', ours has created 'mind grenade'.

Sometimes, however, words die unnatural deaths. Sometimes they are killed off (or at least become victims of attempted murder), and in these instances their demise can be particularly informative about how Anglophones hope to see themselves as well as their language. Aesthetics, both literary and social, have been especially influential in this regard. As I noted in Chapter Two, Johnson for one partly relied on a writer's quality to arbitrate between living and dead words. "Obsolete words are admitted," he says, "when they are found in authours not obsolete, or when they have any force or beauty that may deserve revival."[26] So a word is dead unless a dead but still-read writer uses it, and should the writer fall out of fashion, it would presumably be the lexicographer's duty to kill off the word as well. This attitude towards aesthetic lexical euthanasia persists through the expansion of prescriptive grammars and the many reprintings of the Fowler brothers' *Dictionary of Modern English Usage*, all the way to the comments of modern language mavens like William Safire and John Honey. Among the lexical aesthetic's most eloquent advocates is C. S. Lewis, who sees the beauty of individual words as the moral rationale for their survival or elimination:

I have tried not to obtrude the moral, but I should be glad if I sent any reader away with a new sense of responsibility to the language. It is unnecessary defeatism to believe that we can do nothing about it. Our conversation will have little effect; but if we get into print—perhaps especially if we are leader-writers, reviewers, or reporters—we can help to strengthen or weaken some disastrous vogue word; can encourage a good, and resist a bad, gallicism or Americanism. For many things the press prints today will be taken up by the great mass of speakers in a few years.[27]

When Lewis speaks of Anglophones' "responsibility" for their language, he extends literary issues into concern with another aesthetic—social. And by this aesthetic I mean the use of lexical engineering to shape a particular view of society, or any of the speech communities that make it up. These two kinds of aesthetics may well be inextricably interconnected. As concerned as he was with literature offering the best model for language use, for example, Dr Johnson also saw language—and specifically his dictionary—as a way to cultivate social categories and behaviors. He decried words that showed the undue influence of

French, high society, low society, and so forth, on account of which they deserved to be restricted or eliminated from usage. "Commerce," he similarly notes in his Preface, "however necessary, however lucrative, as it depraves the manners, corrupts the language." And Johnson's definition of 'horrid' engineers still other social behaviors by equating general unpleasantness with gendered slang in the sense "shocking; offensive; unpleasing; in womens cant."[28]

Sometimes words die, then, because at least some speakers try to forget them for reasons of taste or social judgment. We do this with slang, with vulgarity, and with derogatory ethnic terms. 'Ain't', young Anglophones in particular are often told, is not a word at all, even though it occurs with a great deal of frequency throughout the Anglophone world.[29] Regionalisms likewise can become lexis that a community encourages itself to discard, particularly when it advances technologically and its members do so socially and financially. The *English Dialect Dictionary* and DARE are in fact monuments to abandoned and ignored lexis and the lifestyle it supported. *Obstropolous, smothercate,* and *dacious* all fell into disuse in part because of an attitude well expressed by an early reviewer of the *Dialect Dictionary,* who described them as "corruptions of literary English words."[30] And a word like *kinnikinnick* could be discouraged into oblivion for any of several reasons: it's a Native American borrowing (from Algonquian), it was a regional and rural word in the United States, and it referred to tobacco.

As the traditions of prescriptive grammar developed in the sixteenth, seventeenth, and eighteenth centuries, they did so in ways that increasingly marked certain kinds of language, particularly regional language and grammatical errors, as nonstandard, aberrant, and (therefore) expendable. Because of this history, such lexical engineering easily can seem the peculiar exercise that a social elite might use to maintain its status. Yet precisely the same kind of manufactured death occurs when any Anglophone objects on social grounds to the contents of dictionaries. Burchfield, who edited the second supplement to the OED, speaks of some users' insistence that derogatory common senses for words like 'Jew' or 'Turk' be marked as in some way aberrant if not outright eliminated from the OED. There was, he says, "a concerted attempt by various pressure-groups to force dictionary editors to give up recording the factual unpleasantness of our times, and to abandon the tradition of setting down the language as it is actually used, however disagreeable, regrettable, or uncongenial the use."[31] When George Orwell objected to what he saw as the language of political repression and obfuscation, he, too, advocated the elimination of words—even if only for the purposes of a particular piece of writing—as a means to reconstruct society through language: "Never use a long word where a short one will do...never use a foreign phrase, a scientific word or a jargon word if you can think of an everyday English equivalent."[32] Orwell cared what English was because he cared about the world he inhabited. By killing off or nurturing specific words and usages, his reasoning goes, users will transform not only the language but their social reality as well. His dystopian novel 1984 describes just how successful such transformation can be.

This kind of social management through lexical engineering has become increasingly more prevalent in the past half century. Annual lists of neologisms do so perhaps ironically, whether by testifying to the innovations in Anglophone culture or by implying that the new words are unnecessary and that English would be better off without them. In many cases, whatever the impact of these lists, such buzzwords do in fact often go quietly into the night. 2008 alone witnessed the rise and probable demise of 'Obamanation', 'pregorexia', and 'recessionista'. The systematic replacement of 'stimulus' by 'recovery' in economic discussions marks a more concerted attempt to repackage reality through the elimination of words, as do government initiatives to eliminate jargon and thereby allow for greater procedural transparency. In 2007, for example, the United Kingdom's Local Government Association released a 'non-word' list—words that (like non-persons in the Soviet Union) were henceforth to be excluded from official discourse. The list included 'coterminosity', 'empowerment', and 'multidisciplinary', and the expectation was that their disappearance would improve the accessibility of social services. In American politics both 'empathy' and 'kumbaya' have acquired such strongly negative associations with weak-willed, interventionist thinking that many politicians proscribe themselves from using them. More pointedly, Vietnam veterans of Swift Boats (small patrol vessels) have objected to the noun 'Swiftboating', which arose in the 2004 United States presidential election. The Democratic candidate, John Kerry, had served on one of these boats, and when his service and record were questioned as a way to undermine his campaign, 'Swiftboating' came into wide use for a stealthy political attack. Observed one veteran, "It is time to ban a word that is at once offensive, demeaning and obscene both to and for anyone serving in the naval profession."[33]

In the United States, lexical engineering has been institutionalized in the production of literary anthologies and standardized tests for primary and high school students. Driven by the competing political pressures of conservatives (who object to language understood to challenge traditional values) and liberals (who object to language understood to enforce stereotypes), publishers and test-makers have constructed self-imposed bias and sensitivity guidelines for topics, characters, and plots as well as language. Given the size of the American school-age population and the influence of school boards in deciding what books and texts to use, publishers' motives may simply be financial: the need to satisfy a host of conflicting critics in order to turn a profit. The motives of the critics, whatever their political leanings, are to define English—specifically through the elimination of words—in order to bring about a preferred social reality. In the words of Diane Ravitch,

The goal of the language police is not just to stop us from using objectionable words but to stop us from having objectionable thoughts. The language police believe that reality follows language usage. If they can stop people from ever seeing offensive words and ideas, they can prevent them from having the thought or committing the act that the words signify. . . . If they abolish words that have *man* as a prefix or suffix, then women will achieve equality. If children read and hear only language that has been cleansed of any mean or hurtful words, they will never have a mean or hurtful thought. With enough censorship, the language police might create a perfect world.[34]

While Ravitch's rhetoric may be a little over the top, it is nonetheless true that one or more publisher's bias guidelines have proscribed 'bellman', 'laundress', and 'spinster' as sexist; 'bubbler', 'soda', and 'stickball' as regionally biased; 'barbarian', 'cult', and 'dogma' as ethnocentric; and 'cripple', 'fat', and 'lunatic' as insensitive. Any writer wishing to work for such a publisher must comply, and any student reading material issued by such a publisher will not see such words in the classroom.

Whether standard, slang, or vulgar, words can certainly be suppressed, sometimes in a fairly aggressive fashion, though such words can remain very much alive. And part of what it means to be communicatively competent in English is to know the pragmatic impact of certain words—to know that some words are inappropriate in certain domains and that part of contemporary English is virtually dead. Alongside 'bellman', 'barbarian', and 'fat', volatile, offensive, or obscene words like 'nigger', 'wog', 'kike', and 'fuck' exist in the lexicons of all fluent Anglophones, even if they never (or rarely) use them. Studies of speech-related pathologies show just how peculiar and persistent the avoided lexis of blasphemy and vulgarity can be. Individuals who have otherwise lost speech as a result of a stroke, for instance, have been documented as nonetheless retaining the ability to curse; this has even been the case with individuals who prior to the pathology were not known to curse at all.[35] For many speakers, these words, too, live in a kind of vampire state, absent from their active vocabulary but most certainly not dead. And this undead condition reflects the sometimes agonistic relations between Anglophones and English.

The critics Ravitch describes may demonstrate nakedly political objectives in their censorship, but they are not alone in their belief that controlling the definition of English is a way to control the world in which it is spoken. This is the same view, indeed, of many recent philosophers of language, who maintain that it is through language that what we accept as reality comes into being. Such attempts necessarily imply, then, that by eliminating a word, we can eliminate at the same time its reference and effect. Belief in the power of words—and by extension word death—to shape reality is anything but recent or topical, however. Puritan England, with its proscriptions against blasphemy, gave rise to an institutional tradition of monitoring vocabulary for religious purposes that was subsequently extended by groups like the Society for Promoting Christian Knowledge. All such institutions operated on the belief that the absence of expressions like 'Goddamn' would foster a moral and devout society. The non-religious institutional culling of vocabulary can occur, too, as when generations of grammar school teachers try (typically without success) to eradicate forms like 'gonna' and 'wanna', or when governments negotiate a balance between the freedom of speech and the state's right to control obscenity. They can, that is, bracket certain words as unusable, as did the United States Broadcast Decency Act of 2006, which established a government commission to determine what's decent and to set fines for stations that broadcast obscene, indecent, or profane language.[36] The belief that words transform reality occurs at a popular level as well. The word 'coney' (meaning 'rabbit', from Old French *conil*) may well have been excised from the vocabulary by the end of the nineteenth century (it certainly drops from use by that point) because, rhyming as it did with 'honey', it may for some speakers have had what the OED delicately describes as "certain vulgar associations." In all cases, the presumption is that a language that eliminated ungrammatical or indecent expressions would of necessity be one spoken only by an intelligent, morally upright populace.[37]

What vampire words show, though, is that at least in certain cases ideas take precedence over form. In Middle and early Modern English, *swive* prevailed as a vulgar, if not quite obscene, word for sexual intercourse. It's gone, but 'screw', 'bonk', and 'get laid'—all rough modern counterparts—live on, and with them the ability to conceptualize and pragmatically represent casual sex. In a different vein, 'coney' may be gone but the vulgar word that it was associated with, deriving from Old Norse *kunta*, remains, as do small furry leporids and the word 'rabbit' that refers to them. Even if a particular Anglophone never utters 'nigger' or 'fuck', those words, the ideas they represent, and the pragmatic effects they can have likewise continue to exist as well. Euphemisms like 'the n-word' or 'the f-bomb', 'four-letter words', 'expletive deleted', and the comic-book expression '!X% #@*!' are perhaps the most undead of words. For effective communication, they require that a listener know the words they replace, know the pragmatic significance of those words, and know too that the euphemisms have their own pragmatic significance, which depends on the omitted vulgarisms. They become, weirdly, polite ways of saying impolite things. We may try to forget our lexical past and its implications, and we may use dictionaries, peer pressure, and government action to compel English into a particular shape, but ultimately we can control only so much of language, and the language (in turn) only so much of reality. If speakers truly wanted to transform social reality through language, they might begin with their own social behavior, for the 'n-word' would become impossible only if racism somehow managed to disappear.

Even then, forms like 'fuck' and the 'n-word' would retain some utility. Blasphemy, vulgarity, and ethnic slurs are all transgressive language. They all challenge some dominant idea or institution and in the process, inevitably, sustain it. 'Goddamn' can be powerful only if one believes in God or, barring that, in the notion of social propriety, in which case it is not the invocation of God that is transgressive but simply the impropriety of the speech act. It's difficult to imagine a pragmatic contravention like 'Goddamn' in a godless society or in one that lacked any kind of social stratification. The same is true of language that transgresses (and so maintains) distinctions based on class, race, ethnicity, gender, and so forth. Unless one believes a return to a pre-Babel world of perfect communication and social harmony is possible, transgressive language will always serve a social purpose. It's not too much to claim that Anglophones require English to have vulgarity and obscenity, even as they require themselves to suppress it.

When they are encouraged to discard vocabulary that is ill formed or that recalls their native language, second-language learners likewise participate in the constructive disregard of the lexical past. In this case, the injunction 'speak English' can be the response to language that arises from borrowing and code-switching or pronunciations that embody a nativized phonology. Proscribed along with the word, of course, are the speakers and the social processes (of immigration, for example) that they embody. "What's a fi', I don't understand a fi', there's a *v* in the word, it's *five*," Michael Douglas's character says to a

Korean shop-keeper shortly before he destroys his store in the 1992 film *Falling Down*. "You come to my country, you take my money, you don't even have the grace to learn how to speak my language."

When Anglophones try to forget words, then, they also try to fashion a particular version of the present. In a relatively benign version, such forgetting allows us to recall a past of quaint but discarded terms and regionalisms. These in turn allow us both to make the past the object of nostalgia, exemplified by the things and words of a simpler, somehow purer time, and to construct a sadder but wiser present—one that's technologically and even socially more sophisticated but that nonetheless feels a sense of rupture and loss. It's not that we might want to retrieve words for outmoded practices and objects—words like those for the many kinds of Victorian horse-drawn forms of transportation: *phaeton, stanhope, brougham, fly,* and *cabriolet.* We are as glad to discard the words as the things they represent. But by discarding the words and then remembering that we have done so, we comfortably obtain not only a romanticized past but also a measure of our progress, all the while defining English in a way that allows for a trans-historical heritage among only some of its speakers.

The memory of what's been lost plays a far more volatile role when it figures in the reconstruction of a golden age of communication, when words and pronunciations were putatively as fixed as the society they were imagined to construct. Remembering that a word like 'five' had a fixed pronunciation enables a different phonetic realization ('fi') to become a symbol of that memory's loss and, along with it, of the loss of any number of social and cultural associations of the past—however ahistorical or untrue this pronunciation, or what's associated with it, may be. Prior to the fifteenth century, indeed, 'five' would characteristically have sounded like 'feeve', and throughout much of the sixteenth something like 'feyav'; in modern Ireland pronunciations like 'faheev' and 'foive' occur, as do pronunciations like 'fahv' in the southern United States, where they are part of a long-established phonology and not the result of contact with recent immigrant languages. To forget this variation is to remember a sociolinguistically coherent past that has fractured in the modern world, just as to try to forget the contemporary variation—"You come to my country...you don't even have the grace to learn how to speak my language"—is to try to forge this world in the image of something that's been presumed to be forgotten. As many of the examples of this chapter suggest, then, it's probably not so much the words that bother us as it is the speakers who use them and the pragmatic purposes to which they are put. When we try to kill words, whether they're blasphemous, obscene, insensitive, or regional, we really try to kill the speakers and ideas behind the words, along with their historical and cultural associations.

The effort to circumscribe the language—to distinguish what's within English from what should be without—has been terrifically important to Anglophones. It's what led Johnson to anchor his dictionary in the usage of great writers, Webster to see lexicography as a nationalistic gesture, Murray to conceptualize the extraordinary scope of the OED, and modern phraseological dictionaries like Cobuild to construct their definitions from exhaustive corpora. What makes the lexicographical imperative so strong, I think, are several things: a belief since the eighteenth century that English and national identity are tied together; a modern sense of identity politics and their expression through language; and a perhaps primeval notion that if we could define our language once and for all, we might do likewise with ourselves and return to an unscattered moment before Babel. In vocabulary, then, we look for some of the stability and innocence that the world seems to have lost.

This stability may emerge from the exclusion of words and the culture they represent as easily from their inclusion. If this sounds somber and even conspiratorial, I don't mean it to be. Anglophones certainly are responsible for the English they use and the reality it reflects, but their responsibility is typically situational and not indicative of concerted long-term plans to manipulate the world through their words. It is very much we as individuals who decide what makes a word and how it dies, whether by morphemes, sense, or totality. We who decide on shifting criteria which words qualify as English and which do not, and whether English itself is a historical monolith or a modern mélange. And we who do all this in response to the changing experience around us. Words can remain alive, even if no one utters them, so long as speakers conclude that the experience they reflect in some way remains alive as well, just as they can be dead even as someone utters them to us.

CHAPTER FOUR

Space and Time

For several centuries now, in one form or another, tree diagrams have been making their spidery way across the pages of books of all kinds. They trace families for genealogists and the development of species for biologists. Textual critics use them to chart the transmission of literary works. And in linguistics, where they are especially popular, tree diagrams depict the history of related languages.

At its most basic, inverted form, a tree diagram visualizes its subject in a two-dimensional, linear way. At its top is something—a person, animal, or language—from which descends a series of related, stable conditions, each of them marked by a leaf on the tree. In genealogy, these leaves blossom from the grafting (as it were) of a new branch. So a new person might join a family tree through marriage and with the tree's original member produce a number of children, some of whom might also marry and reproduce, and so forth. Movement down the tree is thus simultaneously movement forward in time, and for family trees, as new members appear at the bottom, older ones at the top die, becoming—in terms of the tree diagram—primarily just a link from a distant ancestor to a present life. Theirs is a relational role, without which it's not possible to connect origin and development. The biological counterpart of these leaves would be species, which also evolve and die off, although with considerably more complexity. Since each species has many individuals (not just one) as well as a sometimes arguable integrity, biologists can debate over just where one ends and another begins in a way that genealogists cannot about individual ancestors.

Perhaps the most widely circulated linguistic tree diagram is that of the Indo-European languages, which includes nearly all of the indigenous languages of Europe and many languages of India and Iran. Every stage of this diagram is subject to continual scholarly reconsideration and revision, but a common form begins at the top with the hypothetical Indo-European—both the language and its speakers, who perhaps lived around 5,000 BCE near the Caspian Sea, from where they migrated in all directions, bringing their changing language with them. Moving down the page and forward in time, the tree typically splits the original stage into two different stages (the Centum and Satem branches, reflecting a largely west–east split), which themselves divide into stages labeled Italic, Hellenic, Germanic, and so forth. Positioned below Centum (in this case), each of these stages represents a chronological, geographic, and structural change that renders them distinct from, if still related to, earlier and contemporaneous stages. And so this particular tree diagram crawls down the page through grammar as well as time and space. Germanic, spoken by a people situated in northwest Europe by the second millennium BCE, divides into East, North, and West branches, and the West branch, spoken along the Atlantic seacoast, in turn divides in ways that eventually lead to Old English, which becomes Middle and then Modern English.

Tree diagrams like this have a wonderful logic and utility, allowing us to conceptualize vast stretches of time and significant structural transformation. Ultimately, they respond to something with which we are all familiar in daily language use—variability, whether between our speech and that of a younger generation, or that of a distant group of Anglophones. And they approach this physical and temporal separation with an almost mathematical precision.

As useful as they are, though, tree diagrams do have drawbacks. For one thing, tree diagrams cannot accommodate the lateral influences that adjacent branches have on the character of any one stage in a language's history. Both French in the Middle Ages and Latin in the early modern period significantly reshaped the English lexicon in particular, even though, according to the Indo-European diagram, English is but distantly related to them. For another, tree diagrams can imply a kind of stability at each stage that, while applicable to the individuals in family trees, fits the diversity of any given language even more poorly than it fits the diversity of a biological species. Modern English thus occupies only one leaf on a tree diagram, despite the obvious variations in speech among the world's 1.5 billion Anglophones. Collapsing Old, Middle, and Modern English under the single rubric English, as happens in both tree diagrams and histories of language, can take place only through an even greater suppression of the kinds of historical differences I surveyed in Chapter One. And for a third, as with lexicography's reliance on chronology, English as defined by a tree diagram necessarily becomes a language whose present (and pre-eminent) identity is defined, geographically as well as linguistically, by some selected moment from the past, when the tree takes root.

But the biggest drawbacks with tree diagrams and the linguistic thinking they foster may be with the model they offer for conceiving language change and variation. What tree diagrams seem to demonstrate is how these abstract linguistic forces have affected the history of one particular language. Treating diachronic change (change over time) and synchronic variation (variation within a particular moment) as inevitable traits that exist almost independently of any natural language, they show how Centum disperses into Germanic, and how Old English leads to Modern English. The grammarians' task, in other words, is to connect the linguistic dots that lead to and qualify as English. And they do this (attorneys would say) in a prima facie way that essentially discovers the picture latent in the historical record.

We end up with a much different picture, of course, if we think of diachronic change and synchronic variation not as abstract principles that allow us to identify what is already there but as claims that make it possible for us to create meaningful patterns in language usage. They claim, for example, that the integrity of a language like English persists across time, that at any one moment this integrity embraces and even is defined in part by only certain kinds of variation, and that the identity of the language is fundamentally both abstract and descendent from a single origin. And this latter claim necessarily entails additional claims about speakers, domains, and geography, since the transformation of English from Old to Middle to Modern is equally the extension of English from Britain, to Kachru's Inner Circle, to the entire globe. According to this view of change and variation, definitions of English do not proceed in a connect-the-dot fashion by exposing an image of English that is present whether or not anyone completes its outline. They rather qualify certain dots by selecting and drawing lines among them. In effect, the dots—and the picture—depend on the definition.

This is the approach I will pursue here. From this perspective, diachronic change and synchronic variation are labels we use to designate the linguistic fluctuations that we consider permissible and consistent with the integrity of English. Fluctuations deemed impermissible or disruptive might be errors or evidence of another language, but they cannot be examples of English. And in this sense, change and variation are not immutable linguistic traits but matters of judgment. Rather than manifest something latent in the linguistic record, they legitimate certain kinds of grammatical flux and thereby create English. Or as Heraclitus might have it, they are ways to define identity in change and to locate the main channel of English within a broad watershed, even if the distinctions they draw might seem contradictory and impressionistic. On one hand, for example, to nearly every modern linguistic historian the radical early modern Great Vowel Shift, which accounts for (among other things) why Anglophones pronounce the graph *i* as 'eye' and Francophones as 'ee', would qualify as diachronic change. The same is true of the synchronic lexical variation documented in nineteenth-century dialect studies. These changes are treated as proof that English is a variable yet continuous and still discrete language. On the other, as I discuss in this book, similarly systematic and far less radical phonological and lexical transformations in extraterritorial varieties (i.e., those found outside of England) have been channeled away as 'broken English', creoles, or non-standard language.

In order to draw the language's tree diagram in this view, we require what Dr Johnson described as a "principle of selection":

a way to discern English among a "speech copious without order, and energetick without rules."[1] Like any codifier, Johnson had to distinguish "purity" from "adulterations," and like any historian he had to identify a linguistic past that would lead to his linguistic present and justify his judgments of it. The broad contours of the language's grammar might be acceptable without argument—that English is a language that largely puts subjects before verbs and adjectives before nouns, for example, or a language in which 'dog' refers in the first instance to a domesticated quadruped of the wolf family (*Canis lupus familiaris*). But the specifics of the language's change and variation—the details that constitute historical description and codification, and make possible all that goes with them—depend on the disentanglement of what to Johnson was otherwise confusion. And such selection cannot be based simply on internal linguistic evidence, since this by itself is "energetick without rules."

Johnson anchored his argument about English in extra-grammatical issues, qualifying a lexical usage as English because it appears in Shakespeare's writings, for instance, or a syntactic structure because it imitates similar structures found in Greek and Latin. But this argued sense of English animates not just Johnson's dictionary. From Richard Mulcaster in the sixteenth century to contemporary discussions of global English or claims for alternative histories, codification and linguistic histori-ography have been tools to advance and support any number of non-structural arguments about the character of the language. Whether at one extreme, by luxuriating in what Johnson called adulterations (whatever those would be), or at the other by adhering to acknowledged authority (however it might be defined). Put this way, any principle of selection for framing change and variation and for imagining the history of the language also frames and imagines its political, aesthetic, and social heritage—the things we Anglophones most care about. When imaged in tree diagrams, such selection both emphasizes geography and time in the history of English and de-emphasizes its own active role in producing heritage. Tree diagrams, diachronic change, and synchronic variation can be objective, that is, because (and only if) we overlook how and why they are constructed.

The physical and temporal separation of Anglophones from one another might be called a linguistic fact of life. We don't all live together, and we don't all live at the same time. Rather than impede definitions of English, however, this separation has facilitated them. It has shaped and fortified how we think about the language and provided ways to structure all manner of imaginative arguments about the integrity and continuity of English and its varieties. In fact, without the distance between us and the ways it can be used to frame the inevitability of language change in support of one heritage or another, we Anglophones would have a difficult time defining who we are. Just as any answer to a question about the definition of English's lexicon is an argument, I'm suggesting, so must be any answer to a question about its history.

This chapter and Chapter Five consider two related aspects of my own historical, linguistic argument—here, accounts of change and variation in the language's history, and, in Chapter Five, descriptions of the grammar of English. In these chapters I cut across the categories of codification to consider the imaginative acts by which grammars, dictionaries, and linguistic histories define English and with it a heritage for Anglophones. My interest is not in advancing any particular definition of English, much less in writing a history of the history of English, but in the criteria used to construct such definitions: how and where such definitions are expressed, and what's at issue in them. I emphasize early modern codification in particular, since I see its paradigms as foundational for historical and grammatical discussion. By what principles of selection has the history of the language been written, I ask, and what heritage has accrued to this selection? How and where has this history been expressed, and how does it elide distinctions between the empirical and the imaginative? What categories have framed discussions of the history of English and made conceptions of the language possible? Most generally, how do we utilize space and time in definitions of the language?

ACCOUNTING FOR CHANGE

To the earliest English grammarians, geography provided a way to imagine a language that was at once deformed and coherent. According to John Bullokar's 1616 *An English Expositor*, the first dictionary to define the word, a dialect is a "difference of some words, or pronunciation in any language."[2] Embedded in the landscape, regional varieties were regarded as distinctive if sometimes confusing traits of particular locales, but they also necessarily affirmed that the essence of the language could be located if English were removed from this landscape. And this was what codifiers in fact were trying to do. Were regional dialects simply to disappear, they would take their confusion with them, furthering national linguistic coherence and identity in the process.

This principle for framing change and variation—and the need for them to disappear—has remained powerful and persistent throughout the recorded history of English. Some critics (both early and late) have seen evidence of regional varieties' disappearance already at the end of the Middle Ages.[3] That didn't happen, and so it was in the mid-eighteenth century that Dr Johnson still was claiming dialects "will always be observed to grow fewer, and less different, as books are multiplied."[4] To the neo-grammarians of the next century, the demise of dialects that they saw around them offered the best reason to study regionalisms in the first place. The Victorian Wright undertook his enormous dialect project—a six-volume dictionary along with a grammar—largely because he saw dialects as poised to disappear, leaving behind only the essence of English. And to Wright's contemporary Henry Sweet, since the early modern period "the London dialect...is the only one used in writing throughout England. Henceforth the other dialects of English continued to exist only as illiterate forms of speech confined within narrow areas."[5] Even more optimistically, in 1904 Henry Bradley, one of the early editors of the OED, foresaw the end of linguistic history in the passing of English dialects: "On the whole, it is probable that the history of English grammar will for a very long time have few changes to record later than the nineteenth century."[6] This same desire to transcend geographic dispersal frames equally optimistic contemporary expectations that global English will restore the kind of perfect communication that we lost, according to the Bible, at the Tower of Babel. Once the extraneous forms and varieties of regional dialects have disappeared, what would be left behind (by this thinking) would be a well-defined, expressive, and versatile English. It would be the kind of English that many early grammarians and historians felt was to be found in the southeast British variety (not coincidentally the basis of codification) and that might be defined by what it was not—not the vehicle of regional variations nor an imitator of foreign tongues. "People in former ages were nothing so curious or delighted with varying their speech, as of late ages they are grown to bee," Richard Verstegan claims, "but kept their old language as they did their old fassion [sic] of apparel."[7]

And herein lies a paradox in the use of space as a principle for defining English. By measuring linguistic difference and degeneration, space also identifies the main channel of the language, and this is why regional varieties have remained important in linguistic historiography, even for those who would exaggerate rumors of their death. From a structural point of view, regional varieties are inevitable for any living language, but from a conceptual one they are vital to the definition of a standard. The more critics from Dr Johnson until the present day have castigated, ridiculed, and even denied the extraterritorial English of North America, the South Pacific, and Africa, the more they have been able to identify a normative variety.[8] To define English in their landmark of prescription, *The King's English*, the Fowler Brothers went so far as to label the United States variety as a distinct language: "Americanisms are foreign words, and should be so treated."[9] Without backwaters or even competing currents, there can be no river of English.

Identifying English through geography is by no means idle or even just linguistic speculation, for like all definitions of the language it has economic and social consequences. To the British journalist Raymond Mortimer in 1928, American publishers' ability to secure international copyright for translations of foreign-language books presented a threat to British markets. Beginning with the presumption that the United States and the

United Kingdom in effect used different, mutually unintelligible languages, he maintained that when an American translation is copyrighted, "usually . . . these books remain permanently closed to the English reader." If the linguistic variation born from geographic separation were recognized in copyright, Mortimer felt, foreign books would become available to British markets and readers, since such recognition would allow for translation into British as well as American English. In 1930, with moving pictures just having acquired sound and thereby partially closed the geographic remove of Hollywood from London, the Conservative MP Alfred Knox worried that the new technology might bridge not just physical space but the social difference embedded in it. He proposed that the Board of Trade restrict the number of American-import talkies. The "words and accent" in these talkies, he felt, are "perfectly disgusting, and there can be no doubt that such films are an evil influence on our language . . . What is the use of spending millions on education if our young people listen to falsified English spoken every night?"[10] Modern books like *Lose Your Accent in 28 Days* and *American English Pronunciation: It's No Good Unless You're Understood* define language through geography with even greater economic and social consequences. For readers as well as their publishers, wealth and success depend on recognition of how specific varieties of English are tied to specific locales.

As an imaginative act, then, such linking of geography with language produces powerful yet mutually contradictory definitions of English. From the perspective of speakers like Mortimer and the Fowler brothers, the linking evokes a tree diagram's equation of English with a specific British version that precedes (in several ways) other versions and that serves as their geographic and chronological reference point. This orientation appears already in Laurence Nowell's *Vocabularium Saxonicum*, a Latin dictionary of some 6,500 Old English words that he left incomplete in the 1560s. Although unpublished until 1952, the *Vocabularium* was consulted in its manuscript form, and there its early readers would have seen 173 Anglo-Saxon words marked as still current in Nowell's home county of Lancashire. For Nowell, the integrity of his own regional variety depended on the continuities between it and the language used by his Anglo-

Saxon ancestors.[11] A heritage like this is strong enough to produce extraterritorial speakers who themselves use geography to define English, even when doing so leads to the subordination of their own varieties. "There is not enough distance between the environments of the Englishman and the New Zealander," E. W. Andrews ruefully noted in 1910, "to produce the existing difference in pronunciation. It should evidently be the teacher's aim to stay the process, and if possible restore to the New Zealand speech the culture it has unfortunately lost."[12] And in North America, in one and the same moment, Rev. A. Constable Geikie pronounced "Canadian English" to be a distinct variety and denigrated it as a language whose geographic separation from England mirrored its linguistic separation from English. Canadian English, he believes, is "a corrupt dialect growing up amongst our population, and gradually finding access to our periodical literature, until it threatens to produce a language as unlike our noble mother tongue as the negro patua or the Chinese pidgeon [sic] English."[13] Such linguistic and geographic deviation also serves a vital role for the English left behind, since British English as a distinct variety can exist only if competing varieties of non-British English do, and the same is true of native English as opposed to post-colonial English.[14]

Yet geographic space has been just as useful in locating the language's integrity not at the top of the linguistic tree but among its branches. In Richard Carew's 1606 *The Excellency of the English Tongue*, the finely drawn variability of English attests to the language's integrity. "The copiousness of our Language appeareth," says Carew, "in the diversity of our Dialects, for we have Court and we have Countrey English, we have Northern and Southern, gross and ordinary, which differ each from other, not only in the terminations, but also in many words, terms, and phrases, and express the same thing in diverse sorts." And yet, Carew insists "all write English alike,"[15] a sentiment shared by Alexander Gil in his 1621 *Logonomia Anglica*, which identifies and illustrates six distinct dialects: Common, Northern, Southern, Eastern, Western, and Poetic.[16]

In the United States, this notion that linguistic integrity depends on geographic difference has been crucial for the fostering of a distinct heritage for the country. It was an endorsement of physical and political separation from Great Britain that led John Adams to call for the founding of an American language academy and John Jay (in 1776) to invoke Providence as having "been pleased to give this one connected country, to one united people; a people descended from the same ancestors, speaking the same language, professing the same religion."[17] Because of claims like these, the founding of the country has itself often been treated as a linguistic act, something that regarded a transformed language as foundational to a transformed nation in a transformed environment.[18] Indeed, this is very much how the early American linguist Noah Webster viewed the situation. As he famously declared in 1789, a handful of years after the Revolution had been completed, "We have therefore the fairest opportunity of establishing a national language, and of giving it uniformity and perspicuity, in North America, that ever presented itself to mankind."[19]

Today, especially in post-colonial regions, many speakers evoke this same perspective by promoting recognition of an increasing number of 'Englishes', in the plural and tied to the physical locations of the varieties and an emerging ethnic or national identity of their speakers. By rejecting a paradigm in which the English of the United Kingdom or the United States is normative and their own language a deviation down the linguistic tree, such views endorse Webster's framing of heritage, language, and geography. In this view, post-colonial Englishes linguistically come about through the indigenous convergence of English and other languages, but conceptually express the social identity of their speakers in particular.[20] Geographic distance thereby marks a disconnect with native-based English even as it manifests a distinct, yet still English-based, indigenous heritage. In South Africa, Black South African English has thus been championed as not only a distinct variety but also one that might play a unifying role in the linguistically and culturally diverse region. And in the United States, since at least the 1970s African American Vernacular English (AAVE)—also called Black English Vernacular and Ebonics—has been described (not without controversy) as a distinct, viable linguistic medium whose integrity is demonstrated in part through its linguistic separation from standard American English and the often physical separation of both varieties' speakers from one another.[21]

These disparate perspectives on the relevance of space to linguistic identity necessarily imagine different heritages for English. While critics like Kachru have championed the concept of world Englishes for the way it embeds linguistic and social identity in the landscape, Randolph Quirk has emphasized the landscape's connections with linguistic error and warned against institutionalizing "language activity that could alternatively be seen as levels of achievement." To Quirk, labeling poor achievement an English dialect or even English itself, however much that achievement might be part of its speakers' identity, is the result of a well-intentioned if misguided "liberation linguistics."[22] But simply to dismiss Quirk's views (not to mention those of the Fowler brothers) as antiquated is to miss how easily—maybe necessarily—any definition of English and its history can embed social issues in the landscape. If Quirk's and the Fowlers' principles are indebted to traditions of British grammar and the equation of English with a southeast British variety, arguments about the integrity of AAVE are every bit as indebted to the political, ethnic, and educational history of the United States and of the speakers of AAVE.[23] It's for this very reason that the variety has figured in such a long line of academic, public, and even judicial debates over linguistic integrity and social heritage. For Kachru as well as Quirk, what's at issue, and what we care about, is more than language or geography alone.

Ultimately, such conflicts are irreconcilable, at least from a strictly linguistic point of view. We seem to agree that space provides principles for identifying and talking about English and its regional variations; we all, in fact, rely on geography to define what English is. But as principles, physical space and structural variation are not value-free measures that simply detect a language existing entirely apart from them. Formed by social expectations of language, speakers, and their culture, they are principles that specify how English can be defined, what qualifies as English, and who might be numbered among its speakers. In doing so, the same principles inevitably produce different and sometimes conflicting heritages: England as cultural homeland, Commonwealth countries as deviations from this homeland, and South Africa as a multilingual, multicultural state. The link between geographic separation and linguistic identity that allowed Adams and Webster to imagine the United States as an entity distinct from Britain is the same link that contemporary verbal hygienists now use to describe multilingual variation as a deviation from the country's identity.

ETHICS AND HISTORIES OF ENGLISH

Even as early critics like Nowell and Carew were using a geographic axis to graph an outline of English, others drew a chronological one imagining a past for the language and, in the process, providing another way to identity continuity in the language's development. Both Thomas Smith's and Bullokar's sensitivity to time extends even to minute diachronic details, such as recognition of the fact that English no longer employs the graphs *ð* and *þ*. Of the increasingly common *q*, Ben Jonson says, it is "a letter we might very well spare in our *Alphabet*, if we would but use the serviceable *k*. as he should be, and restore him to the right of reputation he had with our Fore-fathers. For, the *English-Saxons* knew not this halting Q. with her waiting woman *u*. after her."[24]

For the beginning of this past, the moment that stands at the top of the English tree diagram, Camden and Verstegan looked to the fifth-century CE arrival of Continental Angles, Saxons, and Jutes. They thereby established the frame that nineteenth-century philology took for granted and merely extended when it nested the English tree in a larger pre-historical tree diagram. The very first history of English textbooks published for university audiences (those of T. N. Toller and Oliver Farrar Emerson) thus begin above English, with lengthy accounts of the Indo-Europeans and the Teutons. By 1946, principles of time (along with those of space) allowed Otto Jespersen to say simply that the "existence of the English language as a separate idiom began when Germanic tribes had occupied all the lowlands of Great Britain." And contemporary histories typically follow this same pattern, delineating English in spatial-temporal terms that treat Indo-European and Proto-Germanic as the ancestors of a language that began with the migration of the Continental Germanic tribes.[25] Since all these tribes were pre-literate and therefore left no written remains—much less their reflections on migration and language change—we have no way of knowing whether the migration itself had any fundamental effects on whatever it was they spoke. But the relative brevity of the migration period (perhaps 200 years) and the recorded evidence of modern emigration give us lots of reasons to believe that the language spoken in Britain in the year 600 in fact would have remained much like that then spoken in what is now southern Denmark. This chronological model, then, roots the beginning of English not in a major development like the Great Vowel Shift, or even in minor and presumably post-migration phonological changes like what's known as second fronting. English instead takes its origins from Germanic pre-history and from British political geography, well before anything like the state of England existed. Of necessity, moreover, the history of the language thereby becomes the atrophy of Germanic inflections and lexicon rather than the development of analytic word order, the proliferation of non-Germanic vocabulary, syntactic adjustments arising from contact with other languages, or transformations of speakers' demographics. As in treatments of vocabulary, English is what it was.

When time is used in this way, cognates (words that have developed from a common ancestor) provide a way to sharpen the contours of the language and demonstrate its essentially Germanic character. This is how George Hickes employs them in his 1689 *Institutiones Grammaticæ*, the first real description of Old English. By discussing together the grammars of the earliest English and of Moeso-Gothic (an extinct eastern Germanic language) Hickes treats each as a variety of the other. He triangulates the identity of English through both geographic and chronological coordinates, including a dictionary of Old Norse whose translations are variously in Modern English, Old English, Gothic, and Latin. Replete with a "Catalogue of Northern Books," the *Institutiones Grammaticæ* thus roots the heritage of English-speaking people in quintessentially ancient Germanic traditions. Triangulating in the same way with comparative evidence from German, Icelandic, Faroese, Danish, and so forth, Joseph Bosworth later suggested that along with English all these tongues "appear as dialects of one extensive language, branches of one vigorous stock, or streams from the same copious fountain. A recollection of this will, in some degree, restore to order the confusion of Babel, and therefore very much facilitate the acquisition of languages. An appeal to the Germanic languages will be a sufficient proof, not only of their similarity, but of their identity."[26] In essence, recognition of the language's Germanic identity charts the main channel for the river of English and points the direction back to the perfect communication that was lost when we were scattered at the Tower of Babel.

Like Quirk and Kachru, however, Bosworth ends up talking about much more than linguistic structure here, for as with principles of geography, those of chronology can fashion linguistic evidence in support of desirable social truths. By linking English to what was called Teutonic, he and (earlier) Gil, Camden, Verstegan, and Hart all used the history of language to support a heritage of what they regarded as the inherently decent and ethical Germanic people from whom Anglophones descend. "This English tongue is extracted, as the nation," says Camden, "from the Germans, the most glorious of al now extant in Europe for their moral and martial virtues." Not only that, to Verstegan, the German language is the best because it has remained linguistically pure by the Germans ever keeping "themselves unmixed with forrain people, and their language without mixing it with any forrain toung."[27] Through this use of space and time, English will remain English (and estimable) so long as it remains purely Germanic and unaffected by non-English speakers, including anyone outside this Germanic heritage.

Verstegan takes perhaps the inevitable next step in this chronological framing by tracing Teutonic not to the Garden of Eden—though there were early modern critics who did just that—but to the explosion of languages after the Tower of Babel collapsed. He euhemerizes Tuisco, the founding god of the Teutons, by identifying him as the great-grandson of Noah's son Japhet, and very much in an Augustinian linguistic tradition engages in fantastic, self-referential etymologies. In *Ingwaeones*, a Germanic tribe identified by the first-century Roman historian Tacitus, Verstegan sees a reference to the group's physical location: "Inner-woners, that is to say, inward dwellers." And the name 'Eve' he derives from 'even', since she was Adam's companion in Eden. Such derivations show "the efficacie of this toung, that is able to yield as fit and proper significations for these moste ancient names, as the very Hebrew it self . . . yf the Teutonic bee not taken for the first language of the world, it cannot bee denied to bee one of the moste ancientest of the world."[28]

Antiquity in all its forms thereby can be a measure of the integrity of a language and its speakers. And since geography is historically tied to antiquity, the two can provide a mutually reinforcing definition of English: the more recent the variety, the more likely it is to originate outside of England, and the farther it will diverge from English. It is through antiquity that English, in the manner of Heraclitus's river, can transcend and even draw its integrity from particular fluctuations, such as the disappearance of ð and þ and the appearance of q. And by this logic of integrity through antiquity, Smith can ground his discussion of English orthography with an account of Egyptian writing,[29] while a much later writer, Henry Welsford, structures his 1845 *On the Origins and Ramifications of the English Language* by establishing linguistic and cultural connections between English and Persian. Thirty years later, T. L. Kington Oliphant began his history of Standard English with the Aryans and Sanskrit.

Of the ancient languages, however, it is Latin that has played the most significant role in definitions of English. Into the twentieth century, Latin grammatical structures and terminology shaped accounts of English grammar, and, in the early modern period, Latin provided the only (ill-fitting) model for talking about the so-called conjugations and declensions of English. Late in the seventeenth century, John Wallis relies on the antiquity of Latin lexicon in particular in order to verify the age and thus value of English. He regards words like 'wine' as clearly common to Latin and Teutonic, and uses them to conclude that it cannot be doubted that the latter is older—and by this model inevitably purer—than the former. Teutonic even includes, he says, words borrowed directly from Greek that do not appear in Latin.[30] A century before, in a similar vein, Roger Ascham justifies the change and variation that exercised so many early modern grammarians by pointing out a historical precedent in Latin, which retained its purity as a language for only 100 years: "the life of a well aged man."[31]

Like space, time can thus figure in very different ways in definitions of English. Rooting the identity of the language in its past makes any recently developed varieties of English linguistically suspect, situated somewhere on the margins of English; if British English is removed from Teutonic, American or New Zealand English are even more removed, and English as a second language in Asia still more so. Yet the antiquity of English also makes it possible to describe the language by means of the alterations in its structure (like the Great Vowel Shift) that are judged permissible. Time thus produces the fluctuations that define the river of English, allowing the language to be the same and yet different. It does so not by structural criteria alone but through speakers' imaginative engagement with the language and selective judgment about which linguistic phenomena qualify as diachronic change and which as errors or corruptions. The graph þ gradually disappeared from English in the fifteenth century, which happens to be the same century during which the graph q increased in usage. That much is linguistic history. It is linguistic heritage that the former could affirm the language's antiquity and the latter be not only a modern barbarism but also (according to Jonson) specifically female, halting "with her waiting woman u" and opposed to the masculine, "serviceable k" it replaces.[32]

This reliance on time produces dilemmas for language historians, who hope to write the history of the entire language but who must rely for the most part only on the written remains that have chanced to survive. And as much as definitions of English might depend on antiquity, much of antiquity left behind no linguistic record. Early grammarians resolved this dilemma largely by passing over the existence of mostly irrecoverable spoken conventions and instead illustrating the language not even just with written English in general—wills, broadsides, business records, or transcribed conversations—but with literature and literary usage in particular. In effect, the cultivated rhetoric that survives in manuscripts and books, representing only a small fraction of spoken and written English for any historical moment, but especially so for the medieval and early modern periods, often has stood in for the language in the abstract. Carew thus relies on More, Sidney, and Shakespeare; Gil on Ælfric, Robert of Gloucester, and Spenser; and Jonson on the Bible, Chaucer, and Gower.

Even though modern linguistics acknowledges the significance of spoken language, we still often resolve the dilemma of antiquity with the heritage fashioned by Gil and Jonson by imagining the whole of linguistic history through select literary remains and through the works that rely on them. The citations in Dr Johnson's dictionary are nearly exclusively literary and those in the original OED largely so. This is also the case in William C. Fowler's 1855 *The English Language in Its Elements and Forms*, one of the first histories meant specifically for classroom use. In his definition of English of over a half century later, the pre-eminent historical linguist H. C. Wyld similarly collapsed literature, social class, and economic activity: "The makers of Elizabethan English as we know it in the imperishable literature of the period, were the men, illustrious and obscure, who were also making English history, that is, who were living and fighting; sailing strange seas, and discovering new worlds."[33] And this literary and social heritage of English persists in both modern textbooks like Baugh and Cable's *History* as well as many popular modern discussions of the language.[34]

AGONISTIC ENGLISH

As principles of language definition, space and time produce an even more consequential dilemma for language historians, however. How can we truly reconcile the contradictory notions that English changes and yet remains the same? To do this, early codification devised several useful narratives, among them an anthropomorphic vision of languages as engaged in some kind of a contest with one other. The great value of this kind of narrative—besides demonstrating the integrity and continuity of the individual combatants (i.e., they have to be separate to fight one another)—is that it provides reasons for their changes (i.e., the fights themselves). Such narratives also offer yet another way for speakers to distance themselves from their language and its effects: in a world of anthropomorphic language contact, change originates not in particular users, uses, or domains but in languages in the abstract.

Competition with Greek and Latin in particular even might be called the master plot of early grammars, the contest that fostered a sense of English's irregularity and integrity, cultivated belief in its potential to transcend its classical forbears, and gave methods and a purpose to early modern codification. In Mulcaster's famous phrase, "*I loue* Rome, *but* London *better, I fauor* Italie, *but* England *more, I honor the* Latin, *but I worship the* English."[35] Comparing passages of Greek and Latin originals with their English translations, Ascham asserts that English, "auoidyng barbarous ryming, may as well receiue, right quantitie of sillabes [sic], and trewe order of versifying ... as either Greke or Latin, if a cunning man haue it in handling."[36] Anything Homer or Virgil could do, Chaucer could do better.

Contact between English and modern languages as well as interactions among regional varieties of English have produced this same kind of definition through struggle. For Ascham, Italian offers a strong negative example of what Anglophones should avoid. He acknowledges having wasted much time reading an English "toy," the *Morte Darthure*, but maintains that that volume doesn't do a tenth of the harm of books translated from Italian: "These Italian bookes are made English, to bryng mischief enough openly and boldly, to all states great and meane, yong and old, euery where."[37] And as I have noted, the idea that English is synonymous with a standard British variety (itself dependent on dynamics between standard and non-standard language) relied on agonistic struggles between British English and colonial English that helped formulate the distinctiveness of each. The same agonistic dynamic underwrites contemporary arguments that emphasize the aberrant character of extraterritorial varieties like Singaporean English, that define a variety like Hawaiian Pidgin by its deviance from United States English, and that categorize varieties like Chinese English as inadequate levels of achievement.

Like the use of space and time to outline the shape of English, such narratives are ultimately imaginative acts that have the potential to advance conflicting views. Continental French, for example, has been seen to amplify the character of English in ways that, at least as Dr Johnson understood the matter, make it comparable to Latin: "Of many words it is difficult to say whether they were immediately received from the *Latin* or the *French*, since at the time when we had dominions in *France*, we had *Latin* service in our churches."[38] French is likewise the language recognized for its contributions to English vocabulary in prestigious domains, like law, literature, and high culture. But like Italian, French also has helped define English by serving as a model of what the language ought to avoid. For Smith (as I noted earlier), however many words Anglophones acquired from French, the Continental language has had an adverse effect, while Camden felt that the glory of English had been greater prior to the Conquest, with English able to express "most aptly all the conceits of the mind... without borrowing from any."[39] At the end of the sixteenth century, identified with conniving nobles, upstart plowmen, and con-artist immigrants, French was framed as the language that, according to William Harrison, was spoken by "euerie French rascall, when he came once hither, [and] was taken for a gentleman, onelie bicause he was proud, and could vse his own language."[40] This is the sociolinguistic narrative that Sir Walter Scott fictionally (though influentially) manipulates in *Ivanhoe*, and it is the narrative underwriting Matthew Harrison's 1861 attribution of the loss of inflectional endings to Norman linguistic insouciance: "The Normans also, finding the cases and the remaining inflexions of nouns inconvenient, dispensed with them altogether, except in the expression of the genitive case."[41] Substitute Spanish, Hindi, or Zulu for French, and we encounter modern versions of this same anthropomorphic conflict, in each case sometimes to the benefit of English, often to its detriment.

For such linguistic narratives to have any explanatory power, of course, English now and then needs to fight back. And it has done so, remaining English whatever the changes it experienced, in several ways. One way has been through its putative faithfulness to its Germanic origins and character, despite the fluctuations of time and space. Such dependability is in fact a pre-eminent quality for early writers like Gil, who along with Smith and Camden understands the "purity" of English to be rooted in its Germanic past and to endure, despite the many changes effected by the Danes and Normans, whose victory had no impact (he says) on speech.[42] Two centuries later, Richard Trench shared this sentiment, when he too described a victorious English as changed but fundamentally the same after the Conquest: "The Anglo-Saxon is the ruling language in our present English. This having thought good to drop its genders, the French substantives which come among us must in like manner leave theirs behind them; so too the verbs must renounce their own conjugations, and adopt themselves to ours."[43] This principle of the agency of anthropomorphic English remains as well in arguments that explain developments in late-medieval literature and culture by invoking a "resistant vernacular," competing against and eventually vanquishing Latin, French, and the cultural practices they mediated.[44]

Another, more encompassing way for English to fight back against other languages—to engage in what Richard Jones called the "triumph" of the language, which is an anthropomorphic metaphor in its own right—is through the imaginative fashioning of stages for the language. These allow English to transcend moments of mutual unintelligibility and to lead inevitably to an endpoint in the present day. More specifically, by evoking life-stages reminiscent of infancy, youth, and adulthood, linguistic periodization can accommodate certain kinds of change (certainly not all of them) by naturalizing them within the conceptual framework of a single language. It can discriminate among utterances made from the fifth century to the present, using some as evidence for what the language is and some for what it is not. And it can do so as confirmation of a larger linguistic truth, which is that a language like English can change significantly and still remain English.

For English, the conventional historical stages, cultivated since the nineteenth century, are Old, Middle, and Modern—or, as Krapp described them within the spatial-temporal framework of Germanic origins, the period of "full inflections," of "leveled inflections," and of "lost inflections."[45] These have not been the only named categories, of course. Critics like Verstegan drew a difference between Old and Middle English (though not by using that terminology), though they did not draw a similar distinction between their English and that of the late-medieval period. Later critics, in order to emphasize the linguistic and cultural changes surrounding the Conquest, preferred Saxon to designate the earliest stages of what we now call English.[46] In one of the most influential linguistic histories of the late nineteenth and early twentieth centuries, Thomas R. Lounsbury managed to get periodization to work both ways, distinguishing modern English from the language of the Anglo-Saxons but also uniting them and everything in between into the history of one tongue: "It is certainly an argument in favor of the designation as Old English of what is here called Anglo-Saxon, that it makes prominent the continuity of our speech. It is an objection to it that, besides the inevitable ambiguity of the epithet 'old', it suggests wrong ideas as to the nature of that continuity."[47]

As for Modern English, in 1755 it was a century and a half old for Johnson, since Sidney constituted a boundary "beyond which I make few excursions."[48] Wright enacted a narrower definition by restricting the *English Dialect Dictionary* to words in use only in the previous two hundred years, while Wyld defined Modern English as existing from 1400 into the eighteenth century, after which Present Day English came in to use. He further distinguished two classes of the latter: Modified Standard and Received Standard. Karl Luick took perhaps the most expansive approach, identifying historical periods in expansive detail but also beginning his *Historische Grammatik* with a simple exposition of how 'English' refers to the current language *and all* its preceding forms.

Linguistic periodization certainly does rely on structural criteria. As Krapp indicated, the old, middle, and modern distinction reflects a shortening and leveling of inflectional endings that English shares with Norwegian, Danish, Dutch, and the other languages called Germanic.[49] But I am arguing that just as biological metaphors can transform the character of the English vocabulary, so they can naturalize views on space and time in ways that obscure their own impact on our view of language. Linguistic periods allow us to make sense of English linguistic history only by fostering some kind of heritage, and so unlike life-stages like infancy or adolescence, say, they are very much our own imaginative constructs. When we treat the language of, for example, *Beowulf*, Chaucer, and Shakespeare as reflections of three linguistic stages (rather than as three distinct languages) and Hawaiian Pidgin English or AAVE as non-standard varieties or inter-languages, we subordinate all manner of structural matters to issues of heritage, including geography, Germanic origins, literacy, and culture. Indeed, the earliest attempts to define periods for English arose not from linguistic impulses but the gradual equation, in the sixteenth and seventeenth centuries, of pre-modern English with the language of Chaucer as a means for finding a usable pre-Reformation past. In coming to stand in for what we would call Middle English (a role it continues to play in modern histories) Chaucer's poetry provided models for linguistic analysis narrowly based on literature, for the structuring of English as a language that could transcend radical grammatical change, and for the entrenchment of English's history and identity in Great Britain. By this model, English is a language we understand ourselves to share with Chaucer—and Shakespeare and the *Beowulf* poet—even if we can read the first of these only with training, the second only with difficulty, and the third only as a second language. If what you speak does not share this heritage, at least according to some English speakers, you do not speak English.[50]

And so I return to tree diagrams, which, by an additional act of imagination, turn linguistic periods into virtual objects in a sequence of stable, discrete states of English. The identification of Old, Middle, and Modern English organizes what otherwise would be simply undifferentiated historical linguistic data into a kind of coming-of-age romance punctuated by the notion of the language's early modern triumph. And it's a narrative that can accommodate any linguistic data without being disrupted by them. Having defined Middle English, for example, we can use that definition to judge the thirteenth-century chronicler Laȝamon as old fashioned, the fifteenth-century Scots poet Henryson as linguistically precocious, and speakers of interlanguages as not Anglophones at all. Smith laments vocabulary borrowed from French, Trench argues that late-medieval English, emerging "from this struggle of centuries during which it had refused to die, was very different from that which had entered into it," and Krapp claims that at 1100 and 1500 English was changing "more rapidly" than prior to or between those moments. By doing so, all draw factual conclusions from linguistic stages whose history depends on interpretive judgments.[51] In such judgments, indeed, linguistic periods become organizing principles apparently external to definitions of the language when they are in fact a means to write them.

In any of its permutations, the explanatory models that time and space construct for English can be very powerful, even more so than the linguistic details of which they are composed. As David Matthews has said, the Norman Conquest, prior to which inflectional morphology already had begun to atrophy, has in particular "exerted a kind of historical gravitational pull on philology in excess of its actual effect on the language."[52] These models likewise can underwrite linguistic histories and heritages otherwise incompatible with them. When we talk about Englishes or about extraterritorial varieties of English as a way to affirm the integrity of particular varieties, we still graft them onto a historiography of the language that goes back to the early modern period. And when we attribute to such varieties stages of historical development that recall the periodization of English in general, we do so because the spatial-temporal definition has in fact become naturalized. The triumph of a historically rooted English has even been measured by the global expansion of speakers and varieties that otherwise are at odds with many of the traditions I have described here.[53] By identifying new leaves on the English tree diagram, arguments like these recall the strategic use of space and time that I have traced throughout this chapter. And sustained by these principles, the history of English remains a narrative of a well-defined (if variable) language, rooted in British geography and triumphing over other languages and non-standard varieties, preserving in the process its essentially Germanic heritage. In very different circumstances and in very different forms, the river of English flows where and when we direct it.

CHAPTER FIVE

The Genius of Our Tongue

In the Prologue to his 1490 *Eneydos*, William Caxton tells a story that is at once vivid, humorous, and surprising, a story that has become a staple in discussions of English and language change in the late medieval period. I refer, of course, to his account of "certayn marchauntes" who had intended to sail to Zealand, only to have a lack of wind compel them to take land in the Thames estuary. Among this group was a mercer named Sheffield, who entered a public house and asked for food, especially *eggs*, which he designated with that word and not the local form *eyren*. Caxton continues:

And the goode wyf answerde. that she coude speke no frenshe. And the marchaunt was angry. for he also coude speke no frenshe. but wold haue hadde egges / and she vnderstode hym not / And thenne at laste a nother sayd that he wolde haue eyren / then the good wyf sayd that she vnderstod hym wel.[1]
['And the goodwife answered that she couldn't speak any French. The merchant became angry, because he, too, couldn't speak French. He only wanted eggs, and she did not understand him. And then someone else finally said that the merchant wanted eyren, at which the goodwife said she understood him very well.']

As memorable and oft-cited as this story is, I've always wondered about its real point. Caxton uses it in the context of a lament over the condition of English in his day, which varied across England and also differed from what he had spoken as a boy in, probably, the 1420s.[2] His is not so much a theoretical concern as a practical one. When even breakfast becomes difficult to order, how is a printer and, more importantly, a businessman to decide what variety of language will be intelligible and therefore marketable?

But there's more to this story than eggs and cash. Why, I wonder, is Sheffield angry? It might be that he's simply hungry and that further delay, while he and the goodwife sort out inflectional morphology, has put him entirely out of sorts. Or it might be that he's agitated by the additional costs that a delayed sailing will produce—he is a merchant, after all—and that the frustrated meal not only epitomizes his larger frustration but also is just one annoyance too many for him. Or maybe, from a philosophical perspective, he's a kind of proto-Lockean, disheartened over the failure of humans to communicate fully their intentions to one another: "she vnderstode hym not."

Then there's the fact that both speakers admit they cannot speak French. Is there, I wonder, shame in this admission, so that either or both feel that the other has acted with superiority in shifting languages to use a putatively French word? Or is there pride—are the merchant and wife offended that anyone might imagine people of their quality would do something so base as to speak French?

And as long as I'm on this topic, I'll register that it's surprising, too, that a late medieval speaker from Kent should be completely unfamiliar with the form *eggs*. The earliest recorded version of the word is Old English *æg*, a so-called s-stem noun whose plural was *ægru*, reflected in the *eyren* used by the unnamed third person in Caxton's little drama. Deriving from Old Norse *egg*, *eggs* is a form that occurs earliest in the north of England, whose medieval dialects in general tended to be more innovative than those of the south. It would make sense, then, that the southern goodwife would be more familiar with the older, regional *eyren*, but would *eggs* have been unknown to her? By the late-fifteenth century reflexes of many Norse words and forms had dispersed throughout the country, and already a century before, when the Oxford theologian John Wyclif's hens still laid *eiren*, the southwestern poet William Langland's had begun to lay *eggs*.[3] Moreover, not only does the unnamed woman keep a public house, where her own business would have required her to speak with a good many merchants from across England and the continent, but the entire incident is framed by Caxton's acknowledgment that language is a variable phenomenon. If Caxton knew that language changes and varies, why didn't the goodwife as well, since in her line of work communication would have been just as crucial as it was in Caxton's?

But perhaps the most puzzling feature of this story is the matter-of-fact way in which it transpires and is told. For Sheffield, his use of *eggs* qualifies his speech as English, just as surely as his usage disqualifies it for the goodwife. Each seems to know as much instinctively, without the need of English dictionaries or grammar books, which wouldn't exist anyway for another 125 years or so. Further, the merchant and the goodwife both become not just confused but angry over the form *eggs*, and yet Caxton records no surprise—neither theirs nor his own—over this outrage. All three would seem to regard their mutual anger, however inscrutable to modern readers, as well motivated. It's as if we overhear an argument that makes complete sense to everyone else but us.

The simplest conclusion to draw from Caxton's breakfast fable is that to Anglophones, English means more than a collection of grammatical forms. It also means the social implications of those forms—that certain vulgarities, for example, can be known but not used, or that (as for Sheffield and the goodwife) the shape of the language can carry the emotional investment of its speakers. Whatever exactly angers Sheffield and the goodwife, it would seem to be not grammatical issues like phonology and morphology but rather their implications for the larger issue of the definition of English. We care about which words qualify as English, then, and also about what qualitative judgments are associated with them. And just as forms might be better and worse English, so too can be the varieties in which they occur as well as the speakers who utter them.

A failure to communicate like the one Caxton describes thus could owe as easily to a speaker's rejection of another speaker or variety as to genuine incomprehension of an utterance's meaning, and it's not always possible to determine just where the failure originates. Is the goodwife, for instance, only pretending (for whatever reason) not to understand *eggs*? An inability to understand foreign-born workers has in fact figured in numerous legal cases in the United States, and also in complaints by American undergraduates that they cannot understand foreign-born instructors, particularly those in science courses. And yet sometimes such incomprehension is only illusory, rooted in more than linguistic forms alone. In one study, two randomly selected groups of students listened to the same recording of an American-born Anglophone, but were shown one of two photographs: one group saw a young Caucasian woman, the other a similarly aged Asian woman. Students who viewed the latter while listening to the recording not only claimed greater difficulty in understanding the speaker but also scored lower on a comprehension test.[4] Unless this second group somehow contained a high number of weak students, understanding and performance would seem tied to students' expectations of the speaker.

Like physical and temporal distance, then, qualitative judgments about varieties and their speakers are ways to channel the river of English. They structure imaginative arguments involving the integrity of English and its varieties. And this means that grammars, like dictionaries and histories of the language, have an ambivalent relation to English, not so much building definitions out of linguistic experience as categorizing linguistic experience in accordance with pre-existing definitions. How these definitions come about can hinge on non-linguistic issues like speakers' ethnicity, a variety's social uses, or even (as for Sheffield) the circumstances of a conversation. As with space and time in histories of the language, moreover, such qualitative definitions are rationalizing principles. They are ways to frame language that may seem value-free and preparatory to grammatical analysis—simply scientific tools—but that, in contexts as different as early modern codification and contemporary language contact, are themselves embedded in social expectations.

CODIFICATION, LANGUAGE, BEHAVIOR

We accept sentences as well-formed English expressions according to two very different sorts of criteria, each of which has many permutations. We might evaluate them on the basis of descriptive grammar, which simply attempts to describe how speakers form sentences without passing any judgment on the correctness, incorrectness, or infelicity of the expression. Anglophones thus really do say things like 'I ain't never going to join no army', or 'she asked him why didn't he say he was ill', and a descriptive grammar records as much. A prescriptive grammar, conversely, allows only those sentences that meet a specified and sometimes artificially imposed set of standards, regardless both of whether any speakers in fact spontaneously produce qualifying sentences and of how frequently proscribed structures occur. Prescriptive grammar would thus judge both of the sentences I've given as bad English or even not-English, rewriting the first to eliminate the double negatives ('I'm never going to join the army') and the second to regularize the inversion of the subject and auxiliary verb in the embedded sentence ('why he didn't say').

This kind of codification, which is what occurs to most of us when we hear the word 'grammar', first appears late in the sixteenth century and from its earliest stages includes grammars (Bullokar's 1586 *Pamphlet for Grammar*), dictionaries (Cawdry's 1604 *A Table Alphabeticall*), and histories of the language (Verstegan's 1605 *A Restitution of Decayed Intelligence*). Its growth from these beginnings is extraordinary and perhaps the defining characteristic of English language discussion in the early modern period. Following William Bullokar's 1580 *The Amendment of Orthographie for English Speech* and 1586 *Pamphlet for Grammar*, English grammarians published, by the end of the eighteenth century, over 250 grammatical handbooks and over 20 dictionaries, many of which, like Lowth's *Short Introduction to English Grammar* and Murray's *English Grammar*, were issued multiple times. One of the reasons to care about English is indeed the money to be made through its definition.

While the southern British variety used by many of the early codifiers and their readers provided the basis for these grammatical prescriptions, it was Latin and Greek that modeled linguistic regularity, and this tells us that the codifiers themselves were both well educated and financially stable individuals who had the opportunity to pursue a university education when a relative few did. Since English was not a taught subject in universities throughout the period, nor in grammar schools for much of it, codification likewise presumed a narrow audience:

aristocrats, literate merchants, and, to a significant extent, the authors of other metalinguistic discussions.[5] Bullokar, John Hart, Alexander Gil, and William Camden all approvingly refer to Thomas Smith's *De recta & emendata linguæ Anglicæ scriptione*, which they see as foundational for the correction of English orthography; Camden cites Laurence Nowell and other "learned Gentlemen"; Carew commends George Puttenham, Sir Philip Sidney, and Richard Stanihurst; and Carew's own work appears transformed (without attribution) in V. J. Peyton's 1771 *The History of the English Language*.[6]

All of which means that in its inception the codification of English emerged from a limited, literate, and generally affluent selection of Anglophone society, to which it in turn primarily addressed itself. But even though grammars and dictionaries initially reflected the interests of a small and essentially elite group of Anglophones—and not the group of English speakers at large—these same Anglophones, whether as educators, politicians, or financiers, were in a position to mandate specific language usage in many influential domains, both in England and abroad. They—not the millions of illiterate Anglophones in Britain, nor the growing number of speakers in North America and elsewhere—were the ones who formally could define English and its speakers. They were also the ones who had the most to gain from their definitions. In the Standard English that it ultimately produced, that is, codification provided a crucial means for extending (or restricting) literacy and the opportunities, global as well as individual, that went with it, as first England and then the United States became world powers. And so early grammarians perhaps inevitably cultivated a variety closer to what they already spoke than to any other variety.

Much of this early grammatical discussion focuses on what we might call stylistic choices (of spelling, word choice, and sentence structure) that to the grammarians obscured the inherent clarity and even beauty of English. For Bullokar and Hart, the failure of English orthography was essentially disfiguring. Writing in English, says Hart, is in "such confusion and disorder, as it may be accounted rather a kinde of ciphring, or such a darke kinde of writing." For Bullokar, English has been "defaced" by lack of a true "ortography and Grammar." Because of erratic

orthography, he observes elsewhere, "our speech was condemned of those strangers, as without order, or sensibilitie:
whereas the fault was in the picture, (I meane the letters) and
not in the speech."[7] For the sixteenth-century writer George
Puttenham, discriminating among regional and social varieties
of English was also a way to discriminate among English
speakers. According to him, the aspiring poet should avoid the
language of universities "where Schollers vse much peeuish
affectation of words out of the primatiue languages, or finally,
in any vplandish village or corner of a Realme, where is no resort
but of poore rusticall or vnciuill people."[8]

Puttenham's remarks illustrate two important characteristics
of formal descriptions of English from his day to our own.
Firstly, they demonstrate how easily such definitions slide
between matters of style and matters of grammar. In fact, they
often collapse the distinction, so that the use of particular
rhetorical devices can be regarded as not simply undesirable
but ungrammatical. Ben Jonson uses the Bible, Chaucer, and
Gower to illustrate syntactic patterns, while (as I have noted)
dictionaries, from Johnson's through the OED, have relied
heavily on literary quotations to substantiate their definitions of
English. In later works like William and Robert Chambers's 1861
History of the English Language and Literature and T. L. Oliphant's
1873 *The Sources of Standard English* rhetoric and grammar are
effectively synonymous; the latter concludes with 1,200 years of
literary allusions.

This kind of logic entails the second characteristic of formal
descriptions, and that is that they just as easily slide between
linguistic and non-linguistic issues, which then become factors
in defining the structure of English. In theory, of course, evaluation of an utterance might be limited to structure alone, but in
practice it is these non-linguistic considerations that provide the
framework within which comparisons make sense—an often
ethical reference point against which an utterance or variety
might be judged better or worse. So 'between you and I' might
simply be considered bad English, violating as it does prescriptive grammar's edict that the object of a preposition must appear
(when possible) in what's called the oblique ('me'), but the
structure might also be (and has been) considered a sign of a

speaker's lack of intelligence, education, and even moral character.[9] It is in this vein that Puttenham warned against regionalisms as
"primatiue languages" of "poore rusticall or vnciuill people." Hugh
Jones was even more blunt in his 1724 droll assessment of British
dialects:

> For want of better Knowledge, and more Care, almost every County in
> *England* has gotten a distinct Dialect, or several peculiar Words, and
> odious Tones, perfectly ridiculous to Persons unaccustomed to hear
> such Jargon: thus as the Speech of a *Yorkshire and Somersetshire*
> downright *Countryman* would be almost unintelligible to each other,
> so would it be of good Diversion to a polite [i.e., cultured] *Londoner*
> to hear a Dialogue between them.[10]

Even the simple act of defining words through literary quotations
has social implications, since these definitions favor written, educated usage over the oral and everyday. By linking language to issues
of social identity, such qualitative judgments render the definition
of English not simply a gesture of idle or academic curiosity but an
activity of cultural consequence. In effect, the quality of one's
language correlates with the quality of one's character.

The same collapse of style, language, and character continues to
animate the verbal hygienists who engineer guidelines of permissible language for school anthologies and exams. Or a popular
critic such as John Honey, who sees better English as not merely a
linguistic or rhetorical judgment but an ethical opportunity, a way
to provide speakers (specifically children) with "access to a whole
world of knowledge and to an assurance of greater authority" in
the world at large.[11] Put another way, non-standard language is the
language of the ignorant and insecure. An equation like this further
undercuts any claim for the neutrality of grammatical discussion,
since it historically has rested on various kinds of social bias,
particularly in favor of a variety primarily accessible to an educated, upper-rank British social group (especially its male
members). Telling in this regard is the subtitle of Jones's *An
Accidence to the English Tongue*, the first English grammar written
in what would become the United States: *Chiefly For the Use of such
Boys and Men, as have never learnt 'Latin' perfectly, and for the
Benefit of the Female Sex: Also for the 'Welch', 'Scotch', 'Irish', and
'Foreigners'.* The best kind of Anglophones are males who know

Latin, followed by those who know it only imperfectly; after them come females; then members of the United Kingdom; and lastly the English speakers in North America and the South Pacific.

In ways like this, using error to categorize language varieties and forms becomes a way to categorize society, and vice versa. Indeed, like Bullokar before him and Krapp after him, Gil saw dialects as fundamentally measures of difference, specifically of the difference between social inferiors and their superiors: "And whatever I say here about dialects, I want you to understand that it pertains just to rustics; for those who are nourished with subtler wits and culture, there is everywhere one speech and pronunciation and meaning." It is a small but critical next step for Gil from linking a speaker's quality of social background and linguistic competence to supplementing this link with the speaker's ethical character. The western dialect, Gil observes, is "barbarous,"[12] the same word with which Dr Johnson characterizes English spelling; the same word used throughout the nineteenth century to describe extraterritorial English in India, Africa, and North America; and the same sentiment (and sometimes word) used in response to the variety labeled Ebonics and championed in 1996 by the Oakland, California School Board.

A template that links the quality of language to the quality of speakers has terrific explanatory power for English. By means of it, the bad English spoken by children, immigrants, and low-rank speakers as they try to emulate the better English they hear around them can become a source for the transformation of that English. Krapp thus credits the Norman Conquest with removing the de facto habits and rules that had unified and homogenized English until that time. For him, Middle English came about because the errors of the populace, no longer usefully constrained, expanded until they changed the character of the language: "The usages of the radical, the ignorant, and uneducated part of the people were not held in check and the result was that when English began to reassert itself, it was no longer the English of the Old English period, but an English that had been modified by passing through a period of popular and natural development."[13] As in extraterritorial varieties or creoles, the confluence of change and error thus cuts both ways: the worse English of one historical moment might become the better English of another, though that later moment will have its own worse forms, often associated with its own socially marginal groups.

Connections between quality of language and social identity have become so naturalized, so ingrained as a paradigm for modern approaches to English, that they constitute a kind of horizon against which critical disagreements take shape. Such connections define, for example, an argumentative field with Randolph Quirk and his skepticism of liberation linguistics at one end, and modern advocates of creoles or Black South African English at the other. If Quirk relies on the grammatical and political inheritance of Britain to assert a definition of English by which new varieties (and perhaps their speakers) are worse if not simply erroneous, the others seek to advance their cultural independence by severing extraterritorial English from this inheritance and tying it instead to indigenous traditions. Both approaches merge social and linguistic identity, and it is for this reason that this paradigm can fashion diametrically opposed heritages for Anglophones and their language. English thus might take its shape from the Germanic character that someone like Verstegan identified or from the indigenous cultures (e.g., in South Africa) for which the language of Chaucer scarcely occupies some middle status. Qualitative definitions become still more naturalized (mystified, literary critics would say) by reprising the identity-through-contest master plot by means of which many historical discussions of English claim their own objectivity. Honey, for instance, approaches English as a struggle between the academic and non-academic spheres, or between linguistic relativism and the language standards that he sees as ultimately socially liberating.

By linking social and linguistic character in these ways, quality-based definitions of English and Anglophones in general cease to appear argumentative and become instead what philosophers label essentialist: pre-linguistic claims about the fundamental, unchangeable character of the language. In 1762, Thomas Sheridan thus describes the English linguistic repertoire as consisting of stable, clearly defined varieties embedded in social rank. At one end of the spectrum, there is in London a "polite pronunciation"; acquired only "by conversing with people in polite life, it is a sort of proof that a person has kept good company." At the other is Cockney and all other dialects, "sure marks, either of provincial, rustic, pedantic, or mechanic education; and [they] therefore have some degree of disgrace annexed to them."[14] In view of this essentialism, all speakers have what amounts to an obligation to speak a variety that will reflect their birth or occupation and thereby affirm their genuine character as well as that of English. Or as James Cleland observes in a 1607 discussion "How a Noble Man should speake," "Your qualitie being aboue the common, I wish that your speech were also not popular; and with foolish affectation and verbal pride, not ful of triuial words, but plaine and perspicuous as flowing from a natural fountaine of eloquence." Once this naturalness has been disrupted, social disorder occurs as well: "For it is a pitty when a Noble man is better distinguished from a Clowne by his golden laces, then by his good language."[15] The expectation that linguistic and social deviance should confirm one another can be just as strong. It was the failure of early modern rustics to speak according to their station that disturbed Wilson: "And thus we see that poore simple men are muche troubled, and talke oftentymes, thei knowe not what, for lacke of wit and want of Latine & Frenche, wherof many of our straunge woordes full often are derived."[16] And in 1912, anticipating that indigenous Papua New Guineans should constitute a serving class and that their corrupt English ought to be of a piece, Beatrice Grimshaw was disconcerted to discover this wasn't completely the case: "To be addressed in reasonably good English of the 'pidgin' variety, by hideous savages who made murder a profession, and had never come into actual contact with civilisation, is an experience perplexing enough to make the observer wonder if he is awake."[17]

Before we dismiss such thinking as outdated, it's worth recalling the extent to which the integrity of modern varieties like Singaporean English, Black South African English, and Indian English itself depends on a similar linking of language with ethnicity, economics, politics, and so forth. If in these cases the identity projected by language differs completely from what Wilson and Grimshaw imagined, the intensity of the projection—the notion that we are what we speak—does not. As with the principled use of space and time, a paradigm of identity-through-language inevitably produces such opposing views precisely because they all begin with this same presumption.

Codification both depends on such naturalized connections and provides evidence for them. It arranges varieties of English along a continuum of better and worse usage, and binds—or at least has done so historically—that continuum to issues of morality, geography, and social identity, with Standard English at the top and regional dialects at the bottom. Through this model that is at once comparative and qualitative, what might be called a standard ideology makes it possible to define English by the stratification of languages as well as varieties. In essence, a standard ideology offers a template into which linguistic phenomena can be slotted in ways that ultimately validate the template itself—that make it (like other definitions of English) seem to be not an argument but a neutral explanatory structure. And so as the codification of Standard English expanded in the seventeenth and eighteenth centuries, it became possible, even necessary, for speakers to slot varieties into a qualitative hierarchy. As southeast British English might be judged better than northern England's Geordie, then, so British English might be superior to Canadian English and English in general to Hindi, Zulu, or Maori.[18]

This same ideological template made it possible to identify and proscribe various kinds of English as bad language (such as slang, cant, and vulgarity), whether in the explicit form of dictionaries or indirectly through the literary characterization of villains and the like.[19] And as with students' responses to speakers they presume to be non-native, expectations can override linguistic performance. Early modern swearing and blasphemy are cases in point. Whatever the actual specifics of pragmatics—whoever actually used particular blasphemous words and phrases—the usage itself became conceptually identified with lower-rank speakers whose language already placed them, in various ways, at the bottom of the English linguistic repertoire. For the Puritans, censorship of such language easily served as a medium for other kinds of social judgment (such as political or religious). To this day the idea of linguistic vulgarity (specifically, its absence) helps define not simply English but socially desirable behavior of a kind that often is accepted as rooted in class and character. "The picture that emerges," Edwin L. Battistella has noted, "is one in which 'good' language often reflects social desires for uniformity, conformity, and perceived tradition. Bad language is characterized with a range of qualities opposed to these."[20]

EVERYDAY ENGLISH

Against the background of this identity-through-language paradigm, I turn to a specific modern example of definition through codification: *Everyday English for Hawaii's Children*, published in Honolulu in 1935 and intended for children in grades four through nine. As chronologically and socially removed as it may be from the grammars of Bullokar, Hart, and Gil, *Everyday English* shares many of their sociolinguistic presumptions and much of their definition of the language. And it is this shared outlook, as much as any specifics in *Everyday English*, that interests me here.

But first a little history. Hawaii's initial contact with Western Europe and English occurred in 1778, when Captain James Cook chanced upon what he would name the Sandwich Islands. Within a very short period—just over a hundred years—English had become the islands' predominant language. Partly it did so through demographic means. By 1893, due to illness and emigration, the 300,000 to 800,000 people estimated to inhabit the islands prior to Cook's arrival had fallen to about 40,000 individuals, even as the number of Anglophone immigrants increased exponentially. And partly the linguistic shift came about through the managed means that are familiar from other contexts. By the middle of the nineteenth century, American businessmen and missionaries had already come to dominate Hawaii's society, with the result that English became associated with economic and spiritual well-being. In the 1893 Congressional Blount Report that challenged the legality of the United States' overthrow of Queen Liliuokalani and the Hawaiian monarchy, the Honolulu teacher and clergyman Rev. Charles

McEwen Hyde explicitly linked the transference of power to the islands' transition to English:

The Americanization of the islands will necessitate the use of the English language only as the language of business, of politics, of education, of church service; and open the wide field of English literature to a people who have only poorly-edited newspapers and a meager number of very rudimentary manuals as their textbooks in science, as their highest attainments in culture.[21]

Additional management of linguistic history occurred in 1896, when Hawaiian was proscribed in schools and English required, and again in 1900, when the Organic Act mandated that businesses also restrict their activities to English.

By this point, native Hawaiians had shifted overwhelmingly to an indigenous variety of English that likely began as a creole and is known now (oddly enough) as Hawaiian Pidgin English. Rather than bind indigenous people to the ruling class of American businessmen and missionaries, however, the variety became the means for their continued isolation. From its beginnings, Hawaiian Pidgin English has been regarded as stylistically inferior to Standard English—in effect, as a kind of not-English, like that of Somerset (for Gil) or of the United States (for Dr Johnson). An 1886 opinion piece even called it "a sober duty for every instructor of Hawaiian youth to check the use of pigeon-English [sic] ... as we look forward into the years, and think of the possibilities, there is every incentive to make teachers chary in their use of doubtful English, and alert to correct the language of playground and street."[22] One year after the publication of *Everyday English*, H. L. Mencken said of Hawaiian Pidgin, "It resembles vulgar American in its disregard of grammatical niceties, but its vocabulary differs considerably from the speech of the mainland."[23] And despite the self-deprecating humor of a mock phrasebook like the 1981 *Pidgin to da Max*, this attitude remains widespread among not only other Anglophones but also those who speak the variety and often consider it counterproductive to educational and commercial success.[24] As I have argued throughout this chapter, if a variety is judged inferior, so too can be its speakers, particularly if educational practice helps cement connections between the two. The 1924 creation of

English Standard schools in Hawaii did just this, for it used language proficiency to formalize a two-tiered educational system based on whether entering students spoke Standard or Pidgin English. Since native Hawaiians almost exclusively spoke the latter, the policy (which persisted into the 1960s) effectively prevented most minorities from attending the Standard schools and instead diverted them into ones that stressed vocational, agricultural, and manual labor training.

When *Everyday English* appeared, then, it did so as part of a long and complex history of linguistic change, political and financial appropriation, missionary zeal, and racial suspicion. It appeared at a time when Pidgin English was widely regarded as Hawaii's most pressing educational problem, one which available textbooks were ill equipped to resolve.[25] "The purpose of this book," John Ferreiro accordingly says by way of a Foreword, "is to assist the pupil in the grammar grades to speak and write better." He wants to identify and correct the habits of Pidgin English, because language "is largely a habit and it is essential that the bad habits be broken and the good habits formed early."[26] To this end, as a 143-page "activity book," *Everyday English for Hawaii's Children* consists of a linked series of passages identifying bad habits and of exercises by which the boys and girls (as he calls them) can recognize proper forms and correct improper ones. Following pedagogical traditions that originated in the early modern students' learning of Latin and Greek, the boys and girls can rewrite a sentence like "We been got good fun" and affirm one like "We did not come." And they can verify their sociolinguistic transformation through a concluding 11-page test and three-page list of forms for "oral practice."

In an address to the teacher, Ferreiro notes that it is the teacher's responsibility to identify and model proper English but also to refrain from describing forms as bad or wrong, as doing so will intimidate the students. "For this reason," he says, "the typical errors are called poor forms rather than bad forms, and the correct are called better forms rather than correct forms." Ferreiro's address to the "pupils of Hawaii" appeals to the practical emphasis for English education that itself dates to the earliest Hawaiian missionary schools:

Every boy and girl wants to make progress. Every boy and girl wants as good a job as he can get, and he wants to be prepared for promotion when the opportunity for promotion comes. Getting a good job is largely a matter of being able to speak English clearly and correctly. When an employer hires someone, he almost always prefers the one who can speak good English to the one who cannot. It will take you a long time to break your habits of pidgin English and to form habits of good English speech. Do not give up if you think you are not making improvement. It will take you a long time, but it is worth it. You must listen carefully to the speech of others, and, when you hear a poor form, say the better form to yourself.[27]

This is a puzzling if eloquent invitation. All at once Ferreiro invokes a Protestant work ethic, the notion that speech habits are infinitely malleable, the social view that language alone structures Hawaiian society, the possibility of becoming one of the English-speaking peoples, the practical value of doing so, and a view of English as defined by a kind of formal proclamation. With one hand he holds out the possibility of social transformation through language, with the other the explicit classification of Hawaiian Pidgin English as not-English, the intractability of dialect modification, and the promise that with English comes continued subservience. And in doing so, Ferreiro suggests that the boys' and girls' chances for success are slim indeed.

Despite his rhetoric of better and worse forms, Ferreiro constructs a fairly rigid definition of English that collapses a wide array of usages as generically worse. He advocates that the boys and girls "clearly" pronounce words like "going," "yes," and "more," rather than "goin," "yeah," or "mo"; refrain from inserting "you know" as a sentence filler; and avoid the parataxis (excessive coordination) produced by frequent use of "and." He offers a list of words that the children should not use "when speaking English," including common Hawaiian forms like *pau* ('finished') and *wahine* ('woman'), and devotes 13 pages to the niceties of pronoun usage, covering everything from the correct use of "who" and "whom" to the superiority of "it is I" over "it is me." The verb phrase, one of the most distinctive features of any pidgin or creole, is a particular concern for Ferreiro. Marking characteristic structures like "not been play" as worse, Ferreiro observes that "*Been* should never be used when speaking of the past." Other creole verb forms elicit similar comments: "*No going* is misused for the verbs *am not*, *isn't*, and *aren't*," as is the verb phrase 'no stay' for the verb phrase 'am not', 'isn't', or 'aren't'. Ferreiro approaches general non-standard forms in the same way. "The word *never*," he says, is "misused for the verb *didn't*."[28] Style, pronunciation, syntax, word choice, regionalisms, prescriptive grammar, and speaker identity thereby become one and the same in defining English as a language that the children of Hawaii, essentially by birth, do not speak.

Like many works in the codification traditions, *Everyday English for Hawaii's Children* imagines English as an invariable, rule-governed code. It abstracts the language from its contextual usages and presents it as something that the Hawaiian boys and girls must study to learn. And so in the tradition of Renaissance schoolboys learning Latin and Greek, the Hawaiian children need to memorize grammatical paradigms and engage in what are in effect translation exercises. They do so despite the fact that most of the boys and girls certainly couldn't speak Hawaiian, making some form of English their only possible mother tongue, as even critics of Hawaiian Pidgin English (like Mencken) seemed to recognize. Very much through a colonial orientation that saw nativization as a linguistic and social problem, further, Ferreiro attributes any divergence from the forms he specifies not to context, regional variation, or internal structural change—not to anything characteristic of living languages like English—but to speakers' ignorance and inattentive learning. If the boys and girls study and memorize rules, they will learn Standard English, and when they do so, *Everyday English* implies, they will be employable and able to participate fully in Anglophone culture.

By lumping together pronunciation variants, violations of prescriptive grammar, and pidgin forms, the book's codification creates two giant categories of English and not-English. The former is defined both by the traditions of standard language and linguistic historiography and by the habits (as Ferreiro would call them) of the Anglo-American missionaries and merchants who had been fixtures in Hawaii for over a century. Much as with regional dialects and Standard English, in turn, this heritage fashions by comparison the category of not-English out of anything that deviates, in any way and for any reason, from a mainstream of English. In talking only about better and worse forms, Ferreiro demonstrates apparently genuine and certainly laudable concern for the boys' and girls' feelings—and I do not mean to impugn him in any way. But this qualitative judgment, like other qualitative judgments, conceptualizes English in a way that almost guarantees the children's failure. Strictly from the point of acquisition, it seems doubtful that any ninth graders—students approximately 15 years old—could dialect shift so thoroughly as to erase the variety they had used since birth. And this seems particularly the case in light of the fact that, to this day, Hawaiian Pidgin English retains covert prestige, so that shifting from it is likewise shifting from an established social identity that speakers might wish to retain.

From another perspective, even if such a shift were possible, it would occur within an educational system that at least at the time was split primarily between Asian emigrant and native Hawaiian children, who spoke Pidgin, and Anglo-American children. While the latter may not have spoken exactly along the lines Ferreiro described, they did participate in educational and social circles in which the ideas he advocated were endemic. How Ferreiro wrote about language, in other words, would have resonated for them in a way it could not have for speakers of Hawaiian Pidgin English. And part of this resonance lies in the fact that, like the two-tiered educational system, a two-tiered employment system awaited the boys and girls. "Every boy and girl wants as good a job as he can get," Ferreiro observes, and this is certainly true. But in light of the history of the islands' encounter with the West, including the illegal 1893 overthrow of the Hawaiian monarchy, Hawaiian Pidgin English evoked a heritage of subservient positions quite different from the heritage of speaking Standard British or American English.

Above all, in defining English as it does, codification like Ferreiro's creates a paradox. On one hand, it designates the indigenous Hawaiian variety as not-English in several fundamental ways. On the other, by using a qualitative scale of better and worse forms, it defines English in ways that ultimately include and even require Hawaiian Pidgin. Despite the similarity of Ferreiro's pedagogy to that by which Latin and Greek were taught in early modern schoolrooms, the boys and girls are learning not a foreign language but the better form of their own language, which provides the constant of comparison for their usage. In the process, the book produces a heritage that allots them only a peripheral position on the river of English. More generally, it helps sustain traditions that define English through geography, cultural purity, and social identity, and these go back through Mencken and the Fowler brothers, to Sheridan and Verstegan, and all the way to the Proto-Germanic past as comparative linguistics came to imagine it. If it goes without saying that all of this probably happened unbeknownst to Ferreiro, it should also go without saying that this is precisely how a standard ideology works.

IMAGINING ENGLISH

Given their background, codification and standard language easily can be seen as simply and primarily tools of oppression, directed at preserving an elitist social structure and restraining social progress among speakers marginalized by sex, race, class, or nationality.[29] And there's no doubt that, as in literacy tests for voting or citizenship, codification has sometimes served this very purpose. There's also no doubt, however, that many codifiers, both early and late, have understood themselves to be doing something quite different.

For early modern codifiers, English was a language in disarray, lacking standardized orthography and usage, and therefore diminished in comparison to Latin and Greek in particular. Such grammatical inadequacy, according to Joseph Priestley's widely read and reissued *Rudiments of English Grammar*, had significant consequences for British culture. It was "not much above a century ago," Priestley claims, "that our native tongue seemed to be looked upon as below the notice of a classical scholar; and men of learning made very little use of it, either in conversation or in writing."[30]

Yet Priestley (like Richard Mulcaster, Dr Johnson, and others) had conviction that behind this disarray there remained the real English, as it were. This English, in style and expression, could not merely equal its classical models but surpass them. This is Priestley's whole point—that the disarray of English is in the past, as the ascendancy of its speakers is in the present. In matters of orthography, says Johnson, the problem has been a whimsy and novelty imposed on the inherent orderliness of the language: "caprice has long wantoned without controul, and vanity sought praise by petty reformation." He accordingly advocated "few alterations"—there were already too many, he thought—but rather adhered to the principle that in "constancy and stability" there is "a general and lasting advantage, which will always overbalance the slow improvements of gradual correction." What "the corruptions of oral utterance" or the "variation of time or place" obscure is the essence of the language, and it is this that the codifier must not so much define as reveal. To do so, Johnson observes, he has "endeavoured to proceed with a scholar's reverence for antiquity, and a grammarian's regard to the genius of our tongue."[31]

The sense of 'genius' here is crucial not just to Johnson's meaning. It is crucial to the entire enterprise of codification and the grammatical definition of English, whether the definition is Gil's , Ferreiro's, Quirk's, or Kachru's. Johnson means what the OED specifies as the language's "prevailing character or spirit, general drift, characteristic method or procedure" and therefore posits something intrinsic to the nature of the language.[32] It is 'genius' in this sense that underwrites the use of space and time to define English, the linking of the quality of a variety with that of those who speak it, and even transformational accounts of a deep structure underlying superficial variation and error.[33]

In such analyses, English has an identity separate from what speakers do with it, whether by error or design. They may simply misspeak, or they may consistently and intentionally produce utterances like 'I ain't never going to join no army'. For early codifiers, linguistic degradation like this even might be considered one of the characteristics of the genius of English, with the result that when left to the devices of speakers, as Johnson observes later in the Preface, "tongues, like governments, have a natural tendency to degeneration." From this vantage point, however, usage ultimately does not reflect or affect the nature of English, which like a government can be restored to its true order: "we have long preserved our constitution, let us make some struggles for our language."[34] As early as 1586, Bullokar claimed that through his efforts English would be shown "a perfect ruled tung, | conferable in Grammar-art." More generally, according to Mulcaster in his 1582 *English Elementarie*, English has "those thinges…which make anie tung to be of account, which things I take to be thre, the autoritie of the peple which speak it, the matter & argument, wherein the speche dealeth, [and] the manifold vse, for which the speche serueth. For all which thre, our tung nedeth not to giue place, to anie of her peres."[35] Neither fashioned nor enacted, such genius is inherent, with essentialist qualities that render it impervious to what speakers do with the language. And it is revealed not through usage but through the influence of grammarians, lexicographers, and so forth, who like prospectors pan the dross of what is said or written in order to expose the nuggets of language, or who like philologists connect the dots of linguistic history in order to reveal a latent picture of it.

By imagining English in this way, codification offers a heritage that is at once culturally affirming, socially critical, and linguistically liberating. If speech is left unregulated, it will succumb to a kind of speaker-driven decay, even if by its nature it is expressive and ordered. Speech and writing hereby become ways to remind us of the inherent value of our language and so of ourselves, but also measures of our failure to realize that value. Were Anglophones simply to speak real English, all might be well with the present and its continuity with the past. Our failure to do so necessitates codification. Like the role of space and time in fashioning a history for English, codification thus claims an objectivity that allows speakers to view their language from the outside, as it were. Also like space and time, however, codification can blur distinctions between history and heritage. Whether prescriptive or descriptive, grammatical definitions of English reflect what Johnson called principles of selection that are every bit as socially specific as those that underwrite the language's history. If Johnson's principles were rooted in literary tradition and Ferreiro's in Hawaiian history, those of Kachru, Chinua Achebe, and other advocates of new global Englishes are rooted in regional identity politics. That we might share the views of one but not another has no impact on the fact that codification serves social as well as linguistic ends.

I certainly do not mean to downplay the contribution of empirical linguistic data to any sense of a language or its varieties: however defined, English contains some basic structural components of phonology, morphology, and so forth. But if grammar varies significantly within and across time—and it certainly does—so too do understandings of what grammar is and does. I am arguing, then, that even grammatical principles rest on more than structural considerations. Words, forms, and structures can qualify as linguistic facts only if they are acceptable within some kind of precognitive notion of English—Johnson's genius and the philosophers' essentialism. More simply, grammarians, like lexicographers, can look for what they need to find in order to confirm what's already been decided, and principles of space and time or language and identity are ways to get this confirmation. This same thing can happen in histories of the language, whose writers need to decide what the language's history is before they can select the data from which they construct their narratives. The notion that regional dialects and national varieties are poor English or not-English will lead to one kind of history and heritage for the language; the notion that they are reflections of indigenous vernacular culture will lead to another; the notion that some are one thing and some another leads in yet another direction. It was the idea that American English is a linguistic melting pot that led Mencken to focus on slang and collect pages of otherwise ephemeral usage. But even as he was citing the luxuriousness of *hoosegow* ('prison'), *lohengrined* ('married'), and *ossified* ('drunk') to support this idea, Ferreiro, motivated by a much different one, advised Hawaiian boys and girls to avoid slang by substituting 'lazy' for *molowa* and 'work' for *hana hana*. Mencken found empirical linguistic evidence to sustain the heritage of the United States as unconventional and even provocative; the heritage of Ferreiro's evidence was of the United States' conventionality and of the sociolinguistic failures of native Hawaiians.

Like lexicography, then, codification offers ways to define English that might seem rooted in data—and to some extent are—but that in fact rely just as heavily on impressions, attitudes, and expectations. Whether expressed in the inkhorn controversy, nineteenth-century dialect studies, or pedagogical responses to varieties like Hawaiian Pidgin English, the genius of English is not limited to linguistic forms or a single chronological moment, nor is it an antiquated notion unique to Johnson. Imagining the genius of English is instead a necessary historical process for channeling the river of English and establishing coherence among various forms and moments by demonstrating discontinuity with other forms and moments. And it is in this sense that English and its history become arguments, selectively using data for selective purposes that produce selective heritages. Having looked at some of the explicit ways in which such definitions have been constructed, I now turn to the implications of pragmatics. Specifically, I consider how speakers use their own linguistic practices to answer the question 'What is English?' and in the process reveal why they care.

PART THREE

English in Action

CHAPTER SIX

English for the English

The question "What is English?" certainly can be answered through codification. We can and do consult dictionaries and grammars to explain something we've read, to rephrase something we've written, or even just to verify answers in word games. Lawyers use codification to argue intellectual property cases or to explain the meaning of documents. And educators and legislators use it to set various kinds of policy. Even if United States laws like the 2001 'no child left behind' law or the 2009 English Language Unity Act leave the grammatical contours of English undefined, it's a safe bet that what the legislators have in mind by 'English' is something they can find in reference works. So long as the people we're speaking with agree that codification is what defines English, then the definition (or definitions) of grammar will prevail.

But the truth of the matter is that most of us consult codification rarely if at all. We might rely on spell checkers or predictive texting, but we don't carry around pocket dictionaries and grammars, and pull them out in conversations in order to verify the meaning of an utterance, much less whether the utterance qualifies as English. In most conversational and written situations, we instead realize a definition of English through the act of using language to communicate. When we respond without comment to one utterance and fail to make sense of another, we simultaneously accept the first as an instance of the language we speak and challenge the other's appropriateness or even acceptability as English. We do likewise with speakers, when we accept those we say we understand as Anglophones but not those we say we cannot comprehend (for whatever reason). Indeed, a response as simple as "I cannot understand you" can likewise be an assertion that an utterance, barring clarification, does not qualify as English. And when we cultivate these kinds of judgments through group activities, such as education or colonization, we develop a kind of grammatical prescription every bit as powerful as that cultivated by linguists and lexicographers.

How we make such decisions is a complex process, involving everything from structural features (lexicon, phonology, and syntax in particular) to physical environment (including acoustics and weather conditions) to social frame (e.g., whom one is addressing and for what purposes) to personal preference or prejudice. It is factors like these that complicate mutual intelligibility as a simple, straightforward criterion for defining a language. As I noted in Chapter Five, there's reason to believe that asymmetrical comprehension can be as tied to speakers' or listeners' attitudes towards one another as to specific language forms.

Underlying such definitions-by-speech is what Herbert Clark has called "common ground." This is conversants' mutual beliefs, mutual suppositions, and mutual knowledge, the last of which depends on both community membership (i.e., they share some social background) and physical or linguistic co-presence (i.e., they are in close proximity or speaking with one another). Common ground, for Clark, is crucial for all successful communication—it's what allows speakers to determine what they might talk about, when, and how. Given the contextual complications that affect language identification, common ground can also figure in whether conversants understand themselves to be speaking the same language. The goodwife's anger over Sheffield's use of *eggs*, indeed, seems completely comprehensible to them and thereby points to a common ground that they share with Caxton but not us and that explains (or would, if we understood it) why they care what English is. Since common ground may be communal as well as individual, moreover, it also can apply to communication between communities. That is, in interactions between two groups of speakers—such as Anglophones and non-Anglophones, or Glaswegians and speakers of Jamaican English—successful communication depends in the first instance on the degree to which they understand each other. And this success involves, in turn, how much common ground they understand themselves to have.

Clark's metaphor for the location where speakers negotiate common ground and produce meaningful utterances is an arena of language use. It's a wonderfully apt metaphor, emphasizing as it does both language as a process ('use') and the agonistic ways in which the sense of utterances and conversations is negotiated ('arena'). Clark chose 'arena', he says, because language use "is a class of collective activities in which speaker's meaning plays a necessary role. In these activities, speakers take actions by which they mean things, and their partners coordinate with them in trying to understand what they mean. The two of them try to reach certain goals, some joint and others not."[1] For Anglophones to define English in such arenas, of course, they also need some sense of not-English. The goodwife had to know what was and was not English in order to regard Sheffield's *eggs* as French, even as her rejection of the word helped fashion a definition of English for the other guests. Two speakers who share significant common ground likely face few difficulties in any arena (Sheffield and the goodwife, after all, eventually reconcile), but for those who do not, the dynamics of distinguishing English from not-English can prove frustrating, far-reaching, and sometimes volatile.

These dynamics can also be obscure, for when we rely on common ground to define English, we in effect presume— rather than articulate or argue for—one definition or another. And having presumed some definition, we confirm it by demonstrating it in action. Definitions of English that rest on common ground are still more complicated than this, however. Even as arenas of language use produce implicit senses of English, they establish a group identity among native speakers and also dissociate these speakers from conversants with whom they do not share common ground. As with a standard ideology, of course, speakers certainly can be unconscious of such pragmatic definitions and their consequences. Indeed, part of a definition's explanatory power may lie in the fact that it constitutes a naturalized, unexamined horizon of expectations for speakers, who do not need to articulate these assumptions for them to be effective.

This and the following chapters concern themselves with such definitions of English through usage. They shift from metalinguistic discussions that identify the language by identifying acceptable vocabulary, syntax, or linguistic history to institutional or individual interactions that presume and demonstrate some particular definition. And they therefore consider definitions that frequently are not so much intentional as instinctual—the kinds of definitions for which we are all responsible in our speech, even if, as in the case of standard ideology, we sustain them without being aware that we are doing so. Each of these arenas is, I think, a significant and representative place on the river of English. Collectively, they suggest both the diversity of the river and the strength of the argumentative willpower necessary to define it. I begin with the place where most histories of the language presume English began: England.

THE HISTORY OF 'ENGLISH'

One thing few Anglophones have argued about, at least until relatively recently, is the name for their language, which since the Anglo-Saxon period has conventionally been English. Precisely how it got this name is unknown, since the written record preserves no Biblical moment akin to the scene in Genesis when God brings to Adam "every beast of the field, and every fowl of the air... to see what he would call them: and whatsoever Adam called every living creature, that was the name thereof." While its morphology is transparent, this only partly clarifies the origins of 'English'. The word must initially have been an adjective, since it consists of the common Germanic adjectival suffix -*ish* ('belonging to') and the noun *Engle*, which refers to an inhabitant of what is today the Schleswig region of southern Denmark and northern Germany. But while English sometimes modifies nouns like 'language' or 'speech' (or, earlier, *reord* and *spræc*), from its earliest recorded usages, the adjective seems to have been used absolutely—in effect, as a noun as well as an adjective. *Engle* itself probably derives from Latin *Anglus*, which the first-century Roman historian Tacitus and post-classical authorities used for such people, perhaps because it derived from a word that the Continental Germans used to describe themselves.

With the exception of a handful of runic inscriptions, no written examples of anything like the early language of the Engles survives. There are in fact no references to the English language in something that might be considered English until these Engles (along with their neighbors the Jutes and the Saxons, according to the Anglo-Saxon historian Bede the Venerable) migrated to England. They began to do this in earnest in the fifth century, but since they were still pre-literate, they produced no written records in their own language until several centuries later.

By the ninth century, the written vernacular had begun to proliferate in sermons, Biblical translations, histories, and poetry. Variously written as *Englisch*, *Ænglisc*, and (in Latin) *Anglorum lingua*, English had become the dominant name for the language of not only those who might trace their lineage to the Continental Engles, nor even those who resided in the Midlands region of Anglia, which was evidently named for them. Instead, English seems to have been used indiscriminately for any variety of a Germanic language (as opposed to Latin, Welsh, Cornish, or Cumbrian) spoken in what is now Great Britain. And this was the case even though written Old English survives in varieties morphologically and phonologically disparate enough to be considered four distinct dialects: Northumbrian, Mercian, West Saxon, and Kentish, each of which likely reflects pre-migration linguistic variation. In any case, whatever the linguistic differences of these dialects or, indeed, whatever the cultural differences of their speakers, already at this time there were speakers who shared enough common ground to regard themselves as all speaking the same language. They were 'Anglophones', even if that word would not be recorded for another millennium.

The only competition for English, whether in reference to a people or their language, seems to have been 'Saxon'. This is what the sixth-century British historian Gildas uses (in the Latin form *Saxones*), though he qualifies it as an "unspeakable name." According to Gildas, these Germanic invaders, most savage and detested by God and men, were like wolves admitted to a sheepfold.[2] Forms of 'Saxon' are used for the people in the Old English period, and for the language in the Middle English period. But though the latter usage had a brief revival among nineteenth-century philologists and though derivations of the word remain common as nouns or adjectives designating Anglophones or their language in modern Irish (*Sasanach*), Welsh (*Saesneg*), and Gaelic (*Sasunnach*), even 'Saxon' cannot be said to have provided much of a challenge to 'English'.

How and why this nomenclature should have come about may be one of those questions, along with the word's specific origins, that we will never have sufficient evidence to answer. But the issue is worth exploring because the medieval pragmatics of the word 'English' establish a conceptual framework that underlies codification traditions, that has shaped the language's contact with other languages around the globe, and that continues to influence definitions of English. We Anglophones today may share far less common ground than the Anglo-Saxons enjoyed; the history of the language and its users in only the past 50 years demonstrates just how disjointed English-speaking communities have become from one another. But the name of the language, as well as many of the suppositions that support its earliest uses, persists. Even the names of modern forms that classify the language by regional or national varieties, such as South Asian English or Nigerian English, retain a connection (through 'English') to a common ground that may no longer be present.

The dominant Anglo-Saxon kingdom of the late-eighth and early-ninth centuries was Mercia, an area that the Venerable Bede described as having been settled primarily by Angles, rather than the Jutes and Saxons that he claimed had migrated to other areas of England.[3] At the time, Mercia's dominant king was Offa, who had an interest in consolidating his power partly through the production of charters, and in this way he extended the Mercian language outside of Anglia.[4] It was Anglia, moreover, that led Pope Gregory the Great to utter (according to the original Latin of the Venerable Bede, who himself also uses the name *Angli*) a pun on Latin *angelus* ('angel'), saying that some fair-skinned boys he saw for sale as slaves were indeed well named as *Angli*, since they had the appearance of *angeli* ('angels').⁵ All this might justify the generalization of the Anglians' language for all of English.

The influence of Offa and Mercia was brief, however, following as it did the early eighth-century importance of Northumbria and terminating shortly in Viking raids of the mid-ninth century. These raids, in turn, were at least temporarily halted when Alfred the Great ascended to the throne of Wessex, where he fostered a program of literacy and translation that has come to be known as the "Revival of Learning." Wessex's military and cultural prowess continued into the early-tenth century, which generated its own revival of Benedictine practices. Even though Viking raids resumed at the conclusion of the century, thriving literate practices at Winchester and elsewhere in the south produced much of the surviving Old English writing—including works composed in a kind of West Saxon koine (i.e., a common language or variety)—which made the dialect the most politically and literarily pre-eminent variety in the Anglo-Saxon period. All this offers good historical justification for 'English' to have been replaced not by 'Mercian' but by 'West-Saxon' or, with a nod to Thomas Hardy, something like 'Wessexian'.

It is not 'West-Saxon' but 'English' that came to designate the language, of course, often in ways that similarly posit a general geography as the primary criterion in definitions that disregard regional variation, historical change, and political circumstances. Again according to Bede, when Bishop Aidan came to the seventh-century court of King Oswald it was simply "the language of the English" that the bishop could not speak— rather than Northumbrian or Mercian—and so it was left to the king, who had learned Irish in his exile, to translate the bishop's words. Of the place where the Northumbrian king Oswald destroyed the army of the pagan British king Cadwalla, Bede remarks that as Oswald marched to battle he paused there to set up a large wooden crucifix, from which subsequent believers carved relics and by which many miracles occurred. "This place," says Bede, "is called Heavenfield in the language of the English."⁶ Such generic references to English irrespective of regional variety or location persist throughout the Anglo-Saxon period (in Latin as well as English), both in topical comments like these and in longer discursive reflections on language.

When he pondered the decay of learning in England after the Viking raids, for example, King Alfred lamented the loss of the literacy in Latin as well as English that had once characterized the country. He proposed, as remedies, that the most necessary books be translated into "the language that we all know" and that all the sons of free men, to the extent that they were able, be taught to read "English writing." Left unsaid is just what he means by 'English'—his own variety, or that of his Welsh advisor Asser, or even that of Bede. A century later, Abbot Ælfric of Eynsham had only a slightly stronger sense for English in mind when, having been asked to translate Genesis, he lamented the errors that might be produced by false translation or confusion between the literal and metaphorical significances of such a profound book. "We do not dare," says he, "to write any more in English than the Latin has, nor to change the significance with one exception, and that is when the Latin and English do not share an idiom; anyone who teaches Latin or translates it into English must always be careful that the English has its own expression, or else his writing will be very misleading to read for anyone who does not know Latin." Just what the "expression" is that gives English its identity is again left unsaid.[7]

It is not that someone as learned as Ælfric, familiar with the long tradition of codification for Latin, couldn't or didn't see grammatical qualities that were distinctive of English. In his English translation of excerpts from Priscian's *Institutiones grammaticae*, he in fact specifies several vernacular characteristics. "*Littera* is *staff* in English," he notes, and, regarding grammatical gender, that words "are often of one gender in Latin and of another in English." Of the passive voice Ælfric further observes, "It is not very common in Latin nor, indeed, in English."[8] But Ælfric and indeed commentators to the end of the Middle English period wrote in the relative absence of metalinguistic discussion about English, of grammars and dictionaries of the language, and of the kinds of broadly recognized sociolinguistic hierarchies that have organized standard and non-standard varieties in the modern era. In the absence, that is, of the strategies and means for organizing language that

I have discussed, as well as (therefore) without the social practices that depend on codification. In this pre-modern arena,
Ælfric and other medieval English critics relied on the most
general kinds of categorical traits to characterize the vernacular.
"In English," Ælfric simply said, rather than specify grammatical
specifics tantamount to the kinds that Dionysius Thrax had
developed for Greek and Prisician and Donatus for Latin, or
that Johnson and Lowth would develop for English.

To say that in the Middle Ages the word 'English' primarily
projected a geographic locale is not to say that the language
lacked social meaning. A geographically based view of English
still could point to cultural heritage as well as linguistic history,
as in the late-thirteenth-century Icelandic *Gunnlaugssaga Ormstungu*. Set around the year 1000, the saga includes an account of
its eponymous hero's trip to England and the court of King
Æðelræd Únræd, an ineffectual ruler whose nickname has
come down through history as the memorable (if semantically
incorrect) 'unready'. In many ways, Æðelræd's difficulty was that
he was all too ready—to pay off Viking invaders in the vain hope
that they would return home and leave England in peace. In an
offhand comment found in this saga, the anonymous writer
observes: "There was then the same language in England as in
Norway and Denmark. And the languages first separated in
England when William the Bastard conquered England. Afterwards French spread in England, since he was of that lineage."[9]

While this initially may seem an incredible claim, from the
viewpoint of linguistic history it cannot be dismissed out of
hand. Old Icelandic and Old English are closely enough related
on the Indo-European tree diagram (rather like first cousins)
that they did share numerous structural features, including
grammatical gender, extensive inflection of nouns and verbs,
and (to a significant degree) phonology and lexicon. Further,
there's clear evidence that when using English, Norse speakers
refigured Old English forms in accordance with Norse grammar.
Such nativization (as it's known) would seem to suggest that
they recognized similarities between the languages and just
maybe that there was a high degree of mutual comprehensibility
between them. Indeed, the Old English "Battle of Maldon,"
which recounts a heroic but futile Anglo-Saxon stand against

Vikings in 991, offers pertinent evidence. Opening with an exchange between *ealdorman* Byrhtnoth and a Norse messenger, the poem never addresses or even mentions the fact that each of them is presumably speaking his own language as they yell boasts at one another across the river Panta (now Blackwater). A casual reader of the poem or observer of tenth-century linguistic experience might in fact conclude that Norse and English were one and the same language.[10]

At the same time, the remark about English in *Gunnlaugssaga* points to the ways in which the identity of 'English' and its history transcend structural matters and slip easily into arguments over heritage and the pragmatics of how speakers have used the language. Whatever its historical linguistic merits, a claim of supposed identity between Icelandic and English, as against Old French, enhances some of the saga's distinctly rhetorical and political concerns. Like his countryman Egill Skallagrímsson, Gunnlaug is both a warrior and a poet—the quintessential Viking. He is likewise engaged in a quintessential Viking activity: a journey to England, where he can prove himself and gain fame in order to return to Iceland, marry, and prosper. From a literary perspective, the observation on the mutual intelligibility of Norse and English fulfills expectations of the saga genre—it emphasizes the centrality of an English experience to a Norse lifestyle, irrespective of tenth-century linguistic reality.

From a socio-historical one it also evokes late-medieval Norse concerns with political and cultural sovereignty. Written as it was at a time after the mid-thirteenth-century collapse of the Icelandic Commonwealth, *Gunnlaugssaga* offers a nostalgic glance at a moment when Iceland was independent and free of Continental (specifically Norwegian) control. This same nostalgia animates other sagas of the late-medieval period, such as *Egilssaga*, *Njálssaga*, and *Grettirssaga*, each of which is concerned, to some extent, with the deterioration or demise of an independent warrior culture in the face of a powerful European monarchy. And in this regard, late-medieval Scandinavians (the ones who wrote and read the saga, not necessarily the ones they imagined to live in the year 1000) shared something like common ground with their English contemporaries. While

thirteenth-century chronicles from England bear no direct literary connection to these Icelandic sources, several of them do
reveal a similar nostalgia by representing the presence of Francophone foreigners and their king as a symbol of all that had gone
wrong since the Conquest. Writing of the mid-century conflict
between the barons and King Henry III, Matthew of Paris spoke
for a number of writers when he saw the presence of the king's
Continental friends and relatives as the epitome of England's
divisive problems: "With the king's faction thus set against the
queen's, the Poitevins against the Provençals, and with all of
them frenzied because of their many valuables, they rage against
the sleeping English, as if once they eliminated the native inhabitants, they would struggle to determine which of them could
earn control of the . . . kingdom."[11] A century later, writers like
Robert Holcot, Robert of Gloucester, and the forger of the
Chronicle of Ingulph of Croyland amplified such comments
into a tradition claiming that William the Conqueror had
planned, just as King Philip IV and other fourteenth-century
rulers of France allegedly were planning, to drive the English
language and Anglo-Saxon culture into extinction.[12] For both
medieval English and Icelandic, such metalinguistic comments,
telling us as they do about a desirable past that predates contemporary division, define language in ways that sustain heritage as well history, even if they still link it primarily to
geography. English could be the same as Norse, that is, when
their speakers shared a heroic culture undisturbed by Continental influence, uninterested in greed, and unable to sit by pas-
sively while others struggled over their future. In both cases,
pragmatics overrode grammar in the writing of linguistic
history.

Between the tenth and (say) fourteenth centuries, the structure of the language mentioned by Alfred, Ælfric, and the author
of *Gunnlaugssaga* changed to the point where English and Norse
speakers certainly would not have been mutually intelligible to
one another. English lost grammatical gender and most of its
inflections, at the same time it placed much greater emphasis on
word order, and it acquired thousands of words from Latin, Old
French, and Norse. These languages affected different parts of
England in different ways, with Norse having its greatest initial

impact in the Midlands and north, and French its greatest impact in the south. As a result, ordinary patterns of language change and variation were modified by language contact in geographically specific ways: southern Middle English works often contain a higher percentage of Romance words and northern ones a higher percentage of Norse forms. Welsh borrowings, while much fewer, are initially concentrated in the Welsh border area. Perhaps partly because of such localized influences, the regional variation of extant Middle English surpasses that of Old English. And with the proliferation and wider distribution of vernacular manuscripts alongside increased trade and the population movement that accompanied it, such regional variation perhaps became more apparent to speakers than it had been in the Anglo-Saxon period. Indeed, writers as diverse as William of Malmesbury, John Trevisa, Chaucer, and Caxton all note as much.

But despite this variation and its recognition among contemporaries, 'English' persisted as a generic name for the language, continuing to imply (and fashion) common ground among Anglophones. Rather than invent distinct regional labels that might reflect (say) the northern influence of Old Norse, records from across the country continue the Anglo-Saxon habit of using one word, 'English', to encompass all of the regional versions of the language. Chaucer (a southerner) uses simply 'English', as do the anonymous northern author of *Cursor Mundi*, William Langland (a southwesterner), and Dan Michel, a southeasterner who goes so far as to say that he writes in the "English of Kent." Even the sixteenth-century Scots poet William Dunbar, who is otherwise much concerned with native Scots literary traditions, on occasion refers simply to "our Inglis." And all these writers do this despite the persistence of tradition to the contrary, around since the thirteenth century, of claiming that northerners and southerners speak so differently as to be scarcely intelligible to one another.[13]

As in Anglo-Saxon England, such usages of 'English' neither specify the language's structural characteristics nor distinguish systematically among its varieties, and they thereby continue to render English an abstraction generally tied to geography. By a relational rationale, English is the language that is *not* any of several other languages that figure in the late-medieval linguistic repertoire, such as Latin, French, or Welsh, and set against medieval linguistic practice in general, this abstract presentation of English is peculiar. To varying extents, that is, other language traditions do offer the kinds of codification and metalinguistic discussion that specify their grammatical characteristics. I've already mentioned the Latin grammarians Priscian and Donatus, whose works were studied in schools and universities throughout the Middle Ages. While significantly more limited in scope and usage than Priscian's *Institutiones grammaticae*, works like the Welsh *Bardic Grammar*, the four Icelandic *Grammatical Treatises*, the various versions of the French *Second rhétorique*, and Du Bellay's sixteenth-century *Defence and Illustration of the French Language* (not to mention literary treatments like that in the fourteenth-century Old French romance *Florimont*) demonstrate an attention to vernacular poetics and grammar not consistently expressed for English until the seventeenth century. In other words, there's nothing inherent in medieval linguistics that prevented Anglophones from describing their language in grammatical detail.

This abstract sense of English plays out in several ways in the late-medieval period. For one thing, the frequent phrase 'in English' serves the essentially glossarial functions that I've already noted in Old English. "Alfred the king, England's favorite," observes the thirteenth-century poet Laʒamon, "wrote the laws in English, just as they earlier were written in British." With the same sense but more poetic flair, Chaucer meditates on the meaning of the name Cecilia:

> First wolde I yow the name of Seint Cecilie
> Expowne, as men may in hir storie see.
> It is to seye in Englissh 'hevenes lilie',
> For pure chaastnesse of virginitee.[14]

['First I want to explain to you the name of St Cecilia, which men can see in her story. In English, it means "heaven's lily," because of the pure chastity of virginity.']

Here, English might be considered particularly abstract. Chaucer is closely translating Jacobus de Voragine's Latin *Legenda*

Aurea, wherein this passage is labeled *Interpretacio nominis Cecelie* and includes additional etymologizing that Chaucer subsequently translates as well. All of this is linguistically wrong in ways that are not uncommon with medieval etymology, focused as it was less on derivation in a modern sense and more on the linguistic embodiment of eternal truths. But its wrongness allows Chaucer to express "in Englissh" the fundamental qualities of Cecilia that Jacobus had described in Latin. Like Latin in medieval universities, English for Chaucer is a vehicle for truth before it is a variable but structured code for communication.

Another version of this abstract but meaningful sense of English appears in the way that late-medieval English writers relate English to other languages. At least some pre-modern Anglophones commented directly on regional variation evident in extant manuscripts, and others engaged in dialect translation, by which texts written in one regional variety were reworked into another. Yet for the most part medieval English sociolinguistic thinking continued the Anglo-Saxon practice of neither assigning names to particular varieties nor reading social status in them, the way later Anglophones did with Cockney, Geordie, or AAVE.[15] Rather than emphasize the role of individual English varieties within the English linguistic repertoire, they treat languages as indivisible entities. *Cursor Mundi* draws such linguistic distinctions generally on geography infused by social rank:

> And on Inglysch has it schewed
> Not for þe lerid bot for þe lewed:
> For þo þat in þis land wone
> Þat þe Latyn no Frankys cone.

['And it's been written in English, nor for the learned but the uneducated—for those who might live in this land but do not know Latin or French.']

Or again, from the romance *Of Arthour and Of Merlin*:

> Of Freynsch no Latin nil y tel more
> Ac on Inglish ichil tel þerfore:
> Riȝt is þat Inglishce vnderstood
> Þat was born in Inglond.

Freynsce vse þis gentil man
Ac eueric Inglische Inglische can.

['I therefore won't say any more in French or Latin but in English, since English is understood by those born in England. The nobility use French, but all the English know English.']

Connections between languages in the abstract and social rank are expressed with particular emphasis by Thomas Usk: "Let than clerkes endyten in Latin, for they have the propretee of science, and the knowynge in that facultee; and let Frenchmen in their Frenche also endyten their queynt termes, for it is kyndley to their mouthes; and let us shewe our fantasyes in such wordes as we lerneden of our dames tonge" ['Let clerks compose in Latin, since they are intelligent by nature and have learned Latin; and let Frenchmen compose their turns of phrase in French, for it's natural to them to do so; and let us bring forth our imagination in the words that we learned in our mother tongue'].[16] While the specific associations of Latin, French, and English vary in each case, 'English' everywhere points to a language that is conceived as a totality lacking systematic social and regional variation.

As in *Gunnlaugssaga*, then, an indefinite late-medieval sense of 'English' still could have social consequence. The language's definition still could further a heritage of historical and political initiatives reflecting significant common ground among at least some of the language's speakers. Just this sense appears in John Trevisa's English translation of Ralph Higden's early-fourteenth century *Polychronicon*. On one hand, in a dialogue he imagines between himself and his patron (Thomas, Lord Berkeley), Trevisa proceeds in a relational manner reminiscent of Ælfric by, in part, defining English through its divergences from Latin: "In somme place Y mot chaunge the rewe and the ordre of words, and sett the actif for the passif, and ayenward" ['Sometimes I might change the sequence and order of the words, setting active voice for passive, and vice versa']. On the other, he uses the fact that English is the most widely understood language in England's repertoire to justify the translation of Latin works into it. As Lord Berkeley observes at one point, "if this cronicles were translated out of Latyn into Englisshe, than by so meny the moo

men shuld understonde hem as al thoe that understonde Englisshe and no Latyn" ['if these chronicles were translated from
Latin into English, they would be understood by all those who
understand English but not Latin'].[17] To Trevisa, the grammatical shape of English may be fuzzy, but the language nonetheless
plays a socially defining role for English speakers by underwriting the rights of the majority.

For Trevisa's rough contemporaries the Wycliffites, conversely, presumptive common ground that helps define English
is local and theological. Like Trevisa's dialogue, the Preface to
the second Wycliffite Bible translation of about 1395, one of
late-medieval England's most extensive metalinguistic commentaries, does cite some grammatical particularities of English.
Addressing the need to transform peculiarly Latinate construc-
tions like 'ablative absolutes' into acceptably English syntactic
structures, the Preface states: "And þis wole in manie placis make
þe sentence open, where to englisshe it aftir þe word wolde be
derk and douteful" ['And this many times will clarify the sense,
where a literal translation would leave it unclear'].[18] As forces of
religious reform, John Wycliff and his followers most powerfully
used the English language as an instrument of their challenges to
what they saw as the closed hierarchical structure of the medieval church. And their use of English for Biblical interpretation
proved especially provocative to Church authorities. But even
though the Wycliffites cultivated their own idiom, it was not the
distinctiveness of these English grammatical structures that animated them or those who opposed them. It was instead the
symbolic potential of breaking with linguistic norms by con-
ducting Church business in the language of the masses and the
heritage of ecclesiastical reform that this break produced. Once
more as in *Gunnlaugssaga*, the pragmatic meaning of a language
is not necessarily connected to its grammatical characteristics.

A more broadly political use of an abstract sense of English
appears in the various allegations (which I have noted) that
French monarchs planned not simply to take over England but
to eliminate the English language. Already in a royal letter of
1295 King Edward I claimed that such was the plan of Philip the
Fair, and in the following century the forged *Chronicle* of Ingulph of Croyland attributes the same plan to William the

Conqueror; the argument was rehearsed as late as Gil's 1621 *Logonomia Anglica*.[19] At moments of social upheaval like England's episodic medieval conflict with France or the fourteenth-century cultivation of an increasingly urban, moneyed economy, an abstract sense of 'English' could be particularly useful in the construction of shared social identity. During the ongoing struggles with France, the country's population included significant numbers of Francophones who shared numerous traditions, social practices, and ideas with the French from whom (they said) they wished to dissociate themselves. Identification of English as the specific language of England thus had a counterfactual but strategic quality: it was a rhetorical act for denying common ground with Francophones and for constructing something like a sense of national identity among a literally over-taxed and often despairing populace.[20] A 1422 statement by the Brewers' Guild (written in Latin) reflects a related but more inwardly focused strategic use of English in the abstract. It states that the Guild henceforth will follow the example of King Henry V and use English, since it is a language suitable for commoners and nobility alike.[21]

DID PLATO SPEAK ENGLISH?

In the year 1500, at the close of the Middle Ages, the population of England amounted to somewhere between 5 and 7 million people.[22] As small as this number might seem to us today, when the total number of Anglophones in the world is perhaps 1.5 billion people, it's impressive nonetheless. For one thing, 5–7 million people represents as much as a 100% increase from the mid-fourteenth century, when the Black Death had cut an indiscriminate swath through the English population. And for another, these 5–7 million people accounted for virtually all of the world's Anglophones. Only merchants, pilgrims, and clergymen likely would have been speaking English outside of England, with the result that any late-medieval definition of 'English' could bypass a host of complexities that would figure in definitions of the language today; complexities like the relative importance of regional and non-standard varieties, or of official and national versions, or of first- and second-language learners. These are the very issues, of course, that occasion the most heated arguments among contemporary Anglophones. Lacking them, English in the later Middle Ages might well have been primarily defined in geographic terms—as the most widely used language exclusive to what is now England proper. And this in fact seems to be largely how many Anglophones understood their language. One consequence of this early connection between the language and specific geographic space is the very name for the language, English, which has been the conventional term since the Anglo-Saxon period.

'English' did not acquire a more specific sense until well after the casual observations of Usk or the theological claims of the Wycliffites. Indeed, it is not until the end of the sixteenth century that grammar books, dictionaries, and commentaries systematically begin to specify grammatical characteristics beyond either the geographic view that English is what is spoken in England or the essentially relational view that it is the language that is not Latin, French, Welsh, and so forth. Put another way, the language could not have had such substance and specificity until codification began to provide it. And even then, it's worth noting, the abstract and even tautological sense persists. In his 1569 *Orthographie*, John Hart defines 'English' as "that speach which euery reasonable English man, will the nearest he can, frame his tongue therevnto."[23] To Dr Johnson, the definition of 'English' is "belonging to England; thence English is the language of England," which he illustrates with a quotation from Shakespeare that once more contrasts English with Latin, French, and Italian.[24] Webster's 1828 *An American Dictionary of the English Language* nods towards the global population of Anglophones, but however he intends "descendants"—linguistically, ethnically, culturally, or racially—and despite his own rhetoric elsewhere about English and the American nation, his definition follows Johnson's in granting primacy to the language's homeland: "The language of England or of the English nation, and of their descendants in India, America and other countries."[25] And the OED still defines 'English' with an almost airtight succinctness: "The English language."[26]

In this way, whatever its grammatical characteristics, English has also been a kind of Platonic ideal, a language with an existence independent from those who speak it, even as its changeable nature serves as one of their identifying characteristics. To be an Anglophone is to speak English, though to many verbal hygienists probably not as well as it could be or has been spoken. If there are limitations to such definitions, they did work well enough so long as virtually all of the arenas in which English was used were in what's now Great Britain, and when Ælfric, Chaucer, and even Caxton lived, this was largely the case.

Within decades of Caxton's death, this sociolinguistic situation had begun to change radically. Alterations in the verb system and phonology would have made it difficult (but not impossible) for the printer and Shakespeare, born less than 150 years apart, to speak with one another. It was this new version of English that merchants, missionaries, and colonizers carried to North America in the sixteenth century, to the Indian subcontinent in the seventeenth century, and to Africa and the South Pacific in the eighteenth century. In all these locales, English was further transformed, whether by second-language learners who nativized its grammar, or by transplanted English monoglots (i.e., those who speak only English), who borrowed words and structures in response to their new environments and the non-English languages spoken there. The character of Anglophone demographics necessarily changed as well, to a point where Anglophones of Great Britain, even Anglophones of Kachru's Inner Circle, today constitute a clear minority of us. At the very moment when a kind of Whig history of English took shape, anchored in Teutonic tradition and running unwaveringly through Chaucer to a burgeoning Standard English, demographic and sociolinguistic forces were thus transforming the language and the population of its speakers in ways that history had no way to predict, explain, or accommodate. Rooted in Platonic ideals of language that severed English from the specifics of those who spoke it, as well as from where and why they did so, this history was itself a pragmatic gesture that easily could remain impervious to the changes taking place.

CHAPTER SEVEN

Beyond Britain

In 1497 the Venetian John Cabot led an England-sponsored voyage to modern-day Newfoundland—the first of many English trips to the North American continent. Cabot's objectives, like those of his successors, were largely commercial: the discovery of natural resources and a route to the East. Unlike his successors—such as John White, Martin Frobisher, John Smith, Henry Hudson, and William Bradford—Cabot was not a native of England. As the commander of a ship of Anglophones he certainly must have spoken at least some English, but Italian was his language from birth. It remains richly ironic, if also prophetic, that the man who began the transplanting of English outside of England should thus himself have been a second-language learner.

North America was not uninhabited, of course. Anglophone explorers and colonists there encountered not just their French, Spanish, and Dutch counterparts but also Native Americans, who may have spoken, if what is now the entire United States is taken into consideration, 500 different languages. The number and kind of these languages, when added to the diversity of their speakers, made any arena of language use a challenge for Anglophones. Throughout the European Middle Ages, questions about the origins of language, its change, and (therefore) identity could all be answered by reference to the same biblical story: the Tower of Babel. This story explained language change and variation as the unnatural results of God's punishment visited on humans for their pride and presumption. It explained that all languages descended from whatever it was Nimrod spoke (often thought to be Hebrew) and, according to biblical interpretation, that the total of post-Babel languages in the world was 72, the number both of Noah's grandsons and of the translators who completed the Greek Septuagint version of the Bible.

These beliefs certainly weren't easily dropped. Much of the linguistic history of extraterritorial English and its social contexts in the sixteenth, seventeenth, and eighteenth centuries in fact consists of struggles to get indigenous languages and new kinds of English back into the Babel framework. But like speakers of other colonial European languages, Anglophones found themselves in circumstances that forced them to reconsider just what their language was and why it mattered to them. And the North American experience alone invalidated the Babel theory for Anglophones. It made it impossible to believe not only that humans spoke only 72 different languages but that all these languages descended from the top of the same tree diagram.[1]

In this chapter, I am concerned only with the earliest century and a half or so of these struggles. Rather than conventional or simply convenient, this timeframe corresponds to demographic shifts among the language's users and domains. It was only after the mid-seventeenth century, for instance, that English was introduced into much of India, South Africa, Australia, and New Zealand, where many of the issues of the language's first century and a half outside of England were accelerated and transformed. So far as early-seventeenth-century Anglophones were concerned, the last two locales had not yet even been 'discovered'. The year 1630 (or so) also marks a significant change in the status and uses of the extraterritorial English on the North American continent, for it was by this time that the region's formative geographic and political challenges had been identified (though scarcely resolved). While much of the continent remained unknown or unexplored, Anglophone settlements were well established in modern Virginia and Massachusetts and were proliferating along the eastern seaboard, with the result that Anglophone activity concentrated no longer solely on the exploration of additional territory but also on the expansion of these colonies and the creation of others. Settlements in which English was unambiguously dominant were well enough established, indeed, that their occupants had the opportunity to squabble over governance, charters, and the like. Roughly the middle of the seventeenth century, in other words, might be considered (to paraphrase Churchill) the end of the beginning of English's spread around the globe. Already at the close of the century appeared the first British comments about the inadequacies of colonial speech, and shortly thereafter the notion that this English was also distinctively American.

As I suggested in Chapter Six, prior to Cabot, English well might have been defined simply as the most widely used language exclusive to what is now England proper. It certainly wasn't the only language used there, but for the most part, and for quite some time after Cabot came upon the new found land, that was where most of the world's English was spoken and written. Following Cabot's voyage was a 500-year shift for English from the exclusive language of one nation to a global language whose native speakers account for perhaps 25–30% of those who know and use it. Less than 5% of the global English-speaking population now resides in the United Kingdom. What was at issue in the arena of early North American English usage and its pragmatic definitions, then, was not just the theology of the story of Babel. It was how English, Anglophones, and their heritage might be defined in linguistic, cultural, economic, geographic, racial, and political contexts unlike any of those that previously had given shape to the language. What was at issue was whether and how earlier definitions could be maintained despite these differences.

RARE, WONDERFUL, AND GREATLY REGARDED

"Who so maketh Navigations to these countries," observed Dionyse Settle of his 1577 voyage with Frobisher, "hath not only extreme winds, and furious Seas, to encounter withal, but also many monstrous and great Islands of yce: a thing both rare, wonderfull, and greatly to be regarded."[2] Indeed, if the dangers of North America (and of getting there) impressed the earliest Anglophone visitors, so too did its marvels. The common medieval response to encounters with any new lands and people had been to stress their spectacular, other-worldly qualities, as in accounts of the so-called wonders of the East, of which John

Mandeville's *Travels* may be the best-known English example. Largely speculative, and often written by individuals who had never been to the places they described, such works juxtaposed narratives of subhuman and sometimes monstrous people with stories of natural curiosities, such as trees that bore sheep. These works were testaments for the transcendence of Christianity, the superiority of its civilizations, and the 'otherness' of indigenous peoples, who could be defined only in relation to the European explorers who encountered them. Works like André Thevet's *Cosmographie de Levant* (1554) and François de Belleforest's *Histoire des Prodigeuses* (1583) actively cultivated just such an approach to the New World—what the critic Edward Said has labeled orientalism—as did Richard Hakluyt's monumental *Principall Navigations*, the first edition of which (1589) in fact included Mandeville's *Travels*.

But unlike many marvels of the East, those of North America were actually seen by those who described them, and this substance rendered them in many ways wonders as much of metaphysics as of geography or natural history. The Europeans weren't always entirely sure just what they saw. As individuals and groups, for example, Native Americans variously appeared as non-civilized brutes, noble savages, and sometimes both at once. Sailing to the New World even could be like a ride on a time machine, taking visitors back to a people (and moment) comparable to what they understood to prevail prior to the emergence of Greek and Roman culture and the rise of civilization as Europeans understood it. If such people seemed abhorrent, they nonetheless implied some connection with what European powers had once been and perhaps desired (at least in some small part) to become again.

"More than anything else," the modern historian Wayne Franklin suggests, "the West became an epistemological problem for Europe... The issue was not merely an informational one. It involved so many far-reaching consequences that the very structure of Old World knowledge—assumptions about the nature of learning and the role of traditional wisdom in it—was cast into disarray."[3] In order to make sense of such epistemological disarray, Europeans employed a process that has been called 'negation and substitution', by which Native Americans were at once denied civilized status and had projected onto them a supposed innocence that kept them marginalized in European matters.[4] While this process simplified some issues, it did little to clarify epistemological problems of language. The North American experience not only undermined the Babel model for diffusion and change, but also challenged prevailing notions about the immanence of language in culture and statehood—specifically, the idea that English was the language of the English nation in England. In conceptualizing Native American languages, further, Anglophones almost of necessity projected a definition of English as well. And they did so both by imposing inherited views of language and society on the North American experience and by cultivating new epistemological approaches to language, culture, and society.

One common response to North America simply was to maintain silence on the fact of Native American languages. Dialogues frequently take place without any mention of an interpreter or an indigenous speaker's acquisition of English, or any recognition of which language the participants used. And this could be the case even when early writers approvingly quote (in translation) long examples of Indians' skills at oration. Another common Anglophone response, reflecting what the French called the *premiers temps* model of the New World as a place from the past, was to see indigenous languages as simplistic in comparison to English. Such was the case with a 1584 report on two Indians brought to England: "No one was able to understand them and they made a most childish and silly figure."[5] Childishness becomes brutishness and then devilishness in George Percy's account of a 1606 visit to Virginia. He describes the Indians as "shouting, howling, and stamping against the ground" and a sun worship ceremony in which "they began to pray making many Deuillish gestures with a Hellish noise foaming at the mouth, staring with their eyes, wagging their heads and hands in such a fashion and deformities as it was monstrous to behold."[6]

The structural details of Native American languages, in comparison to English, could project this same primitive, even demonic, quality. Describing the language of what was probably a party of Inuit in 1585, John Davis observed, "Their pronunciation was very hollow thorow the throat, and their speech such as we could not understand: onely we allured them by friendly imbracings and signes of curtesie." It was "a lamentable noise . . . with great outcries and skreechings: we hearing them, thought it had bene the howling of wolves."[7] A decade earlier Settle had described perhaps the same language as "straunge shrikes and cryes," while Edward Winslow characterizes an indigenous New England language as "difficult, [a language that] as yet we cannot attaine to any great measure thereof."[8] The Indian language of this area, William Wood says, is a "Language . . . hard to learne; few of the *English* being able to speake any of it, or capable of the right pronunciation, which is the chief grace of their tongue."[9] William Strachey heard similar cacophony farther south. He says of the Sasquesahanougs, whom he describes as "Gyantes to the English," that they "are the most straung people of all those Contryes, both in language and attire: for their language, yt may well beseeme their proportions, sounding from them (as yt were) a great voice in a vault or caue as an Eccoe." Here, linguistic and social primitivism are of a piece, with the simplicity of the language's structure reflecting the simplicity of the people's social organization: "for they haue but few wordes in their language [for king or commander], and but few occasions to vse any officers."[10] As the elegance and emerging codification of English reflect the order of its speakers, then, so the harshness of Native American languages bespeaks the disorder of their speakers and their culture. And whatever communicative difficulties Anglophones face, according to Winslow, owe not to their limitations but to the inadequacies of native languages and their speakers, who "cannot pronounce the letter l, but ordinarily n in the place thereof."[11]

In Massachusetts, Thomas Morton understood such inadequacies not as characteristic of one language or another but as simply endemic to indigenous languages as opposed to English. He notes that because "the nations traffique together," each trying to understand the other's language, they all end up speaking a "mixed language." Given Morton's dismissive attitude, it might seem curious that he identifies the origin of Indian languages as Troy, whose inhabitants wandered through

Italy and eventually to North America. And it might seem even more curious that these peripatetic Trojans, "by reason of their conversation with the Græcians and Latiues [sic], had a mixed language that participated of both."[12] Yet with these interpretations, Morton manages to accommodate North American languages to traditional linguistic thinking, despite disruptive evidence to the contrary. Even as Gil, Verstegan, and others were crafting a history for English as a primarily Germanic language that, though subject to borrowings from other languages, retained integrity and literary potential, Native American 'mixed' languages illustrated the kinds of non-Teutonic, anti-language that contrasted with English. English may have borrowed a lot of words, but its genealogy was not at all as confused as that of Indian languages.

It follows, then, that indigenous peoples might be able to mimic Anglophones in every way but the linguistic one that could be seen to define English identity and achievement. As would be the case in Polynesia, the absence of native writing in particular became by itself a benchmark of the inherent incommensurability between English and indigenous languages. Settle thus tells about a 1577 search for some lost English sailors. Coming upon a party of Native Americans, the searchers use signs to make their desires known, and the Indians, evidently having some prior familiarity with Anglophones, indicate they want pens, ink, and paper. Rather than link Native Americans and Europeans, however, the technology of writing reinforces their differences, since once they get the materials, the Indians simply leave, never to reveal the whereabouts of the lost travelers nor to return at all.[13]

Anglophone visitors seem to have been acutely aware of this linguistic incommensurability, with companions to Davis, Smith, and Hudson all mentioning the necessity of sign language for communication with Indians and Inuit.[14] Similar awareness appeared in 1498, following one of Cabot's North American landings, when three captured (probably Inuit) men were brought to London. According to Robert Fabian,

These were clothed in beasts skins, and did eate raw flesh, and spake such speach, that no man could understand them, and in their demeanor like to brute beasts, whom the king kept a time after. Of the which vpon two years after, I sawe two appareled after the maner of Englishmen in Westminster pallace, which that time I could not discerne from Englishmen, till I was learned what they were, but as for speach, I heard non of them vtter one word.[15]

Ralph Hamor made this same point from the opposite perspective during a 1615 visit to the Powhatans of Virginia:

While I yet remained there, by great chaunce came an English man thither, almost three yeeres before that time surprised as he was at work neere *Fort Henrie,* one *William Parker* growen so like both in complexion and habite to the *Indians,* that I onely knew him by his tongue to be an Englishman, he seemed very ioyfull so happily to meete me there.[16]

A savage might learn to eat and dress like an Anglophone, and an Anglophone might go native. And what was English? It was the indelible mark of England's Anglophones, something that would distinguish the genuine speakers from the false ones and the civilized from the savage.

This imposition of traditional sociolinguistic expectations allowed Anglophones to interact with Native Americans without fully confronting the epistemological problem of which Franklin speaks. In an era of cultivated rhetoric, literary achievement, and codification, English identified not only Anglophones but also the superiority of their culture and political influence. It was Anglophones who brought their language across the ocean, after all, and the only way North American languages came to England was through the involvement of English merchants. Once in England, Fabian's account suggests, Native Americans, whatever language they spoke, remained just that. As the grunts and howls of a primitive people, indigenous languages could be both qualitatively different from European ones but also related to them: primitive versions of what English once had been but was no more. And the result was that the North American experience—the experience of a massive, new, and unexplored continent with thousands of unknown peoples and cultures— could be accommodated with difficulty but without disturbance to inherited ways of conceptualizing language and defining English.

Anglophone approaches to variation and change among Native American languages demonstrate this same kind of epistemological accommodation. While Strachey judged Sasquesahanoug a primitive language spoken by a primitive people, other commentators projected onto the North American linguistic landscape the identification of language, culture, and state that was beginning to influence Europe and that we saw in the earliest English grammarians and their equation of quality of speech with quality of speaker. Thus, Thomas Harriot observes of Virginia in his 1588 *Briefe and True Report*, "The language of euery gouernment is different from any other, and the further they are distant the greater is the difference."[17] Not only does Harriot envision the clustered Virginian tribes as linguistic and political images of the Old World, but in 'government' he adopts a modern word that proliferated in sixteenth-century discussions of political rule and territorial definition. The particular sense of Harriot's use—evidently something like republic or principality—is a still later development that the OED does not record as common until well after Harriot's death.[18] This dynamic between linguistic and political integrity figures in other early accounts, including Smith's *Map of Virginia*: "Amongst those people are thus many severall nations of sundry languages, that environ Powhatans Territories." Smith goes on to name ten such tribes, none of whom "understandeth another but by Interpreters."[19] Smith may well be inflating both the number of tribes surrounding the Powhatans and the extent of unintelligibility among them; he's given to exaggeration in general. But the important point is that he imagines the linguistic situation of Virginia within frames that described the developing character of language and nationhood in Europe and according to which Native American societies necessarily appeared backward. Back in England, Camden indicated that what might be called the linguistic appropriation of North America quickly became well established: "Our Indian or American discoverers say, that in every fourscore mile in America, and in every valley almost of Peru, you shall find a new language."[20]

THE PROMISE OF INFINITE TREASURE

English codification of the sixteenth, seventeenth, and eighteenth centuries had implications for social class and prestige that I already have described. Accessible most readily to the educated and aristocratic, a standard language (spoken or written) served as a way for its speakers to establish their own social standing, along with the moral and personal qualities understood to characterize them as speakers. Of necessity in this dynamic, non-standard languages signified baseness in character as well as social standing. As a sense of linguistic nationalism coalesced in England, this dynamic between standard and non-standard languages became among the most prominent and consequential features of the English linguistic repertoire, put to the service of containing and ordering linguistic fluctuation even as the global expansion of Anglophones made it more likely. More simply (to recall Heraclitus), the fact of varieties arranged in a sociolinguistic hierarchy helped define the language as stable and creditable precisely because it demonstrated historical variation and change. It comes as no surprise, then, that when the earliest North American Anglophones surveyed their linguistic world, they saw evidence of the same kind of linguistic repertoire increasingly cultivated in England. And by seeing this evidence among not only extraterritorial Anglophones but also speakers of indigenous languages, North American Anglophones saw as well confirmation that English was a language that varied in coordination with speakers' character and identity. Its structural characteristics bespoke principles of languages everywhere.

While histories of English often stress the shared southeast England background of many of the original colonists and explorers, the fact is that emigrants represented and so reproduced the entirety of the early modern sociolinguistic spectrum. In 1628, according to Thomas Crosfield, such diversity was in fact a problem in the southern colony: "The plantation at Virginia [is] much hindred by reason of the variety of languages there among them."[21] More generally, along with socially advanced men such as Harriot, North American Anglophones included a Devonshire man like Raleigh; along with the Puritan families in Plymouth were large numbers of legally bound (especially Irish) servants, single men, deported criminals, and (eventually) African slaves in Jamestown. And along with the elegant phrasings of an educated man like Hakluyt were an abundance of writings that showed little awareness of emerging standards in orthography, punctuation, or usage, as in this 1607 letter reporting on the area around Jamestown:

Sir, it had byne my dvty to have wroot the whole Iornye vnto you, & so I wovld have done had not this our evar renowned Captayne, Captayne newport, have cvme him self vnto you, whoe will so Ivstly and trvly declare, better then I cann, all this his discoverye, this is all I will saye to you, that svche a Baye, a Ryvar, and a land did nevar the eye of mane behovld: and at the head of the Ryvar, which is 160 myles longe, ar Rockes & movntaynes, that prommyseth Infynyt treasver.[22]

By itself, the 1585 expedition to Roanoke provided an emblem of the English sociolinguistic spectrum. According to Holinshed's *Chronicle*, there were besides the leader Sir Richard Grenville "diuerse other gentlemen with a competent number of soldiers."[23] And due to the harshness of wilderness life, this changeable population was itself subject to change. During the first 25 years of the seventeenth century in the Virginia colony, as many as six out of seven individuals died at relatively young ages and had to be replaced by new arrivals.[24]

Yet amid all this variability Anglophones continued to hear in the English around them the kinds of sociolinguistic issues that increasingly dominated domestic grammatical discussions. They thereby were able to maintain a specifically British heritage for the language. As I noted in Chapter Five, a particular concern was the use of oaths and blasphemous language that exercised the Puritans. Whether lower-rank individuals in fact cursed any more insistently than upper-rank ones may never be known, but the principles of codification identified such language with the kinds of moral flaws presumed to be endemic among laborers and so forth in North America as well as the British Isles. Smith thus recounts a conflict between the president of the Virginia colony and a metal worker, during which the latter's language coalesces with his social standing and base character and leads to

a punishment evidently considered appropriate for his inso-
lence. He "grew mutinous," says the captain, "in so much, that
our president having occasion to chide the smith for his mis-
deamenor, he not only gave him bad language, but also offred to
strike him with some of his tooles, for which rebellious act the
smith was by a Jury condemned to be hanged." Later, the
president adopts another less stringent if not entirely benign
punishment as a way of maintaining social order through language. He decides to have every man's daily oaths counted "and
at night, for every oath to have a can of water powred downe his
sleeve, with which every offender was so washed (himselfe and
all) that a man should scarse heare an oath in a weeke."[25]
Virginia even enacted legislation to contain lower-rank linguistic exuberance. No one, an early code of law states, "shall dare to
detract, slaunder, caluminate, or utter unseemely, and unfitting
speeches" against the colony's council in England or the council's representatives, and common soldiers in particular were
required to avoid people who are "evill languaged, and worse
disposed persons."[26] In William Bradford's *Plymouth Plantation*,
it is the hand of God and not man that topples a "proud and
very profane" seaman who mocks the ill among the pilgrims,
"cursing them daily with grevious execrations" and threatening
to throw them overboard. "But it pleased God before they came
half seas over," Bradford concludes, "to smite this young man
with a grevious disease, of which he died in a desperate manner,
and so was himself the first thrown overboard. Thus his curses
light on his own head."[27]

Since English, as a living language, embodied such social and
regional differences, finding similar, sociolinguistically charged
paradigms among Native American languages could work to the
same end as locating their supposed origin in Troy. Indian
languages, that is, could display similarities to English without
achieving the status or grammatical regularity that were becoming part of that language's identity. In this way, Indian languages
helped naturalize the regional and social distinctions being
drawn for English—they implied that all languages had such
distinctions—even as by doing so they provided justification for
their own diminished status.

It is Gil's paradigm of English as an amalgamation of dialects, a whole formed from variety, that Roger Williams (as opposed to Harriot or Smith) saw in the languages spoken around him. Like English, these languages reputedly demonstrated an abundance of regional forms but retained a mutual intelligibility that allowed for communication and continuity: "Their *Dialects* doe exceedingly differ; yet not so, but (within that compasse) a man may, by this *helpe*, converse with *thousands* of Natives all over the *Countrey*."[28] In *New Englands Prospect* (1634), Wood explicitly applied England's increasingly discussed regional differences to his understanding of Native American language variation. "Every Counterey doth doe something differ in their Speech," he says, "even as our Northerne people doe from the Southerne, and Westerne from them." Reproducing the social geography of contemporary English dialects, Wood regards the southern New England varieties as more refined than the northern ones: "In serious discourse our Southerne *Indians* use seldom any short *Colloquiums*, but speake their minds at large, without any interjected interruptions from any."[29] Further, in Native American languages Williams sees the same kind of rank-based difference that contemporary discussions described in English. There are two sorts of natives, he says. One group is "Rude and Clownish" and its speakers do not "Salute" but just respond; the other is "*sober* and *grave*" with speakers who are neither socially subservient nor crass. Even as lower-rank Anglophones were presumed to express their identity in the vulgarity and irregularity of their speech—including misapplication of titles of address like 'Mr' and 'Goodman'—so "amongst the more rusticall sort" of Native Americans there is "one Incivilitie...not to call each other by their names, but Keen, *You*, Ewò, *He*, etc."[30]

Because Native American languages were the same and yet different from English, they and their speakers even offered certain benefits for the cultivation of Standard English. Writing in 1624, Richard Eburne championed the colonization of Newfoundland because he saw it as a place wherein English and Anglophones might remain inviolate from the influence of their environment: "the Country, for the most part, is vtterly void of all Inhabitants, *Saluages* or other, so that there is no feare of *Enemies* in it, nor of *Corruption of Language or Bloud* from it."[31] Fabian's account of the three Indians brought to England in 1498 again comes to mind. So long as it remained restricted to its original speakers, and so long as it could remain fundamentally distinct from native versions and conceptually rooted in the geography of England, English could retain its traditional identity. And if neither Eburne nor Fabian mentions a heritage of Teutonic origins, it nonetheless lingers in the back of this paradigm.

Discovery, it often has been suggested, is more of a political act than a geographic one. It involves not simply awareness of a physical place but conceptualization of that place within some political, economic, or religious frame. Accordingly, tenth-century Vikings may have been the first Europeans to set foot in North America, but they did not discover it for Europeans (much less for the Native Americans who had inhabited it for millennia) because they limited their activities to small settlements and trading missions. They did not approach North America, that is, as part of some larger cultural activity of discovery, colonization, conversion, political self-definition, and so forth.

But for later Europeans (who weren't much later, in fact, since a Norse Greenlandic settlement existed into the fifteenth century) the discovery of North America was resolutely political. Already in 1493 the papal bull *Inter caetera Divinae* provided a framework for exploration in this sense by essentially dividing the world in half along a north–south line west of the Azores Islands: unexplored lands west of the line were to belong to Spain, those east of it to Portugal. To get both financial backing and royal support for his 1497 exploratory voyage, Cabot went north to evade the bull, thereby taking a stand as political as the bull itself; the English Reformation, after all, lay 35 years in the future. Beginning as it does with St Helena's 337 trip to Jerusalem, Hakluyt's *Principall Navigations* also situates England's North American activities within a context of historical (and moral) endeavors. By such means of selection as well as by formulaic episodes like captivity narratives, Hakluyt and others used rhetoric to produce what might well be regarded as a Virgilian myth of origins—a coherent story that would justify the presence and political endeavors of Anglophones in the New World and respond to competing European myths. And Anglophones had every reason to be as brazen as they were: the availability of plunder, a need to acquire new territory for an expanding population, the potential for exotic goods and usable natural resources, the opportunity to promote the faith, and expansion of England's role in global dynamics, particularly in relation to France and Spain.[32]

This pattern bears on the early North American definition of English, beginning with the political circumstances of contact between English and other European languages. In the northern part of the present United States, contact between Anglophones and Francophones was catalyzed by colonial activities. Following the death of Henry VII in 1509, England had lost much of its interest in North America, only to have it revived (during the reign of Elizabeth I) by Jacques Cartier's much-publicized explorations of the St Lawrence region in the 1530s and 1540s. It is this revival that led, ultimately, to the settlement in Jamestown. To the south, English contact with Spanish arose from Spain's colonial ambitions. Although most of its concerns lay in the West Indies, Spain established forts in Florida precisely to inhibit the expansion of any other European powers in the region, and at least part of the English motivation in Virginia (in turn) involved the establishment of bases from which the West Indies could be monitored.

Contact with indigenous languages likewise resulted from the colonization and the acquisition of goods that had stimulated English enterprises as early as Henry VII's Letter Patent to Cabot. Authorizing the explorer to plant banners claiming ownership of lands not yet controlled by Christians, the letter's sentiments were echoed in foundational documents for both the Roanoke and Jamestown colonies. Ownership or territory, in turn, enabled Anglophones to take possession of the resources that are prominent in many sixteenth-century accounts, including fish, birds, game, minerals, grains, wood, and arable lands. This is precisely the kind of stuff that Theodor de Bry's colorful illustrations of Harriot's *Briefe and True Report* emphasize. Early explorers of Virginia hoped for precious metals (copper in particular), while Frobisher's second and third voyages to

Newfoundland focused expressly on finding gold as well as establishing colonies.

The search for a Northwest Passage to the Pacific became a crucial strategy in these dynamics, pursued as early as Sebastian Cabot's 1507 voyage and with increasing vigor as the debilitating length of the alternatives—through the Straits of Magellan, or around Cape Horn or the Cape of Good Hope—became clear. In 1745, the English Parliament went so far as to offer £20,000 to the first individual to locate a navigable northwest route. By itself, this search suggests something of the frenzy that drove early Anglophone economic endeavors in North America, for a passage was pursued despite the inevitable and sometimes grue-some failure of repeated attempts, culminating in John Franklin's spectacular debacles of the 1820s to 1850s. Gullibility and even willfulness in the service of territorial expansion allowed Anglo-phones to deny this history and geographic evidence to the contrary in order to imagine that similar latitudes (say) had to produce similar climates.

Even when Anglophones learned Native American languages, they characteristically did so as part of larger political objectives, whether their own or those of native speakers. Writing in 1583 of the Virginia settlement, George Peckham framed acquisition of indigenous languages as a means to a Christianizing process that remained fundamentally English-speaking. Anglophones, he says,

are not so thoroughlye furnished with the perfyectnes of theyr [i.e., Native Americans'] language, either to expresse theyr minds to them, or again to conceive the Savages intent. Yet for the present opportu-nitie, such pollicie may be used by freendly signes, and courteous tokens towardes them, as the Savages may easily perceive, (were theyr sences never so grosse) as a friendship to be offered them, and that they are encountered with such a nation as bring them benefite, commoditie, peace, tranquility and saftie.[33]

All these activities made for a global enterprise that produced a global language. Put another way, the spread of English was a collateral effect of political acts of discovery, colonization, and acquisition, as was the acquisition of indigenous languages by Anglophones. English thereby became something more than a structured grammatical code or a reflection of British social rank, since it served an occasionally crucial role in distinguishing Anglophones from non-Anglophones (whether European or Native American). The real issues in extraterritorial contexts were not the formal characteristics of English but the social qualities of those speaking it and an inconsistent desire to transform them into something more like Anglophones. Friendly signs were presumed to produce comprehension and trust, which would lead to acquisition of English, which would produce conversion. Indeed, Harriot, who more than any other early Anglophone seems to have devoted himself to native languages, understood the primary utility of acquiring Algonquian to be the means it provided for instilling English and Anglophone values in its speakers: "Though conuersing with vs they were brought into great doubts of their owne [religion], and no small admiration of ours, with earnest desire in many, to learne more then we had meanes for want of perfect vtterance in their language to expresse."[34] The role of bilingualism in these larger political processes is clear from a set of instructions for a planned 1582 voyage to Roanoke. These instructions, which likely were echoed in the lost instructions for the 1585 voyage, specify that each colonist should note "the dyversitie of their [Indians'] languages and in what places their speache beginnethe to alter...And the same man to Carry with him an englishe Dictionarie with the Englishe wordes before therein to sett downe their language."[35]

To this end, James Rosier, Smith, Strachey, and others kept vocabulary lists. Harriot, who likely learned Algonquian from Manteo and Wanchese (two Indians brought to England from Roanoke in 1585), wrote but never published a phonetic orthography of the language as well as (perhaps) a vocabulary and phrasebook.[36] And he was not the only Anglophone to achieve proficiency in North American languages. An anonymous 1607 "Relation" about Jamestown claims that its author acquired something like fluency from an Indian guide in an almost casual way: "for Nauirans with being with vs in our boate had learned me so much of the Languadg, & was so excellently ingenious in signing out his meaning, that I could make him vnderstand me, and perceive him also wellny in any thing."[37] John Eliot, who came to Massachusetts in 1631, became proficient enough to write a dictionary and translate the Bible and other religious books into Narragansett. According to John Winthrop, Eliot's customary practice was to take "a text and read it first in the Indian language and after in English. Then he preached to them in Indian for about an hour."[38]

When not pursuing native language acquisition for such practical ends, Anglophones expressed what might be called a kind of idle curiosity about indigenous languages and cultures. Through practical utility and such curiosity, indigenous words, like indigenous things and indigenous speakers, could enter the world of an Anglophone without altering the character of English as a European language spoken by Europeans and therefore without challenging the principles that structured all languages. When interpreters are acknowledged—as in Hamor's 1626 *True Discourse of the Present State of Virginia*—their existence points to such incommensurability.[39] Passing lexical observations like this one in Harriot's *Briefe and True Report* might be seen in the same light: "*Pagatowr*, a kind of graine so called by the inhabitants; the same in the West Indies is called Mayze: English men call it Guinny wheate or Turkie wheate, according to the names of the countreys from when the like hath been brought."[40] For Harriot, things may remain constant across languages, but the languages themselves are distinct: grain may be grain, but *pagatowr* is not *Guinny wheat*, nor is a Powhatan an English speaker. Like Fabian, he sees English as the indelible and self-affirming mark of English Anglophones.

Recounting his 1605 trip to North America, George Waymouth provides an almost mythic illustration of this same linguistic divide. "Then on the shore I learned the names of divers things of them," he notes, "and when they perceived me to note them downe, they would of themselves, fetch fishes, and fruit bushes, and stand by me to see me write their names."[41] Here, Waymouth, English, and writing stand apart from the Indians, Algonquian, and oral tradition. Naming practices in the area of the Massachusetts Bay Colony illustrate this divide more prosaically. While regularly adopting Native American names for natural features like mountains and lakes, Anglophones used only English to name the roughly 60 towns

founded in the Massachusetts Bay Colony prior to 1690.[42]
Anglophones might be removed from England, and they
might encounter all manner of new flora and fauna for which
they consequently had to borrow words, yet English not only
continued to be their language but also to define who they were
and where they lived.

At an extreme, this political and linguistic divide between
English and a non-English language could reflect the savagery
of the latter's speakers. Morton relates that the Indians used to
"call the English Planters Wotawquenange, which in their language signifieth stabbers or Cutthroates." For years the Anglophones, ignorant of the word's true meaning, innocently take it
"for good," until "from a Southerly Indian, that understood
English well, I as by demonstration, made to conceave the
interpretation of it, and rebucked these other that it was not
forborne."[43] More dramatically, Winthrop illustrates how integral to identity English could be when he tells of a girl who as an
eight-year-old was captured by Indians and who was recovered
four years later: "She had forgot her own language, and all her
friends, and was loath to have come from the Indians."[44] Having
lost English, the girl has lost as well the desire to live in what
Winthrop and his contemporaries regarded unambiguously as
civilization. By extension, as the language of the civilized, English becomes a language foreclosed to savages, who could now
number among them the girl who "was loath" to leave them.

In all these instances, Anglophones responded to the epistemological challenge of the new world's linguistic arena by
imposing both traditional principles of language change and
variation, and also the inherent connections between language
and social or moral character that codifiers like Mulcaster were
then developing. Even if doing so took great effort, it was
possible to frame what they saw in North America with what
Bullokar and Gil saw in England. They could measure Native
American languages against English by practices that inevitably
exposed the inadequacies of indigenous speech. And they
thereby could accommodate their discoveries without much
disturbing their epistemology, their definition of English, the
heritage they understood to accrue to it, or its defining connections to the British Isles. Anglophones may never have been to

North America before, but when they got there, they found pretty much what they expected. Or at least some of them did some of the time. This wasn't always the case.

ENGLISH AS A SECOND LANGUAGE

Histories of North American English typically emphasize a grammatical perspective on the phonological and lexical impact that contact with Native American and other European languages had on English. These kinds of changes, which include the introduction of vocabulary for region-specific phenomena like the raccoon and the toboggan, of course characterize natural languages whenever their speakers are isolated in new environments. Indeed, they appeared again with the introduction of English to Africa, India, and Austronesia, and they are common today as English becomes part of linguistic repertoires in Asia and South America.

The spread of English beyond Britain has also meant the acquisition of the language by non-native speakers, however. These affect not simply grammar but conceptions of a language and the linguistic repertoire in which it figures, and in the process they redefine what it means to be a native, indigenous speaker. In England, prior to the North American voyages, Norse and then Normans had been the largest groups to acquire English as a second language. As extensively as they did so, and as large an impact as they had on English, their acquisition occasioned little comment, at least in the surviving records. Things were otherwise in North America, where Native Americans formed the first sizable group outside of the present United Kingdom to become second-language speakers, much to the interest and sometimes chagrin of native Anglophones.

Several issues complicate assessment of the competence of these initial second-language learners. For one thing, given the size of North America and the uncertainty of communication, the status of any specific linguistic contact between Anglophones and Native Americans is often unclear. A particular meeting might or might not be the first time the latter had ever encountered or even heard English. How the Indians spoke thus could reflect the novelty of the situation, the experience of prior encounters, or simply their awareness of rumors about the Europeans that they had heard from other native people. For another, early European accounts like Hakluyt's *Principall Navigations* and Smith's *Map of Virginia* involve significant recycling of the same stories and motifs, undermining the potential authenticity of many comments on or examples of Indians speaking English. And for a third, any examples of Native American English reflect a complex tradition of oral and printed sources, translations, interpreters, and revisions, all of which could be (and were) manipulated both by the political objectives of Anglophones and by the suspicions of Indians.[45]

French practices for language acquisition included both *truchements*, or Francophone boys who lived among the Indians in order to acquire their language and customs and then serve as interpreters, and the lodging in French settlements of Native Americans for similar reasons. Voyagers like Samuel Champlain pursued this policy with a variety of tribes (Huron, Algonquian, and Montagnais), which had the necessary consequence of introducing French to Native Americans. Indeed, in his account of Hudson's 1609 trip to the bay that now bears his name, Robert Juet speaks of an Indian who said "that the French-men doe Trade with them; which is very likely, for one of them spake some words of French."[46]

Although at least one early Jamestown account describes such exchanges as socially (and linguistically) successful, Anglophones seem to have pursued a more aggressive strategy in order to introduce Indian youth to English.[47] Indeed, from the earliest years of the sixteenth century Anglophones made a practice of taking (often by force) Native Americans to England, where they served as cultural curiosities, transports from the *premiers temps* who allowed worldly Anglophones to see how far humanity had progressed—a sort of *memento humanari*. Once in England, such transports helped affirm the integrity and social implications of English by acquiring the language, although only along with Christianity and civilization. The most famous of these transports may have been Pocahontas, the Powhatan chief's daughter who died in England but not until she successfully had transformed her name, her status, and her language. According to Smith, "During this time [1617], the Lady Rebecca, alias Pocahontas, daughter to Powhatan, by the diligent care of Master John Rolfe her husband and his friends, was taught to speake such English as might well be understood, well instructed in Christianitie, and was become very formall and civill after our English manner; shee had also by him a childe which she loved most dearely." From Smith's perspective (and others' as well), all these matters intertwine. Without English, she would have been neither Christian nor married to an Englishman; she would have lacked civility; she even might have remained childless or at least proved an unfit mother. As he proudly observes later, Pocahontas was "the first Christian ever of that Nation [the Powhatans], the first Virginian ever spake English, or had a childe in marriage by an Englishman."[48]

Pocahontas may be the most famous of these Native American linguistic transports, but the Inuk Calichoughe may have had the more moving and emblematic second-language experience. On Frobisher's second voyage (in 1577) he was seized on Baffin Island along with a woman and a child. Presumed to be a family, the three were taken to England. Along the way, Dr Edward Dodding's postmortem report suggests, Calichoughe and the woman (Egnock) seem to have been paired (unsuccessfully) for mating by the observing crew: "although they used to sleep in one and the same bed, yet nothing had occurred between them apart from conversation,—his embrace having been abhorrent to her." Dodding's postmortem further states that the deceased had broken ribs and an infected lung. The injuries were advanced enough to suggest that they may have occurred when Calichoughe was captured. According to George Best (who was present), this capture came at the hands of a Cornish wrestler, who used "suche a Cornishe tricke, that he made his [Calichoughe's] sides ake againste the grounde for a moneth after."[49] Dodding states that the condition was "aggravated by the harmful cold and intensified by the poor diet" of the transatlantic trip. And it must have been aggravated further by the vigorous demonstration of kayaking that the contemporary *Annals of Bristol* attributes to Calichoughe:

Oct 9th, he rowed up and down the river at the Back of Bristol, it being high tide of sea, in a boat, the which was about fourteen feet long, made of skins, in form like unto a large barge or trow, but sharp at both ends, having but one round place for him to sit in; and as he rowed up and down he killed a couple of ducks with his dart; and when he had done he carried away the boat through the Marsh on his back. The like he did at the Weare, and at other places.[50]

After detailing Calichoughe's many injuries, Dodding notes that "there was, you might say, an 'Anglophobia', which he had from when he first arrived, even though his fairly cheerful features and appearance concealed it and gave a false impression with considerable skill." Resistant to Anglophones' food, Calichoughe's health continued to deteriorate, and his response to the first attempts to treat his condition with blood-letting worsened the situation in Dodding's view: "But the foolish, and only too uncivilised, timidity of this uncivilised man forbade it." When Dodding was summoned to Calichoughe's deathbed, the Inuk "came back to himself as if from a deep sleep and recognised us as people he knew." It is at the very moment of death that Calichoughe's language drives home how much he has advanced towards English and civilization but also how far he remains from them:

He spoke those words of ours which he had learned, the few that he could, and in turn replied quite relevantly to questions. And he sang clearly that same tune with which the companions from his region and rank had either mourned or ceremonially marked his final departure when they were standing on the shore (according to those who heard them both): just like the swans who foresee what good there is in death, and die happily with a song. I had scarcely left him when he moved from life to death, forcing out as his last words, given in our language, "God be with you."[51]

In the *premiers temps* tradition, the episode has conflicting implications. Calichoughe's own language sounds like a happy, primeval song—the kind of feral utterance made by birds, animals, and the unsophisticated. But while the Inuit language renders the moment memorable and musical, it is what Dodding labels the Inuk's "uncivilised timidity"—his resistance to English food and medicine—that brought Calichoughe to the point of death in the first place. With his last words Calichoughe switches to English and to the acceptance of Christianity and civilization that the language embodies. Whatever meaning Calichoughe's life has for himself and those around him plays out in these dynamics. They render English as the default language of social progress and spiritual truth, a language that non-native speakers might acquire but only with difficulty and never completely.[52]

Although writers like Waymouth, Smith, and Bradford all mention Indians' command of English in such an offhand manner as to suggest that Native Americans' use of English presented no challenges to contemporary definitions of the language, other accounts portray Native American English in ways that reflect anxiety to maintain the same presumptively inherent distinction between the civilized and uncivilized that appears (far more dramatically) in the story of Calichoughe.[53] Indeed, Indians who commanded English challenged the geographic basis of the language's definition, undermined presumptions about the vast differences between the European present and the *premiers temps* of the New World, and had the means to comprehend the degree to which they were being dominated and displaced from their land.[54] Recalling the notion of discovery as primarily a political act, we might say that an English-speaking Indian represented a challenge to native Anglophones' conceptual and political sense of self. John Brereton's 1602 acknowledgment of Algonquian competency in English, accordingly, registers surprise: "They pronounce our language with great facilitie; for one of them one day sitting by me, upon occasion I spake smiling to him these words: How now (sirha) are you so saucie with my Tabacco? which words (without any further repetition) he suddenly spake so plaine and distinctly, as if he had beene a long scholar in the language."[55] Turning the Algonquian into a mere mimic—a role familiar from subsequent encounters between Anglophones and indigenous peoples in India, Africa, and Polynesia—considerably mollifies Brereton's surprise and simplifies the definition of English behind his remarks. It allows him to recognize the Algonquian's command of English as only apparent and therefore without any obligation that Brereton include him among the group of Anglophones.

Morton expresses similar surprise (even amusement) over this disconnect between grammar and linguistic identity in his account of a *sachem* who "came to the Planters, salutinge them with welcome, in the English phrase, which was of them admired, to hear a Salvage their speake in their owne language, and used him with great courtesie."[56] Wood found this disconnect more potentially disturbing than amusing. He sees Native Americans' competence in English both as an index of their pride and as an opportunity for them to mimic Anglophones by intimidating Indians who cannot yet speak the language: "They love any man that can utter his minde in their words, yet they are not a little proud that they can speake the *English* tongue, using it as much as their owne, when they meete with such as can understand it, puzling stranger *Indians*, which can sometimes visite them from more remote places, with an unheard language."[57] An anonymous 1607 account of Jamestown registers even greater suspicion over second-language acquisition. Within the context of what was understood to be a divinely mandated venture, the Indians' cunning in speech might be used against the Anglophones themselves unless the latter could turn it to their own advantage by channeling it in the service of Christianity: "To conclude they are a very witty and ingenious people, apt both to vnderstand and speake our language, so that I hope in god as he hath miraculously preserved vs hither from all dangers both of sea and land & their fury so he will make vs authors of his holy will in converting them to our true Christian faith by his owne inspireing grace and knowledge of his deity."[58]

Given what was at issue in a definition of English that included the versions spoken by Native Americans, Anglophones often simply denied that they and the Indians spoke the same language. And this, too, is a new development in the history of the language. To be sure, various medieval writers had noted differences between English and Latin, French, or Welsh; many had used the interplay of these languages for aesthetic or political effects; and some had commented on regional differences within English or on the differences between courtly and knavish practices. But the notion that some Anglophones' speech simply might not qualify as English does not arise in the Middle Ages, even if, as in some fifteenth-century business writing or late-medieval sermons, extant documents contain texts that mix languages to such an extent as to leave in doubt just what language the texts are written in.[59] If pre-modern writers in England do not recognize an interlanguage like inadequately learned or ungrammatical English, moreover, neither do they refer to the interlanguages (common in mercantile activities) that modern scholarship designates pidgins: languages that are formed from two or more other languages to satisfy immediate practical needs, as in trade, and that may or may not expand in grammar and usage to the point that they can be considered creoles.

Codification and the investment of social status in language are the necessary prerequisites for assessing whether any utterance is grammatical and, if so, what its sociolinguistic consequences might be. And so it was in the early modern period that Anglophones, buoyed by the spread of codification, began to cultivate a consciousness of interlanguages as a way to draw distinctions between their English and that of second-language learners. The term 'broken English' is in fact first recorded in Shakespeare's 1599 *Henry V*, when the king says to his Francophone wife, "Katherine, break thy mind to me in broken English."[60] Twenty years later an anonymous "Relation" on the Plymouth colony notes the arrival of a "Savage," who "saluted vs in English and bad vs well-come, for he had learned some broken English amongst the English men that came to fish at *Monchaggon*."[61] And a few years after that Christopher Levett tells of the time "the Gouernour was at my house, and brought with him a *Salvage*, who liued not aboue 70 miles from the place which I made choise of, who talking with another *Sauage* they were glad to vse broken *English* to expresse their mind to each other, not being able to vnderstand one another in their Language."[62] Williams illustrates the sociolinguistic implications of interlanguages in his description of a visit to the deathbed of an Indian name Wequash, who voices his regret over not having converted to Christianity: "He replyed in broken English: *Me so big naughty Heart, me heart all one stone*."[63] Failing to follow

Calichoughe's example to convert to the Christianity and civilization of the Anglophones, Wequash fails as well to utter something like the brief but well-formed sentence the Inuk had produced on his own deathbed.

All along the pre-colonial eastern seaboard, such broken English points to the existence of the pidgins and creoles that developed throughout North America and might well be regarded as proof of the impact of Europeans and their languages. Further, whether or not Native Americans ever employed interlanguages to obscure their intentions from Anglophones, Francophones, and other Europeans, the varieties could be regarded as signs of indigenous speakers' ingenuity. In fact, interlanguages acquired a much different status. The typical European response was to see them as reflections of the inadequate intelligence of their speakers in their attempts (and failures) to replicate European speech and custom—much as Ferreiro attributes Hawaiian Pidgin English to laziness and inattentive learning. Trying to learn a Mohawk creole in the 1640s, the Rev. John Megapolensis expresses such frustration with what he takes to be the linguistic and intellectual limitations of his informants. He complains that "one tells me the word in the infinitive mood, another in the indicative; one in the first, another in the second person; one in the present, another in the preterit."[64] While the spread of even a debased version of the language could affirm the power and influence of English Anglophones, the indigenous variety instead marks the second-language speakers of North America as different from England's Anglophones. Serving as a means for non-native speakers to converse with one another and to declare (as it were) their own non-native status, the indigenous variety confirms the spread of English, even as it shows that the savages have far more in common with one another than with Levett and the Governor.

Turning on the definition of English in this period was a dilemma that ran through much of the North American enterprise. On one hand, Anglophones wanted to appropriate territory, goods, and people both for their intrinsic worth and because doing so would justify the rightness of their efforts. On the other, Anglophones wanted to maintain cultural separation between themselves and Native Americans, partly because this too would justify their efforts. If Indians were unable to speak any English, Anglophone attempts to Christianize and civilize them would necessarily fail. But if they spoke virtually the same language as British merchants and traders, they could replicate Anglophones in so many ways as to undermine any distinctions between the groups, including Anglophones' presumption of moral and cultural superiority. Perceived similarities between Native American languages and Greek or (more commonly) Hebrew offered one way to resolve this dilemma. Such descent rendered North America comprehensible within the *premiers temps* frame as a place that evoked a European past but also represented the sociolinguistic equivalent of an evolutionary dead end: Indians were what Anglophones might have been, had the latter not become civilized speakers of English. A widely circulated sixteenth- and seventeenth-century story about the Welsh presence in North America offered another resolution to the dilemmas their acquisition of English presented.

The story's main elements are present already in its earliest version, Peckham's 1583 *A True Reporte of the Late Discoveries*. Building on what were evidently oral medieval legends, it tells of a Welsh prince named Madoc ap Owen Gwyneth, who, following an argument with his brothers over their inheritance after their father's death, left England in about 1170. He came to an island where (according to Hakluyt's slightly later version) "he saw many strange things" and (according to Peckham) he "gave to certaine Ilandes, Beastes, and Fowles, sundrie Welch names, as the Iland of Pengywn, which yet to this day beareth same." Both Peckham and Hakluyt cite other Indian words that betray an alleged Welsh origin and locate this Welsh colony somewhere in Spanish North America, probably in modern day Mexico. Although much of the Welsh force eventually returned home, others remained. "But because this people were not many," Hakluyt notes, "they followed the manners of the land they came vnto, and vsed the language they found there."[65] Joined by stories of blond-haired, blue-eyed Indians that began to circulate after the disappearance of the Roanoke colony between 1587 and 1590, the legend came to identify Welsh-speaking Indians as far north as Jamestown and the Iroquois nations, and (eventually) as far west as the Mandans encountered by Lewis and Clark in 1804.[66]

Motivating the earliest versions of this legend are the same political concerns apparent elsewhere in the North American arena's definitions of English. For Peckham, the Madoc legend, along with the patents Cabot received from Henry VII, demonstrates the "lawfulnes of her Majesties title" to lands England had claimed. "It is manifest," Hakluyt asserts, "that that country was long before by Britaines discouered, afore either Columbus or Americus Vesputius led any Spanyards thither." The Spanish themselves allegedly encountered people who were already Christians, and by the logic of the legend these must have descended from Madoc's colony. It had only been in the 1530s, of course, that the Acts of Union between England and Wales had been passed, absorbing Wales into a united kingdom and proscribing the use of Welsh in Welsh courts and among public officials. And the earliest plantations in Ireland occurred shortly thereafter, while the ascension of Scotland's James VI as England's James I would unite those regions under one monarch in 1603.

In other words, at the very moment when Celtic languages remained dominant in Wales, Ireland, and Scotland, and when England's acquisition of these lands was still in process, an Anglophone United Kingdom was being fashioned. And this presumptively Anglophonic kingdom, in turn, found justification for its heritage as well as its expansion abroad in a Virgilian myth of origins about the interactions between one non-Anglophonic group it had absorbed and another it was about to. If Cabot the second-language learner initiated the historical spread of English as a global language, one might say, Welsh-speaking Indians provided a heritage of political justification for it.

CHAPTER EIGHT

English in the South Seas

To shift from the sixteenth century and the "great islands of Yce" that Settle described to the eighteenth and the South Pacific is to change more than climate. It is to change as well the languages in contact with English, the linguistic repertoire of which English formed a part, and the structure of English itself. Rather than Algonquian and Narragansett, it was Maori and Tongan that Anglophones encountered. Rather than a closely populated and linguistically diverse area, the South Pacific constituted an expansive homeland of what were in many cases regional varieties of the same language. And rather than a language for which codification and the sociolinguistic evaluation of varieties were just beginning to be cultivated—a language that the overwhelming majority of adult speakers remained unable to read and write—English itself was described in monumental dictionaries and grammar books that helped foster the spread of literacy among a population eager for the burgeoning publication of newspapers and novels. As English spread across the South Seas, moreover, it did so with the history of language contact that I have already described. Unlike Harriot or Frobisher, Captain Cook did not need to think about an entirely new definition of English but to extend what had emerged in the language's only protracted contact with indigenous languages outside of the United Kingdom. Indeed, whatever uncertainty or hesitancy appears in North American linguistic commentary is now largely gone, with English firmly identified as the language of a group of first-language speakers from select Anglophone lands, including (if grudgingly so to someone like Dr Johnson) North America.[1]

Europeans didn't become a presence in the South Pacific until Magellan's ocean crossing in 1521, and Anglophones first appeared there when Sir Francis Drake circumnavigated the globe in 1577–80. Already by the seventeenth century, however, regular voyages by Dutch, Spanish, French, and English ships had introduced European languages throughout the region. As in the previous North American encounter and unlike in many ESL and TOEFL (tests of EFL) efforts today, the spread of English in particular was not so much the explicit goal of either Anglophones or second-language learners as the avowed means towards scientific, mercantile, political, and religious objectives. I have already mentioned the voyages dedicated to a search for a Northwest Passage, and the illusory *Terra Australis Incognita* (which the Antique geographer Ptolemy claimed had to exist for there to be global balance of land mass) also motivated exploration until Cook's second voyage of 1772–5 convinced the world that there was no such place. Hydrology, geology, and natural history, best known today through Darwin's Pacific Ocean voyage on the H. M. S. Beagle, inspired additional exploration.

Interest in the *Terra Australis Incognita* or in Polynesian natural history was more than idle or even scientific curiosity, of course. New lands meant new resources and markets, and in fact economic concerns quickly emerged as a primary motivation for exploration. A northern route around North America not only would have shortened sea voyages by weeks but also would have avoided the hazards of a westward journey around Cape Horn. And faster voyages meant less exposure to the dangers of ocean travel and a faster exchange of goods. Even without a northwest passage, eighteenth-century shipping created an economy that spanned the Pacific, linking its disparate parts to one another as well as to Europe and Asia. Bringing in metal goods like axes, nails, and knives, Europeans and Americans harvested sandalwood, bêche-de-mer, breadfruit, and coconut oil; they hunted whales and seals; they acquired food and water for their own use; and they transferred indigenous goods from one region to another, such as cotton from Queensland and salt pork from Tahiti. The need to keep an ambitious economy like this functioning turned labor itself into a commodity, with workers from Asia and across the Pacific mingling in various island communities. In Hawaii, such immigration was largely voluntary, but compelled labor that bordered on slavery occurred too; between 1862 and 1863, Peru forcibly transported approximately 3,000 Polynesians and Micronesians, of whom fewer than 300 remained alive three years later.

Oceania likewise served as a venue for the playing-out of Europe's political controversies. Part of the motivation for finding a northwest passage was that, along with a southern property like the Falkland Islands, it would have bookended the Pacific for British naval power and given the country the upper hand in its struggles for dominion with Spain, Portugal, Holland, France, the United States, and Germany. To some extent, the early South Seas voyages of Joseph Banks, Samuel Wallis, and Cook reflected Britain's rejection of Spain's insistence that the 1529 Treaty of Zaragoza (building on the *Inter caetera Divinae*) effectively kept the entire Pacific region divided between it and Portugal.[2] As a result of such politicking, South Seas locales often became stand-ins for conflicts primarily waged elsewhere. During both the Seven Years War and the American War of Independence, Great Britain blockaded French Pacific ports and engaged in military action around India. The resolution of the War of Independence even involved the redistribution of southeast Asian territory among the French and Dutch as well as the English, whose interest in Australia increased with Britain's loss of influence in North America. For its part, the United States established its first Pacific base in the Marquesas in order to disrupt British shipping during the War of 1812. Manila, which remained primarily under Spanish control until 1898, was briefly seized by Britain (1762–4) because Spain had sided with Britain's then-opponent, France. And Spain finally lost control of the region as a result of yet another non-Pacific conflict, this one with the United States during the Spanish–American War.

Religion figured just as prominently in the spread of English across the Pacific, with the London Missionary Society, the American Board of Commissioners for Foreign Missions, and the Wesleyan Missionary Society all active in the region by the early nineteenth century. Even when explicitly taught, as by these missionaries, English was not an end in itself but a vehicle for religious conversion—knowledge of the language would both introduce Pacific islanders (like American Indians) to Christianity and begin to shift them from barbaric behavior that missionaries understood to be rooted in indigenous languages. Educating and evangelizing from obviously different denominational perspectives, missionaries also played out the West's religious controversies (as in conflicts between Catholics and Protestants in Hawaii) in a region that had as little to do with them as it had to do with Europe's political unrest.

One way to characterize European activities in the South Pacific is to say that they used up the region. In approximately a century of sustained contact between 1740 and 1840, entire industries formed, grew to prosperity, and collapsed due to the exhaustion of the resources they sought. This was true of trade in sandalwood, breadfruit, and bêche-de-mer, and largely of the hunting of seals and whales. Likewise, the demographics of much of the region shifted dramatically. Conflict and disease reduced indigenous populations on the order of 50% in Tahiti, 75% in New Zealand, and 90% in the Marquesas.[3] Movement of laborers from one area to another disrupted these populations still more, as did the influx of European settlers and their families into the void their predecessors had helped produce. The 1840 Treaty of Waitangi in New Zealand (which in the English version effectively established Anglophones as the primary landowners there) and 1848 legislation in Hawaii (which first made it possible for *haole*, or foreigners, to own private property) provided political support to these shifts in population. At roughly this same time, the conversion of island people to Christianity and the production of partial Bible translations in their indigenous languages (Tahitian in 1838, Samoan in 1839, and Fijan in 1847) severed ancient traditions and culturally realigned Oceania with Europe. On many islands, indigenous peoples became politically and socially disenfranchised as well as numerically diminished.

When islanders shifted to English, then, they confirmed the success of Anglo-American business and religious practices and, at least in theory, acquired the ability to participate in the institutions and technologies that had equipped Anglophones to cross the Pacific and colonize it as they had. But if the spread of the language manifested the spread of Anglophone culture, it also paradoxically challenged the special status that that culture claimed, even more so than Native Americans' acquisition of English had. Indeed, the years from 1760 (when Anglophones first became a presence in the South Seas) to 1840 (when most of the area had been explored or colonized) show both repeated attempts to increase the number of non-native speakers, and anxiety over this increase and its implications. In these sometimes volatile dynamics, pragmatic definitions of English impinged on issues like cultural sophistication, national identity, religious conviction, economic opportunity, and personal identity and integrity. And as much as the Polynesian arena offered views specific to one time and place, it also affirmed the well-established main channel of the river of English: traditional associations between linguistic and geographic dispersion, between the quality of a language and of its speakers, and between the character of English and of its imagined Teutonic identity.

A DIFFICULTY NOT EASILY SURMOUNTED

Like their predecessors in North America, Anglophones in the Pacific relied on the dynamics between English and indigenous languages for their definitions of both. Often, Anglophones represent encounters with Pacific islanders as simply unintelligible, and in so doing they drive home the insurmountable cultural differences between what they frame as civilization and barbarity. John Clerke, who accompanied Cook on his third and final voyage (1776–9), thus records that his inability to understand Tongan led to his incomprehension of a ceremony, despite the Tongans' efforts to explain it to him.[4] More pointedly, in a detailed and generally sympathetic account of his eighteenth-century voyage "around the world," Johann Foster notes that he had difficulty identifying the characteristics of individual islands since his "stay among them was so short, and their language so little understood by us." He did observe enough to recognize, however, that while these characteristics differentiated islanders from Europeans, they also associated them with other "barbarians," all of whom he lumps into one category partly by virtue of their inability to speak English.[5] On his first voyage (1768–71), similarly, Captain Cook brought with him a Tahitian named Tupia, whose English steadily improved in his time with Cook and who, because of the structural similarities among Polynesian languages, was able to communicate readily with indigenous speakers in a number of Pacific locales. While it was "an agreeable surprise" to Cook when a group of Maoris understood Tupia, Cook also thought that Tupia, despite his knowledge of English, continued to have far more in common with the Maoris than he did with the ship's Anglophones.[6] As for Levett in his account of New England, knowledge of English is something categorically denied to all "savages," and if some acquire competency, it is of a limited kind that never makes them more like native Anglophones than their barbarian counterparts and that never admits them to the heritage shared by the native speakers.

Hoping to narrow this cultural gap, the London Missionary Society chose to concentrate its activities on the South Seas (rather than Africa, India, or China) precisely because its members believed that island languages would be easy to acquire. One of the directors wrote, "I am assured a corporal of Marines, after three months' stay on the island [Tahiti], spoke it fluently." Despite the missionaries' best efforts, linguistic reality proved otherwise, and persistent difficulties in language acquisition only underscored how different England's language and culture were from Polynesia's. Writing to London in 1798, one missionary noted the consequences these difficulties had for the Society's motivation to be in Oceania, which was conversion of the natives: "The strange construction of their words and sentences, with their quick and vehement mode of pronunciation, is a difficulty not easy to be surmounted. We have endeavoured to lisp out something of the things of Christ, but at present we see nothing to make us hope an arrow of conviction has taken place in any poor heathen's heart."[7] Without English, the Tahitians could not be Christian, but without Christianity they would seem unable to speak English.

In *Typee,* a novel based on his experiences in the South Pacific, Herman Melville presents islanders' incomprehensible differences as more droll ignorance than the sign of barbarism: "I could not but be amused at the manner in which the chief addressed me upon this occasion, talking to me for a least fifteen or twenty minutes as calmly as if I could understand every word that he said. I remarked this peculiarity very often afterwards in many other of the islanders."[8] If the islanders are incomprehensible to Melville, however, they are also transparent in a way widely attributed to primitive peoples: "The lively countenances of these people are wonderfully indicative of the emotions of the soul, and the imperfections of their oral language are more than compensated for by the nervous eloquence of their looks and gestures. I could plainly trace, in every varying expression of their faces, all those passions which had been thus unexpectedly aroused in their bosoms."[9] Able to see an unmediated expression of individual character in the islanders' faces and language, Melville, in the manner of early grammarians projecting personal and linguistic quality onto one another, also can see that their countenances' "nervous eloquence" manifests their language's "imperfections."

For Charles Tyng, who shipped across the Pacific as a boy, the first Hawaiians he encounters are as incomprehensible as another species: "Many of the Indians swam off alongside of the ship, and some of them came on board, but as no one could understand them, they did not stay long, but looked round the ship & then jumped over-board. They seemed to be as much at home in the water as the fish, swam around and dove like porpoises."[10] Unlike the Indians brought to England and dressed as Englishmen, the Hawaiians here seem to be little beyond brute animals, for whom speaking English or any language would be out of the question. In an encounter at the eastern end of French Polynesia in 1767, George Robertson, who accompanied Wallis on the voyage that would land the first Anglophones in Tahiti, likewise stresses the need for non-verbal communication with such alien creatures: "Our men keep Laughing and Making friendly Signs to them—at same time we fired a Nine pound."[11] The explorers' signs may be contradictory, but they do have the desired effect of causing the islanders to lay down their arms. They also mark English as the language of a people technologically and intellectually superior to the Tahitians.

All these examples portray a strategic and imaginative approach that has the result of debasing Polynesian languages in order to distinguish them from and enhance English. Like the linking of geography and language or the construction of narratives of language change, this kind of imagination could identity contradictory qualities in the Polynesians and their language— savagery and also innocence—without challenging the basic dynamic of difference between Polynesian and native Anglophone culture. Pointing to the barbarity of indigenous languages, David Samwell, who was with Captain Cook on his third voyage, thus describes Nootka (spoken on the northwest coast of North America) as "remarkably harsh and guttural."[12] To Banks, a naturalist on Cook's first voyage, it was the language of Tierra del Fuego that was "guttural, especially in particular words, which they seem to express much as an Englishman when he hawks to clear his throat."[13] Darwin thought the sound of a Tahitian sermon boring as well as unpleasant: "The language from the pulpit, although fluently delivered, did not sound well: a constant repetition of words, like 'tata ta, mata mai', rendered it monotonous."[14]

In its strongest forms, such negative imagining goes way beyond Bank's spitting or Darwin's boredom to a perception of savagery as fundamental to Pacific languages and culture. According to Manley Hopkins in 1862, until "taught otherwise by the missionaries," native Hawaiians "had not even a word to express chastity in their language."[15] While compiling evidence for a detailed grammar and dictionary of Tongan, John Martin identified a linguistic counterpart to such licentiousness, remarking that he "discovered where the Tonga language was poor in expression, and where it was more richly endowed; what were the fundamental principles of construction, and what the particular idioms and exceptions to the general rules:—and thus proceeding, step by step, the character and genius of the language were unfolded."[16] With Johnson's term for the essential character of a language—"genius"—Martin roots the considerable linguistic and cultural distance understood to lie between

English and Polynesian languages in grammatical structures that precede and transcend any individual speakers and societies. It's as if by an act of God (or a reflex of Babel) that English should be so superior to Polynesian.

And yet, as I say, Anglophones were also capable of describing the language of Polynesia as one of primeval innocence, at least so long as this innocence affirmed their definition of English. Tahitian, Foster observes, "seems not destitute of some kind of culture, and shews a degree of civilization."[17] While William Brown claims that in Maori the "greater proportion of the sounds being nasal...are not agreeable to our ears," he also sees the language as having the immediate, onomatopoeic quality of primeval speech: "The names of natural objects are frequently very appropriate,—the sound becoming an echo to the sense. For instance, the native name for the wood-pigeon, is 'kukupa', which, as nearly as possible, resembles the cry of that bird."[18] Hopkins characterizes Hawaiian as "so soft as rather to be compared to the warbling of birds than the speech of suffering mortals."[19]

And Banks manages both to identity an innocent beauty in Tahitian and to describe it in a way that affirms and likens the language's undeveloped state to that of the other languages of England's competitors in Pacific exploration. "Their language appeared to me to be very soft and tuneful," he says; "it abounds in vowels, and was easily pronounced by us, while ours was to them absolutely impracticable .... Spanish or Italian words they pronounced with ease, provided they ended with a vowel, for few or none of theirs end with a consonant."[20] This is of course a doubled-edged comment, implying the superiority of English in comparison with the simplicity of Spanish and Italian as well as Tahitian. Melville, who hears the Polynesian language as "beautiful combinations of vocal sounds," directs his own backhanded slap at English in the respect he shows for an innocent speech so different from his own:

I once heard it given as an instance of the frightful depravity of a certain tribe in the Pacific, that they had no word in their language to express the idea of virtue. The assertion was unfounded; but were it otherwise, it might be met by stating that their language is almost entirely destitute of terms to express the delightful ideas conveyed by our endless catalogue of civilized crimes.[21]

If languages can be defined by the vocabulary exclusive to them, English for the peevish Melville could be identified as a language uniquely suited to war and crime.

Through these dynamics, English emerges as a stable, cultivated language lacking the primitive extremes of either innocence or savagery. Without the codification on which Anglophones, more than anything else, had come to base English's claim to stability and prestige, Polynesian grammar offered empirical proof of the languages' innocence or savagery (whatever their true genius). It is for this reason that Anglophones in Polynesia, more so than their predecessors in North America, took pains to describe indigenous languages, and identify dialects and language families: grammatical analysis, comparative linguistics, and literacy all served social as well linguistic ends. And since indigenous Pacific languages could be shown to be everything that English was not, attention to their grammatical deficiencies became at the same time recognition of English's sophistication.

In the simplest form, such recognition appears in the numerous contextually translated borrowings for indigenous food, clothing, and practices that dot journals and accounts of explorations, and cumulatively never allow the reader to forget the Pacific locale of what is being described or its linguistic and cultural differences from Anglophone homelands. More ambitious wordlists occur as well. Cook provides a three-way vocabulary of English, Maori, and "South-sea Islands"; Banks one of Maori and one of "South Seas," Malay, Java, and Prince's Island; Samwell one of Kamtschatka and another of Maori; and Anderson one of Maori. Foster's Polynesian–English wordlist, which remained unpublished in his lifetime, runs to 11 printed pages today.[22]

More expansively, Hiram Bingham observed of Hawaiian in 1826 that "no foreigner or native, at the islands, could illustrate or explain the peculiarities and intricacies of the language."[23] But in fact neither the presumptive inscrutability of Hawaiian (and other Pacific languages) nor the inarticulateness of its speakers dissuaded Anglophones from grammatical analysis that ultimately argued for the superiority of codified English and the sociolinguistic principles on which it rested. The early-nineteenth-century Methodist missionary John Williams thus produced a detailed comparative analysis of what he described as the eight dialects of Polynesia. Williams compares phonology, identifies the presence of dual pronouns, and explains the character of causal verbs. The "fact is," he observes, "contrary to all we might have anticipated, that the Polynesian dialects are remarkably rich, admit of a great variety of phraseology, abound in turns of peculiar nicety, and are spoken with strict conformity to the most precise grammatical principles." All this sounds charitable and tolerant, and Williams is in fact one of several writers who does often display apparently genuine empathy with the Polynesians. But he also documents numerous acts of "savagery" in customs and beliefs, and when he approves of Polynesian language habits, he does so in a way that ultimately enforces British associations between quality of language and social class: "No person speaks incorrectly, and we never hear such violations of grammar and pronunciation as are common in England."[24]

A similar ambivalence animates Martin's 70-page grammar and dictionary of Tongan. He acknowledges that bestowing "much time and pains upon an investigation of the principles of a barbarous language, like the one in question, will, no doubt, in the eyes of many persons, appear more curious than useful; and how far such a view of the subject may be correct, every reader will judge for himself." But, he continues, "to me it appears almost as great a deficiency in the history of a nation to overlook the structure of its language, as to neglect any portion of its moral or political character." Indeed, the Tongan language is the "master-key" to Tongan culture, and its study will help not only philological work on South Pacific languages but also "inquiries into the theory of human language generally." Philologists, Martin asserts, should be interested in a language "which has advanced in its progress up to the present time, among a people who have no conception of any method of noting down their ideas, and yet pride themselves upon the uniform accuracy with which they speak and pronounce their language." What philologists will learn, Martin shows through a discussion of syntax and a section of sample sentences and their translations, is how distinguishing English from non-English necessarily implies the inadequacies of the latter. Anglophones' knowledge of Tongan ultimately will affirm their own superiority, since it will assist them in the "civilization and religious instruction of savage nations."[25]

It was likewise by comparative means that representatives of the London Missionary Society found inherent faults in Tahitian, lamenting the fact that the language had an abundance of homonyms and that its syntax was different "from what an European would naturally do." They further alleged that Tahitian had a one word to one object correspondence, even as in English, through polysemy, a single word could also refer "to the other things of the same kind."[26] Focusing specifically on grammar, Banks exercises a similar pattern of negation and substitution. He notes that "in one respect... [Tahitian] is beyond measure inferior to all European languages, and that is in its almost total want of inflection both of nouns and verbs, few or none of the former having more than one case or the latter one tense."[27] The argumentative character of such linguistic descriptions is clearer still in Kendall and Lee's 1820 grammar and dictionary of Maori. They observe that a "particular object of the work, is the instruction of the European Missionary in the Language of New Zealand...and for this end it was, that Examples in declension and conjugation have been given, after the manner of European Grammars; when, in fact, there exists no such thing in the language in question."[28] Whatever its actual grammatical and pragmatic characteristics, Maori was to be represented through grammatical principles by which it became manifestly inadequate in comparison with European languages.

Melville claims that in the Missionary College at Lahainaluna, he saw "a tabular exhibition of a Hawaiian verb, conjugated through all its moods and tenses. It covered the side of a considerable apartment, and I doubt whether Sir William Jones himself would not have despaired of mastering it."[29] If Melville did in fact see such a table, the 'conjugation' must have resembled those in Kendall and Lee's *Grammar*, with morphological modification (such as it is) limited primarily to the pronouns accompanying a largely unchanging verb form. But more significant here is the evocation of Sir William Jones, for it was his 1786 paper on the relations among Sanskrit, Greek, and Latin that catalyzed Indo-European studies and the production of so many tree diagrams.

Foster likewise subsumes the South Pacific into Indo-European linguistics. Noting that the Germanic languages constitute one language family, he uses this family as a model to classify most of the Polynesian languages, which he traces to an ancestral home-land in and around present-day India. Very much in a compara-tive tradition that would lead to later scholars like Rasmus Rask and Franz Bopp, he supports his conclusions with a table of ten numbers and 36 basic words in each of 15 languages. Of the languages of the Marquesas and New Zealand, he observes that "the differences are hardly sufficient to constitute dialects. The languages spoken at the New-Hebrides, New-Caledonia, and New-Holland, are absolutely distinct from the above general language, and likewise differ among themselves." Foster reaches such conclusions about language families by following the philological tradition conceptually associated with Jones and blending linguistic and physical evidence (such as skin color and hair texture). As for the earliest Germanic tribes and their Indo-European predecessors, for whom language and cultural identity were increasingly understood as synonymous, linguistic evidence thus affords "a further confirmation of the origin and migration of these islanders."[30]

As with many of the linguistic arguments I have considered so far, the responsiveness of Polynesian languages to an Indo-European model of language classification could point simul-taneously to very different conclusions. On one hand, this responsiveness accords the Polynesian linguistic family the integrity accorded to prestigious Indo-European families like Germanic, Italic, and Hellenic. On the other, as with the identi-fication of English dialect patterns among Native American languages, the imposition of comparative paradigms on the South Pacific had the effect of naturalizing the sense of language and English that they crafted. The paradigm, that is, scientifically separates the islanders from the English being spoken around them. It offers a linguistic genealogy and cultural orientation that render English, above all else, a European language and not one of the South Pacific. Hopkins even identifies six Hawaiian words that seem similar to their Greek counterparts (e.g., *rani* and οὐρανός for 'the heavens'), only to conclude that such evidence poorly demonstrates any connection between the languages.[31] In effect, the very fact that the Polynesian languages make sense within comparativist paradigms confirms as well the separation between the genius of Pacific languages and that of English. Because these languages could be categorized as a separate social-cultural group, they evoked the pattern of distinct language families as defined by Germanic, which is a pattern of languages as the expressions of specific peoples and cultures. English as the language of white Europeans could not be spoken by dark-skinned Polynesians, therefore, because it remained tied to a group of first-language speakers and their geography, now half a world away and including North America.

Like formal linguistic analysis, writing and print offered opportunities for Anglophones to define Polynesian languages in ways that diminished them by their distinctions from English. For eighteenth- and nineteenth-century Anglophones, indeed, codification and western writing were the marks of civilization in all its forms. Williams goes so far as to say that the power of writing, along with science and knowledge of natural phenomena, epitomizes what separates islanders from Europeans. Lacking an alphabetic writing, they "kept an account of the number of battles they had fought by depositing a stone, of peculiar form, in a basket which was very carefully fastened to the ridge pole of a sacred home for that purpose. This was let down, and the stones were counted when I was there, and the number was *one hundred and ninety-seven!*"[32] A savage system designed for savage purposes, the Polynesians' own writing only underscores Williams's point. And the fact that the earliest Germanic writing in the runic alphabet was conceptually and formally limited in its own way could be overlooked without challenging the superiority of English and its genealogy. Runes primarily pointed to Teutonic origins, not to the limitations of largely oral culture.

As "strictly oral" (in James Jackson Jarves's description of Hawaiian) Polynesian languages lacked more than a pre-eminent marker of western literacy and culture, however.[33] They lacked as well the most convenient vehicle for the enacting of western business and missionary work. In Bingham's words, the missionaries'

> object was not to change the language of the nation but to bring to their minds generally, the knowledge of the Christian religion, and induce them to embrace and obey it. The sounds of the English being so different from their own, and so much more difficult of utterance, their ignorance of the meaning of English words, and the impracticability of learning them from English dictionaries, together with the intricacies of English orthography, presented insurmountable obstacles to the speedy accomplishment of the main object of a Christian Mission, if the nation were to be confined to that medium.... [T]he vernacular tongue, or a language understood by the learner, must needs be employed to be successful.[34]

Even when Polynesians crossed the great divide of literacy, they could do so in ways that highlighted the inadequacies of their language in comparison to English. C. S. Stewart, a resident of Hawaii from 1823 to 1825, speaks of a woman who "amused herself and us, by writing and reading both in English and in the Hawaiian tongue. She does not understand English, but has learned to pronounce and read it with tolerable accuracy."[35] In the manner of the earliest Native American Anglophones, the woman is presented as a mere mimic, a phenomenon that the London Missionary Society also identified (and lamented) in Tahiti. The Anglophone Tahitians who taught English, the Society discovered, would encourage students to memorize and recite entire books without really reading or understanding their contents. Like a North American dressed in English clothes or the Tahitian "Jonathan," whom Robertson describes as imitating English dress and manners (to the wonder of the Tahitians and amusement of the British sailors), a literate Tahitian could be droll confirmation of cultural and linguistic difference.[36]

Literacy thereby distinguishes native Anglophones from both monoglot Polynesians and second-language learners of English. Recognizing the symbolic but not technological or intellectual potential of literacy, the newest Anglophones cannot be part of the group that includes British and American speakers. When the Tahitian chief Pomare sent a letter to the London Missionary Society's directors, for instance, he first composed it in Tahitian, had missionaries translate into English, and then re-copied it himself, as if he had written the English version that he could not read. William Ellis describes a similarly jarring experience in an 1823 letter he wrote about a missionary ship's arrival at Hervey's Island. Met there by individuals praising God in their own language, the uncomprehending missionaries were skeptical of the islanders' intentions, until the latter "held up" their spelling books "and pointed to their hats, to convince us of the truth and to induce us to let them alongside."[37] Grammar books and (presumably) western clothing here become reassuring gestures, signifying not the islanders' command of Anglophone culture but their submissive recognition of the power and civilization of English and of those who speak it. They know what the heritage of the language is and can use it for their own benefit, even if they are linguistically excluded from it.

In this arena, Anglophones argued for intrinsic connections between writing and English in the grammars, wordlists, and translations they wrote and published but also in the abundance of journals and letters that characterize this period, even more so than they had on the North American seaboard in the sixteenth and seventeenth centuries. For Cook's third voyage alone we have, besides his own journal, accounts by three crew members. And journals survive for each of the two preceding voyages as well. Reminiscent of modern castaway motifs, Cook even made a habit of writing down messages and leaving them in bottles in the various Pacific locales he passed through. Beyond recording and passing on to other Anglophones the events and specifics of a faraway place, the written channel is thereby also one more sign of the distinctions between literate English and oral indigenous languages. As a language-defining characteristic, literacy had an associative quality that becomes especially apparent in those cases where the Anglophones themselves were not in fact literate. Even as they encouraged the translation of the Bible into indigenous languages, that is, many of the earliest eighteenth-century missionaries were themselves 'mechanics'—laborers who lacked the ability to read and write, much less advanced education. Like John Smith in North America, Robertson writes with an erratic orthography that deviates considerably from highly developed late-eighteenth-century school standards. Even later Wesleyan and Calvanist missionaries, in comparison to their Protestant contemporaries, placed more emphasis on faith and zeal than on learning. But just as upper-class speakers in Britain could be imagined to be less vulgar by nature than lower-class ones, so Anglophones could be thought to be inherently more literate (and therefore civilized) than speakers of Tongan or Hawaiian.

The sixteenth-century poet Edmund Spenser once expressed a sentiment with which many Anglophones in the South Seas would have concurred: "for it hath ever been the use of the conqueror, to despise the language of the conquered, and to force him by all means to learn his."[38] For all their efforts to transcribe Pacific languages and translate the Bible into them, and despite the fact that some Anglophones, such as the infamous Captain William Bligh, became nearly fluent bilinguals, missionaries as well as merchants and explorers clearly expected that it would be not they but the indigenous people who would be the ones to learn another language. The demands of business and politics, in which Anglophones held several kinds of advantages, pushed the sociolinguistic equilibrium in this direction, as did the various missionary schools that quickly sprang up across the region. As a result, and despite the anxieties Anglophones showed in their desire to emphasize difference between themselves and the Polynesians, English spread just as quickly and, combined with the decline in indigenous populations, became established throughout the region. When the whaling industry approached its peak in 1830, even tiny Wallis Island, situated just west of Samoa and only 77 square kilometers in size, had speakers with at least some knowledge of English.[39]

BROKEN ENGLISH

As much as the spread of English might be considered confirmation of Anglophones' missionary and economic success in the South Pacific, however, what stands out most prominently in the records are the limitations of the second-language Polynesian variety. Frequently characterized as fractured and limited, the islanders' speech could resemble English, but it remained fundamentally not-English. Like their commercial counterparts in colonial North America, the first missionaries to Tahiti heard only "a few broken sentences of English...often repeated," as did Darwin in his own 1835 visit to Tahiti: "Nearly all the natives understand a little English—that is, they know the names of common things; and by the aid of this, together with signs, a lame sort of conversation can be carried on."[40] Some 50 years later, by which time many indigenes had lost their ancestral tongue (whether it be Hawaiian, Maori, etc.), Isabella Bird still described the English spoken by Hawaiians as "abrupt, disjointed, almost unintelligible."[41] In this context of diminished expectations, Vernon Lee Walker, resident throughout the South Pacific at about the same time as Bird, regarded a high degree of second-language competency as downright suspicious in the way the anonymous 1607 'Relation' on Jamestown had: "I find from experience that the ones that are the worst are those that have been to the white man's country and can speak English, they are the biggest rogues & the ones to be most carefully watched." Distrust of such competency motivates Tommo's own shock in *Typee*, when the mysterious Marnoo, having been engaged for some time in conversation with the other islanders, suddenly asks about his well-being in English: "Had I been pierced simultaneously by three Happar spears, I could not have started more than I did at hearing these simple questions."[42]

Like Marnoo himself, his English is what other colonists called 'broken': "'Ah! metaboo,—me go Nukuheva,—me go Tior,—me go Typee,—me go every where,—nobody harm me,—me taboo!'" It is as if Marnoo, like the Tahitian chief Pomare, can masquerade as an Anglophone for only so long before his language manifests his dissociation, otherwise apparent in manners and religion, from Tommo. When he meets a young chief in Malava, Papua New Guinea, Williams experiences a similar disjunction between the chief's apparent and actual command of English: "On entering the house, to my surprise, he saluted in English, with 'How do you do, Sir?' I instantly replied, 'Very well, I thank you, Sir: how do you do?' 'O', he answered, 'me very well: me very glad to see you; me no see you long time ago; me away in the bush making fight; oh! plenty of the fight, too much of the fight!'"[43] The grammar of the chief's language deteriorates as he describes his increasingly violent behavior, and as his grammar collapses, so too does any claim he might make to be counted among the civilized Anglophones.

Examples of such broken English abound in dismissive (even scornful) accounts of the Pacific from the late-eighteenth and early-nineteenth centuries. Due to the Tahitians' physiological limitations, Ellis observes, their English is so broken that in Tahiti at least it should be the missionaries who learn a second language:

This was the more necessary, as the natives who reside in those parts visited by shipping, soon pick up a few of the most common English phrases, which they apply almost indiscriminately, supposing they are thereby better understood, than they would be if they used only native words; yet these words are so changed in a native's mouth, who cannot sound any sibilant, or many of our consonants, and who must also introduce a vowel between every double consonant, that no English-man would recognize them as his own, but would write them down as native words.

What bothered Ellis as much as Tahitian pronunciation of English words was their 'application':

the most ludicrous mistakes were made by the people. "Oli mani," a corruption of the English words "old man," is the common term for any thing old; hence, a blunt, broken knife, and a threadbare or ragged dress, is called "oli mani." A captain of a ship, at anchor in one of the harbours, was once inquiring of native something about his wife, who was sitting by. The man readily answered his question, and concluded by saying "Oli mani hoi," she is "also an old man."[44]

Englishmen might grant in theory that words change in form and meaning—that Old English *wif*, pronounced 'weef' and meaning 'adult female', might become Modern English 'wife'. But they would not accept Polynesian nativizations of form or meaning as English.

Brown contends that he had met only two Maoris who could speak English and that one of them had been to England. As for the rest, they lack Standard English models and have (he main-tains with Ellis) a physiology that prevents them from learning the language: "This apparently natural defect in their organs of speech has been consolidated and rendered permanent from the missionaries having discarded" certain letters (i.e., sounds), such as *b* and *c*. Physically as well as socially inferior to Anglophones, Maoris are unlikely to acquire English and, along with it, civilization: "The difficulty which the natives experience in pronouncing our language has probably had its influence in deterring the missionaries from attempting to teach them English." But doing so "would have done more for their civilization than teaching a hundred merely in their own language." "The necessary consequence is," Brown concludes, "that before they can ever be expected to make any progress in knowledge, they must yet be taught English, or some other European language."[45] Participating in their own subordination, the islanders are said to embrace the primacy of English, its native speakers, and the entire English linguistic hierarchy. George Turner thus notes that Fijians did not want to learn English through a Tongan or Samoan intermediary but only directly from a native Anglophone: "Nothing will satisfy them but a white missionary."[46]

Yet learning English from native Anglophones had its own drawbacks. Jarves claims, for instance, that Kamehameha II of Hawaii had lost interest in learning English until "vagabond whites about him, taking advantage of his inquisitiveness, corrupted his mind by teaching him the basest phrases of their own languages."[47] If the king's debased language disadvantages him in his dealings with Anglophones, it provides them with another way to make sense of their Polynesian experience. By citing disreputable influences like "vagabond whites," Anglophones, like their North American predecessors, at one and the same time could explain the islanders' errors and affirm the moral implications of their own language's codification. Bingham thus notes that the "English as spoken by sailors on heathen shores at that time, was the language of Pandemonium; and the thought of making young men and women better able to comprehend and use that language, while subjected to the influence of frequent intercourse with an ungodly class of profane abusers of our noble English, was appalling. We could not safely do it until we were able to exert a strong counteracting influence."[48]

Comments like these enforced sociolinguistic hierarchies developing in England and already witnessed in North America. They implied (or, better, argued) that codification was not only universally applicable but inherently characteristic of at least English. In doing so, they also confirmed cultural and linguistic disjunctions between upper-class, native Anglophones and whomever they encountered in their travels around the world. Indeed, categorization of islanders' speech—whether as English, broken English, lower-class English, or something else entirely—did more than describe linguistic relations among them and native Anglophones. It also placed the islanders and their language within a nexus of the social institutions that language helped maintain, including class-structure, personal refinement, individual integrity, religious faith, and national affiliation. Like the basest first-language speakers in the English linguistic repertoire, whether those of a dialect like Cockney or an emerging national variety like Canadian English, indigenous peoples spoke a fundamentally flawed, even unnatural variety that barely qualified as English and that affirmed the rightness of the repertoire.

Few native Anglophones, for example, seemed willing to accept what they heard in the Pacific as English, plain and simple. Some went so far as to suggest that the individuals they encountered lacked any language—and by implication any humanity—at all. John Meares mentions a Nootkan he met in 1788 who "had become very deficient in his native tongue, and he now spoke such a jargon of the Chinese, English, and Nootkan languages, as to be by no means a ready interpreter between us and the natives"[49] And of the Malays Banks observes, "The language spoken among them is entirely Malay, or at least so called, for I believe it is a most corrupt dialect...[in Java] none use, or I believe remember, their own language, so that this *Lingua Franca* Malay is the only one spoken in this neighbourhood, and, I have been told, over a very large part of the East Indies."[50]

But if second-language speakers in Polynesia were not Anglophones, what were they? Even though Anglophones resisted acknowledging as much, South Seas English persisted in rule-governed ways across time and among numerous speakers, and it therefore functioned just as other kinds of English did according to the burgeoning nineteenth-century field of dialectology. Pitcairn English thus blends Tahitian lexis with an atrophied pattern of English inflections; Melanesian Pidgin employs lexical and phonological change to produce familiar structures like 'bilong olfala' [literally, 'belong [to] old fellow'] for 'an old person's'; and Hawaiian Pidgin accommodates English to indigenous phonology and also systematically deletes the copulative verb (i.e., a linking verb like 'is') in sentences like 'mai sista wan bas jraiva' ['my sister [is] a bus driver'].[51] There's nothing peculiar in the lexical and syntactic features that resulted from Pacific language contact. Indeed, some of these patterns already had appeared in the history of British English: the development of Middle English well might be described as the same kind of blending of simplified English morphology with foreign lexis (specifically French and Norse) that appears in Tahiti.

Further, like many such interlanguages worldwide—and, for that matter, like natural language in general—these Pacific versions of English embodied their own systematic variations and occupied stable positions in the linguistic repertoires of the South Seas. In Hawaii and elsewhere, interlanguage varieties co-existed with versions of British and American English in a stable relationship reminiscent of the regional dialect repertoire in England; without this relationship Ferreiro's *Everyday English* would not have been possible. For its part, the development of Melanesian Pidgin facilitated the transfer of indigenous laborers across the region and with them the growth of Anglophone business interests, while what began with language contact is now one of the most widely used indigenous languages in New Guinea (Papua Tok Pisin).

Ultimately, the problem of English in the South Seas arena was that it was a linguistic code that Anglophones could understand but did not want to accept as part of the language's heritage. Simply calling the variety broken had much to commend it, since doing so affirmed the integrity of English as defined through codification and pragmatic experience in North America. But Anglophones did not seem content with this category, since other ones, specifically pidgin and creole, begin to gain traction at this time. To identify a variety as one or the other is to make a claim that is at once historical and linguistic—a claim about how a variety came into being and about what it is in relation to other linguistic codes. Marking a variety as a pidgin or creole, even an English-based one, categorically separates it from English and its various regional and social dialects. The variety becomes a subset not of English as a natural language but of language contact between English and other languages, with whatever English features it has—such as words or syntax—becoming shared features and not variants of a common origin. And given philology's arguments about the immanence of culture in language, pidgins and creoles necessarily reflect something other than an English-speaking society. To pick up Heraclitus's metaphor, such varieties become less channels or tributaries of the river of English and more adjacent streams in the watershed.

By this thinking, English involves a historical narrative of continuity and change from the Old to the Middle and the Modern eras. But interlanguages represent the grafting onto English of another language with its own related but distinct narrative. English and creoles are imagined to hang, as it were, from the spidery legs of different tree diagrams. And this is the case even when the grafting may be more social than linguistic and when the linguistic narrative, if severed from its origins, describes a variety that can be structurally indistinguishable from what are conventionally called natural languages. Indeed, the modern conventions of creole studies have the effect of concretizing linguistic differences that can sometimes be more apparent than real. As a student of mine once pointed out, if we were to use the phonetic transcriptions of creole studies for representing any language varieties, all would appear deviant from English. "'I live in Wisconsin,'" she said, "makes me look like I speak English. 'Ai lIv en WeskahnsIn' makes me speak something else."[52]

Designating a variety a pidgin or creole may solve certain categorical problems about that variety's origin and history, and it may be a way for linguists to make sense of the world. But speakers make sense of it by understanding one another (or not) in an immediate context and not against a larger backdrop of language classification. We don't ask, 'Am I being addressed in an English-based pidgin or creole' but, based on cultural as well as linguistic expectations, 'Do I understand this utterance?' And, as I say, one of the biggest problems presented by the versions of English that developed in Polynesia (and elsewhere around the world) is that however wrong or bad or comical Anglophones might have thought them to be—and it's worth recalling that Ferreiro's *Everyday English* was meant to save Hawaiian children from their pidgin English—they nonetheless often understood what the Polynesians said. Within the eighteenth- and nineteenth-century context of prescriptivist anxiety over non-standard varieties and language change, broken but still comprehensible English challenged Anglophones' sense of themselves and their language. Within the context of mercantile and missionary activities, such English also challenged the self-proclaimed moral and cultural superiority that Anglophones used to justify their activities in the South Seas. Above all, political right and personal identity depended on difference, and this is precisely why some speakers cared so much about what English was. Islanders' language might be demeaned as broken English or legitimized as a creole or pidgin (labels that became widely used only in the twentieth century), but it never could be equated with the language of those who regarded themselves as native Anglophones.

A DIFFERENT PEOPLE,
SPEAKING A DIFFERENT LANGUAGE

A different people, speaking a different language—this was how Captain Cook distinguished the aboriginal people of New Guinea from those of Australia, groups that in fact had been geographically, culturally, and linguistically separated for a very long time.[53] By the end of the 300 or so years that I have considered in this chapter and Chapter Seven, the same distinction might well be drawn between the innermost of Kachru's Inner Circle (England) and the small but expanding populations of extraterritorial Anglophone communities that had sprung up across North America and the South Pacific. Formed within the context of increasing standardization and dialectal stratification, these speech communities spontaneously helped sustain a definition of English that included them in a burgeoning global

Anglophone population but also excluded them from the group of native speakers of what grammar books, dictionaries, and histories of the language would present as English itself. Extraterritorial English became evidence of the global achievement of Anglophone business and colonial aspirations and also of the new speakers' presumed intellectual and cultural limitations. Put another way, the earliest extraterritorial versions of English affirmed and justified Anglophone expansion. They made possible definitions of the language that drew on the increasing codification of the seventeenth and eighteenth centuries but also on religion, economics, and politics. Through the Age of Exploration, geography, grammar, and ethnicity came to figure equally in definitions of English.

Extraterritorial versions likewise provided a model for much that later would transpire linguistically in Africa, India, Asia, and elsewhere. In every case, pragmatic uses of English have drawn categorical distinctions between (initially) British English and colonial varieties such as American or New Zealand English, and then between the English of Kachru's Inner Circle and that of post-colonial expansion. And in every case as well moments of incomprehension, broken English, or shared language reflect attitudes about the desirability of mutual heritage in economics or culture. At times, as when Robert Bridges discussed the reasons for creating the Society for Pure English in 1913, all these distinctions seem to focus as much on speakers as on their language:

It would seem that no other language can ever had had its central force so dissipated—and even this does not exhaust the description of our specific peril, because there is furthermore this most obnoxious condition, namely, that wherever our countrymen are settled abroad there are alongside them communities of other-speaking races, who, maintaining among themselves their native speech, learn yet enough of ours to mutilate it, and establishing among themselves all kinds of blundering corruptions, through habitual intercourse infect therewith the neighbouring English.[54]

Described so baldly by Bridges, an Anglophone is not just the person we understand. It is the one we want to understand and want to be one of us.

This sorting-out of the definitions of English and its extrater-ritorial varieties accompanied the continued global expansion of Anglophones through the nineteenth and into the twentieth century. While Britain had roughly the same population as Spain in 1790, by 1930 it had twice as many people (even though the population of Spain also had grown). Its population growth rate surpassed that of Russia, China, and India as well, but not that of the United States—a predominantly Anglophone coun-try that contributed its own share to the global English-speaking population.[55] Even though Spain, Portugal, Holland, France, and Russia all engaged in their own colonial expansion, then, the population momentum of nineteenth-century Britain put Anglophones in particularly advantageous position for spread-ing their language around the world, as did the fact that Britain had the most versatile and effective navy in the world as well as a particularly aggressive merchant fleet. English is a global lan-guage today, and not just the dominant language of the United Kingdom and North America, largely because of Great Britain's superior sea power in the eighteenth and nineteenth centuries.

Buoyed by this sea power, a developing sense of British identity also contributed to evolving definitions of English. Following the 1707 Acts of Union between England and Scotland, this identity took shape in various, sometimes conflicting ways: resistance to a common enemy in France; reliance on a Protest-ant ethos; advocacy of trade, patriotism, and the monarchy; indulgence in public spectacles; the forming of an elite class through education and military service; and the cultivation of specifically national views on everything from slavery to the social roles of men and women. These individual acts of imagin-ation in the eighteenth and nineteenth centuries forged a greater imaginative act, and that was the notion of British exceptional-ism as defined by external conflicts and internal practices as divergent as military marches, religious observance, and social activism. Having lost its first colonies in 1783—and thereby given rise to just the second Anglophonic political state—Britain employed the dominions and colonies of its empire for this same definition by contrasts. To the extent that English figured in the developing notion of British identity, British identity required linguistic differentiation between itself and other English-speaking territories, including Polynesia.[56]

To make sense of extraterritorial definitions of English in this context, I would argue, we need to turn to the diglossia model that had informed England's linguistic repertoire for centuries. Referring to the functional distribution of languages, diglossia is a sociolinguistic dynamic in which one language (or variety thereof) serves as a so-called High language in prestigious domains like education, politics, or religion and another language (or variety) as the Low language in domestic and casual domains. Found in many multilingual cultures around the globe, diglossia appeared in England beginning with the Norman Conquest, when (generally speaking) English assumed a diminished status in a primarily three-way distinction. The High languages were Latin and French, which predominated in religion, government, literature, and education; as the Low language, English was used nearly everywhere in oral channels and also in popular and often ephemeral kinds of writing. But while Latin and French gradually lost their cultural roles in early modern England, diglossia has never entirely gone away.[57]

As English spread around the globe, it began to figure in two new diglossic relationships. The first of these involved the dynamic arrangement of English sociolects and dialects. As non-standard forms of the language, these varieties helped define an increasingly standardized form that, in turn, depended on the subordination of them and their speakers. The linguistic repertoire fashioned in this way remains powerful. It could accommodate (at its base) first the regional varieties maligned by early modern grammarians, then national Englishes like that of the United States, and then post-colonial ones. It's a repertoire that continues to exercise a hold over speakers' imaginations about which dialects are the better or more financially remunerative ones.

The second new diglossic repertoire responded to many of the same sociolinguistic forces that underwrote codification, but did so from a broader linguistic perspective. It situated English in the abstract not as a Low language alongside Latin and French but as a High language in relation to colonial languages largely unknown to Anglophones before the modern period: Hawaiian,

Maori, Zulu, Bengali, Chinese, Algonquian, and so forth. Indeed, the written language of speakers bureaucratically, technologically, and militarily superior to nearly anyone they encountered, English quickly—within two centuries of leaving England at the most—became entrenched as a language of colonial administration and economic aspiration. By the end of the South Seas period, English had become a language that demonstrated the ascendancy of Anglophone culture and seemed to offer second-language learners a means to join that culture. But whether these new speakers spoke a variety of English or continued to speak their native language, a firm diglossia kept English and English-speakers (however they are defined) at the top. In particular, comparative linguistics joined codification and creole studies in advancing a hierarchical linguistic repertoire that had southern British English as the highest variety; followed by British regional dialects and transplanted national varieties like American English; then by urban varieties like Cockney and the English cultivated in India, the South Pacific, and throughout the world; and finally by the remaining indigenous languages.

Versions of both kinds of diglossia persist to the present day, apparent whenever, for historical, grammatical, or political reasons, distinctions are drawn between the English of Kachru's Inner Circle and that of the rest of the Anglophone world or between English and indigenous languages. Substantive challenges to the distinctions I have traced here do not in fact appear until the latter part of the twentieth century, at which point linguistics, law, and education across the globe begin to suggest reassessment of the status and definition of English. The first large-scale dictionaries of specifically national forms of the language (such as South African, Jamaican, or Australian) all date to this period, as do descriptive grammatical analyses of extraterritorial varieties like Singaporean English or Nigerian English. By establishing legal status for non-English languages, legislation like the constitution of the new South Africa, the Welsh Language Act, the Australian National Policy on Languages, and the Native American Languages Act in the United States all disrupted the superiority that accrued to English in the colonial period. In the United States in particular, the 1974 Supreme Court decision in Lau vs. Nichols legally recognized the rights of non-native Anglophones to freedom from linguistic discrimination in their education, while the so-called Ann Arbor Black English case of 1979 extended these rights to speakers of non-standard varieties. Native-language schools in Hawaii, New Zealand, and elsewhere have likewise displaced 'the means of education' as a criterion exclusive to a definition of English in English-dominant regions.

It is easy to describe the pragmatic senses of English to which such actions respond as tools of imperial expansion. From a retrospective, panoptic view, there is in fact much to be said for this description. What reasonably might be called Anglophone empires—American as well as British—did spread in the sixteenth through nineteenth centuries, and the English language did serve not only as a vehicle for this spread but also, in some religious and political contexts, as an instrument of political expansion. All that's true enough. It's also true that the individual, interpersonal contexts in which this spread occurred lacked any kind of panoptic vision. As I suggested in Chapter Four, it is not languages that anthropomorphically come into contact with one another but speakers who literally do so. When English explorers and American whalers addressed natives of Virginia, Newfoundland, Tahiti, Fiji, and Hawaii, they did so as individuals, with the same kinds of discursive expectations of all such speakers, even if these expectations were framed by the specific pragmatics of colonial expansion. They sought to buy breakfast, to trade, to convert, or even to swindle, but not to further the global domination of the English language. If the spread of English was a collateral effect of political acts of discovery, these were the acts of specific Anglophones and not of Anglophones in the abstract. And this means, as I argue throughout this book, that definitions of English are not impositions against which we are powerless, but imaginative acts that we have the ability to control.

CHAPTER NINE

English in the Classroom, I:
American Indian Boarding Schools

By the time European exploration and colonization of the South Pacific had come to an end, English-speaking communities were well established not only there but in North America, India, China, and Africa. In many communities, especially those in North America, Australia, and New Zealand, Anglophones were so numerous and their influence so strong that they linguistically and socially overwhelmed non-English speakers, whether indigenous or themselves immigrant from some other place. It became incumbent on these non-Anglophones, in turn, to learn English if they were to function successfully in English-speaking communities, and on Anglophones (as the dominant speakers) to decide how they wanted to respond to the English of non-native speakers. This is largely how diglossia works, and it certainly worked this way in the Middle Ages, when Anglophones were subservient. In theory, they might acquire Latin or French and thereby improve their social standing, but they could do so only with the assistance of clergy and aristocrats, who could and did exercise considerable discretion over whom to admit to the universities or noble households, where the languages most easily might be learned.

In the nineteenth century, in North America and elsewhere, this discretion belonged to Anglophones who themselves sometimes still were the objects of linguistic discrimination. As Americans might not accept second-language learners from Europe, Asia, or even (in the case of American Indians) North America, so the Fowler brothers rejected American English and its speakers from the Anglophone mainstream. And as in the Middle Ages, such linguistic repudiation could take specifically pragmatic forms, including the denial of access to citizenship, property, jobs, and education.

All this might be called a bend in the river of English, a vista of new arenas wherein definitions of the language take a new direction, even as previous definitions continue to flow through them. By the nineteenth century, under the influence of standardization and the formative extraterritorial experiences in North America and the South Seas, English had acquired more than grammatically precise definitions or general social implications. It also had acquired what might be called a frame for organizing and interpreting linguistic experience. This was a frame shaped by principles like the judgment that some words were more English than others, the equation of speakers' ethics with their speech, and the use of space and time to measure a variety's authenticity. And it was a frame that made it possible for Anglophones to assign any number of social, cultural, and political significances to a linguistic code and its variations. Historically speaking, by the nineteenth century, definitions of English followed patterns flexible enough to accommodate new arenas without disturbing old principles.

Education has been among the most consequential and controversial of the domains that define English in the language's original and expanding homelands. For one thing, in English-dominant nations since the close of the early modern period, English has been the means of education in grammar schools (and eventually secondary schools) in all manner of subjects. With the exception of fairly recently developed foreign-language immersion schools, English has had this status whatever a student's background and wherever the school. And for another, English has also been a subject onto itself, whether in the form of grammar instruction, spelling, oral recitation, or reading. If schools (to a significant extent) are instruments of socialization, enforcing in children social practices along with academic knowledge and skills, then English has been the pre-eminent means of socialization—more so, indeed, than courses on history or politics. And it is this influence that can make the consequences of English in education so controversial. Depending on one's social vision—that the world is (or should be) one of multicultural equality, for instance, or that racial and cultural distinctions are fixed, or that logic and rhetoric exist independently of any particular content conveyed by them—the role of English in education will vary considerably.

In this chapter and Chapter Ten, I focus on two educational arenas on this new stretch of the river of English: American Indian boarding schools of the late-nineteenth century and what I call the American industrial schools of the early twentieth. Both arenas are from roughly the same time period in the same region, of course, and that choice needs to be explained. It is during this very period that the population of the United States surged past that of Great Britain. The number of American Anglophones didn't just grow, however; it grew through the terrific influx of non-English immigrants, most of them from Europe. If Americans thereby became the largest component of the Anglophone population, American English became the target of one of the largest language shifts in recorded history. Additionally, the increase of American business and military activity abroad rendered American varieties the face (or at least a face) of English for many individuals who did not live in English-speaking communities. For a stretch of time that now may be coming to an end, American English even might be described as the language's main channel and (to mix metaphors) gravitational center.

One reason to focus on two specifically American arenas, then, is that the pragmatic bend in the river of English corresponds with this sociolinguistic bend. Another is that the events described in this chapter and Chapter Ten are related not simply in geography but in presumptions about grammar, speakers, and national identity. They describe related responses to related problems, and together suggest how complex (and conflicting) definitions of English can be. And a third reason is that like all of the illustrations in this book, the American examples are not unique but suggestive of general trends—in this case, trends in how established extraterritorial Anglophones have responded to the newest generations of second-language learners. Many of the relations and expectations that I trace in this chapter might also be traced in the nineteenth-century English education of Celtic speakers, of southeast Asians, of east Africans, of Maoris, of speakers of Aboriginal languages, and so forth.

ENGLISH AND IDENTITY IN EARLY AMERICA

"The preservation of the *English language* in its purity throughout the United States," John Pickering observed in 1816, "is an object deserving the attestation of every American, who is a friend to the literature and science of this country."[1] Already well established by Pickering's day, such linking of the definition of a language with the definition of a country follows generally from nationalistic discourse of the eighteenth and nineteenth centuries. German Romantics like Johann Herder, Wilhelm von Humboldt, and Johann Fichte all saw languages as fundamental traits and expressions of a people's individuality. To them, language doesn't simply articulate ideas: it fashions culture and nationhood. Perhaps because it took initial shape during this period, the United States proved especially receptive to such thinking. Indeed, already to early political figures like John Adams, John Jay, and Thomas Jefferson, managing the character of English became (and remains) a way to manage the character of the nation.[2] This was the case in proposals to create a national language academy, to curtail the use of German in Pennsylvania and Spanish in New Mexico, or to prohibit foreign-language instruction in wartime. And the connection appears again in recent legislation directed against bilingual education or for the creation of an official language amendment to the Constitution.

The name most associated with the formative period of this association between English and national identity is that of Noah Webster, author of the first dictionary of American English. A Federalist in his political inclinations, Webster believed that a strong, centralized government was the best way to resist the economic and social fragmentation that easily might overtake a country as new and socially diverse as the United States. His linguistic views were of a piece. To Webster, the American Revolution was an opportunity for crafting English into a unified expression of a unified national will: "Now is the time to begin the plan. The minds of the Americans are roused by the events of the revolution . . . and the danger of losing the benefits of independence, has disposed every man to embrace any scheme that shall tend, in its future operation, to reconcile the people of America to each other, and weaken the prejudices which oppose a cordial union."[3] As a former school teacher as well as a Federalist, Webster believed that since a *"national language* is a band of *national union*," education was the best way to cultivate this language and thus this union. "Nothing but the establishment of schools and some uniformity in the use of books," he observed in a 1785 speech, "can annihilate differences of speaking and preserve the purity of the American tongue."[4] If we substitute 'genius' for 'purity', we return to Dr Johnson's essentialist view of English as a language that can rise above the corruptions perpetrated by those who speak it. For Webster, though, the imagined essential character of American English retains a distinctively Federalist twist. This English may be like Dr Johnson's in that both are understood to be fixed, commonly shared, and transcending regional variation. But for Webster, American English had this shape because it reflected the character of the new country as a presumptively egalitarian, predominantly agricultural, and non-aristocratic place. Such a society had no place for dialects, not because (as for Dr Johnson) a standard language would triumph by its nature but because, by their nature, dialects reflect social difference of one kind or another. And so Webster simply excluded all regionalisms from his dictionary.

The educational heritage of this sociolinguistic beginning has been twofold. The first heritage has involved versions of verbal hygiene—professional and popular tinkering with the specifics of usage. Webster's spelling reforms for words like 'honour' and 'theatre' are but the first (and most trivial) in an extensive American history of language planning and reform focused on everything from graphs and orthography to lexicon and even the language's name. It is a history that has played out in public venues (e.g., William Safire's long-running column on language) as well as grammar books and universities.[5] And rather than idle linguistic play, such regulation of usage and vocabulary, particularly in classrooms, has served as a forum to negotiate larger political issues involving national identity. For those who immediately followed Webster, these issues continued to focus on the cultural separation of the United States from England. More recently, verbal hygiene has shaped discussions on immigration, citizenship, and the extent to which English is a (or perhaps *the*) pre-eminent defining characteristic of the country. Constantly acrimonious, these discussions give a sense of just how deeply engrained the link between language and national identity remains in the United States.

The second part of Webster's sociolinguistic heritage has been a broadly shared conviction that it is the business of education—and specifically of education about English—to foster an egalitarian society peopled by individuals who are morally upstanding as well as intellectually accomplished. And society's interest in the individual is ultimately self-interest, since by this conviction moral, responsible citizens of necessity will contribute to and protect the interests of a moral, civically responsible society. As Edward Everett observed in 1839, "Education is a better safeguard for liberty than a standing army."[6]

In the colonial period, education of any kind was largely limited to the socially elite and largely conducted in private academies emphasizing the kind of instruction in languages and philosophy that dominated traditional English grammar schools and that might be seen as preparatory for the growing number of American colleges and universities. But as the nineteenth century progressed, a strain of populism expressed itself in everything from Alexis de Tocqueville's praise of what he saw as the non-aristocratic American character (*Democracy in America*) to the mythologizing of Abraham Lincoln's beginning as a simple, self-educated frontiersman. And to such populism, English education had a responsibility not to foster the cultivated rhetoric of an elite, but democratically to develop a citizenry in ways that would allow the best individuals to emerge from any social rank. Rather than protect social difference, schools would equalize social inequity, and it would be the government's responsibility to see to it that they did so.

This thinking informed both pedagogy and the institutional character of early American schools. In this regard Webster's *American Spelling Book*, originally issued in 1783, was both prescient of future goals in American education and influential in the methods classrooms took to reach these goals. The most widely used grammar and reader throughout the first half of the nineteenth century, the *Spelling Book* was thoroughly traditional in design, following the grammars of Bishop Lowth and Joseph Priestley (and, indeed, most early modern grammarians) by building incrementally from pronunciation and accent to syllables, phrases, parts of speech, and then reading lessons. These lessons, however, reflect distinctively American views on education, English, and citizenship. With a stated purpose "to teach children to read, and to know their duty," Webster's readings emphasize veracity, obedience, piety, modesty, caution, and so forth. "No man may put off the law of God," reads one lesson; "My joy is in his law all the day." Much as he had with his *Dictionary*, where he illustrated 'love' with "The *love* of God is the first duty of man" and 'patriotism' with "*Patriotism* is the characteristic of a good citizen," Webster used the *Spelling Book* to cultivate civic responsibility among what he imagined to be a class-free American society.[7] And when the *Spelling Book* declined in popularity, the lessons of the grammar and reader that replaced it, that of William McGuffey, duplicated its emphases. McGuffey's *Second Eclectic Reader*, intended for beginning students, offers lessons such as "A little play does not harm any one, but does much good. After play, we should be glad to work." The more advanced *Fifth Eclectic Reader* includes selections from principled and popularly treasured writers like Tennyson, Bryant, and Longfellow, the latter represented by a moralizing poem on death, beginning, "There is a Reaper, whose name is Death."[8]

When McGuffey's first readers appeared in 1836, the common school movement was taking shape in the United States. Seeking to make education truly common to all the children of the country, advocates like Horace Mann championed the structural reorganization of schools in ways that both furthered the reaction to the perceived elitism of academies and provided a definition of public education that has remained influential to the present. Seeing education as primarily the responsibility of state and local governments, the common school movement advocated increasing professionalization in the form of teacher training and certification, the distribution of students by grade and age into separate classrooms, and the organization of schools by district and state.

Within this framework, the purpose of education remained less to prepare students to enroll in universities than to socialize them for entrance into society. And to do so, schools had to assume authority, firstly, for educating all children regardless of social class, and secondly, for cultivating in them appreciation not just of decency and honesty but also of civic duty, political engagement, and economic responsibility. With a startling directness, in his 1843 report to the Massachusetts Board of Education, Mann equated knowledge with morality and the personal with the communal. It is, Mann observes, an "eternal truth, that, *in a Republic, Ignorance is a Crime; and that Private Immorality is not less an Opprobrium to the State than it is a Guilt to the Perpetrator.*"[9] Whatever social ills existed, whether crime, poverty, or violence, would thus be rectified through the study of writing and arithmetic. "When will society," Mann asked elsewhere, "like a mother, take care of *all* her children?"[10] And while this question might strike us as self-indulgent and even patronizing, its presumptions help account for the emergent predominance of women teachers in the nineteenth century: understood as more attuned to morality than were men, women would therefore be better able to cultivate it among students.[11]

As shaped by early American nationalist discourse and the common school movement, American English, particularly in the by-then well-developed standardized variety, was increasingly defined in terms of cultural expectations. What was English? Already the measure of personal worth and social standing through the codification of Lowth and Dr Johnson, as well as the characteristic of Inner-Circle Anglophones through its contact with second-language learners in North America and the Pacific, English became both the means and the measure of non-linguistic issues of civic responsibility and performance. In effect, grammar and civic duty encoded one another, and in this context speakers could not answer the question 'Do you speak English?' simply by producing specific linguistic forms or by identifying themselves as from a geographic area traditionally associated with the language. They needed as well to acknowledge and demonstrate the nationalizing values that were defined by the language.

STRANGERS IN A STRANGE LAND

Where such attitudes towards education and English left non-native speakers—whether American Indians or immigrants from Europe—is a complicated matter, beginning with the substantial size of this population. At least in areas with high concentrations of immigrants (such as rural Nebraska or the lower East Side of New York City) non-native speakers in fact would have outnumbered native ones. And while these nineteenth-century demographics of Anglophones do not match the minority–majority dynamics of global English today, they do show a non-native population large enough to have a significant and variable impact on American English and the national character. Words like 'tipi', 'jazz', 'schmaltz', and 'cruller'—and thousands of others—all demonstrate this impact, as do changes in pronunciation (e.g., simplification of the *th* sound to *t* at the beginning of words) and usage (e.g., 'by' in the sense 'to', under the influence of German *bei*).

Webster and the common schools, however, had fashioned a definition of English that challenged non-natives' attempts to speak the very language on which they had such demonstrable impact. To acquire English, non-native speakers needed to achieve the task of becoming fluent in social expectations as well as grammatical nuance. And this already challenging task became all the more challenging because non-native speakers were in many ways categorically excluded from the social promise of linguistic codification. For Native Americans, the acquisition of English was complicated all the more by the fact that, unlike speakers of Italian or Polish, they had not chosen to immigrate to the United States, bringing their language with them. They were indigenes who, by end of the nineteenth century, often were unable to speak the language of another, more socially powerful group that also then claimed indigenous status in a land it had transformed completely. In effect, Native Americans had become linguistically isolated foreigners without ever emigrating.

Acquiring the social as well as grammatical nuances of English as it had come to be defined in nineteenth-century America, like acquiring Latin in medieval England, depended on more than chance. It necessitated formal education, which for Native Americans, in the early colonial period, took place only in missionary schools. With the founding of Dartmouth College in 1769 this situation changed. Or it did so at least symbolically, because, while established for the expressed purpose of educating Indians, Dartmouth silently evaded this responsibility for a considerable time. Like many American colleges and universities, in fact, Dartmouth did not aggressively recruit Indian students until the latter part of the twentieth century, by which time most Native American students (or rather their parents and grandparents) had already shifted language. When all students had to have competency in English to gain admission and successfully complete their courses of study, their acquisition of English had become a moot point.

The growth of English education for Native Americans, in any case, remained desultory throughout the nineteenth century, due in part to racial segregation but also to the fact that they had in effect been designated as foreigners by the 1790 Naturalization Act, which excluded them from citizenship. It was not until the 1819 Civilization Fund Act that federal money was set aside to support schools for Indians, and by the 1860s only 48 day-schools (mostly still associated with missionaries) existed on or near reservations. The first genuine impetus to the English education of Indians came the following decade, partly from what's traditionally described as the closing of the West and partly from a shift of national attention away from freed slaves following the 1877 withdrawal of federal troops from the South. The Carlisle Indian Industrial School, the first of the federally funded off-reservation boarding schools for Native American children, opened its doors in 1879 and, by 1900, 25 such schools, annually teaching 6,000 students, existed alongside 81 on-reservation boarding schools and 147 day-schools. Between 1877 and 1900, enrollment in federal Indian schools of all kinds rose from 3,598 to 21,568, while governmental annual expenditures on Indian education climbed from $20,000 to $2,936,080.[12]

"If the common school is the glory and boast of our American civilization," asked the Board of Indian Commissioners in its 1880 annual report, "why not extend its blessings to the 50,000 benighted children of the red men of our country, that they too may share its benefits and speedily emerge from the ignorance of centuries?"[13] And so it was by design that the English these schools taught combined the traditional pedagogical objectives of the common school movement with objectives dependent specifically on the non-native status of Indian students. To Col. Henry Pratt (Carlisle's founder), education at boarding schools ought to provide Indians with "enough of the English language, intelligence, industry, and discipline to enable them to find a welcome in our American schools and families and thus enable them to earn their own way by labor out of school hours and during vacation."[14] As the Indians were to learn it, then, English not only would offer the training and means to succeed in further academic learning but also would develop character and integrity. A grammatically regular code, English would also be both morally uplifting and civically responsible. In the words of Thomas J. Morgan (the Commissioner of Indian Affairs) in an 1889 report on education, "It is of prime importance that a fervent patriotism should be awakened in their minds. The stars and stripes should be a familiar object in every Indian school, national hymns should be sung, and patriotic selections be read and recited."[15]

Where the English instruction of Native Americans diverged from that of Anglophone students in common schools was in the way Indian schools channeled broader notions of civilization through the language. Speaking for a host of public officials, Carl Schurz (the Secretary of the Interior) maintained that, left to their own devices, Indians were a barbarous people on the point of extinction. Survival lay only in civilization, which, Schurz felt, was therefore "an absolute necessity, if we mean to save them."[16] According to the motto of Carlisle, "To civilize the Indian, get him into civilization. To keep him civilized, let him stay." And to keep him (or them) civilized, many boarding schools dressed their students in military garb and followed military practices after the model of the Hampton Institute, which was founded in 1868 to educate newly freed slaves and where Pratt spent the year prior to his arrival at Carlisle.[17] In these racially charged contexts, culture is something that white American Anglophones seem to have by nature and can pass on to Indians and African Americans only by compulsory training, including instruction in the English language.

The terms of this discussion shock today, and in many instances self-interest clearly proved the strongest motivation. Morgan, for example, saw the domestication of Native Americans to be something primarily in the best interests of settlers. To allow "Indian children to grow up in ignorance, superstition, barbarism, and even savagery," he said, "is to maintain a perpetual menace to our western civilization, and to fasten upon the rapidly developing states of the West...an incubus that will hinder their progress, arrest their growth, [and] threaten their peace."[18] But some educators and critics also demonstrated genuine concern for the Indians in the difficult and weird situation in which all Americans then found themselves. Showing empathy with former slaves as well as Native Americans, for example, Pratt vigorously and consistently argued that it was a moral responsibility to grant both groups the legal and constitutional protections afforded Anglophone white citizens. "If enforced," he asserts, "the Declaration of Independence and the Constitution of the United States, as they read, amply provide the complete and economical cure for our every Indian trouble...[the Declaration] meant nothing unless it included the native Indian even more than the foreign immigrant."[19] Alice Fletcher, a teacher at Carlisle, was just as emphatic: "We desire the Indian's education that he may be fitted to enter upon the duties of manhood and cultivate the gentle graces of Christianity, but we cannot successfully accomplish this desire if we disregard his rights as an individual, or if we fail to recognize what was noble and worthy in his past history."[20] Said Emily Cook, from the Office of Indian Affairs, "Let the Indian keep both his personal and his race identity."[21]

My concern here, however, is not with boarding schools as such but with the definition of English that they fostered. The schools and federal officials in fact treated the language as absolutely crucial to the processes of assimilating Indians into American society. As early as 1868, at the outbreak of the Plains conflicts and a decade prior to the founding of Carlisle, a 'Peace Commission' of army generals asserted that through "sameness of language is produced sameness of sentiment and thought."[22] So long as Native Americans remained physically walled off from society by reservations and linguistically so by their own languages, many argued, they could not join the American experience. "It would be in vain to destroy the imaginary line which surrounds the reservation," the Rev. Lyman Abbott observed in 1888, "if we leave the Indian hedged about by an ignorance of the language of his neighbors"; this "would be to convert him from the gypsy isolated into a gypsy of the neighborhood."[23] In effect, sentiments like these extended Webster's views of the symbolic power of English to include (in theory at least) Native Americans in the culture that the language was understood to fashion.

Beyond English's patriotic implications and whatever moral qualities that accrued to the language through the common schools movement, however, the instruction of Indians responded to the beliefs (similar to those evident in the South Pacific) that through language would come civilization. In an 1887 report mandating that English be the only language of instruction in federal boarding schools, thus, Commissioner John Atkins comments, "The first step to be taken toward civilization, toward teaching the Indians the mischief and folly of continuing in their barbarous practices, is to teach them the English language."[24] Teaching English to Native Americans, even as their own languages were discouraged and perhaps eliminated, would enforce the notion that the language was a medium of national unity and that by acquiring the language Indians were acquiring civilized status, if not citizenship.

As distinctively American as this definition of English was becoming, it nonetheless built on earlier traditions, since like Standard English, it marked variation as a social debility in need of correction. The "number of Indian vernaculars," says Atkins in support of his argument for Indians shifting to English as a means to civilization, "is even greater than the number of tribes."[25] And as in New Zealand, Australia, and elsewhere, the definition rendered English preeminent over issues of personal freedom, since its acquisition justified the forced isolation of

Indians in boarding schools. Indeed, compulsory and almost ritualistic haircuts, changes in clothing, and adoption of western names corroborated the transformative power of language for Native American students as well as the social power of their white Anglophone teachers.

Instruction methods for non-natives similarly extended in two directions, incorporating traditional pedagogical strategies with ones developed specifically for the American experience. Under the aegis of the Bureau of Indian Affairs and with Carlisle as the preeminent pedagogical model, Indian education was meant to be as rigorous and structured—maybe more so—than anything that occurred in the common schools.[26] Besides taking the unprecedented American step of isolating school children from their families, boarding schools also formally mandated the use of English, even if in the form of what would then be judged an inadequate variety. Luther Standing Bear records that at Carlisle, "We were not allowed to converse in the Indian tongue, and we knew so little English that we had a hard time to get along."[27] As in Ireland, Wales, and Scotland, which employed their own English-only policies in nineteenth-century schools, students themselves could (and did) enforce this policy by informing on each other for speaking their native languages.

Also as in these locales, little attention was paid to the structural differences between English and indigenous languages. Modern English, that is, is an analytic language, one in which speakers determine meaning largely through word order and inflectional morphology, while many American Indian languages are agglutinative, forming words and meanings by compounding semantically distinct elements. There are as well numerous phonological disconnects between English and American Indian languages. Navaho employs tones (like Chinese) and has a class of voiceless consonants (unknown in English) called ejectives, in which the glottis produces the air-expulsion necessary for all consonants by definition. And it lacks some ubiquitous English sounds like the vowel [u] (as in 'boot') and the diphthong [au] (as in 'about'). Pratt mentions that Indian students (like many European immigrants, one might add) had difficulty with the *th* sound in particular.[28] Together, sound, syntax, and morphology—all taught in a formal class-room setting that itself was uncharacteristic of native Indian education—presented structural obstacles that surpassed any-thing encountered by a native speaker of a European language trying to learn English.

Within the Indian classrooms, English was taught with a pedagogy similar to that found in the common schools or, indeed, in British schools since the eighteenth century. Many employed the same bottom-up methods, without regard for use or users, or even for how native Anglophones themselves might have acquired the language. Through this model, English was defined as the accumulation of isolatable, interlocking, and increasingly complex elements in a putatively regular code that speakers, whether through social class or ignorance, tend to diminish. And so Carlisle stressed phonics in the earliest grades, introduced grammar (including the parts of speech) in the fifth grade, and moved to phrases and clauses for students who remained in the school after that.[29] Carlisle as well as the Hampton Institute utilized the 'objective method', by which students were shown an object and told its English name, and it also adapted methods from the education of the deaf.[30] And as in the common schools, English instruction in Indian schools also relied heavily on rote memorization and recitation. Every grade at Carlisle, for instance, demanded in-class oral exercises and declamation of poems and speeches. A debating society met regularly to discuss motions such as: "That New York City has made greater progress than Philadelphia since the Colonial Period" or "That an increased navy tends to peace."[31]

Like their counterparts in Anglophone classrooms, students used some of the most popular grammars and readers of the day. At least some and probably many schools used the ubiquitous McGuffey readers, which, like Webster's and Lowth's before them, begin with letters and pronunciation and move gradually to reading.[32] Carlisle used J. Russell Webb's 1874 *Model First Reader*, and the Bureau of Indian Affairs recommended similar works, such as A. C. McLean's 1903 *Steps in English* and Robert Metcalf's 1894 *English Grammar for Common Schools*.[33] Charles Eastman, who attended the Santee Normal Training School, Knox College, and Beloit College before moving on to Dartmouth, describes the challenge of this pedagogy, specifically of beginning to read with "words of three letters."[34] And like second-language learners everywhere, this system also made it possible for Native American students to become the kind of mimics present already in colonial North America, knowing how to pronounce English words without knowing what they mean or how to use them. The students who did progress enough to review complex grammatical issues did so via edifying readings from the McGuffey *Reader*, the Bible, or even *Pilgrim's Progress*. At Carlisle, high school students were expected to compose on topics like "We Ought to Be Saving" or "Work Makes Us Strong" and to read essays entitled "Dignity of Labor," "Mercy Better Than Justice," and so forth.[35]

One grammar written specifically for the instruction of Native American students was C. E. Birch's *Methods of Teaching English*. First published in 1912 and reissued in 1914, Birch's grammar was based on his experiences at Haskell in Kansas but, he hoped, would help address the "errors which seem common to nearly all Indian children," regardless of their native language. "Every teacher who has had experience in teaching Indian pupils," he begins, "realizes the peculiar difficulties under which these children labor in their attempts to master the intricacies of the English language." These difficulties arise because their native language "depends quite largely upon signs and the inflections of the voice—a language meager in descriptive powers if robbed of these two aids to expression."[36]

Recalling Anglophone comments about Polynesian languages, such premises may strike us as arrogant and condescending, but the fact is that Birch's *Methods* in many ways did surpass McGuffey's grammar (or Webster's or Lowth's) for the instruction of non-native speakers. The readings, for example, are not moral or patriotic platitudes but accounts of familiar objects like butterflies or models of business letters. Moreover, Birch emphasizes vocabulary before everything else, maintaining that students need words and the contexts in which to use them before they can appreciate the abstract subtleties of syntax or parts of speech. (The book concludes with a list of the "Five Hundred Words Most Frequently Used in Speaking and Writing.") Accordingly, much of *Methods* consists of gradated vocabulary exercises that ask students to define particular groups of words and then use them in sentences. Syntax, including negation and verb phrases (perhaps the biggest stumbling blocks in acquisition), is taught through the recitation of questions and answers, the construction of paraphrases, and reading comprehension exercises. If *Methods* identifies and responds to few structures that seem distinctively Native American, it does presume that the students already know English, that they constitute a coherent speech community, and that the book's task is to improve students' knowledge, not teach them a language with which they have no familiarity. This alone sets it apart from McGuffey's as well as Ferreiro's grammars.

THINKING AS A WHITE MAN

On his initial recruitment trip to the South Dakota Rosebud Agency in 1879, Pratt said to a skeptical parent, "Spotted Tail, you cannot read or write. You cannot speak the language of this country. You have no education."[37] For Pratt, the goal of Indian education from the outset was to transform indigenous nonnative speakers into Anglophones who had complete access to all the cultural power of their language. Judged in these terms, or even by a straightforward linguistic measure, the success of Indian English education was mixed.

Pratt's own assessment was particularly positive. Prior to Carlisle, he had supervised a group of Indian prisoners at Ft Marion in Florida, where he was already promoting English. The result (he claimed) was the kind of linguistic and social assimilation he sought to foster at Carlisle: "Most of the young men learned to write fairly intelligent letters during the three years of their imprisonment, and the English language became the common tongue among them, thus breaking down the wall of language which separates the tribes as fully as between them and our own people."[38]

From a non-native speaker's vantage, Eastman provides similarly positive testimony about the acquisition of English. In his second year at Knox College he still lacked the ability to speak the language, but he "could translate every word of my English studies into the native tongue." By the time he had arrived at

Beloit College, he considered himself a dedicated Anglophone: "Every day of my life I put into use every English word that I knew, and for the time permitted myself to think and act as a white man." Thinking as a white man meant more than language. It meant sentiments that Pratt readily would have embraced, including seeing Christian civilization "as the development of every natural resource; the broad brotherhood of mankind; the blending of all languages and the gathering of all races under one religious faith." Within a short period Eastman came to imagine himself as not simply a fluent Anglophone but a native one: "My understanding of English was now so much enlarged as to enable me to grasp current events, as well as the principles of civilization, in a more intelligent manner."[39] For better or worse, Eastman here does not seem to be exaggerating. His entire life story, which he writes with a rhetorical elegance that would have pleased McGuffey, testifies to his acquisition of the power of English. Beginning life as an Indian on the Plains, he graduated from Dartmouth and Boston University Medical School before taking up a career as a physician in the Health Service of the Bureau of Indian Affairs, where he was a tireless advocate for Native American causes.

The success of Pratt's Ft Marion students or of Eastman's transformation into an Anglophone is remarkable; it would be remarkable for any speaker anywhere to acquire a second language as effectively as Eastman did English. And the truth of the matter is a good many other Native American students never seem to have mastered even the grammatical components of English as defined in its nineteenth-century American context. Those who did acquire competence and perhaps fluency were in fact so rare as to be valuable to the superintendents of competitive Indian boarding schools, since an adept Anglophone student body provided one way for schools to achieve distinction. To this end, schools recruited students from one another, with the Phoenix Indian School intentionally diversifying its student body out of a sense that the local Pimas and Papagos were inherently deficient at English.[40] The meaning of English in this arena thereby acquired yet one more nuance: a language from which credit might accrue to native speakers through the correct use of non-natives.

In a letter he wrote to Haskell's superintendent, one student probably spoke for many in his mixture of formal grammatical errors and features suggestive of incomplete learning: "I am write a few lines to you this evening and I am going to tell you that I am been sick about two weeks on my back, may be consumption, and I don't think that I never get well again, and so will you please kindly help me?"[41] Birch quotes another as writing, "There were four brothers they father and mother had died. One of the brothers wented and spoke to the chief."[42] And as positive as Pratt's assessment of the Ft Marion prisoners was, a letter from Paul Tsait-kope-Ta, one of his students there, suggests otherwise: "I suppose you think I ought very good English speak by this time, but I cannot very well yet. I know a great many words, but not how together to put them."[43] To white Anglophones, such language was not simply ungrammatical but characteristically non-native. Dr Samuel Porter, a specialist in pedagogy for the deaf and dumb who visited Carlisle, felt that this kind of English was as much in need of eradication as the Polynesian varieties had been:

There is a point upon which I should think there would be need of very determined effort on the part of the instructors. I refer to the tendency to employ broken English. I think that may prove one of the greatest difficulties you will have to contend with. With this also, and of course the tendency to use Indian idioms and Indian order of words, the only way must be not even to allow, except in extreme cases, any such violations of correct usage to go uncorrected.[44]

This language had enough of a perceptual integrity that it could be mimicked in manufactured conversations like this one (recorded in 1869), between a Chinese immigrant and a Native American, who speaks first:

"Say John!" says the Digger Chief, "What do you want here?"
"Me workee. Who you?"
"Me Piute Cappen. Me kill plenty Melican [American] man. Dis my lan. You payee me John. No payee me, gottam, me killee you!"
"No got—velly poor Chinamen; how muchee you want?"[45]

Just as blasphemy became a marker of lower-class speech, whatever the reality of usage, so ungrammatical expressions like these were accepted as characteristic of Native American Anglophones.

Whether such speakers even could be called Anglophones depends on the definition of English, and usage alone would have disqualified any whose language included pidgin forms like 'am been' or 'Me workee'. Despite his optimism Pratt himself recognized the prevalence of such structures, noting that he was "bothered with their [the Carlisle students'] limited acquirement of English." His memoirs in fact frequently record characteristic interlanguage utterances like the following, which lacks copulative verbs and collapses the subject pronoun 'I' into the oblique 'me': "Captain, two just same. Me no understand which cleanest."[46] Francis La Flesche, who attended a Presbyterian school on the Omaha reservation, similarly refers to Indian students' "peculiar English," which he illustrates with 'fool bird' for 'quail' and 'first time' for 'long ago' and which he claims he accurately represents in his autobiography.[47] Far more simply and less sympathetically, in his 1898 report, Sedgwick Rice, the Commissioner of Indian Affairs, judged English acquisition at the San Carlos agency to be a dismal and even grating failure. The students, he observes, used little English outside of school, and what they did use was "so broken that only a careful observer can distinguish it from the Indian tongue, which is very difficult and guttural."[48]

Reminiscent of what codification treated as lower-class, socially unprestigious varieties, this kind of English was not without value to native Anglophones, since it facilitated a familiar way of ranking speakers and their varieties. Recalling British speakers' skepticism about colonial American English, Commissioner Rice and other descendants of colonial Americans faulted the English usage of Indians but also, as in the Digger Chief's imagined conversation, used it to justify their constricted social status. In 1905, the Commissioner of the Bureau of Indian Affairs, Francis E. Leupp, went so far as to argue that the goal of English instruction for a Native American should be only that he or she "can read the simple English of the local newspaper, can write a short letter, intelligible though maybe misspelled, and knows enough of figures to discover whether the storekeeper's cheating him."[49] In effect, failure to achieve fluency could be a pedagogical objective guaranteeing preservation both of the social status that English education in general promised to transform and of a prevailing view of what English was.

Whether by circumstances or design, then, a good many American Indians, like a good many second-language learners everywhere, must have failed to gain anything like grammatical competence (much less fluency) in English. Indeed, while the records aren't entirely clear, it seems to be the case that in its 39 years of existence, Carlisle actually graduated a fairly small number of students with the equivalent of a grammar school education.[50] How many children simply and intentionally refused to learn English, or to acknowledge that they knew it, is of course impossible to say. Pratt tells of an Indian interpreter in Florida who was asked about whether some whiskey was of high quality. "No! Good whiskey Fort Mead," he responded, and Pratt continues, "Those were the only English words I heard them use, although I was told that all the men could speak some English."[51] By refusing to speak English with him or to acknowledge what they can understand, speakers like these rejected associations between English and national identity that went back through the common schools to Webster. Even those whose failure was genuine—that is, the children who earnestly tried and failed to learn English—undermined definitions of English as an inherently transformative language. And having acquired English, a Native American speaker still could use his knowledge to challenge the Anglophone culture in which he lived. Asked at a public event by an Anglophone to say something in Sioux—a language he ordinarily was forbidden to use—Luther Standing Bear uttered a sentence that meant "If I talk in Sioux, you will not understand me anyhow." He translated it as "We are glad to see you all here tonight."[52]

What never seems to have been considered is that even without any formal mandate, many off-reservation Indians likely would have shifted to English for the same reasons of social utility that speakers everywhere acquire languages. Indeed, one way for Native Americans to learn English was simply through the happenstance of proximity to Anglophones. Pratt credits to this very cause the widespread use of English near Fort Griffin, in modern-day Texas: "Practically all the Tonkawas spoke English, having lived so many years near the fort."[53] The 'outing' system pioneered by Pratt thus rendered superfluous some of the English instruction at Carlisle. In this program, in what could amount to little more than indentured servitude, Indians periodically worked and resided off-campus in Anglophone homes and businesses specifically because Pratt saw these as opportunities for them to learn more English. This same speaker-motivated functional utility, however, could animate Native Americans who never attended a boarding school. Or, for that matter, students who never left campus, where English offered a lingua franca among linguistically diverse groups. Students at Carlisle spoke as many as 75 native languages, and those at Chilocco (in Oklahoma) over 30.[54] At Haskell, English became the lingua franca that enabled students to share experiences and even forge a sense of Indian identity as strong as that achieved through native languages.[55] This social utility of English helps account for the fact that, as repressive as United States policies for Native Americans could be, many individuals followed Luther Standing Bear in expressing their desire to learn English and their gratitude, at least in this one regard, to the schools for providing them the opportunity to do so. Indeed, the Carlisle student newspapers are filled with student-written articles entitled "Talk English," "Not Good English," "A Letter by a Sioux Boy Who Knew No English When He Came," "Talk Only English," "Speak Only English," and so forth.

But to learn English outside the common and boarding school traditions would be to learn the language not only grammatically transformed but also stripped of its social meanings. And as much as feigned or genuine ignorance, such learning would challenge prevailing definitions of the language. Through their usage alone, inevitably, Native American speakers did indeed transform the meaning of English. Like all natural, living languages, for example, Native American varieties developed group-specific lexicon and structures. Haskell's local usage included 'your aunt' (for a boy's girlfriend), 'bad case' (for a serious romance), and 'a pleasant' (for a smile). This variety of English was so engrained in the boarding school culture and student identity that older students could good-naturedly use it to deceive the newly arrived, telling them, for example, that *kale* was local dialect for 'orchard' or 'bakery' when it in fact meant 'money'.[56]

In a different vein, Indian students' nativization of English appears in rhetorically sophisticated student compositions or in the use of English for the expression of students' non-Carlisle lives. While perhaps stilted ('when the solar orb comes forth'), student poetry published in the Carlisle newspapers can demonstrate a sound grasp of meter and rhyme, and a composition like "Iniskin or the Buffalo Rock" uses lucid, grammatical prose to tell a Blackfeet myth as a class assignment.[57] This same nativization underwrites student pieces in the newspapers on topics like "Iroquois Burial Customs" and "The Thunder Tradition," as well as, more pointedly, opinion pieces that utilize the rhetorical devices cultivated in classrooms (such as sarcasm) against the institution and its presumptions to civilize Indians by means of English. One anonymous editorial opined, "Some white people do not like to let the Indians have an education.... If all the Indians had an education like some whites they would be wise and have great minds to think.... If the Indians had more chance they would soon learn how to do most everything like the whites."[58] Students at Genoa Industrial School in Nebraska put their new artful English to much the same subversive effect in order to question school policy and to champion the use of Indian languages.[59] If these students internalized the dictates of codification, others internalized Anglophone ways for thinking about their own language, including a standard ideology. La Flesche describes his native Omaha not only as a standard language by nature, but also as one that lacks—improbably—profanity, slang, and regionalisms.[60] Omaha, it seems, is exactly the language that Priestley, Lowth, and Dr Johnson had in mind.

Luther Standing Bear so adopts English as his own language that he chastises the white Anglophones who misuse it when they mistranslate Indian languages. "The Sioux name for railroad was Maza Canku," he observes, "or Iron Road. The term 'Iron Horse' is merely a white man's name for a moving-picture play." Having taught for many years at a reservation school, he's even more critical of the methods Anglophones use to teach the language they share. These seem designed to produce the incomprehension that Eastman describes and the failure that Leupp envisioned: "The Indian children should have been taught how to translate the Sioux tongue into English properly; but the English teachers only taught them the English language, like a bunch of parrots. While they could read all the words placed before them, they did not know the proper use of them; their meaning was a puzzle." The irony of such pedagogy, Standing Bear seems to enjoy pointing out, is that rather than turn Indians into Anglophones, it sometimes turned Anglophones into Indians. One school brought 60 Native Americans from the Pine Ridge agency to study with white students, thinking "the Indians would learn English language faster by this arrangement. But lo and behold! the white boys began to learn the Sioux language! So they discharged all the white boys and kept the Indians."[61]

SEPARATED BY SPEECH

When we look at Indian boarding schools in the context of the American West, they can appear as a distinctly nineteenth-century colonial practice.[62] And in many ways their pedagogy does repeat a more general movement and restraint of native populations through treaties, reservations, and so forth. But in their definition of English, the boarding schools also further sociolinguistic patterns established in the early modern period, when English was no longer geographically restricted and its varieties began to acquire the socially differentiating characteristics previously associated with distinct languages—specifically, Latin and French as well as English. Through this transformed diglossia (evident already in Polynesia) and sustained by a standard ideology, English and its varieties became, to an extent, ciphers to which any number of non-linguistic, social meanings might be attached—they provided what I earlier called a frame for organizing and interpreting linguistic experience. As the early modern period's definition of English had distinguished gentlemen from clowns, and the common school definition responsible citizens from irresponsible ones, so the boarding school definition discriminated between the civilized and the uncivilized. From the viewpoint of Leupp, Atkins, and other officials, any assessment of the success of English instruction for American Indians depended on how well non-native speakers met the requirements of this definition.

Above all, educators and legislators alike cared what English was precisely because it was more than a grammatical code. Competence in the language included the ability to use it in socially constructive ways. And for Native Americans to be Anglophones, this in turn meant that they needed to use English in ways that would affirm their civilized status from the point of view of white Anglophones. Pratt's objective at Carlisle, as he said in a private 1878 conference with Secretary of the Interior Carl Schurz, was to create a school where this kind of English could be learned, in conjunction with the manual arts for which he saw, at various times, Indians to be destined by either their limitations or society's: "Let me prove it is easy to give Indian youth the English language, education, and industries that it is imperative they have in preparation for citizenship."[63]

Consistent with Leupp's linguistic aspirations for Indians, however, social aspirations, reflected in the training at Carlisle and other boarding schools, typically extended not to the medical profession that Eastman achieved but only to various kinds of skilled and unskilled professions. As the common schools had tied English education to morality and religion, so Indian schools (like Hawaii's English language schools) tied it to manual labor, even while continuing to endorse the civic responsibilities and heritage emphasized in non-Indian schools. Many of the Carlisle students who did not graduate were awarded 'industrial certificates', which invariably divided along sex lines. From the class of 1911, thus, the boys took certificates as bakers, painters, printers, compositors, blacksmiths, carpenters, florists, pressmen, carriage-makers, tinsmiths, carpenters, and farmers. Girls' certificates were in farming, dairying, laundering, plain dressmaking, plain sewing, and (nearly all of them) general housekeeping.[64] English was always taught with these objectives in mind. In the words of one of the school catalogues, "The purposes of English in vocational courses are (1) as a means for leisure occupation and general culture, (2) for utilitarian value. While the first of these purposes is not minimized, it must be remembered that it will function only to a limited extent in the lives of most persons actively engaged in a trade, manufacturing and agriculture or home making."[65] Classroom lessons were designed to implement this conception of English: the boys required to write about manual labor, the girls housekeeping. A list of spelling words in the hand of a first grade girl consists of 'clothes', 'soak', 'wash', 'rinse', 'tubs', 'irons', 'starch', 'boards', 'bluing', 'soda', 'driers', 'water', 'stove', 'steam tables', 'smooth', 'sprinkle', 'pins', 'lines', and 'baskets'.[66] Those Indian students who did manage to acquire the grammatical competence implicit in the day's definition of English had little chance of pursuing the liberating social expectations it also implied.

Beyond the irony of English as an instrument to civilize Native Americans for menial jobs is the irony that in many cases even these jobs didn't exist. Girls trained as domestics could find little work if they returned to reservations with dirt-floor houses, where boys taught to be shoemakers, carpenters, and blacksmiths had little opportunity to exercise their craft. Trained as a tinsmith at Carlisle and accustomed to send to his family the goods he produced, Standing Bear notes, "After I had left the school and returned home, this trade did not benefit me any, as the Indians had plenty of tinware that I had made at school."[67] Equally telling of Anglophone Native Americans' marginal status is the fact that in some areas the only speakers with whom students might use their new language were their teachers or other students. Acquiring English invited them to join a group that didn't exist.[68]

As defined by the boarding schools, English promised to assimilate non-natives to a set of values (not just jobs) that many likewise neither could attain nor even desired. "We need to *awaken in him wants*," said the educator Merrill Gates of the proto-typical Indian student. "Discontent with the tepee and the starving rations of the Indian camp in winter is needed to get the Indian out of the blanket and into trousers,—and trousers with a pocket in them, and with *a pocket that aches to be filled with dollars!*"[69] The wants to which Gates alludes, then, were the wants that would remake Native Americans according to the model of a burgeoning Anglophone consumerism, which their economic limitations would allow few to realize. In 1887, indeed, Henry L. Dawes sponsored legislation that sought to break up reservations by dividing the land in severalty to individuals (often in parcels too little to provide subsistence) and allowing the land eventually to be resold to non-Indians.

Such inconsistencies, complexities, and self-interest lie at the heart of any definition of English in any arena. In an 1899 incident at the Phoenix Indian School, for instance, maintenance of native languages amounted to a small act of rebellion that became much larger through the difference between the students' definition of English and their teachers'. Frustrated by superintendent Samuel McCowan's long history of abusive behavior, the students sent an unsigned letter of complaint to the Bureau of Indian Affairs. This documented, among other incidents, an occasion on which McCowan beat a newly arrived Papago boy nearly to death and even threatened to kill him because the boy failed to understand and follow the instructions he was given. When the Bureau refused to address the students' concerns, its silence demonstrated its authority over English as well as the students, whose own (broken) English provided the justification for McCowan's behavior and the Bureau's response.[70]

More generally and less brutally, while Anglophone educators and legislators understood English to be an issue of assimilation and identity, Native Americans often saw it in strictly practical linguistic terms. They sought to acquire the language, that is, perhaps because, as Sitting Bull said to Standing Bear, "there was nothing left for the Indians," but they did not necessarily seek to abandon traditional values and adopt Anglophone culture in its place.[71] It was recognition of this practical utility that, probably more than anything else, accounted for why some students embraced English the way they did. Even as many students lamented the loss of their native languages, the various Carlisle student newspapers regularly produced enthusiastic student testimonials to the value of learning English. Said one boy, "Dear friend I wish you would try to speak only English now. I know you improving fast than some of the other Sioux boys. But don't try to speak only English therefore I am grieved for our relations sent us to learn the English language, therefore we must try to speak only English...I wish all the Sioux boys would try to speak only English now."[72] The students' and parents' strategic endorsement of boarding school English also appears in an ironic consequence of what was essentially a hostile English immersion program. Such an experience, that is, sometimes helped maintain native languages by fostering their covert prestige. Despite formal prohibitions, students continued to speak them out of necessity or as defiant acts that expressed resistance to school values, established emotional connections among native speakers, and maintained connections with their pre-school life. At Haskell, some students even preserved Ojibwe better than did those who remained home.[73]

Many students and parents simply hoped to remain English-speaking Indians, however much this seemed a contradiction in terms, if for no other reason than the fact that what English as defined by the boarding schools offered was not really available to them. With or without the structured English of McGuffey or Birch, few Native Americans had the option of following Eastman by pursuing advanced education, moving into a city, and adopting the lifestyle of white citizens. An almost preternatural quality thereby accrued to the language as magically acquired and capable of magical transformation. Standing Bear thus speaks of his companions' belief that "some morning we would awaken and discover that we could talk English as readily as we could our own. As for myself, I thought if I could only be permitted to sleep in a white man's home, I would wake up some morning with a full knowledge of the English language."[74] But the only children who might awake in such a house would be white Anglophone children, for many of whom English provided realizable social opportunities as well as a means of communication.

The incommensurability between Anglophones divided by their definitions of English is summed up in a story Standing Bear tells of his trip to England as a member of Buffalo Bill's Wild West, in which, as literate as he was, he rode among the "wild" Indians. After a command royal performance before Edward VII in London, "Buffalo Bill brought the King over to me and we were introduced. We shook hands, although neither of us said a word."[75] There's much more here than the glibness about England and the United States being two nations divided by the same language that is often attributed to George Bernard Shaw. Many of us Anglophones are separated. And what separates us is the reality that we don't, in fact, all speak the same language.

CHAPTER TEN

English in the Classroom, II: Industrial English

"History is more or less bunk," said the industrialist Henry Ford in a 1916 newspaper interview.[1] It certainly wasn't the case that the ever-practical Ford saw no purpose in confronting the complex interrelations of economics, politics, and culture. Indeed, at the time of the interview, he recently had returned from organizing and sailing a "peace ship" to Europe in the hopes that the heads of state might be reasoned out of war. What Ford claimed to resent, rather, were history books and their stories of the past, which he disdainfully called tradition. "We don't want tradition," Ford continued. "We want to live in the present and the only history that is worth a tinker's dam is the history we make today."

Two, interconnected pieces of life in the present especially affected Ford: an increase in immigration into the United States in the decades surrounding 1900, and an increase in the industrial economy that this immigration made possible. According to the 1850 census, the first to ask about place of birth, 9.7% of the United States population was then foreign-born. In every census between 1860 and 1920, this percentage varied generally from 11 to 14, with the result that during this same period the total number of foreign-born residents in the United States increased from 2.2 million to 13.9 million among a population that itself rose from 23 million in 1850, to 76 million in 1900, to 105 million in 1920.[2] The 1908 Immigration Commission estimated that students with foreign-born parents accounted for 72% of the student population in New York City, 67% in Chicago, 64% in Boston, and 60% in Cleveland.[3]

The same Commission determined that over 60 nationalities were represented in 37 industrial cities, but after 1890, and coincident with the rise of industry, immigrants overwhelmingly came from eastern and southern Europe in particular.[4] During the first decade of the twentieth century, in fact, 72% of all immigrants can be traced to these regions.[5] Unlike earlier generations of immigrants from the United Kingdom, these new immigrants were thus characteristically non-Anglophones as well as non-natives. Among the 1910 population of 91 million Americans, for example, there were approximately 13.3 million foreign-born residents, perhaps as many as 5.5 million of whom had come to the United States in just the previous 13 years. Of these, only 3.3 million spoke English as a mother tongue; nearly another 4 million spoke one of the Germanic languages, 1.3 million one of the Scandinavian languages, 2.2 million one of the Romance languages, and 1.7 million one of the Slavic languages. While only 3.1 million of the foreign-born residents were recorded as not having the ability to speak any English, many of the others likely would have been bilingual and/or spoken English in a limited way or with a distinct non-native accent.[6] Altogether then, in 1910, 10 million individuals born in Europe (or 11% of the United States population) either spoke English as a second language or did not speak the language at all.

And these numbers do not account, of course, for the children of an earlier generation's immigrants, many of whom, particularly if they lived in rural or metropolitan enclaves of non-natives, maintained some degree of bilingualism or even lacked the ability to speak English. It likewise does not account for the varied patterns of immigrant settlement, by which some locales might be virtually entirely Anglophonic, while the labor-intensive cities might resemble Detroit, which had an average immigrant population of 25% throughout the first decades of the twentieth century. And neither do figures for the non-English population account for the nearly 300,000 Native Americans who were estimated to remain in 1910—a population of speakers who were at once indigenous, non-native, and often bilingual or even unacquainted with English. Nor do the figures account for the fact that illiterate, non-native speakers like immigrants and American Indians constituted a group that was particularly unlikely to participate in an English language census. All this means that the 11% of non-native speakers in the United States population of 1910 is undoubtedly an understatement and that in any case these speakers accounted for a new and sizable current in the river of English.[7]

Just as the predominance of southern and eastern European origins distinguished what's often called the third wave of immigration to the United States from the second one, so too did the clustering of the new immigrants in urban environments, where they became integral to the expanding industrial workforce. It was largely through immigration that Detroit, the center of the fledgling American automobile industry, grew from a population of 285,000 in 1900 to one of 1.7 million in 1930. As of 1916, one-third of Detroit's residents were foreign-born and three-fourths were either foreign-born themselves or the children of those who were.[8] The growth of Henry Ford's company epitomizes this transformation through immigration. At its 1903 founding, the Ford Motor Company had a workforce of 125. By 1921, this had increased to 33,000, largely, as will become clear, through workers newly arrived in the United States.[9]

The United States has always been a place peopled by immigrants, a place that even embraces its role as a homeland for those leaving other lands. At the same time, the presence of immigrants has been consistently controversial, drawing attention to issues like race, religion, economic stability, and nativism. This has been the case from the first Puritan settlements in New England, to the arrival of Irish immigrants in the 1840s, to the current influx of South American and East Asian emigrants. Responses to the southern and eastern Europeans who made possible the automobile industry were no exception.

"In every city the tendency of the foreigners is to colonization," observed Peter Roberts, a widely read social critic of the day. "The foreigner is ignorant of our ways, but let us remember that he comes from countries that are backward."[10] In fact, by settling in ethnic neighborhoods, individual immigrant groups often were isolated by religion, customs, and language. They likewise came to dominate certain factories, departments of those factories (low-paying, unskilled jobs in particular), and even trade organizations—all of which helped maintain their social and linguistic isolation. Further, with generally high birth rates in addition to a steady stream of new arrivals, immigrants easily produced the impression of a surging population. For Anglophones suspicious of these circumstances and the people in them—"colonization" is the word Roberts uses—immigrants' health, personal habits, cleanliness, and language all became signs of inherently flawed character, much as they already had been for Native Americans. And these suspicions were developed enough and widespread enough that they make it possible to construct the era's collective ranking of foreigners, beginning at the top with Germans (typically considered a model immigrant population) and moving precipitously downward through Poles and Italians to Hungarians and Greeks.[11]

In the years surrounding the First World War, an aggressive, even militant Americanization movement transformed these suspicions into connections between English, civilization, and citizenship. Perhaps the most benign form of this identification of English with the United States was a prohibition on non-English telephone conversations in some areas. The definition of English acquired much greater legal and civil consequence through laws that declared it the official language in several states or that curtailed and even eliminated instruction in non-English languages. And the nationalistic rhetoric of critics such as Frances Kellor went farther still, equating English not only with patriotism but with financial success and international harmony: "The road to American citizenship, to the English language, and an understanding of American social and political ideas is the road to industrial peace."[12]

Such connections between personal character, language, and national identity rested on more than suspicion, however. They had an allegedly scientific basis as well. By the 1890s, as the ideas of Darwin (and eventually Mendel) filtered into the popular imagination, responses to immigration had become racialized in discussions that represented the newest immigrants not simply as undesirable but as genetically inferior and therefore a threat to the country's racial purity and intellectual achievement.[13] Building on tests he had designed for United States servicemen, which involved pictures and pantomimes to accommodate the illiterate, Carl Brigham assembled statistical data to support a theory of race-based intelligence. The most intelligent, according to Brigham, was the "Nordic" race, with its English-speaking component (such as the United Kingdom and Canada) scoring higher than non-Anglophone Scandinavians and northern Germans. The next two groups, which scored closer both to one another and to the lowest group than they did to the Nordic, were the "Alpine" (Poles and Russians) and the "Mediterranean." At the bottom of the racial-linguistic spectrum was the "American Negro." By Brigham's reasoning, knowledge of English correlates with natural intelligence, so that southeastern Europeans were not simply dirty and non-English-speaking; they were genetically limited. On the basis of his work, Brigham concluded that "the average intelligence of our immigrants is declining," and that, should all four races continue to blend, it is "a foregone conclusion that this future blended American will be less intelligent than the present native born American." There was therefore need for immigration laws to "not only be restrictive but highly selective" and for the revision of naturalization laws to prevent "the continued propagation of defective strains in the present population."[14]

Before we dismiss Brigham as a crank and a racist, we should recognize that at the time he wrote (1923), his were anything but fringe views. The same pseudo-scientific reasoning had led the psychologist Henry Goddard a few years earlier to argue on behalf of eugenics and race-based intelligence differences. Similar reasoning provides at least part of the context for the Immigration Act of 1917, which expanded the categories of undesirables to include criminals, alcoholics, and the feeble-minded. The Immigration Act of 1924 additionally restricted the number of immigrants from any one country to 2% of that group's immigrant population in 1890 (i.e., prior to the period of greatest influx of southeastern Europeans). Brigham's own work made its greatest impact in academic assessment, through the Scholastic Aptitude Test (SAT). First administered in 1926 to those aspiring to attend American universities, the SAT remains an important admission criterion to this day and has inspired similar tests as well as a lucrative industry of courses devoted to improving students' scores and thus the likelihood of their acceptance at prestigious institutions. Not only did Brigham's work on language and intelligence underlie the first version, but Brigham himself chaired the committee that prepared the test.

From this arena of early twentieth-century immigration, I argue in this chapter, definitions of English emerged that were marked both by the kind of history Ford valued and by the kind of tradition he rejected. Responding to the dramatic increase of a non-Anglophone yet vital workforce, and to educational practices that stretched from the Puritans to the Indian boarding schools, these definitions differentiated civilized, socially responsible Anglophones from the uncivilized, vicious immigrants around them. By a logic that would have pleased Webster, the definition of English, with or without any legal sanction, included citizenship as one of its senses. Yet the definition of English in this context also evokes traditions of the sort Ford said weren't worth a tinker's dam. Like the new Anglophones of the South Seas, the growing population in the United States affirmed the desirability of the country and English, even as it found itself and its English continually marked as non-native. And as in traditions of codification that began in the sixteenth century, Anglophones used geography, time, and a standard ideology to write definitions that were arguments about personal and national identity. Downriver definitions of English, it seems, are always subject to the currents of what has flowed before.

IMMIGRANT ENGLISH

In his final report as Secretary of the Massachusetts Board of Education, Horace Mann imagined education as an opportunity democratically available to all Americans: "Education, then, beyond all other devices of human origin, is the great equalizer of the conditions of men—the balance-wheel of the social machinery."[15] As places where the best and brightest children, whatever their social backgrounds, could realize their potential for the benefit of society as well as themselves, common schools would foster what was imagined to be an "aristocracy of talent." To participate in this aristocracy, non-Anglophone immigrant children, like their counterparts in the Indian boarding schools, needed first to acquire English in its preferred linguistic form and with that form's social implications.

For immigrant children, as for Indian children, this meant that English channeled anxieties about morality, health, and intelligence, but also—since immigrants constituted a much larger and growing portion of the populace—about employability, social coherence, and the heritage that Americans identified for themselves. The late-nineteenth-century emergence of vocational tracks provided one way for schools to socialize these children, training them to assume, again like their Indian counterparts, low-paying and sometimes menial positions with little opportunity for advancement. But schools also began to offer classes in English as a second language that could and sometimes did lead to social mobility. Initially, private enterprises like the Education Alliance in New York City offered the only such training, but as of 1904 the city of New York itself began to offer tax-supported transitional programs in the public schools. While underfinanced and under-enrolled, 'vestibule' or 'steamer' classes nonetheless provided five or six months of language work preparatory to a child's placement in an appropriate grade and thereby constituted a significant improvement over the previous practice of placing all non-Anglophone students, regardless of age, in the lowest grade. In 1913, William Maxwell, New York's Superintendent of Schools, framed this instruction in a way with which Mann would have agreed: "It is the great business of the department of education in this city…to train the immigrant child from the shores of the mediterranean [sic] Sea to become a good citizen."[16]

Things were otherwise for the parents of these children. Indeed, when the third wave of European emigrants acquired English and entered the American economy, the workforce took a shape distinctly different from the egalitarian one Mann had imagined. To the early-twentieth-century economist Isaac Hourwich, surveying the distribution of workers in skilled and unskilled positions, "The effect of immigration upon the occupational distribution of the industrial wage-earners has been the elevation of the English-speaking workmen to the status of an aristocracy of labor, while the immigrants have been employed to perform the rough work of all industries."[17] American industries thus found themselves in a bind. On one hand, distinction between Anglophones and non-Anglophones sustained their employment hierarchies, with knowledge of English (in the broad sense from the common school traditions) serving a gate-keeping function that allowed advancement only to select individuals. On the other, the vital and expanding presence of non-English speakers in factories created efficiency and safety issues. The Ford company alone posted safety notices in eight languages at its Highland Park Crystal Palace factory near Detroit, whose workforce represented as many as 50 different nationalities.[18] Compounding the problems of this linguistic diversity is the simple fact that printed notices can benefit only the literate. Dangerous to begin with, factory work thus resulted in frequent accidents, maimings, and even deaths that were traceable to linguistic confusion of one kind or another.[19]

Public schools were in no position to remedy this situation. Some did offer night and summer English classes for adult foreigners; this was the case in industrial cities like Cleveland, Chicago, and Milwaukee. And so, too, did the North American Civic League for Immigrants and the YMCA, which in 1914 could count 30,022 students, from 42 nationalities, who were taught in 272 branches nationwide.[20] While these numbers may seem impressive, against a non-English- or partial-English-speaking population of perhaps 10 million people, even the efforts of the YMCA seem paltry. Indeed, because of limited funds and commitments to other enterprises, these organizations had few opportunities to teach English to adults. All such schools additionally suffered from inadequately trained teachers and a curriculum that targeted children, not working adults, with the result that large numbers of disaffected students failed to complete the courses. Still more never enrolled, or were unable to do so. In Detroit, for instance, a total of approximately 3,500 students registered for the adult English classes, even as the city's foreign-born population was roughly 157,000 in 1910 and 290,000 in 1920.[21]

Likewise in Detroit, beginning in 1914, the Board of Commerce worked with the Board of Education, the Boy Scouts, the Recreation Commission, Juvenile Court, the public library, industries, and virtually every other civic organization in an effort to make the city English-speaking in just two years. Some 27 night schools were intended to teach citizenship as well as English and to assist workers in the naturalization process, emblemized in a tri-colored poster distributed by the National Americanization Committee. This showed Uncle Sam greeting an immigrant and then showing him the public school and the road to English and citizenship. In order to reach the immigrant women involved in home upkeep and therefore excluded from factory and night-school opportunities, the Board proposed establishing afternoon classes in the public schools. Its efforts received boosts from the Committee for Immigrants in America, which distributed promotional material in pay envelopes and on factory floors, and advised employers of the disadvantages of non-Anglophone employees. The Employers' Association showed its support by restricting services to English-speakers and by distributing a film (made by Ford) that showed immigrants being turned away from employment offices because of their limited command of English.[22]

As with the education of foreigners in general, the key words here might be functionality and efficiency. "Evening-school students wish to know the vernacular, both spoken and written," William Chancellor noted in his 1904 textbook, "and are not concerned with language as a means of understanding literature. They study English for the sake of communicating with others."[23] To this end, books like Chancellor's advocated the kind of recitation that formed the basis of common school education, as well as the objective method (used in Indian schools) that introduced concepts and related lexicon through familiar objects and pictures of them. Prefacing his textbook with an excerpt from the popular poet Longfellow, "America the Beautiful," and an early version of the "Pledge of Allegiance," Isaac Price emphasizes real-life situations or introductions to American cultural institutions as ways to teach grammar and pronunciation. And Sara Redempta O'Brien's book, reflecting skepticism over the primitiveness of foreigners, introduces English by way of lessons on hygiene, health, home furnishings, citizenship, and letter-writing. Unlike McGuffey's stories of virtue and vice, her readings include explanations of occupations like manufacturing, coal mining, and meat-packing.[24]

The most influential of these textbooks for foreigners, however, was *English for Coming Americans* by Peter Roberts—the same Roberts who excused the foreigner's ignorance by explaining that "he comes from countries that are backward." The objective of his course, which he initially developed as a YMCA program for factory workers, was "to give foreigners a practical knowledge of English for daily use in the home, in work and in business." Of the 30 lessons in Roberts's program, ten illustrated domestic issues, ten industrial ones, and ten commercial (i.e., social) ones. Like his peers, Roberts emphasized recitation, the objective method, and lessons that taught grammar indirectly through readings and vocabulary. And also like his peers he drew a distinction between English and the form of the language as used by second-language learners. Foreigners have particular trouble with verbs, he believes, and part of the difficulty is that they "have tenacious memories" that allow them to mimic correct forms without learning them. That some might be using a simplified verb structure of the sort evident in pidgins and non-standard varieties (like Hawaiian Pidgin English) is not something Roberts considers.[25]

Selectively rewriting history so as to exclude or marginalize African slaves and American Indians as well as Spanish, French, and Dutch speakers, Roberts also believes the United States to be inherently Anglophonic. Prior to 1880, he asserts, most passengers to America "knew the English language and practically all of them were of the Keltic and Teutonic stock." And if American citizenship is one of the senses of English, another is civilization. Of more recent foreigners Roberts observes, "These people are not as fastidious as English-speaking people, and their ideas as to the amount of room a family needs and the privacy necessary for the members are very different from ours." Degrees of citizenship and civilization are thus proportionate with knowledge of English: "The wives of the new immigration are more backward than the men, for they seldom leave the foreign colony, rarely have an opportunity to hear the English language, and hardly ever enter an American home."[26] Elsewhere Roberts tells of 15 Greeks living "several degrees below the standard of Christian civilization" whose appearance and habits improve markedly after they enroll in a YMCA English class. The socializing and even moralizing power of English affects native speakers as well, as in the case of a "bachelor in Boston" who "was drying up and soon would be wretched and bitter" but who was "renewed" and "saved" by teaching English to foreigners.[27] For all speakers, whether civilized Anglophones or uncivilized immigrants, English affirms what it is to be a cultured American.

Recalling the Indian boarding schools, the English taught in this way might be described as something between disingenuous and deceptive. Held out as a vehicle towards citizenship and realization of the American Dream, English for European immigrants more closely served the needs of the industries that taught it. The language was intended to be limited in its corpus and domains of usage, and limiting in the opportunities it provided to those who learned it. Immigrant English was intended as well to differ from the language spoken by those who owned and ran the industries. As George Mason said in 1916, there were then "still many thousands of workers in Detroit who know not the language of Shakespeare, but the number drinking at fountains of knowledge in the night schools" was larger than in the previous year and growing.[28] Ultimately, Roberts's YMCA program had the same discriminatory effect. The three-part 30-lesson course was in fact meant only as the first of three such courses, after the third of which students would be "able to read, write, and talk fairly well in the English language." By extension, of course, this judgment meant that for all its rhetoric about decency and helping immigrants to achieve social equality through language, the first course did not yield conversant Anglophones, a point made by the language of a letter from "an Italian in the Western Penitentiary of Pennsylvania" who wrote to express his gratitude for what the prison's YMCA course had done for him: "I will thank the Lord for produce me here...because I could not even write my own name, and now that I can write little bit it make me represent self better man than I ever was."[29]

For Native Americans and immigrants alike, definitions of English promised social mobility through grammar. The wildly popular *Sherwin Cody 100% Self-Correcting Course in English Language*, whose earliest versions appeared in 1903 and which was advertised from 1919 to 1959, perpetuated this same promise for the next generation—the children of the immigrants who might have taken Roberts's course or who were educated in steamer classes. Bluntly challenging readers to stop abusing English by making mistakes in speech and writing, and offering to sell them the means to do just that, Cody explicitly tied language to class and employment. Bad English may have been the indelible mark of social failure, but Cody's book, like the earlier *Poor Letter H* and the later *Lose Your Accent in 28 Days,* insisted that if it were remedied, failure would turn to success.[30]

The pragmatic sense of English that runs through the efforts of Brigham, Roberts, and Cody offers the same contradiction that runs from Horace Mann to the Indian boarding schools. On one hand, English means a non-varying grammatical code embedded with shared cultural values. It is accessible to all, and once acquired it affirms acceptance into American society and its economic opportunities. On the other, English as framed by a standard ideology serves as a means to discriminate among individuals otherwise distinguished by race, class, and ethnicity. The form of the language that such speakers acquire only confirms the rightness not just of their social standing but of their children's as well. If 'broken' or regional, the inadequacy of this form of English is self-evident. And if apparently standard, speakers' inability to advance socially and economically points necessarily to perhaps hidden but patently debilitating flaws. Anglophones and native speakers thereby become categories based as much on non-linguistic issues as on matters like communicative competence and geographic origin.

THE FORD ENGLISH SCHOOL

This pragmatic sense played out nowhere more clearly than at the Ford Motor Company. From its beginnings, the company capitalized on a one-size-fits-all approach best expressed in Ford's comment on the 1908 introduction of the phenomenally successful Model T: "I will build a motor car for the great multitude. It will be large enough for the family, but small enough for the individual to care for."[31] This approach animated the methods of production, most famously in the assembly lines wherein laborers were as interchangeable as parts and which could produce a complete automobile in about 90 minutes—down from the 12 or more hours that workers previously had required to do the job. And it rested on principles of scientific management that are often called Taylorism, after the work of Frederick Taylor.[32] These principles included efficiency, the fostering of cooperation between workers and employers, and the education of workers.

By the late-nineteenth century, as a reaction to the practical excesses of industry and the theoretical ones of social Darwinism, an evolving social gospel advocated attention to the good of workers. Partly such advocacy focused on workers' basic human rights, but also partly on the notion that workers who were healthy and content would contribute more usefully to society than would those who were not. Attention to workers' housing, medicine, recreation, and education thus would benefit the industrialists as much as the workers. Perhaps more so. Education in particular served as a way for industrialists and entrepreneurs to enact this social gospel, whether on the local level of an industrial plant or on the grander stage of a university. Ezra Cornell, Leland Stanford, and John D. Rockefeller all took the latter route by establishing (respectively) Cornell University (1865), Stanford University (1885), and the University of Chicago (1890). Befitting his professed commitment to the common man, Henry Ford took his educational stand on the factory floor.

Already in the earliest issues of the *Ford Times*, a monthly that began publication in 1908, the company expressed interest in the personal well-being and habits of its employees, using stories, articles, and direct advice to show them how to live cleanly and work productively. But by 1914, it was the company's own well-being that needed attention. While in just six years Ford had grown exponentially, it also confronted staggering difficulties in its workforce. In response to nine-hour shifts at a mind-numbing assembly line, workers quit in droves, some staying less than a week and so many that Ford annually needed to hire 52,000 individuals to maintain a workforce of 14,000.

The demographics of this workforce presented its own problems. As I have noted, at the Crystal Palace in Highland Park perhaps 50 languages could be heard, reflecting the fact that in the plant's early years three-quarters of the workers were foreign-born, most of them in southern and eastern parts of Europe. According to a press release from November of 1914, among the approximately 9,100 foreign-born workers at the company, fewer than 900 originated in what Kachru later called the Inner Circle. While the balance included some French, Danish, and other workers Brigham would have classified as Nordic, the overwhelming majority came from the Alpine and Mediterranean areas where alleged intellectual deficiencies (and the inability to speak English) ran the highest. Over 2,600 Poles worked at Highland Park, then, alongside over 2,000 Russians, 750 Romanians, 269 Hungarians, 690 Italians or Sicilians, and so forth.[33] Three years later, the workforce exceeded 40,000 and among the most recent immigrants included 7,525 Poles, 1,954 Italians, 1,750 Romanians, 1,437 "Jews," 1,160 Russians, and 690 Hungarians.[34] Native Americans from the Carlisle Indian Industrial School, whose social status at best mirrored that of the Mediterranean group, were also present—25 in 1916 and 68 two years later.[35]

In 1914, at Henry Ford's instigation, the company took two, related actions to address these workforce problems. Firstly, the work day was shortened to three eight-hour shifts, for which qualified laborers, though a profit-sharing plan, would receive the equivalent of five dollars a day—twice their current pay or the pay at other factories in Detroit. It was a plan that James Couzens, the company's Vice President, framed very much in the social gospel tradition: "We believe that social justice begins at home. We want those who have helped us to produce this great institution and are helping to maintain it, to share our prosperity. We want them to have present profits and future prospects. Thrift, good service and sobriety will be encouraged and recognized."[36] And secondly, Ford created the Sociological Department. In a 1915 speech to the Industrial Relations Committee, Ford himself situated this Department within the frameworks of both the social gospel and his own personal conviction that individuals needed to live a committed, responsible life. Its purpose, he said, was to "explain opportunity, teach American ways and customs, English language, duties of citizenship... The whole effort of this corps is to point men to life and to make them disconnected with mere living."[37] More particularly, the Sociological Department—whose name was changed to the Educational Department when its directorship passed in 1915 from John R. Lee to the Rev. Samuel S. Marquis—had responsibility for evaluating each of the company's workers in order to determine who qualified for the profit-sharing plan. To do so, the Department employed up to 200 doctors, nurses, and investigators who went into the community to interview workers and their neighbors about issues like housing, health, and lifestyle.

The immediate objective of the Department was to identify workers whose personal habits required corrective attention if they were to disconnect "with mere living" and reform enough to participate in profit-sharing. Rev. Marquis claimed, in fact, that Henry Ford was not an automobile maker. He simply "shoots about fifteen hundred cars out of the back door of his factory every day just to get rid of them. These are the by-products of his real business, which is the making of men."[38] This objective also required enforcing what might be called middle-class values, which the *Ford Times*, much like a modern-day McGuffey Reader, emphasized through accounts of pluck, determination, and hard work. In the company's vision of America, success or failure originated not simply in the character of the individual but in that individual's relations through the family to shared social and cultural values. Workers who drank excessively, gambled, or failed to provide for their families were a special concern (and, by implication, problem). According to Rev. Marquis, "We have made the discovery at the Ford [sic] that the family is also the basis of right economic and industrial conditions. The welfare of the factory, no less than the welfare of the state and church, depends upon the home. We therefore keep a close watch on the home."[39] The groups that qualified immediately for profit-sharing, according to Lee, were thus married men taking good care of their families, thrifty single men over the age of 22, or single men under 22 or women "who are the sole support of some next of kin or blood relative."[40]

The Educational Department certainly offered a more compassionate view of human society than that offered by social Darwinism. "The right relationship between employer and employee," Rev. Marquis maintains, "follows naturally in the wake of the things we try to do for our men. The spirit of the Ford school is not that of paternalism but of fraternalism."[41] But the company itself obviously had a vested interest in this spirit, for it produced the very consumers who might purchase its product. Or as Rev. Marquis put the matter (recalling Merrill Gates's advocacy of providing Native Americans with trousers and pockets that ache "to be filled with dollars"), "The Ford Idea is to increase a man's capacity for happiness and at the same time to increase his efficiency, his earning capacity, his worth to society, so that he may have access to the things he has been taught to enjoy."[42] The company's treatment of education was no exception.

The Ford Motor Company ran a variety of educational programs, enrolling as many as 25,000 employees in compulsory courses on thrift, domestic economy, and community relations. Among these programs was the English School, which began in May of 1914. At the time, Ford employed 13,000 workers, 5,000 of whom, according to a piece in the *Ford Times*, "could not speak, read nor understand the English language. Of these 5,000 only a few could say the simplest words, disconnectedly." Altogether, these 13,000 workers represented 53 "different nationalities, speaking something more than one hundred languages and dialects" and requiring 25 interpreters in the factory.[43] Efficiency, cost, and worker safety, then, were significant motivations for the school, and the latter in particular is cited repeatedly in Ford documents of the period: "Learn the English Language—It will insure safety, and save money."[44] But the company's avowed commitment to social justice was a factor as well. "The foreigners are good workers and are treated like those of native birth and parentage,"[45] Ford observed in an interview, and like wages required like treatment and abilities. Since both native and non-native workers were to receive the same $5.00 per day, they all (according to the *Ford Times*) had to speak English: "If the man who could not speak the language and who could not understand his foreman was to receive $5.00 a day, surely the intelligent English-speaking men were getting less than they deserved, was the thought that occurred to more than one man." Equity and workplace harmony depended on a shared knowledge of

English, and so too did the ability to function successfully in American society:

It was found, by the investigators, that a majority of the non-English-speaking men were incapable of taking care of the share of profits given them by the Company. Through their inability to speak the language, and their ignorance of the customs of the country, these employees were the prey of sophisticated and unscrupulous fellow countrymen familiar with their adopted tongue.[46]

Beginning with one teacher and 20 pupils, the school enrolled 2,700 students taught by 163 instructors in 1916 and 3,200 students (spanning the ages from 18 to 72) the year after.[47] Organized in a Teacher's Literary Club devoted to debate, singing, and socialization, the instructors were by design all volunteers with just three months of training.[48] The arrangement saved Ford money, of course, but it also had the presumed advantage of the faculty having much in common with their students in terms of background, work experience, and daily contact. Consisting of two 90-minute sessions each week, which took place before or after work both outside and in conventional classrooms, a typical English course required 36 weeks for completion.[49] Enrollments in these classes reflected the predominance of immigrants from southern and eastern Europe throughout American industry at the time. One class of 518 students from 1916, for instance, consisted of 163 Poles, 134 Russians, 46 Austrians, 28 Italians, 23 Hungarians, 20 Germans, 16 Romanians, 13 "Jews," and 11 Bohemians. Some 28 other nationalities made up the balance of students, and as many as 55 different nationalities were represented in the school in its few years of operation.[50]

"The object of the English school," Rev. Marquis observes, "is not only to make the men more efficient in our work in the shop, but also to prepare them for citizenship." The Ford school thus followed traditions established in the connections forged between linguistic form and social identity that first appeared in the standardization process and that the common schools movement fostered in the United States in particular. Much like the *vulgaria* taught to early modern students or the social lessons of McGuffey's readers, the first sentence learned by Ford students was one that expressed their satisfaction with their situation in life: "I am a good American."[51] The school's principal, Clinton C. De Witt, viewed this connection between citizenship and English as an industry-wide reason to employ workers as instructors:

When industries wake up to the fact that their plants are full of potential teachers and are willing to give recognition to their talent, then our Americanization problem will practically have been solved, for it takes only a short time to teach the American language with a broad knowledge of civil government, which is one of the many byproducts given with a well-outlined course.[52]

Inspiration for the course came from Roberts's *English for Coming Americans* and Francis Gouin's eighteenth-century "cumulative method," both of which emphasized the need for students and teachers to dramatize conversational situations.[53] Ford maintained its approach differed from these and all other pedagogical systems, however, because it furnished "instruction sheets and classroom programs for the guidance of the teacher."[54] The very first of these lessons emphasized the hygiene and personal habits that provided much of the motivation for the Sociological Department: "I wash myself," "I comb my hair," "I put on my collar and necktie." Relying on recitation and the objective method, the school used the eagle, emblem of the United States, as an object of study that was among Ford's personal favorites.[55] Later lessons involved sentences and conversations that stressed cooperation and civic responsibility. One of these imagined a worker going to the public library in the evening and involved sentences like "I finish my supper at 6 o'clock P.M.," "I clean my overcoat with a hand broom," and "I say 'Goodnight' to my family." While pantomiming the action being described, the teacher was to recite the sentence and the students to repeat it.[56] Ford materials insist

the men thoroughly enjoy this form of instruction, because it presents the carnival spirit, a sense of co-operation. Twenty-five men shouting the lesson together arouse a great deal of good feeling, and in a few minutes, the day's work is forgotten. The time flies, and the hour and a half session is all too short. So interested are some of the men that they will remain long after the class is dismissed in order to receive special instruction.[57]

Classes were grouped according to the students' ability (e.g., those already literate in a native language were placed in the same class), and the more advanced lessons utilized 111 conversation cards, each holding one sentence of an exchange meant to teach students the appropriate English to use in a variety of workplace situations. Beginning with discussion of a laborer's home, job, and transportation to work, one conversation underscores proper work habits: "Where do you keep your tools?" "I keep them in a box." And it offers a model of on-the-job behavior:

> "Is the foreman kind to you?"
> "Yes, if I do what he tells me."
> "Do you always do what he tells you?"
> "Yes, I try to, but sometimes I don't understand."

In their nine months of limited instruction, Ford workers could never have progressed beyond Roberts's introductory lessons. But if they had, they would have confronted a familiar emphasis on civic responsibility at the expense of linguistic niceties. Roberts's Second Reader, for example, is subtitled "Readings and Language Lessons in History, Industries, and Civics," and it includes passages on the discovery of America, "American Aborigines," Ulysses S. Grant, and "Dying for the Flag." And those who graduated were understood by the federal government to have demonstrated sufficient knowledge of English to qualify immediately for the first stage of naturalization.[58] In this vein, it's significant that Ford papers frequently refer to the students learning not English but the "American language."[59]

While Ford may have run the largest and most influential of the industrial English schools, other employers shared its interest in cultivating both an Anglophone workforce and an educational program consistent with their own production objectives and those of an increasingly strident Americanization movement focused on English education. In the early part of the twentieth century, thus, US Steel, the American Bridge Company, the Illinois Steel Company, Keystone Works, International Harvester, and the Pfister and Vogel Tannery all ran English classes.[60] What these industries understood English to be, for the most part, was a set of basic grammatical features (functional lexis and simple syntax) that would facilitate production and preserve safety, but also a vehicle for citizenship and for the advancement of industrial values. By learning English, workers would learn as well about the dangers of workplace insubordination, unions, and Communism. To Boyd Fisher, vice president of the Executives Club of Detroit, the employer should be "a co-partner with the teacher, the minister and the social worker in the business of reforming men."[61]

Workers at International Harvester thus attended classes on discipline, safety, and welfare, and learned simple sentences that would improve their job performance: "I hear the whistle. I must hurry," or "I leave my place nice and clean." While more linguistically ambitious than much of what Ford taught, subsequent lessons at Harvester placed a similar stress on worker responsibility: "When you are sick or hurt report to your time-keeper and the doctor at once."[62] At the Keystone Works, English classes included mock naturalization proceedings that produced dialogues illustrating language, citizenship, and economics all at the same time:

TEACHER: Who is president now?
ALIEN: Mr. da Wils.
TEACHER: Could you be president?
ALIEN: Excuse me please, I got pretty good job on the Keystone.[63]

Those who finished the Ford course might participate in a lavish graduation ceremony that underscored, above all, a social as well as a linguistic definition of English. Staged on a baseball field or in an auditorium, accompanied by a brass band, and thronging with workers and families, the ceremony typically began with a procession of students descending from a boat representing the one that had brought them to the United States, or, dressed in their pre-American national costumes, singing non-English songs, dancing folk dances, and carrying the flags of Europe. In each case, overseen by a master of ceremony dressed as the proverbial Uncle Sam, students entered a wooden container seven and one-half feet high and 15 feet in diameter. Stirred by teachers holding ten-foot paddles, the container was emblazoned 'Ford English School Melting Pot'. Above it hung a banner with the national motto: 'E pluribus unum'. Inside the pot, the students changed from national garb to the derby hats, collars, and ties of American dress, and they exited, in some cases, waving American flags or singing the "Star Spangled Banner." Commencement also might include speeches from judges, other public figures, and students, as well as the singing of patriotic songs.[64] Afterwards, graduates might meet Henry Ford himself, along with other company leaders, and participate in a day-long family picnic.

As a spectacle, then, the entire graduation event emphasized and dramatized the connections between English as taught at the Ford school and civic responsibility, moral respectability, and patriotism. Indeed, the school maintained a close connection with Americanization Day ceremonies, holding banquets in honor of it and marshaling thousands of students to march in commemorative parades.[65] Even the diplomas make these connections. One side verifies an individual's ability to "understand the English language to write it and read it within certain limitations," the other attests to a candidate's "definite comprehension of the rudiments of Government, National, State and Municipal, and fits him to become a Citizen of the United States and to understand the obligations therein."

Ford maintained that when its 36-week initial course was completed "the pupils, whatever the land of their birth, are able to read, write, and speak simple American language."[66] It quoted Gust Papas, a Greek immigrant who gave an address at one commencement, as saying in improbably stylized prose, "That we may lay aside thoughts of the old world, and strive to become true American citizens in the new, is my heartfelt desire for the class."[67] And it sponsored an American Club, to which all students were admitted upon graduation and which held weekly meetings to discuss historical, civic, and national matters of interest, sometimes with guest speakers and entertainment for families.[68] The Club's "fundamental purpose," as the company described it, was "to promote good American citizenship."[69] All contemporary accounts of the school, whether written or planted by Ford, describe it as a success in enthusiastic, even jingoistic, terms.[70]

But given the linguistic diversity of the students' backgrounds, their age, and the brevity of the course, it is difficult to believe that most of them (or of those at other industrial schools) would have acquired anything beyond a bare minimum of morphological and syntactic complexity. Speaking primarily with one another, they would have acquired even less Standard American phonology. They would have spoken, that is, broken English with a foreign accent, a fact borne out by the Ford school's graduation rate: of the 14,000 to 16,000 workers who enrolled in the program between 1914 and 1917, only 1,500 received diplomas for completing the course.[71] Ford's own definition of English was certainly a factor in this failure rate, since, as the diploma indicates, completion depended on civic as well as linguistic achievement. Indeed, English-competent students could not graduate if they lacked "familiarity with the principles of the government of the state or the nation. Every graduate must be thoroughly familiar with the basic principles of civil government."[72] But even without this civic emphasis, circumstances scarcely favored the cultivation of more than rudimentary knowledge of the language.

At the same time, the Ford school did achieve its goals. Along with the elementary vocabulary, cleanliness, and civic lessons that they learned, non-native Anglophones would have become well aware of the connections Ford posited between patriotism, virtue, and language; of their own linguistic limitations; and of the workplace demeanor that went with these. To this end, the company actively discouraged workers from taking any of the public school options for learning English rather than its own classes.[73] And despite the beneficent rhetoric of Ford and Rev. Marquis, the English School had a kind of corrective, even punitive quality that assured workers as much of their subservience as of the transcendent value of the American experience. At just three absences, students were severely reprimanded.[74] Rev. Marquis himself goes so far as to say, "This course is not exactly optional. A man who declines to take it is laid off for a couple of weeks in order that he may have time to think it over. If after further persuasion he refuses to attend the classes he is given an opportunity to find employment elsewhere."[75] According to Ford's autobiography, 38 workers were in fact let go in 1919 because of a "refusal to learn English in the school provided."[76]

And if the Ford school instilled patriotism and discipline, it was also measurably successful at teaching its definition of

English, whatever the accents and linguistic deficiencies of its workers. Between 1914 and 1917, the percentage of non-English workers at the Crystal Palace declined from 33.5 to 11.7.[77] In 1917, indeed, Ford recorded just 4,772 non-English-speaking workers (from a workforce of over 40,000), and by 1920, the company claimed that "the proportion of foreigners in the Ford Factory is less than in the average factory. Not more than one-half are foreigners."[78] In response to this decline, as well as to the increased production demands of World War One, Ford down-sized the English School from 22 classes to three by the end of 1917. Partly the drop in enrollment might be attributed, of course, to the decline in immigration that accompanied restrictions in federal policies during and after the First World War. And partly it might be due simply to the fact that by 1917, workers who could not speak English when they began working at Ford in 1914 had had three years of experience with the language. But partly credit must be given to policies that in the first years of the program had exposed a great many workers to some kind of formal training in English. "Whereas three years ago," Lee said in 1916, "we, of the manufacturing department, used to be able to use the phrase 'hurry up' in forty or fifty languages or dialects, at the present time this expression is rarely, if ever, heard."[79]

Put another way, one might say that the workers acquired just what the school had hoped they would: obedience to their Ford employers as well as the functional English necessary for improved production and their own employment. They spoke better and worked faster. As odd as it might seem in the twenty-first century, moreover, like many Native Americans thinking back on their boarding school experiences, at least some Ford workers had good memories and a strong sense of gratitude for their experience at the Ford school. "There never was a man who did so much for his employees as Mr Ford," said one worker; "I am proud to be a workman in his plant. I want to learn something about the United States' Government after I have mastered the English language sufficiently well."[80] And in 1915 the company claimed "That the men appreciate what is being done for them is clearly shown by the number of letters received from employes [sic], which are sent without

solicitation, and express, in good English, the sincere obligation they feel toward the work, which is enabling them to enjoy
the advantages and comforts previously unknown to them."[81]
In 1921, in any case, the Educational Department (as the Sociological Department was then called) merged into the Service
Department, where it fulfilled essentially a charitable function
and no longer focused on the workforce. Lacking its larger
institutional purpose, the Ford English School ceased to exist
in 1922.

The Ford school's English program certainly made it possible
for immigrants to retain their jobs—attendance was a stipula-
tion of employment, after all. And in all likelihood the program
made their sometimes dangerous jobs considerably safer. But
given the brevity and character of the Ford school's English
program, one wonders whether workers who participated in it
achieved a transition to the English used outside of the Crystal
Palace that was any more effective than the ones who did not
participate. As the Indian boarding school experience shows, we
are social creatures with innate linguistic capacities who by
nature have the urge and ability to acquire the means to speak
with those around us. For immigrants to the United States, with
or without educational programs or legal mandates, this acquisition typically has followed a three-generation path: an initial
generation of monoglot or dominant non-English speakers,
a generation of variable bilinguals, and a generation of monoglot Anglophones. In either case—self-managed immersion or
brief formal instruction—at least the first generation of
speakers, the ones who would have been working at Ford, is
marked by lexical and phonological hallmarks that have distinguished non-standard speech since the early modern period.
Lee's claim that knowledge of English and American customs
would "liberate" workers "from the bondage...under which
they have unconsciously been placed" thus rings hollow.[82]
Even setting aside whatever Lee might have meant by "bondage,"
non-native workers most assuredly were not liberated by their
English, marking (as it did) their ethnicity, social class, and level
of education. For all its promises of opportunity and mobility,
English simply became a new way to designate the same
categories.

Employment patterns at Ford during this period make this point particularly well. In a 1917 study for the United States Bureau of Labor, Boris Emmett identified strong correlations between level of employment and ethnic background at the company. The rigor with which the Sociological Department applied its evaluation process, he found, depended on "the specific character of the group of employees concerned." The company paid "very little attention to the manner of life, etc., of their office employees," who were in fact mostly "native Americans with some education." The welfare program, including the Ford English School, thus was concerned chiefly with "the manual and mechanical workers, many of whom are of foreign birth and unable to speak the English language."[83] Immigrants, in other words, could qualify to learn a kind of English that in turn would qualify them to work on the factory floor but not in the better-paying, more publically visible commercial and clerical sectors. Commissioner Leupp's English aspirations for Native Americans well might describe Ford's for its workers—that he or she "can read the simple English of the local newspaper, can write a short letter, intelligible though maybe misspelled, and knows enough of figures to discover whether the storekeeper's cheating him." Like the Indian boarding schools or Cody's *100% Self-Correcting Course*, indeed, the Ford school produced (whether intentionally or not) speakers whose language marked them as socially subordinate and whose sense of English rendered them complicit in the subordination of their own variety and, by extension, their own social status. What industrial English was depended on why industrialists cared.

No doubt some workers did manage to acquire proficiency in Standard English, but whether even they found the promised social mobility seems doubtful. Reflecting the prevailing attitudes towards the southeastern European workers who dominated the Ford workforce, the company early on linked language, moderation, and employability. One group of suspect workers, it claimed in 1914, consisted of "the men who do not speak English or who live in dirty squalid conditions, who are improvident, and who, unfortunately for the most part, have not squared away for a number of reasons."[84] 1920 Ford statistics reinforce this same correlation between language, ethnicity, and employment. Some 32.5% of native-born white employees held office jobs, as did 17.6% of British immigrants and 23.1% of Canadian immigrants who were British born. Conversely, no Italian or Armenian immigrants held white-collar positions.[85] For its next level of employment, skilled workers, the company employed primarily native-born Americans, immigrant British, and immigrant German workers—or native Anglophones and individuals from the longest entrenched group that was consistently evaluated as most in sympathy with American culture. And for the bottom level of unskilled employment, Ford utilized Americans, Germans, and Austrians for the better-paying machine work and Russians, Poles, Croats, Hungarians, and Italians for the lowest-paying positions as press operators, grinders, and laborers.[86] In the racialized environment, of course, one group came even lower in the hierarchy of American labor than did immigrants from southeast Europe. Mason thus tells of a plant that "has been forced to employ Negroes because of the scarcity in Detroit of white workmen who speak English."[87]

HISTORY, HERITAGE, AND NOSTALGIA

A commanding, transformative figure in the history of the United States, Henry Ford was also a mass of contradictions. He was a self-made man who carried his own well-thumbed copy of Emerson's "Self-Reliance" and who made genuine efforts to help others follow his path, all the while regarding it as "self-evident that a majority of the people in the world are not mentally—even if they are physically—capable of making a good living."[88] He employed and educated thousands of immigrants, provided them (through his profit-sharing plan) with substantial, steady incomes, and demonstrated an ongoing commitment to furthering opportunities for women and the disabled. But he did so in discriminatory ways, advocating an anti-Semitism so virulent that in 1938 he received the Grand Cross of the German Eagle, Nazi Germany's highest award for a non-German. The product of rural America and Yankee ingenuity, Ford became the very image of the modernism and efficiency that he fostered in the assembly lines and that opened up something like a middle-class lifestyle to millions previously living in abject poverty. All the labor-saving devices of the modern world could well be considered the heirs of Ford's imagination. At the same time, particularly in the years after the Ford English School flourished, he cultivated nostalgia for the rural America that his industrial efforts had helped destroy. It was his wealth and technical know-how that allowed him to imagine and construct both Greenfield Village and Fordlandia—the former an outdoor museum near Detroit where Ford brought everything from the bicycle shop where the Wright brothers built their plane, to the house where William McGuffey was born, to Noah Webster's homestead, to replicas of Thomas Edison's workshop and the school house where Ford had studied as a boy; the latter a self-sufficient town carved into the middle of the Amazon rain forest where Ford hoped to cultivate his own rubber for tires, alongside the clean and orderly lifestyle that he understood to lie at the heart of the United States. And if it was only Ford who had the wherewithal for such undertakings, it was likewise only Ford who had the sentimentality and selective vision that provided inspiration for such grand and, in the case of Fordlandia, ultimately failed endeavors. No one else had the means to create what no one else had the nostalgia to imagine.[89]

The industrial definition of English cultivated by the Ford school and other industrial schools manifests these same contradictions. Grammatically, the language was nostalgically rooted in the regularity and standard ideology of McGuffey and Webster but conceptually in the modernist pragmatism of Roberts and Cody. English was to be the language that united all Americans, immigrants and the long-established, even as structural differences among users and usages identified various groups by ethnicity, job, and level of education. If the Ford company distinguished itself simply by its willingness to educate immigrants whom many regarded as genetically inferior and irredeemable, the education it provided reinforced a sense of the workers' inferiority. The vehicle of Americanism and liberation, English was also the means for maintaining hierarchies of employment and social opportunity.

Ultimately, in fact, the language in this definition only obscures the influence of the issues like race and ethnicity that it promised to transcend. Part of the ultimate lesson both at the Ford school and in Sherwin Cody's book was that if workers learned English and nonetheless failed to advance, their failures owed to their incompetence in English, which they therefore needed to study all the harder, and not to issues of prejudice or even job availability that were beyond their control. Like the Sociological Department in its treatment of lifestyle and, indeed, the assembly line in its production of cars, the Ford English School homogenized the teaching of English, applying the one-size-fits-all attitude that lay at the root of Henry Ford's industrial vision. Also like the Department and the assembly line, the Ford school reproduced, whether incidentally or intentionally, the very distinctions that it aspired to eliminate. Undermining the shop mentality that prevailed in nineteenth-century American production, the assembly line offered an industrial model in which unskilled workers were interchangeable, expendable, and clearly demarcated from the skilled ones, who were themselves demarcated from the office staff. And through the efforts of the Sociological Department, southeast European immigrants tended to obtain not clerical jobs but manual labor ones, to which their command of English was well suited.

Although Greenfield Village did not open until 1933, Ford first began to conceive the project in 1919, when he won a libel suit against the *Chicago Tribune* for calling him an anarchist. It was then that he decided to reconstruct a vision of America prior to the advent of his own modernism, something so historically accurate that it could not be considered bunk.[90] One irony, therefore, is that bunk might be the very word many would use today to describe the hodgepodge of sanitized, improbable juxtapositions and restorations that make up Ford's village—a material history more real for him than the written versions that he found so unreliable. Another would be that in English education as well as national history, the bunk of self-interested interpretations—heritage, we might call it—was perhaps the only thing that Ford could perpetuate. The implication of criticism like Bullokar's, Johnson's, Webster's, and Chomsky's, indeed, is that the genius of English exists only within such interpretations, which become as much a part of the alleged grammatical abstraction that grammarians see, as Ford's sentimentality became a part of the material history in Green-field Village. And a third irony would be that the particular bunk of the English School had a very long history of its own. Far from originating with Ford's efforts, the definition of English as a language consisting of differing and sometimes inadequate versions that inherently mark the qualities and potential of the speakers who use them recalls the definition of English in Indian boarding schools, in the common schools in general, and in fact in the earliest formal analyses of English, its history, non-stand-ard language, lexicon, and the connections between language and social standing. Once English became the vehicle for non-linguistic issues—a cipher, as I have called it—there seems to have been no limit to the issues it could carry, whether of race, economics, ethnicity, nationality, gender, or intelligence.

And so by the time the Ford school drew its last graduate from its melting pot, one answer to the question 'What is English?' would be, 'The means and measure of a number of categorical distinctions, including civilized / barbarous, civic / anarchic, capitalist / communist, and patriotic / traitorous'. And these are on top of inherited distinctions like educated / illiterate, noble / rustic, male /female. Given the malleability of the mean-ings of English, in turn, these kinds of distinction could be extended to include native / foreign and Anglophonic / indigen-ous. To speak English is to be on one side of a divide. Not to speak it, or just as importantly to be judged not to speak it, is to be on the other. In this way, English functions as far more than simply a linguistic code or communicative medium. For soci-eties that consider themselves Anglophone, English becomes as well an ordering principle that is and can be implicated in any number of social issues. And this is yet another reason why we care what English is.

CHAPTER ELEVEN

The English-speaking Peoples

If World War One was the Great War, the war to end all wars, World War Two was that and then some. Everything about the challenging events of 1939–45—their geographic scope, the number of people and nations involved, the loss of lives, the armaments, the horror of the Holocaust—was unprecedented and would have been difficult to imagine before they occurred. Even the name of these events presented a challenge. At the time, British government offices in Whitehall preferred simply 'the War', an expression that was (and remains) widely used in the United States as well. If in the abstract 'the War' seems vague (almost inviting the response, 'Which war?'), the immediacy of current events would have eliminated any vagueness. As an abstraction, further, 'the War' refrained from drawing a parallel with what had occurred between 1914 and 1918. In fact, already in 1941, prior to the formal military involvement of the United States, President Franklin Roosevelt did just this. What Britain had called the 'Great War', the United States had called the 'World War' and Germany the equivalent *Weltkrieg*, and so Roosevelt by extension began to refer to 'World War Two', perhaps in part to prod his country from its isolationism. By 1947, Winston Churchill had adopted 'Second World War', and others across the globe quickly followed suit.[1]

This war truly was a world war, with participants from each of the six permanently inhabited continents and with battles fought across the globe. But the crux of the conflict was a struggle between the Axis (Germany, Italy, and Japan) and the Allied powers (the United Kingdom, the United States, and the Soviet Union). Described (and simplified) in this way, World

War Two also became a struggle in which distinctions could be drawn among the combatants based on whether or not they spoke English, and this is precisely what the Allies in particular did. Their side was, many said, that of the English-speaking peoples.

To define English in support of its military effort, the Allies treated the language as the embodiment of virtue, social identity, justice, and political loyalty. English became nearly synonymous with their cause, although as in every grammatical and pragmatic context I have considered, this definition was above all an argument, functioning almost despite the evidence of speakers and usage. Not all the English-speaking peoples spoke English, while some of their enemies did. Further, in this wartime arena definitions of English required the suppression of sociolinguistic tensions that had been building since English left England. Indeed, two long-flowing currents were about to intensify and redirect the river of English still more: truly global extension of the language, and a population of second-language speakers vastly greater than that of the first-language ones living in the historical English homelands.

These are the concerns of this chapter: the pragmatic definitions of English that underwrote military, political, and cultural practices during World War Two. How, I ask, did the concept of the English-speaking peoples extend prevailing grammatical traditions and pragmatic practices for defining the language? How, whether in formal domains like military orders or informal ones like radio broadcasts, did the concept define the language as well as the combatants and their heritage? Simply put, what did English do in the War?

IT WAS THE LANGUAGE'S FINEST HOUR

Framing the Allied effort as simply English-speaking represents the culmination of a long sociolinguistic tradition that, at least early on, scarcely seemed to be pointing in this direction. North American colonists of varying social backgrounds utilized variations in English as a way of drawing distinctions among themselves, and between themselves and Native Americans. And no sooner had the language achieved a secure foothold in the western hemisphere (in the period just after the conclusion of Chapter Seven) than Anglophones began to emphasize the differences and deficiencies of colonial English in general as opposed to the variety spoken in Great Britain. Of a book he reviewed in 1756, one year after his *Dictionary*'s publication, Dr Johnson observed, "This treatise is written with such elegance as the subject admits, tho' not without some mixture of the American dialect, a tract [i.e., trace] of corruption to which every language widely diffused must always be exposed."[2] Later in the century, according to an American visitor to England, British speakers regarded North American English as "a colonial dialect, with a corrupt and barbarous pronunciation, and a vocabulary, interspersed with strange and unknown terms of transatlantic manufacture."[3]

Already in the nineteenth century, the status of colonial Englishes, particularly American English, began to improve. They and their speakers (or at least some of them) became, if certainly not the superiors of British English, then partners in a Greater Britain, united by language and culture against the rest of the world. The suspicion and distrust between Americans and Britons that date to colonial days continued, but it was joined by a grudging recognition of shared interest and identity. "America is becoming," commented Charles Dilke in a lengthy and widely read 1868 book on his travels to English-speaking countries, "not English merely, but world-embracing in the variety of its type; and, as the English element has given language and history to that land, America offers the English race the moral director-ship of the globe, by ruling mankind through Saxon institu-tions and the English language. Through America, England is speaking to the world."[4] Or, in the words of a late-Victorian music hall song, "It's the English-Speaking Race against the World."[5]

If such views foreshadow the Anglophone confederation that would define Allied efforts in the Second World War, they also embody a certain amount of ambivalence about this union. The concept of Greater Britain (the title of Dilke's book) may identify a community of English-speaking peoples, but it also identifies the United States and Great Britain—and ultimately England—as the first among equals. This same ambivalence governed the Society for Pure English, founded in Oxford in 1913 and arising from two competing beliefs: one, that the global spread of English was laudable, and, two, that new speakers were squandering the integrity and quality of the language.[6] And it governed the creation of the English-Speaking Union in 1918. Now with nearly 100 branches distributed almost equally throughout the United Kingdom and around the world, the Union was founded to promote debate, public speaking, and student exchange among the English-speaking peoples. It also offers scholarships and sponsors seminars involving a host of high-profile individuals that focus directly on current events and indirectly on the use of the English language. But while the Union's focus is expressly global, its point of reference is just as expressly the United Kingdom, where it is registered as a charity. According to the Union's website, "Our vision is to provide people in the UK and internationally with communication skills, confidence and networking opportunities."[7] Prince Philip, Duke of Edinburgh, has been president since 1952. In 1921, the chairman was Churchill.

It was of course Churchill who made the phrase 'English-speaking peoples' famous, although others used it before him, including contemporary Conservative statesmen Arthur Balfour, Robert Gascoyne-Cecil (the Marquess of Salisbury), and Stanley Baldwin, who twice served as an enormously popular Prime Minister before the War. Baldwin in particular liked to evoke English as the crucial, moral determinant of the British people—as the continuity among the rural and ancestral traditions that promoted a sense of national heritage and unity. Extending eighteenth-century traditions that had forged British identity, Baldwin understood England to be as much a national character trait as a geographic and political place, and so anything that was immoral, unethical, or unpatriotic was perforce un-English: "Underlying everything in the English-speaking peoples there has been . . . that belief in God and in the responsibility not only of the individual, but of the nations, for his actions and their action on earth."[8] To speak English was not merely to follow grammatical rules but to be dutiful, industrious, respectful, and devout. It was a large part of what made Great Britain exceptional.

But Churchill remains the one who, inimitably, rendered the concept of the English-speaking peoples as both a rapier and a bludgeon. He seems to have been so dedicated to the exceptionality of English that he even insisted on saying 'Nazi' not like a German but like an Englishman. As Christopher Ricks imaginatively recalled, one of "the reasons why the British won the war against Nazi Germany... was Churchill's refusal to pronounce the word *Nazi* as the Nazis might have wished and as weaklings and quislings did. 'Nar-zee', he growled, and crouched around the radio we felt better at once. Not only did 'Nar-zees' sound more sleasily nasty, but we took them over, we did not acquiesce, we anglicized. No pronunciation could have been less welcoming."[9]

As early as 1898, in a letter to his mother, Churchill wrote that, "One of the principles of my politics will always be to promote good understanding between the English-speaking communities."[10] In a 1911 pamphlet on Irish home rule, he identified the English-speaking peoples as one of "the four consolidations of the human family," the others being "the Russian power, the Yellow races, [and] the Teutonic alliance."[11] While not at all unique to Churchill, this collapse of language, race, nationality, and (in fact) morality into a single category would prove to be a hallmark of the role of 'the English-speaking peoples' in the Second World War. Indeed, even in a 1917 speech, before the Great War had ended, Churchill averred that the "comradeship and reconciliation" of Great Britain, the United States, Australia, and New Zealand (Kachru's Inner Circle again) would make "the mainstay of the future world when the war is over."[12] In 1932, he gave a United States lecture tour entitled "The Pathway of the English-Speaking Peoples," in which the primary threat to any American-British alliance was said to be Bolshevism, and this was a year after he had engaged in perhaps his most imaginative use of the concept—a speculative essay on what might have happened if General Robert E. Lee had won the Battle of Gettysburg and (therefore) if the South had prevailed in the United States Civil War.[13]

Had Lee been victorious, Churchill speculates, slavery would have ended (though without the "idiotic assertion of racial equality"), the turmoil of reconstruction would have been avoided, and the South would have seceded successfully as an independent nation. Spurred on by the 1905 Russo-Japanese conflict, Great Britain (led by Balfour), the North (led by Teddy Roosevelt), and the South (led by Woodrow Wilson) would have signed the "Covenant of the English-speaking Association," with the result that "henceforward the peoples of the British Empire and of what were happily called in the language of the time 'The Re-United States', deemed themselves to be members of one body and inheritors of one estate." The English-speaking Association would have found a peaceful way to prevent the Great War, avert the worldwide economic downturn of the 1920s, and inspire in-progress attempts to create a United States of Europe.

Churchill's most extensive pre-war use of the English-speaking peoples as a moral and political concept appears in this four-volume *History of the English-Speaking Peoples*. The book was largely finished in 1939, but the next year, following the Nazis' seizure of Norway and just prior to their invasion of France, Neville Chamberlain resigned and Churchill was asked to become the Prime Minister of a coalition government. He laid aside his *History* for the position for which he saw his entire life as preparation, and again later, first to write an even longer history of the Second World War and then once more to serve as Prime Minister from 1951 until 1955. It was only then that Churchill returned to the *History of the English-Speaking Peoples*, whose first volume appeared in 1956.

Like any historian, Churchill inevitably selected and described events as reflections of his own critical interpretations—"re-enacting for himself," as R. G. Collingwood said of historians in general, "so much of the experience of the men who took part in them as he wishes to understand."[14] Accordingly, Churchill's history has blind spots, perhaps the biggest of which is the title of the book itself. For Churchill 'English-speaking peoples' serves as an unexamined concept, as the constant that he can take for granted and thereby use to anchor his historical discussion. Whose history will he re-enact for himself? The history of the English-speaking peoples. As for who they are or what English is, Churchill has little to say. In fact, he addresses the issue head-on only once, in the Preface. There he states: "I use the term 'English-speaking peoples' because there is no other that applies both to the inhabitants of the British Isles and to those independent nations who derive their beginnings, their speech, and many of their institutions from England, and who now preserve, nourish, and develop them in their own ways."[15]

There's sleight of hand here, of course. While Churchill defines what seems to be a stable linguistic concept, he does so largely through non-linguistic criteria. Anglophones are not simply those who speak English but those whose culture can be said to originate in England and who now work to maintain that same link. In practice, this means England proper, since he writes about the rest of the United Kingdom only as it relates to England. And it means the United States, with which he was already (in the late 1930s) cultivating a special relationship in the hope that it would join as an ally in the war Churchill felt to be inevitable. Perhaps a third of the final volume is devoted to "The Great Republic," and most of this concerns the American Civil War, which Churchill, I think with an uneasy eye towards Nazi Germany, describes as "the noblest and least avoidable of all the great mass-conflicts of which till then there was record."[16] Other areas of the Commonwealth figure only in accounts of British imperial expansion—in chapters entitled "The Indian Empire" or "The Migration of the Peoples II: Australia and New Zealand." And of what we would today call second-language learners, the millions of English-speaking peoples in Asia, Africa, South America, and Europe, Churchill has virtually nothing at all to say.[17]

Churchill's treatment of 'English-speaking peoples' had strong statistical support, even if he didn't say as much. In 1939, when he finished the bulk of the book, British and American speakers accounted for over half of the total number of Anglophones in the world, while the economic and cultural status of these two nations in the War years made the preservation of their beginnings and institutions, along with their speech, an acknowledged and pursued goal in many global regions. In 1939, indeed, Canada, Australia, and New Zealand all retained formal political ties with Great Britain. Many colonial regions—including India, Nigeria, Zimbabwe (formerly Rhodesia), and much of the West Indies—had not yet achieved any degree of independence. It's not surprising, then, that of the 13,000 identified pieces of English linguistic criticism published prior to 1922, only 28 can be considered 'Colonial English'.[18] Numerically and conceptually, much of Churchill's thinking would have made good sense to many of those who were English-speaking peoples, as well as, probably, to many of those who were not.

In this context, it also makes good sense that Churchill should state the following as his "theme" for the first volume of his *The Second World War*, published between 1948 and 1953: "How the English-speaking peoples through their unwisdom, carelessness, and good nature allowed the wicked to rearm."[19] It is a theme to which he returned time and again throughout the War, using the English-speaking peoples as a leitmotif to drive home the virtue and presumed commonality of the Allies' endeavors. In a 1939 radio broadcast, for example, he maintained that the Anglophonic core of the Empire shared the enthusiasm and means to prevail over Nazi Germany: "We have the freely-given ardent support of the twenty millions of British citizens in the self-governing Dominions of Canada, Australia, New Zealand and South Africa."[20] Some 11 months later, in his stirring speech after the evacuation at Dunkirk, Churchill went beyond vowing to fight the enemy on the beaches to asserting the shared sympathies natural to Anglophones—including those in the United States—that would lead them to rally and deliver Great Britain: "And even if, which I do not for a moment believe, this island or a large part of it were subjugated and starving, then our Empire beyond the seas, armed and guarded by the British Fleet, would carry on the struggle, until in God's good time, the New World, with all it power and might, steps forth to the rescue and the liberation of the Old."[21] After France fell a few weeks later, Churchill insisted that he had heard from all the dominions and that all "declare themselves ready to share our fortunes and to persevere to the end." Speaking after the death of Neville Chamberlain still later in 1940, Churchill asserts that "no future generation of the English-speaking folks ... will doubt that" the British wanted to avoid bloodshed. These future Anglophones alone are "the tribunal to which we appeal," so that English unites not only the Allies among themselves but the Allies with their partners after the War. Six months later, before quoting from Arthur Hugh Clough's "Say But the Struggle Naught Availeth," Churchill again links present with future Anglophones and both to liberty, saying that Clough's lines "seem apt and appropriate to our fortunes tonight, and I believe they will be so judged whenever the English language is spoken or the flag of freedom flies."[22] Even once the United States had entered the War and Churchill no longer needed to appeal to the presumption of shared fellow-feeling based on language, he continued to invoke the English-speaking peoples, as in a 1943 speech at Harvard. There he advanced the cause of a special relationship between Britain and the United States by citing law, language, literature, morality, justice, and personal freedom: "These are common conceptions on both sides of the ocean among the English-speaking peoples. We hold to these conceptions as strongly as you do."[23]

And while the War itself was perhaps the finest hour for Churchill's concept, the idea of the English-speaking peoples continued to resonate afterwards for him and for others. Indeed, it was by asserting the importance of the English-speaking peoples as allies in the Cold War that Churchill found purpose for his own, personal post-War experience and his eventual return as Prime Minister. It was this view of a language-based morality and commonality to which Churchill appealed in his 1946 speech at Westminster College in Fulton, Missouri, the one in which he popularized the phrase 'Iron Curtain': "It is necessary that constancy of mind, persistency of purpose and the grand simplicity of decision shall guide and rule the conduct of the English-speaking peoples in peace as they did in war." In turn, these peoples will provide the leadership essential to the formation of a peaceful post-War world: "Neither the sure prevention of war, nor the continuous rise of world organization will be gained without what I have called the fraternal association of the English-speaking peoples. This means a special relationship between the British Commonwealth and Empire and the United States."[24] Later, as he contemplated the 1954 speech he would give upon leaving office and public life for good, Churchill returned yet again to the language-based union of the United States, the United Kingdom, and the former dominions. In a letter to Dwight Eisenhower (then President) he expressed skepticism that colonial regions were ready for their own democracy and self-government: "The British and American Democracies were slowly and painfully forged and even they are not perfect yet. I shall certainly have to choose another topic for my swan song. I think I will stick to the old one: 'The Unity of the English-speaking peoples'. With that all will work out well."[25]

Partly because Churchill so strongly and eloquently professed the commonality of Anglophones, the phrase 'English-speaking peoples' resonates with a kind of moral imperative that by necessity underwrites the conflict with the Axis. Britain, for Churchill, was not simply at war; it was fighting for the survival of civilization. From his very first speech as Prime Minister, in fact, he frames the cause of the English-speaking peoples in this way. Great Britain's policy, he noted, would be "to wage war against a monstrous tyranny, never surpassed in the dark, lamentable catalogue of human crime." Just a few days later, in his first speech as Prime Minister to the House of Commons, Churchill emphasized that without victory, there would be no survival: "Let that be realised; no survival for the British Empire, no survival for all that the British Empire has stood for, no survival for the urge and impulse of the ages, that mankind will forward towards its goal."[26] When he spoke on June 18, 1940, following the fall of France and in anticipation of Nazi invasion, Churchill brought together both the communal and moral aspects of his theme. "Upon this battle," he observes in imagining the Battle of Britain, "depends the survival of Christian civilization. Upon it depends our own British life, and the long continuity of our institutions and our Empire." The survival of Christian civilization depends, then, on the English-speaking peoples, and yet again looking to the future, Churchill not only sees continuity with this group but hears what it has to say: "Let us therefore brace ourselves to our duties and so bear ourselves that, if the British Empire and its Commonwealth last for a thousand years, men will still say, 'This was their finest hour.'"[27]

There's no doubt that the English-speaking peoples could be an ennobling concept for Churchill and others as they sought to hold together the Allied confederacy and champion the moral righteousness of war against an enemy that, initially, seemed invincible. At the outbreak of aggression in 1939, then-Prime Minister Chamberlain himself had imagined the War as between not so much nations but primeval forces of right and wrong: "It is evil things that we shall be fighting against: brute force, bad faith, injustice, oppression and persecution."[28] In his Order of the Day to the Allied Expeditionary Force landing in Normandy on June 6, 1944, similarly, Eisenhower, the Allies' Supreme Commander, invoked imagery of the conflict understood to be the archetype of all struggles between the Christian and pagan worlds: "You are about to embark upon the Great Crusade, toward which we have striven for many months."[29]

But there likewise can be little doubt that the 'English-speaking peoples' served as a vehicle for assumptions and beliefs that we today might call jingoistic and even racist. While Churchill referred generally to the Empire, it was the dominions, not the colonies, that most exercised his imagination, that supplied reinforcements to the Allied armies, and that (all things considered) had the most to gain by an Allied victory. Indeed, although he once claimed that Britain had "the heart and moral conviction of India on our side,"[30] even during the War he devoted a great deal of political effort to resisting independence for the colonies and other territories, particularly India. For his part, Jawaharlal Nehru (India's first Prime Minister) always saw the War as a confrontation among competing imperialist powers.

Churchill's personal views on Empire, which in any case are far more nuanced than is often granted, are not here my concern. Nor is the fact that to some observers during the War, and to many afterwards, Churchill's belief in a special relationship with the United States and in an inherent bond among nations of the Commonwealth was misguided and even self-destructive. Churchill's rhetoric, some have argued, obscured obvious cultural differences and in effect rendered post-War Britain subservient to the United States.[31]

Rather, I want to emphasize once more how definitions of English come about in specific arenas, how they can obscure the inconsistencies of their formation, and how powerful they can be, even when they only partially reflect the demographics of uses and users. Despite the global scope and democratizing rhetoric of the Second World War, Churchill's 'English-speaking peoples' had the effect of further identifying English with Kachru's Inner Circle in general and with England in particular. And in this identification the concept emphasized a moral trait rooted in the English language. It is no coincidence that Churchill saw the King James Bible as "a splendid and lasting monument...to the genius of the English-speaking peoples."[32] What is English? English is a language anchored in history and geography, and expressing the word of God, morality, cultural unity, and resistance to evil, each of these a very good reason indeed to care about the language's definition.

GERMANY CALLING

As tidy, useful, and even powerful a concept as the English-speaking peoples could be, it did indeed obscure the inconsistencies of its formation. While it is true that most of the Axis combatants spoke German, Italian, and Japanese, some spoke other languages, including English. As a vehicle for the ambitious Nazi Ministry for Propaganda, the radio in particular became a vehicle for Anglophones to disseminate Axis propaganda that was heard by civilians as well as soldiers around the world. Diverse by nationality and degree of participation, Axis broadcasters differed as well in their motivation. Some used their English to advance anti-Semitism, others to resist Communism, others to advance (so they believed) their own patriotism, and still others merely to cooperate and stay alive. They were alike in the popular and sometimes formal perception among the Allies that their activities qualified as traitorous, with the result that after the War many were tried, some convicted, and some even executed.

They were also alike in the indirect but unavoidable implications of their speech. Once Radio Normandie and Radio Luxembourg ceased broadcasting in English in 1939, the English heard around the world was mostly that of the American Forces Network or the BBC. The latter in particular, especially in the accent known as BBC English, often assumes a kind of mythical status as the voice of the Allies' war effort. At the very least, with the guidance of the Ministry of Information, the BBC disseminated news and entertainment and, along with the British Council, played a critical role in introducing the language and its speakers' values into non-English environments abroad.[33] Listeners picking up BBC broadcasts in Asia or Africa might not know precisely what was being said, but they would know that the language was English, that the BBC version was the accent of English, and that English was a language heard everywhere, even in places where it was not understood. By broadcasting on the very medium that Churchill used so effectively to champion the English-speaking peoples and in the same language he claimed formed their unity and identity, Anglophones in the service of the Axis offered a direct challenge not only to the presumptive status of the BBC but to the stability and validity of prevailing definitions of English.

At one end of the Anglophone Axis-sympathy spectrum may have been the novelist P. G. Wodehouse, who was arrested and interned in France from 1940 to 1941. There, the creator of Bertie Wooster, perhaps the embodiment of a conventional English-speaking person, wrote and broadcast several humorous pieces about his life as an internee. Since he did so with the cooperation of his guards, the broadcasts were perceived as pro-Nazi, though their substance would not seem to support such a charge and in fact accusations that Wodehouse was a traitor were never proved. At the other end was a host of clearly pro-Nazi broadcasters, born variously in Germany, Britain, and the United States. Constance Drexel, for instance, emigrated to the United States as a child and became a naturalized citizen, as did Max Otto Koischwitz. Both returned to Germany for the War. Frederick Kaltenbach, Edward Delaney, Jane Anderson (the 'Georgia Peach'), Robert Best, Douglas Chandler, and Donald Day were all born in the United States. Among the best-known of this group of periodic broadcasters was the American Mildred Gillars. Known as Axis Sally, she transmitted pro-Nazi propaganda from Berlin, where she was arrested in 1946. Tried and convicted of treason, Gillars was imprisoned until 1961.[34] Perhaps even more disruptive to the notion that English was synonymous with the Allies, effort were Ezra Pound, who made pro-Axis broadcasts from Rome throughout the early part of the War, and George Bernard Shaw. While he never broadcast from Germany, Shaw did produce, before and during the War, a series of articles and talks in support of Germany, where he was quoted and regarded as a friend of Nazi propaganda.[35] And more disruptive still may have been the Duke of Windsor, who, at the outbreak of war, urged appeasement in a radio broadcast carried on American but not British radio.[36]

The news, music, and drama of one broadcaster might be indistinguishable from that of another. But the important fact is that throughout the War, Axis use of English was frequent and diverse. Turning on their radios, the English-speaking peoples might get Churchill talking about toil and duty, but they might also get Day ranting against the Soviets or Koischwitz championing the order and virtue of the Third Reich. They might even get the parodic jazz songs of Charlie and His Orchestra, which reworded "Stormy Weather" for Churchill in a broadcast during the Battle of Britain:

> Don't' know why
> I cannot blockade the sky.
> Stormy weather,
> Since my ships and the German planes got together
> I'm beaten every time.[37]

As prominent as radio was in the United Kingdom and the United States, much of the English-speaking audience would have known that its language served both sides of the conflict. Perhaps because it cared about the definition of English, the same audience helped keep alive, however unintentionally, what it regarded as the language's perversion by the Axis Anglophones to whom it listened. In this regard, I now want to focus on two of the English-speaking Axis voices: William Joyce and Iva Toguri.

While he always claimed to be British citizen, Joyce was in fact born to Irish parents in the United States. He emigrated to Ireland as a child and eventually pursued a post-graduate degree in London, where he came under the influence of Sir Oswald Mosley, founder of the British Union of Fascists. Joyce visited Germany in 1939 and was prevented from leaving by the outbreak of war. He began broadcasting on behalf of Germany already in September of 1939 and by the following spring had achieved the nickname 'Lord Haw Haw', a name that was meant to mock his presumptively aristocratic accent and initially was applied to another pro-German British broadcaster.

From then until the end of the War in Europe, Joyce used his program, known as "Germany Calling" from his call sign, to broadcast a steady stream of mostly lies and invective directed at Jews, Communists, the British press, international capitalism, and major Allied figures. While Joyce displayed genuine sympathy for Nazism, he always insisted that it was patriotism for Britain that had driven him to the Nazis. The British, he believed, had reneged on their ideals—the principles that would in fact have made them English-speaking—and the only way to recover them was through the guidance of the Reich. Joyce thus took terrific pride in his efforts, and in the spring of 1941 even announced on-air that he and Lord Haw Haw were one and the same. Captured at war's end, Joyce was imprisoned and tried as a traitor in England. There the fact that he was not an English citizen (despite his lies) presented difficult but not insurmountable problems for the prosecution, with the result that he was executed in January of 1946.

As offensive as Joyce's broadcasts may have been and as much as they challenged the neat contours of the English-speaking peoples, the fact of the matter is that this linguistic and political traitor was to a significant extent the creation of the very audience that tried him for treason. In 1939 and 1940, the Ministry of Information and the BBC shared a concern that the Nazis were winning the propaganda war. Joyce's broadcasts, despite their obvious errors, assumed grave consequence in this war within the War and had to be taken seriously. In the process of demonizing the broadcasts, of course, the Ministry inevitably gave them substance and rendered Joyce a declared threat to Britain, leading to his eventual arrest. Even the name Lord Haw Haw was a creation of the British press, and by collapsing at least three individuals and assigning a British sociolect to him, the press increased this figure's materiality and treachery. Through his reputed aristocratic background, Lord Haw Haw encouraged as well the notion of a People's War, conducted by common people throughout Britain and immortalized in the popular film *Mrs Miniver.* For its part, the listening public engaged in a kind of mass hysteria that attributed to Lord Haw Haw no limit of insider's knowledge on the gravest military initiatives or the smallest details of everyday life, such as the stoppage of local church clocks. Listeners swore to having heard Lord Haw Haw broadcast gossip and information on munitions that, recordings of his shows demonstrate, he never in fact said. He became a subversion of the ideal of the English-speaking peoples that the peoples themselves helped manufacture.[38]

The same can be said of Iva Toguri, better known as Tokyo Rose. Born in the United States to Japanese immigrants, Toguri was visiting a sick relative in Tokyo in 1941 when the United States' declaration of war prevented her from returning home. With American citizenship and a minimal command of Japanese, Toguri by 1943 had become involved with Charles Cousens, an Australian prisoner of war, in the production of radio news and drama aimed largely at American military personnel in the Pacific. Like Cousens and unlike Joyce, she did not reject her country, did not embrace her captors' cause, and did not broadcast anything that can be considered propaganda. She didn't even have a particularly good radio voice, and this was why Cousens had sought her out—to discredit the very programs he was producing.

None of this prevented service personnel, like the British audience of Lord Haw Haw, from fabricating a dangerous, on-air personality. Only one of at least 27 women who broadcast in English on Japanese stations during the War,[39] Toguri made her first broadcast well after the *Chicago Daily News* had identified a voice as that of Tokyo Rose, "the female Lord Haw Haw of the Son of Heaven."[40] As with Lord Haw Haw, listeners collapsed the distinct voices of individual broadcasts into a single individual, for whom they manufactured an identity as treacherous as that of Lord Haw Haw's. Perhaps given the isolation of military personnel in the Pacific and playing off of Hollywood stereotypes of the inscrutable femme fatale of the East, Tokyo Rose assumed a distinctly sexualized persona: a sultry voice that predicted defeat, gloated over victory, and taunted GIs with memories of the girls they left behind. Or that's what GIs swore they heard. But again as with Lord Haw Haw, transcriptions of Toguri's broadcasts, all of which were delivered in her croaky voice, suggest otherwise. Tokyo Rose became a figure as sought after by the American military as Lord Haw Haw was by the British. She, too, became a spectacle after the War, accused and convicted of treason, for which she was imprisoned until 1956. Some 21 years later President Gerald Ford pardoned her.

The simple question 'Was there a Tokyo Rose?' thus proves difficult to answer. On one hand, United States reporters and military personnel used the term, fashioned an identity to go with a voice, credited that voice with specific broadcasts, and invested a great deal of effort in finding someone by that name to arrest and imprison for treason. On the other, the broadcasts credited to Tokyo Rose were given by numerous different women (none of whom styled herself with that name), and they did not contain the words listeners insisted they had heard. In some ways, however, Tokyo Rose the persona may have been more real than Iva Toguri the person. Created by the English-speaking peoples (or at least the American portion of them), Tokyo Rose allowed those peoples to define themselves in ways that maintained a definition of English as the language of the Allies. Tokyo Rose might have spoken English, but she did so in violation of national, political, and sexual propriety. She therefore did so in ways that justified her forced exclusion from the English-speaking peoples, with the result that the peoples maintained their integrity.

Before leaving this topic, I want to say something about the quality of English in Axis broadcasts. If the BBC and Churchill alike defined English as an aristocratic language, acceptance of foreign broadcasters' language as English required a much looser definition. In both Europe and the Pacific, Axis censors had no experience with either colloquial English or the subtleties of regional and social variation. As a result, German scripts could contain lines like the following, broadcast on Christmas Eve of 1939: "I know that what I am going to say may revolt some of you. But, Honest Injun, have you ever tried to rely on clear sober thinking, rather than on sentimental prejudices?"[41] Such stilted language appeared in Toguri's scripts as well, though there perhaps as an intentional subterfuge of their credibility. "Hello, you fighting orphans in the Pacific. How's tricks?" she once asked, sounding rather like Hollywood's version of a hipster. On other occasions she observed, "With the exception of one dead, all on the exchange ship were in the best of spirits," and "Japanese men look furious but they are sweet inside."[42] And even Ezra Pound, in a pro-Mussolini broadcast of 1943, said of Americans: "You have been hugger-muggered and scarum-shouted into a war and you know nothing about it."[43] Not so much ungrammatical as unidiomatic, expressions like these stretch considerably the notion of English as a unified, unvarying code. They are not at all the language that Churchill had in mind when he rooted his own utterances in the King James Bible and declared English the common ground of an inherently virtuous people.

As such, one response to Tokyo Rose might have been simply to exclude her language from the scope of English, just as she was excluded from the English-speaking people. Saying she or Lord Haw Haw just did not speak our language ought to have simplified things by moderating the danger they seemed to present. But the perverse thing is that the English-speaking peoples did the exact opposite. They expressed a strong desire to claim the language of foreign broadcasters as still English in order that the broadcasters then could be excluded from their midst and in the process contribute to a stronger sense of just who the 'we' of the English-speaking peoples were. In the case of Lord Haw Haw, this desire extended to identifying the specific accent of a speaker partly fabricated by his audience. In October of 1939, a BBC monitor said simply, "There's a new announcer on these stations who speaks perfect English, but with a much less ironical tone than the other English announcer." But a month before a columnist in the *Daily Express* had zeroed in on the variety in order to extrapolate the appearance and dress of a pretentious aristocrat: "From his accent and personality I imagine him with a receding chin, a questing nose, thin, yellow hair brushed back, a monocle, a vacant eye, a gardenia in his button-hole. Rather like P. G. Wodehouse's Bertie Wooster." A later writer in the *Times* rejected the accent (if not the physiognomy), using the speaker's phonology as evidence. Lord Haw Haw commits "such solecisms as accenting the second syllable of 'comment'. I shouldn't call it 'public school English.'" Still others contended that Lord Haw Haw's speech placed his origins in northern England, Scotland, Germany, and even Chicago.[44]

This attempt to identify Lord Haw Haw's linguistic provenance in fact proves doubly ironic. To the extent that his listeners' fabricated him, he might indeed have come from any of those locales, as well as many others. The *Daily Express* commentator who coined 'Lord Haw Haw', after all, used it to refer to another broadcaster, Norman Baillie-Stewart. Joyce—an American who was raised working class in Ireland—in fact spoke a kind of English that in the pre-War BBC never would have passed muster as having an authentic upper-class accent. That Baillie-Stewart's supposed accent simply could be reassigned to Joyce suggests just how impressionistic and self-serving the characterization of speakers can be.[45] For the wartime definition of English to prevail, Lord Haw Haw needed to be accepted as a member of the British upper class and his language needed to qualify as the appropriate variety of English. And so that, despite all evidence to the contrary, is precisely what happened.

THE ONLY AUTHENTIC VERSION

In the 'them-us' rhetoric of war, the equation of the Allies with the English-speaking peoples, and the presumption of a moral basis for this equation, had much to commend it as a tactical and propagandistic weapon. Non-Anglophone portions of the Empire—Singapore, Hong Kong, Malaya, Burma—were the first to fall (in 1942) into Axis hands, leaving the English-dominant portions to provide the greatest resistance. And of the European powers it was Great Britain alone that managed to prevent Nazi invasion. Once the United States entered the War, this identification of English with the Allies became even stronger. In announcing the D-Day invasion of June 6, 1944, Eisenhower broadcast the following: "People of Western Europe, a landing was made this morning on the coast of France by troops of the Allied Expeditionary Force."[46] Even if the announcement eventually was translated into French, Dutch, and other languages, it was a declaration of Allied unity initially directed at an audience that for the most part could not be presumed to understand it.

Perhaps reinforced by the fact that Eisenhower seems to have been an English monoglot (as was most of the force he commanded), the presumption that the war effort was in English easily followed.[47]

As defined by knowledge of English, however, both the 'them' and the 'us' of war rhetoric inadequately (even poorly) matched the combatants. I have just argued that 'them' did not exclusively speak German, Japanese, or Italian, but included some Anglophones in ways that challenged the stable, moral concept cultivated by propaganda and governmental policy. Just as misleading is 'us', since it included individuals who either were not English-speaking or whose English (like Joyce's and Toguri's) in its own ways challenged the integrity of the English-speaking peoples.

Foremost of the non-Anglophone Allies, of course, was the Soviet Union, which far and away suffered the greatest number of civilian and combat casualties, and without which an Allied victory would have been much more difficult, perhaps even impossible. Despite the significance of its wartime contribution, however, the Soviet Union always made an awkward ally for the English-speaking peoples. Indeed, in the 1920s and 1930s, much of the West regarded Communism as a graver threat than Nazism. In a 1932 speech, Churchill even identified the "great opposing forces of the future" as "the English-speaking peoples and Communism."[48] When the Soviets invaded Finland and began the Winter War in 1939, the view that the Soviet state was the totalitarian equivalent of Nazi Germany deepened the unease and suspicion of many in Britain, and it was not until June of 1941, when Germany invaded the Soviet Union, that the latter became a peculiar (and temporary) member of the English-speaking peoples.

Always uneasy, the alliance became even more so towards the War's end, when the United States seemed agreed with the Soviet Union against Great Britain on issues like the creation of an additional front (whether it would be in southern France or Italy) and on the post-War administration of Europe. Following the 1943 Tehran conference of the "Big Three" (Churchill, Roosevelt, and Stalin), Roosevelt even hinted that the conference testified to a special relationship between the United States and not Britain but the Soviet Union: "Things of that kind take quite a while to work out with people who are five or six thousand miles away, who don't talk our language, English—and we certainly don't know Russian. And yet we are getting somewhere with them."[49] In late April of 1945, when he wrote to ask Stalin for restraint in the Soviet approach to Poland, Churchill continued to describe the world in terms of the English-speaking peoples, from which he now expressly excluded the Soviets. Churchill took "not much comfort" in a future divided between, on one side, Communists and Communist-dominated countries and, on the other, "those who rally to the English-speaking nations and their associates or Dominions... It is quite obvious that their quarrel would tear the world to pieces."[50]

As vital if overlooked as the Soviets may have been, a host of other non-Anglophones also participated in Allied war efforts in both Europe and the Pacific, whether as formal soldiers or as members of the resistance. Speakers of Norwegian, Danish, Polish, Dutch, Czech, and French thus all contributed significantly throughout the War and particularly during the Normandy campaign. In turning back a German counterattack near Mortain on August 7, 1944, the 123rd wing of the RAF used pilots from Britain, of course, but also Belgium, France, Norway, Poland, Argentina, and even Germany, as well as Canada, Australia, New Zealand, and South Africa.[51] Besides the Polynesians participating in the Pacific, Allied efforts there and (to a lesser extent) in Europe utilized the so-called Code Talkers: Native American speakers of Navaho, Choctaw, Lakota, and Comanche who transmitted intelligence in their own languages, which proved untranslatable to the Axis.

And as much as this multilingual confederacy may have shared a desire to defeat the Axis powers, the notion that it was English-speaking could prove not simply inaccurate but inflammatory. In 1943, a conference on the production and distribution of food for war-occupied areas took place, and the British report on it implies tension among the Anglophone powers as well as between them and the non-Anglophone ones:

There was to be one official language—English. This provoked a characteristic protest from the French, who demanded that French should be adopted, in accordance with precedents, as a second official language. The proposition was turned down by the Conference. It was, however, only the first of a series of clumsy and childish manoeuvres designed to assert the rights of France as a Great Power. These tactics failed in all respects save one: they succeeded in irritating the Americans to the point of frenzy.

The Soviet delegation to the same conference "were a strong and businesslike team, but they were always a doubtful factor because the heads of the delegation spoke no English. They had their own interpreters, but it was never possible for any member of the British delegation who knew our own views and policy to talk directly with the Russians."[52]

A 1944 *List of Publications for Training* gives a sense of just how broadly the English-speaking peoples recognized their alliance to be. Itemizing the phrase books and language guides available to United States personnel, the list mentions Portuguese, Spanish, French, German, Icelandic, Italian, Japanese, Moroccan, Dutch, Norwegian, Swedish, Danish, Hungarian, Turkish, Arabic, Persian, Chinese, Cantonese, Malay, Russian, Bulgarian, Serbo-Croatian, Romanian, Greek, and Albanian.[53] Even the BBC acknowledged the multilingual nature of the English-speaking peoples, continuing to broadcast in Welsh and Gaelic throughout the War; providing air time to émigrés and exiled governments from Holland, Norway, Greece, and France; and, by the end of 1943, transmitting in nearly 50 different non-English languages.[54] In contrast with the pro-Axis English broadcasts of Pound and Shaw, the Nobel Laureate Thomas Mann, from 1940 until the end of the War, produced monthly anti-Nazi addresses in German that the BBC transmitted to Europe. Yet English remained first among equals. On May 8, 1945, when Germany formally surrendered, the Declaration was "drawn up" in English, Russian, French, and German, of which the "English, Russian, and French" versions were "the only authentic texts." Four months later, Japan's formal surrender stated that it was "drawn up in the English language, which is the only authentic version."[55]

Even restricting the 'us' of the English-speaking peoples only to those who in fact spoke English (however broadly defined) points to a group far more sociolinguistically diverse than wartime uses of the concept typically implied. Churchill's rhetoric, for example, evoked a common heritage of fortitude and democracy for all Britons, regardless of class, sex, or locale. And as depicted in wartime propaganda and celebrated in film and song, the common people—and the People's War—displayed the determination and sacrifice that were understood to characterize them and Great Britain in general. Or as the vicar says in a stirring sermon at the end of *Mrs Miniver*, "This is not only a war of soldiers in uniform. It is a war of the people. And it must be fought not only on the battlefields, but in the cities and in the villages, in the factories and on the farms, in the homes, and in the heart of every man, woman, and child who loves freedom. This is the people's war."[56] As in the American industrial schools from earlier in the century, citizenship and linguistic competence depended as much on morality and ethics as it did on birth certificates, and required that what individuals did for themselves they also did for the public at large.

Yet the English-speaking peoples themselves ill-justified the model of commonality implicit in the People's War. While the model imagined a unified, unchanging nation, motivated to cultivate security at home for all, the impact of the War, perhaps necessarily, affected different groups in different ways. Evacuation of poor children from London to the country, for example, faced active resistance from wealthy landowners, the same class that seemed largely able to avoid the conscription of its unmarried women and avoid many of the War's deprivations in goods and services. It was thus not a coincidence that a posh accent was projected onto Lord Haw Haw, though it, too, points to inconsistencies in the definition of English. Some aristocrats (such as the Duke of Windsor) might be credible as Nazi sympathizers, but others, like Churchill, were certainly part of the English-speaking peoples. Prevailing wartime images of quintessential Englishness embodied similar contradictions. Was the ideal English-speaking person a heroic fighter, like those evacuated at Dunkirk, or a civilian like Mrs Miniver, who kept the home fires burning, or (somehow) both?

In transforming the character of the British workforce and its home life, the War itself accentuated these kinds of inconsistencies and contradictions, leading in July of 1945 to the ouster of Churchill and the election of Clement Atlee, the Labour Prime Minister whose government ushered in the radical introduction of the welfare state and with it social security, national insurance, and the National Health Service. One might read this transformation as a rejection of the governmental restraint in economics and social policy that had prevailed since the Victorian era. Or one might read it as so much illusion, masking long-standing imbalances and built on merely the language of equality that the Thatcher 'revolution' exposed.[57] One might even read it as simply an extension of policies put in play during the First World War. But whatever the case, the English-speaking peoples clearly constituted a far more divergent group, in social outlook as well as language, than the 'us' of wartime rhetoric allowed.

By extending the concerns of Great Britain to Greater Britain and imagining the People's War as the Empire's War, the concept of the English-speaking peoples in theory could accommodate citizens of Commonwealth countries as well as the United States. Inasmuch as the model had certain fractures at home, however, it's not surprising to see still more abroad. Indeed, the more geographically and socially removed that wartime Anglophones were from England, the more they diverged as well from the ideal of the English-speaking peoples. By September 6, 1939, all members of the Commonwealth save the Irish Republic—what Churchill later would call "one melancholy exception, round the corner"—had committed their support to Britain.[58] But they did so for reasons other than the allegiance to Poland that officially motivated Great Britain: opposition (variously) to anti-Semitism, Communism, paganism, and Kaiser Wilhelm and the First World War, as well as a sense of loyalty to the Empire. And the War's impact on the Commonwealth further worked against the unity of the English-speaking peoples. Already in the Great War, Australia's and New Zealand's military efforts began to have the perhaps unforeseen results of distancing both countries from Britain, fostering their individual and joint histories, and aligning them more closely with Polynesia than had previously been the case.[59] The Second World War accelerated this realignment: it was only after the War (1947) that

New Zealand ratified the 1931 Statute of Westminster, which formally allowed it self-governance. Australia already had done so in 1942, but with the conclusion of the War it began to encourage emigration from throughout Europe, not just Britain. Put another way, by working on behalf of Churchill's English-speaking peoples but anxious that Britain might not adequately support them against the Japanese, both Antipodean countries further separated themselves from Britain and produced another definition of English in the process.

The disunity of the English-speaking peoples broadly conceived appears with even greater clarity when one turns from the Dominions to what, from the Boer War until World War Two, had been distinguished as colonies: Nigeria, Kenya, Malaya, and so forth. As much as wartime rhetoric cultivated the notion of the Empire's War and of the Empire itself as multinational and multiracial, clear sociolinguistic demarcations ran through the Commonwealth. English-speaking peoples needed to embrace Anglophones from Africa, Ceylon, and so forth if they were to represent themselves as a global, moral power. But as in colonial America and Polynesia, some of the peoples also evidently needed to distinguish themselves from others in ways that sustained racial as well as economic categories. During the War, for instance, the Colonial Office in Africa made concerted efforts to stress the peaceful, beneficial, and collaborative success of the Empire but could not claim (or did not seek to claim) much of a moral high ground vis-à-vis Nazi belief in the Aryan race, since doing so could have challenged the Empire's own racial policies. Hence, drawing on a Conservative Party solution that went back to a similar dilemma during the Boer War, emphasis on commonality through English—even when there wasn't such, much less commonality through civil and social rights—became a less disruptive, socially acceptable way to maintain the useful idea of a Greater Britain.[60] In light of social and political changes around the globe, even this solution had its limits. The inter-war Pan-African Congress, for example, used the colonizers' English as a means to express its opposition to colonialism. And during the War, South Africa, a sovereign state in the British Empire, experienced significant tensions between the English-speaking and Afrikaner populations. A 1942 Cabinet report pointed to still more fractures among the English-speaking peoples by warning that "the relation between Boer and Briton will be as nothing compared with the obstinacy and danger of the problem that will arise when the white people of this country, in the not distant future, are confronted by the effective pressure of the non-European people for their rightful opportunities in the political and the economic spheres."[61]

As the immediate post-War period developed, the traditional ideal of the English-speaking peoples became still harder to maintain in the Commonwealth. Beginning with early modern writers like Verstegan and continuing through the nineteenth-century nationalist reflections of writers like Matthew Arnold and historians like E. A. Freeman, Englishness had been conceived as a stable ethnic category that depended significantly on Teutonic traditions. Contact with French and Francophones affected this ethnicity only from the perspective of an English-dominant absorption of external influences. Through identification of a people and place with a language—"English is the language of England," says Dr Johnson—this same model shaped the responses of comparative philology to change and variation. While English in theory might be spoken by anyone, in practice its speakers were limited to a largely white population resident in Kachru's Inner Circle. But global demographics of Anglophones, shifting already in the sixteenth century, undermined this merger of race with ethnicity. And when Anglophones in India, Pakistan, and Ceylon achieved the same independent status as those in Canada or Australia, they undermined this merger still more. In response, into the 1960s, selective immigration policies throughout the former colonies and dominions attempted (without success) to reassert traditional definitions of the language and its speakers by restricting the movement of Asians and Africans.[62] Even Stalin, upon hearing Churchill yet again invoke the English-speaking peoples in a 1946 speech, claimed that this was a racial theory based on language.[63]

Changes in the Anglophone demographics contributed in other ways to the fracturing of Churchill's ideal. To modern independent nations like Nigeria or India, the speech of the United Kingdom (along with the technology it supports) may remain important, even politically vital, but British institutions do not necessarily hold the foundational role Churchill imagined. In the post-colonial world, indeed, these institutions—literary, economic, cultural—are as likely to elicit outrage and rejection as admiration and emulation. And so having spent much of his career writing in English, the Kenyan writer Ngũgĩ wa Thiong'o eventually decided that the language could not be freed from its colonial associations and wrote a dramatic farewell to it. His countryman, the political writer Alamin Mazrui, has described the "hidden push for English . . . as part of a right wing agenda intended to bring the world nearer to 'the end of history' and to ensure the final victory of capitalism on a global scale." Less confrontationally, Kachru has championed the acceptance of transplanted English varieties, in South Africa or Singapore for example, as structurally defined codes that take their significance and purpose in relation to indigenous cultures. For Kachru, a variety like Indian English seeks to "preserve, nourish, and develop" not British institutions but those of the subcontinent.[64] The constant that Churchill could take for granted—the English-speaking peoples as understood in the Second World War—no longer seems so incontestable, if it ever was.

Perhaps not surprisingly, it was the United States, with whom Churchill claimed the special relationship that was one of the cornerstones of the English-speaking peoples, that presented the most significant challenges to the concept. The entire idea of Empire, while probably only dimly understood, was anathema to a nation that traced its beginning to a rejection of colonial allegiance to Britain. And the result was that British policies in India and other colonies became one of the few continuous sources of American-British tension during the War. The Anglophones of the United States differed from their British counterparts as well in the degree of enthusiasm with which they entered the conflict. Isolated by an ocean as well as by political inclinations, fully three-fourths of the American population in the fall of 1941—well over a year after Churchill had memorably vowed that Britain would never surrender—continued to support the current practice of providing aid but refraining from active military engagement.[65]

The idea that political and moral associations might derive from language also achieved far less traction in the United States than in it did in Britain and the Commonwealth. Both American policy and individual Americans certainly acknowledged a kinship with the British. By the 1941 Lend Lease Act, for instance, the United States supplied Britain with matériel throughout the War, while in a 1954 letter to Churchill on his 80th birthday Eisenhower observed, "We have seen our great Anglo-American partnership grow and flourish, with you as one of the staunch advocates. In the dark times of war, and the anxious ones of uncertain peace, this partnership has sustained us all and given us strength."[66]

But nowhere does the concept of the English-speaking peoples even enter into American policy or what might be called the American imagination, which explicitly used the language (as Chapters Nine and Ten have shown) to unify and structure the country, not fashion a global community. Neither the language itself nor a wider global kinship based on language engaged prominent Americans like Roosevelt, Eisenhower, or General George Marshall. Instruction manuals prepared for United States service personnel do discuss language, but they emphasize only the practical importance of English for stating procedures and saving lives. One such manual states:

Therefore, it is clear that you prospective officers must learn how to explain, both orally and in writing, for the purpose of both understanding and instructing. You are not here concerned with the niceties involved in telling a good story or in describing a beautiful scene that has aroused you emotionally. You are rather concerned with the logical presentation of facts and inferences based on facts in such a direct, concise and clear language that your meaning cannot be misinterpreted.[67]

And while American wartime films certainly stressed the history shared by Britain with the United States, they did not render the English-speaking peoples the topic of a film or a cinematic theme. Popular writers like Ernie Pyle bypassed the issue as well, and others viewed English's variations simply as a source of bemusement.[68] Given a historical background of British antipathy to American speech, followed by the American fostering of its English as a nation-defining feature, it's difficult to see how shared language ever could attain the heritage and significance in the United States that Churchill understood it to have.[69]

Even if we focus solely on linguistic forms rather than on the pragmatic meanings of English, we see the sometimes illusory quality of the English-speaking peoples. And this quality is not something identifiable only in retrospect, since at the time there was a clearly expressed awareness of the diversity of English and the problems this could create. As much as the posh BBC accent defined wartime broadcasting, for instance, the BBC itself made conscious if sporadic attempts to reflect the voices of the People's War by employing a variety of regional and class accents to broadcast features, news, and entertainment, of which "Post-scripts" by the Yorkshireman J. B. Priestley may be the best known.[70] In Australia, where throughout the War Received Pronunciation remained the prestige accent by which some speakers judged the inadequacies of their own variety, the radio program "The Lawsons" nonetheless focused on the issue of a rural family whose Australian accents were encouraged as realistic touches.[71] And a 1944 United States War Department manual for soldiers in the Pacific echoed the earliest views of Polynesian English by accepting it as a version of the language but also by denigrating that version and framing it as poorly learned English:

Although native languages vary widely most natives of the southwest Pacific area are familiar with 'pidgin English', and often, provided it is spoken slowly and distinctly, can understand correct English. Their replies in pidgin are fairly easily understood by anyone familiar with English, although the limited scope of pidgin does not permit involved or technical discussions. In Central America, Spanish is spoken except in rare instances. A working knowledge of this language is easy to acquire.[72]

Like Axis radio broadcasts, Polynesian speech could qualify as English but only in ways that confirmed its marginal status. And English is a language that has correct and incorrect versions and that allows its speakers to comprehend not only these incorrect versions but other languages as well.

As much as Churchill relied on Britain's special relationship with the United States, it's not surprising that he could overlook linguistic difference in order to pronounce the countries (and their languages) as entirely mutually intelligible to one another. When American troops arrived in Tripoli in 1943, he wrote his wife that the unprecedented cooperation and ultimate success of the Allies were rooted in their shared language: "There is no doubt that these high officers, spending practically twelve hours of the day in each other's company, and speaking the same language, have got to know each other in a way never before achieved between Allies."[73] Yet Eisenhower, who as Supreme Allied Commander had a more immediate vantage on wartime communication, took a different view. While he by no means presents language differences as a severe or persistent obstacle, he does note their occurrence. A letter of January 1943 mentions communication difficulties based on differences in conversational style between British and American soldiers. And in a letter from the previous August, wherein Eisenhower discusses differing plans and objectives for Operation Torch (the upcoming British-American invasion of French North Africa), he seems to allude to the potential (and potentially fatal) miscommunication that can arise in such circumstances: "It is clear that differences of opinion as to concepts must be disposed of by definite language in the final directive."[74]

Eisenhower himself fell victim to the problems of indefinite language in an exchange with Field Marshal Bernard Montgomery. In a letter from the fall of 1944, he took Montgomery to task for his open questioning of Allied plans and successes. When Montgomery replied that he'd meant no such thing, Eisenhower apologized, saying he had misread Montgomery's language.[75] It was Eisenhower as well who agreed to a request for linguistic clarifications made, in fact, by Churchill. In a note prior to Operation Husky (the 1943 Allied invasion of Sicily), the Prime Minister had requested that the Allied forces' terminology be regularized thoroughly, with 'aircraft', for instance, used in place of 'aeroplane' and 'airfield' in place of 'aerodrome'. This would be "good English," said Churchill, "and good American."[76]

For its personnel serving abroad, the United States military distributed pamphlets to address the fact that the English-speaking peoples did not all speak the same language. *A Short Guide to New Zealand*, issued in 1943, offers a casual introduction to the culture and lifestyle Americans would encounter and includes a passage on "How They Talk." "As in Australia and Great Britain," it observes, "many words have different meanings or are used differently," and there follows a glossary of basic words and their translations, such as "Cookie—biscuit" and "gas—petrol." A section on "Slanguage" begins by noting, "You won't find New Zealanders taking any back seat when it comes to tossing the lingo around and you may find yourself slow on the uptake until you get hep." The adjoining brief "Glossary of Slang" contains equivalents like "Bloke—man" and "Torch—flashlight."[77]

Far more extensive is the 1943 *British Military Terminology,* which applies a tradition of foreign-language manuals to British English.[78] Intended for officers, who were just then beginning to arrive in numbers in the United Kingdom, the volume has sections on American military terms with their British equivalents, British terms with their American equivalents, RAF terms, general differences between British and American English, and abbreviations. The primary impediments to communication arise, we are told, not from differences in lexicon but from differences in meaning: "British Military Terminology includes a number of words unfamiliar to U.S. troops. However, a more serious difficulty is caused by the fact that British usage includes many words identical with ours but having important differences in meaning; for example, *gallon, ton, battery* do not have the same connotations for U.S. and British officers."[79] Spelling presented fewer complications, though the volume does note variations that dated to the early-nineteenth-century adjustments of Webster: *ll* for *l, re* for *er, our* for *or,* and *s* for *z.*[80]

In phonology, *British Military Terminology* recognizes significant differences, although in documenting them it draws a distinction between intonation and pronunciation that is not at all clear: "There is in general an audible difference between British and American intonation, but there are few actual differences in pronunciation."[81] These "actual differences" are introduced in a way that makes clear that just as English in some generic sense embraces but still stands superior to the pidgin varieties heard in the Pacific, so American English now surpasses the variety from which it historically derived: "Chief of these [differences] are the British slurring of polysyllables and predilection for the broad 'a'." This "broad" *a*, along with the "short" *i* of 'civilization' or 'futile' and a host of miscellaneous words like 'been' and 'clerk' and proper nouns (such as 'Gloucester' and 'Greenwich') are said to account for the main differences in pronunciation.

"Of the several hundred thousand words in the English language," we are further told, "all except a very few have the same meanings in British usage and American usage."[82] There nonetheless follow seven pages of equivalents, categorized by topics like business, clothing, food, motoring, and travel. We thereby learn that an American 'overcoat' is a British 'greatcoat', 'oatmeal' is 'porridge', and a 'construction crew' a 'gang of navvies'. Perhaps the most striking feature of the lists is how poorly they match the usage of any of the English-speaking peoples just 70 years later. It's true enough that in the United States 'elevator' prevails over 'lift', but many if not most American and British speakers would know both terms, and the same is true of 'gas' for 'petrol'. And it seems doubtful that anyone, American or British, has much occasion these days to talk about 'coal/coals', 'radio tube/valve', 'crank/starting handle', or a 'roadster/two-seater'. British speakers might still serve a 'joint' for Sunday dinner, but no American serves a 'roast of meat'. Whether a majority of British Anglophones prefers 'geyser' to 'water heater' seems unlikely, if only because the over-the-sink devices to which the word specifically refers are themselves no longer common.

Another recognition of this same problem—the linguistic differences among the English-speaking peoples—appears in British wartime emphasis on Basic English. Formulated by Charles K. Ogden in his 1930 *Basic English: A General Introduction with Rules and Grammar*, Basic English attempted to stabilize English as a secondary language for technical discourse by reducing its vocabulary to just 850 words. Beginning with the suppositions that a global language was a political necessity (particularly between the two World Wars), that an artificial language like Esperanto was not viable, and that of the natural languages English was the most logical choice, Ogden's goal was not to produce an interlanguage—a creole or pidgin—but to create a simplified version of English that would serve as a lingua franca helping to foster global understanding and forestall military conflict. According to I. A. Richards, Ogden's colleague and champion,

If a language is to be easy to learn we must not only cut its words down to a minimum and regularize its grammar; we must also study very carefully the meanings of every one of its words and decide upon the central, pivotal or key meaning of each one of them. Parallel to the reduction and ordering of its vocabulary, there must be a reduction and ordering of the meanings of the words it recommends.[83]

Basic English, then, arose from recognition that English alone could not guarantee communication among the English-speaking peoples.

Embracing these sentiments, the British War Cabinet formed a committee to survey the value of Basic English as well as of Oxford Progressive English, Essential English, and 1000-Word English—alternative simplified varieties that relied more heavily on ordinary word frequencies. Information was culled from a variety of linguistic experts and from reports by the British Council and the military, and the committee issued its own report in December of 1943. According to the report, "A useful Memorandum was provided by Mr I. J. Pitman, Director of Organisation and Method at the Treasury, stressing the need for some standardization to avoid increasing corruption of the English language by 'backward peoples'."[84] What the committee found was that Basic English had varying success. It was well received in China and parts of India, but in "Africa, Basic had not achieved general popularity, partly on account of a tendency for the natives to consider it an inferior substitute for the full English that they wished to acquire."[85] In support of Basic English, the committee noted that the simplification process resulted in a variety still intelligible to native speakers: "The striking fact about this remarkable performance is that the result is still perfectly adequate English."[86] While the committee felt that Basic English might be excessively artificial and that it in no way challenged genuine English, it also felt that the version could serve as a useful first stage for "the learning of normal or wider English," as an auxiliary language for scientists, and as a medium for the distribution of health information in largely illiterate areas.[87]

In recommending that development of Basic English should be encouraged by diplomatic and commercial interests, the British Council, the Ministry of Information, the Colonial Office, and the BBC (which broadcast lessons and programs in Basic English alongside its various non-English programs), the committee also saw the variety as a way to protect, in effect, the integrity of the English-speaking peoples and their language. The danger of the global spread of English, according to the committee is that,

like Latin on the downfall of the Roman Empire, it may get debased, and that local forms of 'pidgin English' may develop on their own and supplant, or an any rate infect, the present language. A universal standard vocabulary, simple enough to be easily learnt, and naturally linked with normal literary English, would, it is suggested, afford a real protection against this danger.

Basic English might prove useful for scientists and for the distribution of health information, but its fundamental value (in Pitman's words) would be as a means "to avoid [the] increasing corruption of the English language by 'backward peoples.'" Judgments like these recall American authorities' evaluation of Pacific pidgins, popular assessments of the English in Axis broadcasts, and, in fact, early British authorities' opinion of all extraterritorial forms of the language. Like all of these varieties, Basic English would and would not be English. Its cultivation would expand in the most general way the population of the English-speaking peoples, even as it maintained clear sociolinguistic differences among those speakers and impeded any claims that extraterritorial varieties be considered proper English.

MOBILIZING ENGLISH

As imagined communities, nations can depend on rhetorical acts that flatten tensions, discontinuities, and alternative histories in order to champion the views and institutions that are understood to be foundational for them. Nations remember what makes them nations and forget what does not, with the result that nations tend to think of themselves as nurturing (if not always safe) and unchanging places. In the imagined consistency of their history and heritage, nations offer security and a sense of belonging to those who live there.[88] The imagined nation, in turn, embodies imagined individuals, whose characteristics include speech.

And so it was during World War Two, particularly in Britain, definitions of English came to disregard division in order to posit an unreal, if often useful, unity for the English-speaking peoples. Distinguishing Allied from Axis powers in ways that did not match the combatants' language patterns, these definitions also sometimes posited a unified speech community among individuals whose speech it on other occasions qualified as wrong or partial varieties. If the People's War achieved mythic status, so, too, did the unity of English and the success attributed directly to it. Indeed, no sooner had the War ended than formal reports appeared that identified differences in language as among the specific problems arising from a reliance on civilians in the European theater. Or that anchored the success of military planning in English, as did this report from 1945:

It would have been impossible for SHAEF [Supreme Headquarters of the Allied Expeditionary Force] to have functioned as an integrated operational headquarters with the same organization and methods if the other major power had not been an English speaking one. Difficulties in language alone would have rendered it impossible. While long and intimate associations with the British have eliminated confusion and friction in staff procedures, it must be remembered that in the initial stages they existed in pronunciation, custom, terminology, operating methods, organization, staff procedures and basic military policy to an extent now difficult to recall.[89]

English was the means both to victory and to the cooperation necessary for that victory.

If this were only a wartime story, it would have limited interest. But it is more than that, for what happens with the definition of English during the Second World War in many ways foreshadows and prepares for post-War contradictions about the language and its speakers that remain operative today. As Churchill indulged in counterfactuals regarding the Battle of Gettysburg, we might speculate on how the state and character of present-day English would be different if the Nazis, as they planned, had successfully invaded Britain in 1940. Historians might disagree on whether the United States would have seen sufficient provocation to declare war on Germany at that time, or on whether Hitler, with all of western Europe in his power, still would have turned on the Soviet Union the following June. But in either case, with the English homeland under Nazi rule and the Commonwealth cut adrift, it seems difficult to imagine that the language would have emerged from the War still rooted to its British geography and Germanic past, and as well-positioned economically, educationally, and socially to become the global language it is today. The Allies might have won the War anyway, but the fate of English would have been considerably different.

The irony is that while Churchill's English-speaking peoples did prevail, the War has still perhaps proved to be their undoing. Energized by the global spread of English, all the contradictions that were held in check during the War—for that matter, since Cabot landed in Newfoundland—have led to a situation in which not only are English monoglots a minority among the current English-speaking peoples but any sense of Britain as the exclusive historical or sociological determinant of the language has been (or should be) significantly undermined. To be somewhat arch, one might say that by winning the Battle of Britain, the English-speaking peoples lost the war of resistance to the political, social, and economic transformations that have rendered their identity more tenuous than before. If one major result of the Cold War was an expansion of the alliance of the English-speaking peoples, another was a shift of these peoples' gravitational center to the United States, which after the 1945 Yalta conference would not let any Anglo-American special relationship prevent it from determining its own foreign policy.

The "danger" of global English that the Committee on Basic English foresaw has perhaps come to pass: the structure and uses of English are now much changed by the global population that the committee described as "backward." But building on the arguments I have made throughout this book, I would argue that post-war transformations to the definition of English represent nothing subversive. Nor do they constitute any kind of a break with the traditions of the language that go back to the medieval period. The definition of English and its people has always involved pragmatics, and once the river of English flowed out of England, these increasingly have evolved speakers and domains with ever more slender ties to Great Britain or the United States. Indeed, as the post-War gravitational center of English shifted from Britain to the United States, so it is now shifting to a globally dispersed population of second-language learners.

In a phrase as memorable as many of Churchill's own utterances, the correspondent Edward R. Murrow suggested that during the War the Prime Minister had "mobilized the English language and sent it into battle."[90] We may disagree with precisely how this army mobilized. We may disagree with a wartime sense of the moral and intellectual unity and superiority of the English-speaking peoples. But to dismiss such mobilization out of hand is to overlook the means and roles of language definition in any social endeavors; for the fact of the matter is that all definitions of English, not just Churchill's, are identity-driven. Impulses to acknowledge non-standard varieties like Ebonics as suitable for classroom use, or to accept regional varieties like Singaporean English as every bit as English as are Standard British or American English, or (most broadly) to define the 'we' of the English-speaking peoples in ways that include all or only some of the perhaps 1.5 billion people using some form of the language today—all of these share little conceptual common ground with English as it was defined during the War. Pragmatically, in the fact that they define the language discursively as well as grammatically, and link a social heritage to their definitions, they share everything.

PART FOUR

Beyond English

CHAPTER TWELVE

Defining Moments

Histories of English often label the Middle English period, the years from about 1100 to about 1500, as the period of the language's greatest diversity. And in fact prior to the advent of print and Standard English, written forms of the language did vary significantly, from the modern-looking expressions of Chaucer, to the exotic ones of *Sir Gawain and the Green Knight*, to the sometimes almost inscrutable ones of early Middle English works like the *Peterborough Chronicle*. Yet when we ask what English is, none of this diversity compares with what we hear around us today among the world's 1.5 billion Anglophones.

Expressions that earlier generations might have described as broken English or non-standard English or even simply unusual English now appear so regularly in print and speech that they have to be regarded as examples of stable new varieties of the language. The *Times of India* thus writes of an actor who "has been suffering from the pain in his jaw since 2007 while shooting for 'Partner'. It got worse last year following which he decided to undergo a surgery"; Singapore's *Straits Times* relates that "Officers from Jurong Police Division, who were acting on information received, closed in on the three youths and seized loanshark-related paraphernalia, including three bottles of paint and mobile phones containing suspected debtors' records that were found in their possession"; and the *Guardian* of Nigeria tells of an attorney who "has tendered unreserved apology for telling lies and conspiring with his client to discredit the Commissioner of Police," acknowledging to "newsmen that he was constrained to tell the public the truth since his conscience was no longer at peace due to the fictitious petitions he had written against the senior police officer."[1] I completely understand all of these expressions, and none violates any prescriptive grammatical rule that I can find. Yet in one way or another each sounds somehow unnatural to my American ear, even as each also reflects the habits of well-established speech communities.

It is not simply the number of speakers and usages or the prestige of formats like newspapers that establish new varieties of English. Since the 1960s, dictionaries, grammars, and critical discussions have framed extraterritorial varieties with the kinds of codification that in the seventeenth and eighteenth centuries fashioned Standard English alongside notions of regional, non-standard varieties. And so we have dictionaries (hard copy or online) of Jamaican English, South African English, Australian English, New Zealand English, Singaporean English, Chinese English, Nigerian English, Indian English, Japanese English, and Korean English. We have grammars and analyses of the phonology, lexicon, syntax, and morphology for varieties as narrowly circumscribed in geography as the Orkney Islands and the Falklands. And these kinds of works appear with increasing frequency, even insistence. For the years 1990 to 1999, online search engines record 506 linguistics publications with the keyword 'Englishes'; for the years 2000 to 2010, 1,085 entries are listed. Published several times each year since 1985, the journal *World Englishes* is devoted to such issues, featuring articles on (say) Asian varieties of English, pedagogical practices, the multilingual contexts of specific new Englishes, the English of particular areas (e.g., Cameroon or Turkey), English in non-native advertising, and so forth.

One way to approach the question 'What is English?' would be to attempt to synthesize grammatical analyses of new varieties into a comprehensive or presumptively core grammar for English today. I haven't done this, of course, even though we now have enough cross-linguistic data to make confident characterizations of what is and is not grammatically possible.[2] Human languages in general do not seem to be infinitely variable in their structure, for example, and some critics have argued that at least in syntax, all languages are merely variations of the same universal pattern, which itself may be a function of human biology.[3] With rare exceptions, further, certain types of syntactic structures co-occur. A language like English (however defined) thus has verbs that ordinarily precede direct objects and prepositions that ordinarily precede dependent nouns, while a language like Japanese has verbs that follow their objects and prepositions that follow their nouns. A mixed combination—verbs preceding direct objects and dependent nouns preceding prepositions—does not seem grammatically possible. Any speaker who produced the combination would not seem to be speaking English or any language at all.

To get from linguistic generalizations like these to particular languages, again at a purely grammatical level, we can use the 'principles and parameters' approach, which explains that language-specific structures can arise in particular environments but still must be consistent with a universal grammar of human language. For an utterance to qualify as English, then, it must coordinate the placement of verbs and prepositions, and it must pass what's called the cleft structure test, which demonstrates that English sentences consist of constituent parts that function as units. And so 'I heard a two-part invention of Bach' is a well-formed sentence, as is the cleft 'It was a two-part invention of Bach that I heard' but not 'It was a two-part invention that I heard of Bach' because 'the two-part invention of Bach' is (evidently) a constituent structure. If part of a constituent is moved to the front of the sentence after the cleft 'It was', all of it must be. Otherwise, an expression not only will sound odd to any Anglophone ear but will violate what seem to be the syntactic rules that make any English sentence possible.

Above all, then, language is not simply a case of anything goes. There are limits, whether neurological or physiological, to the kinds of grammar that seem humanly possible in general or recognizable as English in particular. For any one language (like English), these elements might be regarded as an abstraction of the language's core grammar—or, as I have said, a synthesis of various grammatical analyses. In linguistics since the early-nineteenth century, an idealized grammar in fact has constituted the essence of any language—the thing whose history the neogrammarians could describe; that Ferdinand de Saussure could name the *langue* of linguistic structure and distinguish from the *parole* of what we say; and that Noam Chomsky could anthropomorphize as the competence of an ideal listener-speaker and designate the primary concern of linguistic theory.[4] And such essentializing dates back before the nineteenth century, of course: we saw it in Dr Johnson and in medieval linkings of English and geography. All such arguments treat language as an autonomous system that operates irrespective of (maybe despite) its speakers and the contexts in which they use it. And in doing so, as I say, they expose universals of language structure.

But in dismissing de Saussure's *parole* as only usage, such arguments also bypass the ways in which lexicon, grammar, the history of a language, and the principles by which we frame all of these are themselves malleable arguments subject to non-linguistic social criteria. They exclude non-structural issues not simply from the language's definition but from the theory of language. They do not allow for the fact, in other words, that performance—how we use and understand English—might be not simply and tautologically what we do with language but itself a fundamental component of typological variation and linguistic integrity.[5]

We see this component particularly well whenever grammatical and pragmatic definitions diverge from another, as they consistently have throughout the language's history. I noted in Chapter Six, for example, that already in the earliest English records of the eighth century there's evidence of regional differences in phonology, morphology, and (to a much lesser extent) lexicon. Since the Anglo-Saxons used only 'English' (actually, in Old English, *Englisc*) to describe the language used in Northumbria, Mercia, Wessex, and Kent, they evidently regarded all these regional forms as varieties of the same language. And this is the linguistic identity that we echo whenever we speak of four distinct regional dialects of one discrete language in one distinct period of the language.

Yet these were not the only Germanic varieties used in Anglo-Saxon England, and they alone did not define what Anglophones understood. From the mid-ninth century Danish and Norwegian Vikings, speaking what's generically labeled Old Norse, settled in the midlands, Northumbria, and Scotland, where they intermarried with Anglo-Saxons and where their language, despite the sociolinguistic divergence of Norse and English ancestors as much as a millennium before, may have functioned as a kind of regional variation in a continuum of dialects. While the Anglo-Saxons document the use of interpreters in many of their dealings with the Continent or the Celtic borderlands, no mention is made of the need for such an interpreter with the Norse, suggesting that none may have in fact been needed. Several literary works (undoubtedly with some poetic license) certainly represent the languages as mutually intelligible if not the same, and others contain English representations of Norse speech that seem to reflect personal knowledge of the Scandinavian language. When projected across the Anglo-Saxon population, such intimate knowledge (along with structural similarities and overlaps between Norse and English) could well explain developments in English's history. It would provide, for instance, a grammatical basis for the terrific influx of Scandinavian words into English in the centuries to come. And conversancy of Norse and English speakers with each others' languages likewise would account for the atrophy of inflectional endings that began already in the tenth century, when these endings would have been non-functional among speakers who otherwise could understand one another by the roots of words alone. The point is that while we may regard Norse and English as distinct languages, and while we have good grammatical reasons for doing so, in Anglo-Saxon England the pragmatic distinctions between them were far more complex and perhaps even tenuous.[6]

From grammatical perspectives in the later Middle Ages, similarly, distinctions between English and French or Latin also are easily drawn. In fact, both of the Romance languages already had their own extensive codification traditions at that time, distinguishing each from the other and also both from English, which had no such traditions. Yet outside of schoolrooms, speakers used not codification but their own sociolinguistic experience to define languages, and because of this, they did not always produce the same definitions. The merchant Sheffield and the goodwife he met at a public house, it will be recalled, disagreed strongly over which words were and were not English. In some arenas, such as fourteenth- and fifteenth-century business records, pragmatic definitions point to an even murkier situation. Rather than promote a social or regional variety of English for their business activity, some late-medieval London merchants developed a language composed of Latin, French, and English elements, as in "Item por jarlandis de rosis por le feste."[7] In this passage, *item* is Latin, *rosis* from Anglo-Saxon, and the remaining words from French, though *jarlandis* and *feste* had both been borrowed into English by the early-four-teenth century. Syntactically, the sentence works well as French or English and well enough as Latin. Is this, then, French with Latin and English borrowings or English with Latin and French ones or Latin with English and French ones? Or would the London merchants have understood it to be still something else, a language in its own right? One thing that is certain is that however grammatically obscure the variety might be, it was widely used and therefore understood.

By the seventeenth century English had its own traditions of codification that used grammatical criteria to mark off (in part) that era from an earlier one and that offered a precedent that later linguistic historians could use to string together a sequence of disconnected structural moments into one language. But from a pragmatic perspective, again, the medieval linguistic repertoire certainly did not end decisively with the arrival of the printing press, the Great Vowel Shift, the Protestant Reformation, or any of the other events that have been used to signify the conclusion of the Middle English epoch. From this perspective, what codification did was not so much revolutionize the repertoire as transfer to English the qualities and practices that had sustained Latin's privileged status in the Middle Ages. In effect, English became Latin, with its grammar and rhetoric the focus of critical discussion, its varieties arrayed vertically in a version of diglossia, and its value rooted in the transcendent value of Anglophone nations. These are traits that were dominant through the era of Churchill's English-speaking peoples and that (in some places) remain operative today, with the result that as neatly as grammar might distinguish Middle from Old or Modern English, pragmatics unites many of us to a stage of the language otherwise long defunct. Entrenched distinctions between varieties of English and broken English or creoles similarly transcend grammatical periodization. They echo, that is, early modern thinking that linked the former to British geography and descendants of English (and American) speakers and the latter to a proliferating extraterritorial population using the language for reasons that have nothing to do with Kachru's Inner Circle. In this case, grammar, including principles of lexicography and language history, actually becomes a way to affirm definitions based on pragmatic considerations and the heritage they imply.[8]

The reason I have not tried to write some kind of composite grammar of English, then, is not that I don't believe it could be done. It is because I believe, and in this book have tried to demonstrate, that any definition of English depends significantly, perhaps even primarily, on non-structural criteria rooted in specific arenas of use. This is true for linguistic principles, such as those identifying acceptable or current vocabulary, describing regional dialects in relation to a standard, equating a language with its history, or positing deep structures. And it's true for specific contexts like the early modern codification of English through the principles of Latin grammar, American Indian boarding schools, Polynesia in the age of European exploration, or the early-twentieth-century industrial expansion of the United States. Through tree diagrams and discussions of language change as anthropomorphic struggle we may naturalize a sense that English is what it was or that the language exists apart from its speakers, and we may substantiate that sense with grammars, dictionaries, and enterprises like the Early English Text Society. But the fact remains that neither definitions of English nor the principles we use to write them are value-free. They are all situational and strategic.

In fundamental ways, much of what we accept as English we understand almost instinctively, without any act of will or choice. On this probably most linguists and speakers in general would agree. My argument is that this understanding derives not only from an abstract grammatical structure latent in our minds but also from our experiences and expectations. It is in specific contexts, or in even more individual circumstances at grocery stores or bus stops, that speakers encounter one another and instinctively (if subconsciously) ask themselves: are these people speaking English? And as in all the arenas in the language's history, from the first moments when English left Britain to those when it helped forge a global war-time confederacy, speakers answer this question not with reference to a dictionary nor subject to the qualification of some structural analysis but in relation to their prior sociolinguistic experience, the context of their conversation, the identity of those speaking to them, and their sense of themselves.

And it is these same experiences and expectations, in turn, that lead to abstract or prescriptive grammars and the definitions that underwrite sociolinguistic actions like university admission, employment, and the naturalization of citizens. Since these actions themselves shape Anglophones' definitions of their language, grammar and pragmatics have a kind of symbiotic relation. The genius of English (to recall Dr Johnson) always has been as much the product of pragmatic effects as grammatical forms, because usage is more than simply usage—it is in part what the language is. Purely structural definitions that disregard these fundamental determinants of language identity produce an artificial reality rather like the subatomic particles or chemical elements that exist only in laboratory settings.[9]

Accordingly, English might be described as what John Searle labels an institutional reality, something whose objective properties are objective only because we accept them to be.[10] The sounds that speakers utter have an empirical existence measurable by spectrographs and the like, that is, but they become phonemes or words when we—or, more consequentially, grammar books and dictionaries—designate them as such. We do all this not in the abstract but within contexts that might be linguistic (such as codification), pragmatic (like the ones I surveyed in the second half of this book), or both. Comparable to money or personal property, English is intentionality-relative. It is a thing independent of the mind that requires mental states for its existence. English has the particular shape and function it has, then, because speakers (both Anglophones and non-Anglophones) grant these qualities to it and act accordingly. And this is true as well for the analytic principles that we use to explain permissible synchronic variation and diachronic change. They have factual status because we the speakers grant this status to them, and they thereby become institutional realities of language activity that support a larger institutional reality of English itself. In effect, through speech acts (called declarations) we transform empirical reality by stating that something exists, thereby bringing it into existence. So we say that English consists of certain grammatical characteristics, that certain words fit within the lexicon of the language, that diachronic change and synchronic variation characterize any individual language, that language qualities reflect personal traits, and that language competence can be a vehicle for all manner of social distinctions. And in saying so we turn linguistic principles and the language into factual objects that can then be verified in language use through discrimination between utterances that comply with these pre-determined categories from those that do not. Even the simplest utterances, such as 'I do not understand you' or 'Do you speak English?' have this same declarative impact on the shape of the language.

None of the principles or arenas I explored suggests that we do this to carry out some vast Anglophone conspiracy. Rather, like all institutional realities, English is the expression of collective intentionality. It is as discrete individuals in banks and at lunch counters that we understand English to be something in particular, just as we understand certain individuals to be English-speakers. We certainly do so in relation to grammatical structure and under the influence of social institutions and beliefs, but the definition of the language ultimately remains the cooperative endeavor of (now) 1.5 billion Anglophones, most of whom will never have the opportunity to speak with one another. Part of what it means to speak English is to recognize the nature of this cooperation and to accommodate it in our own speech. Further, while such collective intentionality requires non-linguistic common knowledge, it by no means depends on agreement, since cooperation can result as easily from simple acceptance or recognition of (in this case) what constitutes the language. Certainly, many Native American children and immigrant Europeans at the Ford factory recognized the operative definition of English without also embracing it.

We map and channel the river of English at the same time, then. As an institutional reality English has an objective shape by virtue of the fact that certain kinds of flux—and only certain kinds—are treated as evidence of continuity. We Anglophones agree on this reality because we must if we are to communicate and further the social institutions and objectives that shape our language and that our language, in turn, furthers. English survives (so far) because it is changeable, because we continually redefine it, and it, like Heraclitus's river, continually replenishes itself. Were the language ever to be held to just one definition, this river would cease flowing. And since English achieves an objective shape only through subjective judgments, its shape will change as much due to variation in pragmatic circumstances (which themselves affect grammatical principles) as to variation in structure. The language can have a specific shape as an institutional reality only so long as Anglophones are willing to recognize as much. And so it is that with every word and sentence we utter we are always in the process of defining English.[11]

WHY WE CARE

At the beginning of *Slang in America*, a short prose piece in his 1888 collection *November Boughs*, Walt Whitman observes:

View'd freely, the English language is the accretion and growth of every dialect, race, and range of time, and is both the free and compacted composition of all. From this point of view, it stands for Language in the largest sense, and is really the greatest of studies. It involves so much; is indeed a sort of universal absorber, combiner, and conqueror. The scope of its etymologies is the scope not only of man and civilization, but the history of Nature in all departments, and of the organic Universe, brought up to date; for all are comprehended in words, and their backgrounds. This is when words become vitaliz'd, and stand for things, as they unerringly and soon come to do, in the mind that enters on their study with fitting spirit, grasp, and appreciation.[12]

Animated in a distinctly Whitmanesque way as an absorber and combiner, language contains multitudes—of forms, varieties, and historical stages. And in so doing it epitomizes humankind. Mirroring the boundless and fertile universe of Whitman's imagination, English is at once the essence of language and the essence of experience. It is the image of what Whitman values in life.

Even for Whitman such a claim is not really provable. Skeptical of science, he would have been unconvinced by anything that nineteenth-century philologists might have demonstrated (to borrow the wording of his "When I Heard the Learn'd Astronomer") through "the charts and diagrams, to add, divide, and measure" language.[13] In fact, had their science affirmed his comments, the contrarian Whitman might well have then rejected them himself. His views rest instead on an idea, a kind of essentializing of English that precedes and even bypasses inductive or deductive reasoning about linguistic structure to express the essence of the language. English is what Whitman, in an almost precognitive manner, understands it to be, with the result that any instances of language use can do only one of two things: affirm what Whitman has already essentialized or fail to qualify as English.

As distinctively Whitmanesque as such thinking might seem, it echoes much of what I have traced in formal and pragmatic definitions of English. In fact, Whitman's remarks summarize just why it is that we care about the identity of our language: because we have come to see English as a mirror of ourselves and our heritage. In the words we accept as English and the principles by which we write its history, as in our educational, commercial, and legislative practices, we circumscribe the speakers making up the group of which we understand ourselves to be part. In the ways we teach English, understand its roles in multilingual environments, and define native competency, we flesh out—literally—the ethnic, racial, sexual, educational, economic, and national profile of this group. More generally, to follow Searle's thinking, in institutional realities like citizenship, government, commerce, and civilization we use English to define the material world we inhabit. And we do all this whether we share Churchill's sentiments about the English-speaking peoples or the sentiments of the modern critics who champion extraterritorial Englishes or even those who warn against the threat English presents to other languages. It is because English is an institutional reality that we can have so many competing definitions of the language: the definers may all agree on how to define English, but the definers themselves are not all the same.

By defining English we are also defining ourselves, and to do this, we begin as much with an idea of English as with any particular words, sounds, or syntactic structures. Grammarians like Bullokar, Dr Johnson, or Ferreiro may have assembled evidence of usage to support their claims about what constitutes correct or even just better English, and they may have rooted these claims in the superiority of Latin or Standard English. But they also relied on simply a sense of the genius of the language and the character of its speakers to motivate what they looked at and how. This is a sense often expressed in a kind of structuralist dynamic that defines English by comparing an idea of it to ideas of other languages, irrespective of any grammatical considerations. For earlier critics, the dynamic appears in anthropomorphic comparisons between English and classical or European languages, but once the idea of English became synonymous with a Standard British variety, comparative comments (now derisive) focused on extraterritorial English and the characteristics of it and its speakers. Indeed, pragmatic definitions that emerged in colonial North America, the South Pacific, or twentieth-century industrial schools all began with an idea of the language that extended ideas about culture and heritage, and that found in the language support for these non-linguistic concerns. In effect, speakers fashioned their own Platonic ideals and then found evidence for them.

Philology's emphasis on geography and the Germanic heritage of English provided theoretical justification for this pragmatic strategy. Wanting not to see Indians or European immigrants when they looked into the mirror of English, American Anglophones saw a language that marked non-native utterances as non-standard, uneducated, and even uncivilized. And they saw a language that, as Whitman said in his preface to *Leaves of Grass*, equated with an idea of the United States: "The English language befriends the grand American expression...it is brawny enough and limber enough and full enough...it is the dialect of common sense. It is the speech of the proud and melancholy races and of all who aspire."[14] Whatever grammatical specifics it may have, American English here begins with the ideas of Emerson and de Tocqueville that the United States is a novel, fundamentally democratic, and revolutionary place, open to all and offering endless possibilities. In describing the American variety as brawny and limber, Whitman projects onto grammar the qualities that he and others had seen as characteristic of the United States, and he then projects American English onto English in general.

Such ideas and their pragmatic impacts are tenacious, maybe more so, in fact, than grammatical structure. Shortly after Whitman published *Slang in America*, for example, Krapp, the most prominent American linguist of his day, also acknowledged the slanginess of which Whitman spoke, asserting that American English "is a restless, rapid, animated style, a sparkling if not a profound style. In short, American style . . . is taken to be a style of wit, whereas British style is a style of thought and constructive understanding."[15] To Mencken, initially writing in the Jazz Age of the Roaring Twenties, American English was "the common materials of English dumped into a pot, exotic flavorings added, and the bubblings assiduously and expectantly skimmed."[16] The best-known expression of this idea, however, is perhaps that of the poet Carl Sandberg, who said of slang, again as a synonym for language in the United States, that it was "a language that rolls up its sleeves, spits on its hands and goes to work."[17] This same colloquial lack of restraint continues to figure in modern textbook discussions that describe slang and regionalisms as some of the most distinctive features of English in the United States.[18]

Equally tenacious have been the equation of social rank with grammatical correctness, the linking of civilization with pronunciation and word choice, and the primacy of history and geography in definitions of English. As with Webster's confident assertion that there was a new English in a new land, such ideas can become communal ways to affirm social heritage in linguistic forms, reflecting an image of what some of us (at least) want to see.[19] And this means that they can become more tenacious and important than the evidence of speakers and usages. Regional writing that featured slang did indeed proliferate in Whitman's day and well afterwards, for instance. But this was only one strain of stylized rhetoric that also included

newspapers, textbooks, business accounts, government documents, and formal speeches. And stylized rhetoric itself represents only a narrow slice of English in the United States. Then as
now, ordinary conversations and the ephemera of letters and
notes made up the greatest portion of language usage, and since
we cannot easily access such usage, we also can't say much with
authority about just what English was in the nineteenth-century
United States. When histories of English feature authors
like Mark Twain and Joel Chandler Harris as illustrations of
nineteenth-century American usage, they follow Whitman in
using a brawny, limber language in order to project linguistic
forms onto a vision of the United States and its citizens.[20] It is
the same kind of projection used by antiquarians like Nowell,
John Leland, and Robert Cotton, who searched old books in the
lexicographical and grammatical projects that would establish
the history of English literature and culture, and sustain their
emerging claims to greatness.[21] And as projections onto language, ideas like these easily can draw on the same linguistic
evidence to support opposing conclusions. As I noted in
Chapter Five, at the very moment when Mencken was documenting what might be called the vernacular luxuriance of
American English, Ferreiro was telling the boys and girls of
Hawaii that they needed to avoid local slang if they were to
aspire to the better, more staid form of the language as it was
spoken in the United States.

Again, I certainly do not mean to downplay the fact that
empirical linguistic data contribute significantly to any sense
of a language or its varieties. But I am arguing that definitions
of English, in theory as well as practice, rest on more than
structural considerations and that these other concerns are
what we care the most about because these directly determine
what we see in the mirror of the language. In light of how much
grammar varies in and across time, decisions about the relative
significance of various linguistic facts turn on the non-structural
influence of how a particular idea might help us imagine the
language. Put another way, the empirical data sometimes
become motivated by and confirm what's already been decided.
This is especially the case in histories of the language, which
need to decide what the language's history is before they can

select data that will confirm it. The notion that regional dialects are broken English or not-English will map the river of the language so as to lead to one kind of history and heritage for the language; the notion that they are reflections of vernacular culture will yield a quite different map.

Like many linguistic attitudes in the modern world, equating English with identity might seem so entrenched as to be, apparently, a natural feature of the language. But the fact of the matter is that we have not always maintained this equation, nor has it always functioned in the same way. Neither Bede nor King Alfred understood English to be the mirror of personal identity, and even Chaucer, as skillful as he was at matching personal temperament with linguistic nuance, manifests little interest in defining language so as to define ethnic or national character. It's in the early modern period that this interest quickens and becomes expressed through a thriving industry of codification, which histories of the language often present as a motivating force, a cause behind transformations in Anglophone society, literacy, education, and (indeed) conceptions of English.

No doubt this is true, but it's not the whole story. The pragmatic definitions I have considered here suggest that an at least equally powerful motivation behind these transformations and behind codification itself was the introduction of English to speakers outside of Britain, the establishment of extraterritorial Anglophone communities, the political impulses that underwrote contact among all these new speakers of English, and (therefore) the changing image of Anglophones. Contact between British English and extraterritorial varieties, or (more generally) between standard and non-standard ones, produced the dynamics not only of attitudes about English but also of the language's grammar and history. By drawing distinctions between indigenous varieties and Polynesian and other extraterritorial ones, or between a standard variety and the English used by non-prestigious speakers like American Indian students and immigrant factory workers, Anglophones defined their language, themselves, and their culture. We continue to make such sociolinguistic distinctions because doing so enables us to make sense of our world and because codification can be a way to define the socially marginal in the act of defining the language. And so long as some

Anglophones speak better English than others, these others can recognize the distinction and turn it to their own advantage, as Polynesians did when they insisted on learning English from British speakers, or as Native Americans did when using English to argue for their own personal dignity, or as members of the Commonwealth did when they rejected Basic English.

It has been argued that in the seventeenth, eighteenth, and nineteenth centuries Great Britain emerged as a nation through its dynamics with Continental and other extraterritorial concerns. I am extending this argument. I am suggesting that the sociolinguistic characteristics of the English linguistic repertoire—the reformed diglossia that placed English above indigenous languages and Standard English above regional varieties—likewise took shape in response to the spread of the language and the changing demographics of its speakers. Driven by goals like scientific exploration, economic expansion, and colonization, Anglophones required the services of non-native speakers as workers, consumers, and the objects of missionary activity. The acquisition of English by these speakers was a clear measure of the success of Anglophone policies. But it was also a source of the considerable anxiety that I have documented among speakers from the historical homelands of English, since non-native Anglophones redefined what appeared in the mirror of English. As a strategy to forestall this redefinition, insistence on the inadequacies and obscurities of extraterritorial or non-standard English, which appears in every one of the modern case studies I considered, was both desperate and doomed. The fact is that for Anglophone influence to spread, the language had to do so as well. And however much British or American Anglophones might have wanted to exclude Native Americans or Africans or Tahitians from their own 'us', transplanted English was mutually intelligible with the one defined in grammar books and dictionaries. Codification, then, was as much an effect as a cause. It was a response to and the means to control and resist the transformation of English and through it the changing demographics of Anglophones and their culture. Like so much of what I have discussed in this book, however, codification supports more than one heritage. English began the early modern period with grammatical descriptions that lagged behind those of contemporaries like French and Italian, but it ended it, catalyzed by encounters with non-Anglophones, with perhaps the most sophisticated metalinguistic traditions of western Europe. Codification testified for both the superiority of English and the inadequacies of those who would learn it.

There is a paradox here, of course. Anglophones endeavored to produce the very situation they also endeavored to prevent, with the equally paradoxical result that the faster Anglophone demographics changed, the more insistent the codification of linguistic change and grammar became. And ultimately, the sociolinguistic forces Anglophones unleashed in North America, the South Pacific, and elsewhere proved irresistible. It is only with great difficulty that many of us still can see Churchill's English-speaking peoples mirrored in our language, though just what we do see is something not at all easy to agree upon. Indeed, one of the most significant transformations of the modern era—specifically, a contraction—has been to the common ground that Anglophones can claim to share. Flowing wider and deeper than ever before, the river of English today has become a vast delta whose main channels are as contested as they are muddied. And that is all the more reason to care what English is.

A FINAL WORD ABOUT US

We like predictions. Even if we are not weather forecasters or political analysts, we like to speculate on what the future will bring, partly, I suspect, because the future we imagine would provide some confirmation of the present we inhabit. A world that we think is going to Hell in a handcart inevitably will end up down below, just as one that we see filled with power and vigor will discover a new frontier.

Linguistic predictions are especially popular. Long ago Alfred the Great predicated the survival of English civilization on the revival of vernacular and Latin literacy in England, and several centuries later King Edward I speculated that unless stopped, the King of France intended to wipe out the English language. Later still (in 1789) Webster believed that the American experience would "produce, in a course of time, a language in North America, as different from the future language of England, as the modern Dutch, Danish and Swedish are from the German, or from one another."[22] Nearly a century after this Henry Sweet predicted that within another century "England, America, and Australia will be speaking mutually unintelligible languages, owing to their independent changes of pronunciation."[23] More recently, various American critics, linguists, and elected officials have asserted that Spanish promises one day to become the dominant language in the United States, an eventuality variously seen as laudable or lamentable. Others have described English as a global killer language that will eliminate indigenous languages and cultures as a means to advance Anglo-American imperialism, while Nicholas Ostler foresees that "the world is moving not to English monolingualism, but a much more multilingual, diverse, and potentially incalculable future." "The forces making for the spread of English will soon peak," he believes, "and the sequel will be a long retrenchment, as auxiliary English comes to be less widely used, but no single language takes its place. There is no convincing reason to think that the future of English will diverge from the pattern of all the great world languages that have preceded it."[24]

The fact is that most linguistic predictions, perhaps like most predictions in general, do not come to pass, at least not precisely in the ways that were foreseen. King Alfred may have revived vernacular writing but within two centuries of his death England and English still were overtaken by Francophones; Philip IV of France didn't really try (and probably didn't want) to eradicate English; and Australian, American, and British English remain, for the most part, mutually intelligible. A record like this doesn't instill confidence in predictions for the future, and, indeed, these seem on shaky ground as it is.

It is true that in the United States, Spanish has grown at an unprecedented rate. According to the 1940 census, just 1.6% (1,858,024 individuals) of the white population spoke Spanish as a mother tongue. Because census categories have varied over the years, exact comparisons between then and now are difficult to make, although as of 2007, in a population of 281 million individuals over the age of five, about 35 million—or 12.5%—were reported as speaking Spanish or Spanish Creole at home.[25] That's an eightfold jump in population percentage in 70 years. But before we conclude (as many do) that Spanish soon will overtake English, we should exercise caution for two reasons beyond simply the poor record of linguistic prognostication. Firstly, with every day that passes English becomes more entrenched as the country's national language, mandatory in education, vital in business, and exclusive in all manner of powerful domains. There's every practical reason for non-native speakers, Spanish-speaking or otherwise, to learn a language so associated with economic success and (for similar reasons) for businesses and schools to continue to depend on it primarily or even exclusively. It's worth recalling that these same factors, present throughout the nation's history, led to language shift among even higher percentages of non-native speakers in nineteenth-century rural America and in early twentieth-century industrial cities like Detroit. Boys and girls want jobs as good as they can get, said Ferreiro, and for children in Hawaii or the United States mainland those jobs continue to demand English.

The second reason to be skeptical of predictions about the future of Spanish is that the post-War social factors that made possible a twenty-fold increase in speakers were completely unforeseeable in 1940. These included the Civil Rights movement; the 1965 elimination of immigration quotas; the expansion of American industry and farm production; the increasing refusal of native Anglophones to take on many service and manual labor jobs; the reluctance of employers to pay many kinds of tax and insurance; persistent poverty and political unrest in Central and South America; and (therefore) increased emigration from there. On the basis of what was known in 1940 about birth rates, immigration patterns, and educational practices, no prophet could have predicted the subsequent changes in linguistic demographics. And this means, by the same token, that no one today can foresee future sociolinguistic developments that might maintain Spanish, increase or decrease the shift of its speakers to English, or advance the presence of some other non-English language in the linguistic repertoire of the United States.

Predictions about English's global future are likewise unconvincing. The population of Anglophones today obviously exceeds that of any previous era, just as the number of non-

English languages obviously has decreased. But as I have argued throughout this book, the river of English has altered and adapted throughout its history, and where we stand today, with monoglots a distinct minority and the whole concept of native speaker difficult to define, looks nothing like where the Venerable Bede, John Smith, Captain Cook, or even Churchill stood. Not only have the demographics of Anglophones been transformed completely, but so too have the proliferating and regional and social varieties. With the guarantee—and I do mean guarantee—that natural language will continue to change, whatever the grammars of these varieties look like in the future, they will not look like they do today. To reduce all this variation and change to the simple label 'English' and to represent it as some irresistible sociolinguistic killer monolith engaged in an anthropomorphic struggle with other languages is to endorse a historical-geographic definition of English (i.e., English is what it was, from where it has been) that silences both the historical individualizing arenas I have described and the contemporary ones so well described by others. It is to silence as well the predominant group of Anglophones—second-language learners who may speak English for reasons that, again, have nothing to do with Kachru's Inner Circle and whose grammar and pragmatics are shaped accordingly. As Standing Bear discovered when he met the king of England, all of us English-speakers do not speak the same language.

But the prediction that English will follow the pattern of previous lingua francas and retract its domains and users seems no more convincing. The fact is that there is no pattern. Not Persian nor Greek nor Latin was used in a geographic or sociolinguistic world remotely comparable to the one through which English has flowed. English is a language that by means of writing has become increasingly pervasive, not simply for epic poetry or history but for holiday cards, tax codes, and job applications; that extends literacy past socially elite males to all ranks of society; that sustained and accelerated this record by first print and then electronic communication, making possible a unique awareness of the language and its history; that technological developments in transportation carried and established around the entire globe and not just the known world; and that is now spoken by nearly one-fifth of the largest ever population of humans. With nothing like English in the past, we have little way of knowing, really knowing, what the future will bring.

Indeed, as with the growth of Spanish in the United States, a great many factors crucial to the spread of English would have been unforeseeable until they took place. In 1800, when English remained localized in the United Kingdom and the United States, it would have been impossible to predict not only technological developments in transportation and communication but also the confluence of socio-political events—including the rise and failure of Nazism and Communism—that would draw on these developments to elevate the global status of the United States and to disperse British and American influence and, therefore, language around the globe since then. If it had been, and if anything could have been done, even Anglophones surely would have avoided many of the events that enabled this dispersal. Had these events and their impact on English in fact been avoided, Sweet might well have proved right in foreseeing that England, Australia, and the United States would now be speaking different languages. But in view of all this unpredictability it remains the case that, however confident we might feel about the linguistic future, we lack crucial data for our predictions. We do not now know what individuals, global events, economic developments, natural catastrophes, political realignments, population shifts, national and international laws, and technology lie in our future. And so we cannot know how these will affect us and the definitions of our language, dependent as those definitions are on usage.

One thing we do know, based all on the moments I have considered in this book, is that phenomena like these have had significant impact on English and Anglophones. And we know that if the reason we care about English is that we have come to use it as a mirror of ourselves, then we will evaluate what we see in the mirror, even with the most critical and discerning eye, against some pre-linguistic notion of who we are. We might identify ourselves in relation to traditions of Teutonic origins, those of variation as error, and those of language as the expression of ethnicity and nationality. Or we might identify ourselves as part of a global, racially and ethnically diverse population that is at once united and divided by English. Or we even might identify ourselves as speakers in effect held hostage by a language that is the vehicle of an internationally aggressive economic and military culture. In every case, perhaps depending on our outlooks more generally, we might be pleased by seeing just what we hope to see or appalled by seeing what we fear. And depending on our influence, depending on whether we are speakers like Pratt and Ford or ones like the Inuk Calichoughe and the Tahitian chief Pomare, we may be in a position to try to engineer a linguistic reality that matches our linguistic idea.

All definitions of English are moments on a river that is itself continually remapped by those moments. We might criticize some speakers and arenas for the character and implications of their definitions of English, and we might be morally well justified in doing so. But we cannot dismiss them simply on the grounds that the definitions they advance are invested in extra-structural concerns, since there are no definitions, critiques, or linguistic principles that are not themselves so invested. Because each moment on the river of English links the ones before it to the ones after it, further, all these necessarily provisional definitions become part of the language's identity as fashioned by those who count themselves among the language's speakers. And it is for these reasons that when, like Narcissus, we look into the river's mirrored surface, we see ourselves, even if we do not all see the same reflection.

Notes

CHAPTER ONE

1. "Overseas Applicants."
2. Lewin, "Foreign Students Take More Seats on Campus," A21.
3. Kennedy, *A Bibliography of Writings on the English Language*, 480–9, 505–10, and Alston, *English Grammars*, 42–8. On grammar's financial rewards in the early modern period, see further Mugglestone, '*Talking Proper*,' 50–76.
4. Fewer than 20 grammars appeared in each decade of the eighteenth century; from 1810 to 1900, the number per decade is never less than 60 and once is as high as 120. See Tieken-Boone van Ostade, *The Bishop's Grammar*, 261.
5. "Pronunciation Workshop." See further Roberts, "Unlearning to Tawk Like a New Yorker."
6. "International Poll Finds Americans Twice as Frustrated with Bad English," and Chiswick and Miller, "Language Skills and Earnings among Legalized Aliens," 77.
7. Holborow, *The Politics of English*, 1.
8. Quoted in Ostler, *The Last Lingua Franca*, 45.
9. Chiswick and Miller, "Language Skills," 81; Hamilton et al., "Measuring the Wage Costs of Limited English," 268.
10. Dávila et al., "Accent Penalties and the Earnings of Mexican-Americans," and Hosada and Stone-Romero, "Effects of Foreign Accents on Employment-Related Decisions."
11. Quoted in Dorman, "L.P.G.A. Sees Use of English as a Facilitator." The Association eventually rescinded the directive and instead arranged for language tutors to work with players in person and through video conferencing. See Crouse, "Mastering the Language Game."
12. "U.S. Citizenship and Immigration Services." The United Kingdom and New Zealand have a similar requirement; Canada specifies speaking ability in either of its official languages, French or English; Australia requires candidates for naturalization to pass a citizenship test, which is administered in English.

13. Article 20, sec.8. Just what it means to speak English was at the heart of a legal challenge to one candidate's eligibility for a seat on the San Luis city council (Lacey, "Arizona Candidate Challenged").
14. Kron, "For Rwandan Students."
15. Phillipson, *English-Only Europe?*, 4.
16. Mojsin, *Mastering the American Accent*, vi.
17. "The Elementary and Secondary Education Act," Title IX, Part A, sec. 9101, and "Glossary of Terms."
18. Sec. 3, ch. 6, sec. 161.
19. *Beowulf and the Fight at Finnsburg*, lines 1–3.
20. *Paradise Lost*, ix, 846–9, in *Complete Poems and Major Prose*.
21. Kelman, *How Late It Was, How Late*, 6.
22. Quoted in Siegel, *The Emergence of Pidgin and Creole Languages*, 61.
23. Cassidy and Hall (eds), *Dictionary of American Regional English*, s.v. 'off ox' n.
24. Filppula et al., *English and Celtic in Contact*.
25. Morley, "Perspectives on English for Academic Purposes," 155. In 1936, H. L. Mencken put the population of native Anglophones at 174 million and that of total Anglophones at 191 million (*The American Language*, 592). *The World Almanac Book of Facts for 1950* (ed. Hansen, 218) estimates the native-speaking Anglophone population at 270 million (against a total global population of 2.3 billion), to which it adds another 47 million speakers of English as a second language for "barter, trade exchange, or other manner of communication" in the former British empire. By this reckoning the global Anglophone population would have been about 320 million, but earlier historical data makes me think that the estimates of both of these studies are low.
26. Crystal, "English Worldwide," 425.
27. Truss, *Eats, Shoots & Leaves*; McWhorter, *Doing Our Own Thing*.
28. Kachru, *The Other Tongue*.
29. See Schneider, *Postcolonial English*; Mesthrie and Bhatt, *World Englishes*; Wierzbicka, *Experience, Evidence, and Sense*.
30. Belich, *Replenishing the Earth*, 126–7 and 82–3.
31. Kahn, *The Art and Thought of Heraclitus*, 52.
32. An exception to this generalization would be in service industries, where many times every day of the week clerks might have to utter the same phrases without any measurable pragmatic difference.
33. Wright, *The English Dialect Grammar*, vii.
34. For various reasons, including the difficulty of counting speakers and uncertainty about the level of competence required for a speaker to qualify as an Anglophone, exact numbers of English

speakers today are impossible to produce. The 1.5 billion estimate is the most common one, however. The most recent *Ethnologue: Languages of the World* (ed. Lewis) records just 328 million first-language Anglophones in 112 countries (21), an estimate that seems significantly low. If accurate, then first-language speakers would account for no more than one-fifth of the global Anglophone population.

35. Novick, *That Noble Dream*, 316.
36. On heritage and history, see Considine, *Dictionaries in Early Modern Europe*, 1–18.
37. See further Schildkraut, *Press 'One' for English*.
38. Lass, *Historical Linguistics and Language Change*, 377.
39. *The Collected Tales*, 361–6.

CHAPTER TWO

1. Durkin, *The Oxford Guide to Etymology*, 34–43.
2. Crystal, *The Cambridge Encyclopedia of the English Language*, 119. This notion was popularized in Payack's *A Million Words and Counting*, which, along with the website Global Language Monitor, actually offered a countdown to the moment when the one-millionth word would be uttered. While such a countdown, as a spectacle, attracts the attention of the popular press, it has little value or even meaning in light of the arguments of only this chapter.
3. Crystal, *The Cambridge Encyclopedia*, 123.
4. Crystal, *The Stories of English*, 162. Even if exaggerated—and the claim isn't provable one way or the other—this figure does point to the significant impact of Norse on the English lexicon by the late Middle Ages.
5. *A New English Dictionary*, 1, part 1, xvii.
6. Garner, "Shakespeare's Latinate Neologisms."
7. Pinker, *The Stuff of Thought*, 17.
8. Skeat, "Report upon 'Ghost-Words'," 353.
9. Machan, "*forlynen*: A Ghost Word Rematerializes."
10. Dood, *The Reverend Guppy's Aquarium*; Burridge, *Blooming English*; Garg, *The Dord, the Diglot, and an Avocado or Two*. The number of such whimsically titled books is enormous and expanding. I can also mention here Burridge, *Weeds in the Garden of Words*; Oliver, *March Hares and Monkeys' Uncles*; McKean, *Totally Weird and Wonderful Words*; and Butterfield, *Damp Squid*.

11. Richler, *A Bawdy Language.*
12. "Report upon 'Ghost-Words'," 351.
13. Osselton, "The Early Development of the English Monolingual Dictionary," 149. Osselton notes that the dictionary's editor—listed only as "J. K."—is commonly understood to be John Kersey.
14. "On Some Deficiencies in Our English Dictionaries," 4–5.
15. Quoted in Mugglestone, "The Oxford English Dictionary," 244.
16. Johnson, *A Dictionary of the English Language*, i, no sig.
17. Camden, *Remains Concerning Britain*, 38–40. See further Vine, *In Defiance of Time*, 51–79.
18. Stockwell and Minkova, *English Words*, 2–4. It was the eighteenth-century writer Horne Tooke who was perhaps the greatest proponent for the notion that the meaning and character of English is best understood through its etymologies.
19. Considine, "Literary Classics in *OED* Quotation Evidence," 625. More generally, see Brewer, "The Use of Literary Quotations in the *Oxford English Dictionary.*"
20. Krapp, *Modern English*, viii.
21. E.g., Leech et al., *Word Frequencies in Written and Spoken English*, and de Klerk, *Corpus Linguistics and World Englishes.*
22. Trench, "On Some Deficiencies in our English Dictionaries," 57, 59, 15.
23. *A New English Dictionary*, 1, part 1, xix. On the hesitant inclusion of extra-British words and senses in the OED, see Oglivie, "Rethinking Burchfield and World Englishes."
24. Burchfield, *Unlocking the English Language*, 85–94. For recent discussions of the procedures and principles of the OED over the years, see Mugglestone, *Lost for Words*, and Brewer, *Treasure-House of the Language.*
25. S.v. 'chip', n.1, sense 2b. See further Algeo, "British and American Biases in English Dictionaries," 208–10. In American English, 'chips' might be recognized as the British equivalent of 'French fries' but ordinarily would mean only the equivalent of 'crisps', a sense that the OED records under 'potato chip' and to which readers are directed only as an ancillary meaning.
26. Landau, "Major American Dictionaries," 207.
27. Murray, "Ninth Annual Address," 134.
28. Verstegan, *A Restitution of Decayed Intelligence*, 204.
29. *The Arte of Rhetorique*, 86r.
30. See further Blank, *Broken English* and "The Babel of Renaissance English," and Mugglestone, *'Talking Proper.'*
31. "On Some Deficiencies in Our English Dictionaries," 69–70.

32. Willinsky, *Empire of Words: The Reign of the OED*, 23–4.
33. Quoted in Sledd and Ebbitt (eds), *Dictionaries and THAT Dictionary*, 78. See further Morton, *The Story of 'Webster's Third'*, and Machan, *Language Anxiety*, 186–91.
34. Allsopp, "Dictionaries of Caribbean English," 353.
35. See further the discussion of Randolph Quirk's notion of "liberation linguistics" in Machan, *Language Anxiety*, 228–31.
36. *A New English Dictionary*, 1, part 1, xvii.

CHAPTER THREE

1. *Epistles*, lines 60–3.
2. *A New English Dictionary*, 1, part 1, viii.
3. Mackay, *The Lost Beauties of the English Language*, v–vi.
4. Kacirk, *The Word Museum*, 9. Linguistic textbooks rarely take notice of word death. Katamba's *English Words* addresses the topic only in passing, while it doesn't figure at all in Harley's *English Words: A Linguistic Introduction*.
5. Dearborn, *The Columbian Grammar*, 135, 133.
6. Cassidy and Hall (eds), *Dictionary of American Regional English*, s.v. 'dare' v, A.4.c.
7. *Adventures of Huckleberry Finn*, 300.
8. In 2008 a speaker from Lancaster county, Pennsylvania—an isolated, rural, and largely Amish community—produced 'daresn't' (Mummert, "Sounds Like Home"). 'dustn't' and 'dursn't,' evidently British equivalents, occur in Dickens's fiction (*Bleak House*, 689, 701), and in *The English Dialect Dictionary* Wright records these alongside 'dazzent' in largely northern examples ('dare', v.1 and sb.1).
9. Alter, *Darwinism and the Linguistic Image*, esp. 52–79.
10. Lyell, *The Geological Evidences of the Antiquity of Man*.
11. Darwin, *The Origin of Species*, 466.
12. Pinker, *The Stuff of Thought*.
13. See Hughes, *A History of English Words*, 44; and Bauer, "Competition in English Word Formation," 183.
14. Pinker, *The Stuff of Thought*, 115. Zipf once claimed that "Different meanings of a word will tend to be equal to the square root of its relative frequency" ("The Meaning-Frequency Relationship of Word," 255). Durkin has argued that words simply do not have the kinds of fixed categories of meaning that dictionaries imply

but are inherently polysemous, with meanings that shade into one another (*The Oxford Guide to Etymology*, 68–79).

15. Schmid, "New Words in the Mind."
16. See Babbitt, "College Words and Phrases"; and Zandvoort, *Wartime English.*
17. For additional examples, any of the books cited in note 4 can be consulted, along with Abley's *The Prodigal Tongue.*
18. The examples come from Coleman, *A History of Cant and Slang Dictionaries*, 95. More generally, see her *The Life of Slang.*
19. See Starnes and Noyes, *The English Dictionary*, 41–2; Norton, *A History of the English Bible*, 26–8.
20. None appears in a listing of the top 40 most popular names for baby girls for 2012 ("Popular Baby Names for 2012").
21. See further Hughes, *A History of English Words*, 95–7.
22. For further discussion of changes in morphology, usage, pronunciation, and meaning, see Durkin, *The Oxford Guide to Etymology*, 179–265.
23. Wright, *The English Dialect Grammar*, 297.
24. Bauer, *Watching English Change*, 29.
25. Barfield, *History in English Words.*
26. Johnson, *A Dictionary of the English Language*, i, no sig.
27. Lewis, *Studies in Words*, 6–7.
28. *A Dictionary of the English Language*, s.v.
29. A simple Google search of 'ain't' produced over 82 million hits.
30. "The Varieties of English Speech," 87.
31. Burchfield, *Unlocking the English Language*, 111.
32. "Politics and the English Language," 138.
33. Quoted in Zernike, "Veterans Fight to Reclaim the Name 'Swift Boat'," A15. Also see Hulse, " 'Recovery' is in" and Mallet et al., "The Most Annoying."
34. Ravitch, *The Language Police*, 158–9. On the policing of language more generally as a way to shape social reality, see Cameron, *Verbal Hygiene.*
35. See Pinker, *The Stuff of Thought*, 334–7; and Allan and Burridge, *Forbidden Words*, 11–12. Pinker notes that such language may be mentally stored as a unit in a part of the brain other than the one associated with language production.
36. See further Pinker's discussion in *The Stuff of Thought*, 323–72.
37. Sensitivity to the word remains. In the blockbuster 2001 film *The Fellowship of the Ring*, the character Sam, holding a pair of rabbits, refers to them as "conies" (using the word that occurs in the

book), which he pronounces so that it rhymes (unhistorically) with 'ponies.'

CHAPTER FOUR

1. *A Dictionary of the English Language*, i, no sig.
2. *An English Expositor*, s.v.
3. E.g., Kaluza, *Historische Grammatik der Englischen Sprache*, i.29, and Wogan-Browne et al. (eds), *The Idea of the Vernacular*, 362.
4. *A Dictionary*, i, no sig.
5. *A Short Historical English Grammar*, 11.
6. *The Making of English*, 11.
7. *A Restitution of Decayed Intelligence*, 197. See further Marshall, *Language Change and Sociolinguistics*.
8. All of these might be considered, ultimately, as varieties of south-east British English. See Lass, "Where Do Extraterritorial Englishes Come from?"
9. Fowler and Fowler, *The King's English*, 23.
10. Mortimer, whose comments appeared in *Nation and Athenaeum*, is quoted from Mencken, *The American Language*, 42. Knox's comment appears on p.32. On such criticism more generally, see Bailey, "American English Abroad," 493–5.
11. See Considine, *Dictionaries in Early Modern Europe*, 164–8.
12. Quoted in Gordon et al. (eds), *New Zealand English*, 6.
13. Quoted in Chambers "Lawless and Vulgar Innovations," 6. Also see Bailey, "The English Language in Canada." The earliest recorded example of 'Americanism,' explicitly coined by John Witherspoon in 1781, is less condemnatory but still scarcely enthusiastic. See Cassidy and Hall, "Americanisms," 185–6.
14. Algeo, "What is a Briticism?"
15. "The Excellency of the English Tongue," in Camden, *Remains Concerning Britain*, 49.
16. *Logonomia Anglica*, 16–9.
17. Quoted in May, *Language and Minority Rights*, 209.
18. See, for example, Simpson, *The Politics of American English*; Algeo, "External Factors"; and Howe, *Language and Political Meaning in Revolutionary America*.
19. *Dissertations on the English Language*, 36.
20. See Schneider, *Postcolonial English*, 30.
21. See, for example, Titlestad, "English, the Constitution and South Africa's Language Future"; Gough, "Black English in South

Africa"; Makoni et al. (eds) *Black Linguistics*; Perry and Delpit (eds), *The Real Ebonics Debate*; and Smitherman, *Word from the Mother.*

22. "Language Variety: Nature and Art," and "Language Varieties and Standard Language."

23. At issue here is what might be called a tendency in ethnographic history to advance a particular modern position in part by claiming for it the vantage of dispassionate science in comparison to preceding positions, which are dismissed as invested in specific theological or political agenda. See Herbert, *Culture and Anomie*, 150–203.

24. *The English Grammar*, 47.

25. *Growth and Structure of the English Language*, 17. A characteristic modern treatment is Hoad, "Preliminaries: Before English." In imagining English as produced by a post-migration 'koineization', Mesthrie and Bhatt bring together the most traditional kinds of historical thinking with the most recent post-colonial work. See *World Englishes*, 13. For a Foucauldian critique of such analyses, see Watts, *Language Myths*.

26. *The Origin of the English*, 162.

27. Camden, *Remains Concerning Britain*, 24, and Verstegan, *A Restitution of Decayed Intelligence*, 43.

28. *A Restitution of Decayed Intelligence*, 14, 191–2.

29. *De recta & emendata linguæ Anglicæ scriptione, dialogues*, 9r.

30. *Grammatica Linguæ Anglicanæ*, 126–7.

31. *The Scholemaster*, 58v.

32. The material manifestation of this conceit would be early modern editions that used black letter font for early English works and Roman for glosses and facing-page Latin translations. A format like this stresses both the antiquity and the modern comprehensibility of the works it contains. For a discussion of Old English works see Echard, *Printing the Middle Ages*, 21–59. For Middle English see Machan, "Kynaston's *Troilus*."

33. *A History of Modern Colloquial English*, 101.

34. A recent example of a literary-based account of English is Lerer, *Inventing English*. Non-literary works have become more common in studies of synchronic moments within the language's history. See, for example, Wright, "Macaronic Writing in a London Archive," and Nevalainen and Raumolin-Brunberg, *Historical Sociolinguistics*. For the dependence of the OED on literary citations, see Considine, "Literary Classics in *OED* Quotation Evidence," and Brewer, "The Use of Literary Quotations in the *Oxford English*

Dictionary." Corpora of popular speech and writing (e.g., magazines) are also beginning to have an impact on linguistic analysis, though the farther back in time one goes, the more likely even corpora are likely to be based on literary sources.

35. *The First Part of the Elementarie*, 254.
36. *The Scholemaster*, 24r. The whole of Carew's 1606 *Excellency of the English Tongue* is devoted essentially to demonstrating that English surpasses other languages in its spelling, palindromes, proverbs, and semantic richness.
37. *The Scholemaster*, 27v.
38. *A Dictionary of the English Language*, i, no sig.
39. *Remains Concerning Britain*, 29.
40. Holinshed, *The First and Second Volumes of Chronicles*, 13–4. This edition was revised by Harrison. See further Machan, "French, English, and the Late Medieval Linguistic Repertoire."
41. *The Rise, Progress and Present Structure of the English Language*, 47–8.
42. *Logonomia Anglica*, B1r.
43. *English Past and Present*, 32.
44. For example, Wogan-Browne et al. (eds), *The Idea of the Vernacular*.
45. *Modern English*, 62.
46. So John Earle, *The Philology of the English Tongue*; Marsh, *Lectures on the English Language*; Craik, *A Manual of English*; and Fowler, *The English Language*. For an overview of the development of histories of the language in this period, see Cable, "History of the History of the English Language."
47. *History of the English Language*, v.
48. *Dictionary*, i, no sig.
49. Lass, "Language Periodization and the Concept 'Middle.'"
50. See further Machan, "Chaucer and the History of English."
51. *English Past and Present*, 68, and *Modern English*, 62.
52. *The Invention of Middle English*, 7.
53. McCrum's *Globlish* in fact uses the modern diversity of English as testimony to the greatness of the language of Chaucer, Shakespeare, and so forth. Valuable critiques of such approaches can be found in Mufwene, "African-American English," and Poplack et al., "'Deformed in the Dialects.'"

CHAPTER FIVE

1. Crotch (ed.), *The Prologues and Epilogues of William Caxton*, 108.
2. Blake, *Caxton and His World*, 13–25.

3. OED, s.v. 'egg,' n., 1.a.
4. Lippi-Green, *English with an Accent*, 149–81, 92–6.
5. While English was not an explicit subject until late in this early modern period, exercises in spelling, recitation, and the like certainly did incorporate the language. See Michael, *The Teaching of English*.
6. For the interconnections among some of the early modern grammarians, see Parry, *The Trophies of Time*.
7. Hart, *An Orthographie*, 2r; Bullokar, *Pamphlet for Grammar*, 55r; and *The Amendment of Orthographie for English Speech*, 1.
8. Puttenham, *The Arte of English Poesie*, 120. See further Machan, *Language Anxiety*, 191–231.
9. See Williams, "'O! When Degree is Shak'd'."
10. *An Accidence to the English Tongue*, 11–12.
11. *Language is Power*, 42.
12. *Logonomia Anglica*, 19, 18.
13. *Modern English*, 75. John McWhorter recently has revived virtually this same argument. See *Language Interrupted*, especially 59–103.
14. *Course of Lectures on Elocution*, 30.
15. *Hērō-paideia*, 185–6. A century later Lord Chesterfield expressed similar sentiments: "The common people of every country speak their own language very ill; the people of fashion (as they are called) speak it better, but not always correctly, because they are not always people of letters" (quoted in Wyld, *A History of Modern Colloquial English*, 19–20).
16. *The Arte of Rhetorique*, 87v.
17. Quoted in Mühlhäusler, *Pidgin & Creole Linguistics*, 27.
18. See further Machan, "When English Became Latin." On standard ideology see James Milroy and Lesley Milroy, *Authority in Language* and James Milroy, "The Consequences of Standardisation in Descriptive Linguistics"; and for its sense of dialectal difference as a measure of social difference, see Blank, *Broken English*. On the development of codification for Standard English more generally, see Leonard, *The Doctrine of Correctness in English Usage*; Vorlat, *The Development of English Grammatical Theory*; and Görlach, *Explorations in English Historical Linguistics*, 137–212. For pointed critiques of this tradition, see Crowley (ed.), *Proper English?*, and *Standard English and the Politics of Language*.
19. See in particular Coleman, *A History of Cant and Slang Dictionaries*.
20. *Bad Language*, 149. Also see McEnery, *Swearing in English*.
21. Quoted in Schütz, *The Voices of Eden*, 351.

22. Quoted in Schütz, *The Voices of Eden*, 301.
23. *The American Language*, 373.
24. Simonson et al., *Pidgin to da Max*, and Siegel, *The Emergence of Pidgin and Creole Languages*, 265.
25. See further *A Survey of Education in Hawaii*; Wist, *A Century of Public Education in Hawaii*; and Benham and Heck, *Cultural and Educational Policy in Hawai'i*.
26. *Everyday English for Hawaii's Children*, 3.
27. *Everyday English for Hawaii's Children*, 5.
28. *Everyday English for Hawaii's Children*, 7, 17, 23, 21.
29. See, for example, Crowley, *The Politics of Discourse*, and *Standard English and the Politics of Language*.
30. Priestley, *Rudiments of English Grammar*, ix.
31. Johnson, *A Dictionary of the English Language*, i, n. sig.
32. S.v. 'genius' n., 3c.
33. The nineteenth-century philologist Matthew Harrison even entitles one section of his *The Rise, Progress and Present Structure of the English Language* the "Genius and Character of the English Language."
34. Johnson, *A Dictionary*, i, n. sig.
35. Bullokar, *Pamphlet for Grammar*, A4r; Mulcaster, *The First Part of the Elementarie*, 80.

CHAPTER SIX

1. *Arenas of Language Use*, xvii. More generally see 3–59 and also Clark's *Using Language*, 92–121.
2. *The Ruin of Britain and Other Works*, 97.
3. Bede makes the claim in Chapter 15 of Book 1 of his *Ecclesiastical History*. Its accuracy, and whether Bede's assertion amounts to anything more than circular reasoning (Anglia must have been settled by Angles), has been the subject of much scholarly discussion.
4. Toon, "The Social and Political Contexts of Language Change."
5. *Historiam Ecclesiasticam Gentis Anglorum*, 80.
6. *Historiam Ecclesiasticam Gentis Anglorum*, 132, 129. The Old English translation of Bede's history simply uses "English" in both cases (*The Old English Version of Bede's Ecclesiastical History*, 158, 156).
7. Cassidy and Ringler (eds), *Bright's Old English Grammar & Reader*, 182, 253–4.

8. *Grammatik und Glossar*, 4, 18, 134. Despite the structural differences between Latin and English, the Grammar says enough about English in particular that it could be argued it was designed to improve students' facility with both languages.

9. Foote and Quirk (eds), *Gunnlaugssaga Ormstungu*, 33.

10. See further Fjalldal, "How Valid Is the Anglo-Scandinavian," and, more generally, Townend, *Language and History in Viking Age England*.

11. Matthew of Paris, *Chronica Majora*, v.352.

12. Machan, *English in the Middle Ages*, 82–5.

13. Machan, *English in the Middle Ages*, 95–96.

14. *Brut*, lines 3148–9; and *The Canterbury Tales*, VIII.85–8.

15. In the OED, the first use of the noun 'Scots' for that variety is dated to 1494. This is likely to be among the earliest references by name to any regional variety. The MED records for 'English' the sense "Of the regional dialects in England" (sense 2c), but in the only example with an attributive adjective ('south'), the meaning is geographical, not sociolinguistic. The OED dates this usage to the nineteenth century (A.3.b). When the Anglo-Saxon abbot Ælfric says that Aidan was unable to turn his speech to the 'Northumbrian language' ("norðhymbriscum gereorde"), the history of the adjective again suggests that reference is to a region or people, not dialect. See *Lives of Saints*, 3:130.

16. *Cursor Mundi*, lines 5–8; *Of Arthour and Merlin*, lines 19–24; and Usk, *Testament of Love*, 2. See further Machan, *English in the Middle Ages*, 86–96.

17. Wogan-Browne et al. (eds), *The Idea of the Vernacular*, 134–5, 132.

18. Hudson (ed.), *Selections from English Wycliffite Writings*, 68.

19. Stubbs (ed.), *Select Charters*, 480; Woodbine, "The Language of English Law," 403; and Gil, *Logonomia Anglica*, B1r.

20. See Butterfield, *The Familiar Enemy*.

21. Chambers and Daunt (eds), *A Book of London English*, 139.

22. Grigg, *Population Growth and Agrarian Change*, 83; Bacci, *The Population of Europe*, 8 and 81; Freedman, "Rural Society," 90; and Biller, *The Measure of Multitude*, 112.

23. *Orthographie*, 21r.

24. *A Dictionary of the English Language*, s.v.

25. *An American Dictionary of the English Language*, s.v.

26. OED, s.v., adj. (and adv.) and n., II.2.a.

CHAPTER SEVEN

1. See further Machan, *Language Anxiety*, 81–95.
2. Quinn et al. (eds), *New American World*, iv.210.
3. *Discoverers, Explorers, Settlers*, 7.
4. Sayre, *Les sauvages américains*, 138–43.
5. Quinn (ed.), *The Roanoke Voyages, 1584–1590*, i.116n.
6. Barbour (ed.), *The Jamestown Voyages under the First Charter*, i.136, 143.
7. Quinn et al. (eds), *New American World*, iv.235.
8. *Good Newes from New-England*, 60.
9. *New Englands Prospect*, 91.
10. *The Historie of Travaile into Virginia Britania*, 48, 59. Completed about 1612, Strachey's *Historie* was not published in his lifetime.
11. *Good Newes from New-England*, 28.
12. Quinn et al. (eds), *New American*, iv.209; Morton, *New English Canaan*, 20. William Wood (see note 9) cites this same inability to so say [l] or [r].
13. Quinn et al. (eds), *New American World*, iv.212.
14. Quinn et al. (eds), *New American World*, iv.231; Barbour (ed.), *The Jamestown Voyages* i.82; Edwards (ed.), *Last Voyages*, 155.
15. Hakluyt, *The Principall Navigations*, 515. Despite Hakluyt's certitude, the precise date of the Indians' arrival is uncertain: they may be from John Cabot's 1497 voyage, from a later voyage led by his son Sebastian, or from some other voyage to the lands John Cabot discovered.
16. *A True Discourse of the Present Estate of Virginia*, 44.
17. Quinn (ed.), *The Roanoke Voyages*, i.370.
18. Sense 5.
19. Barbour (ed.), *The Complete Works of Captain John Smith*, i.150.
20. *Remains concerning Britain*, 7.
21. *The Diary of Thomas Crosfield*, 19.
22. Barbour (ed.), *The Jamestown Voyages*, i.107. Smith's written language is notoriously idiosyncratic.
23. Quinn (ed.), *The Roanoke Voyages*, i.175.
24. Bridenbaugh, *Jamestown, 1544–1699*, 45.
25. Barbour (ed.), *The Complete Works*, i.41, 238.
26. Strachey, *For the Colony in Virginea Britannia*, 13, 83.
27. *Of Plymouth Plantation*, 58.
28. Williams, *A Key into the Language of America*, A3r.
29. *New Englands Prospect*, 91–2.

30. *A Key into the Language of America*, 1, 5–6. On Elizabethan titles of address, see Williams, "'O! When Degree is Shak'd.'"
31. *A Plaine Path-Way to Plantations*, 105.
32. See Hulme, *Colonial Encounters*; Greenblatt, *Marvelous Possessions*; Fuller, *Voyages in Print*; and Read, *New World, Known World*.
33. Quinn (ed.), *The Voyages and Colonising Enterprises of Sir Humphrey Gilbert*, ii.451–2.
34. Quinn (ed.), *The Roanoke Voyages*, i.375.
35. Quinn (ed.), *The Roanoke Voyages*, i.52.
36. On Harriot's linguistic undertakings, see Salmon, "Thomas Harriot (1560–1621)." A cumulative record of Indian words recorded by early Anglophones in Virginia can be found in Quinn (ed.), *The Roanoke Voyages*, ii.884–900.
37. Barbour (ed.), *The Jamestown Voyages*, i.94.
38. *The Journal of John Winthrop*, 683. Despite his fame and his own claims to linguistic proficiency, Smith may well have been among the Anglophones who did not learn a native language. See Sayre, *Les sauvages américains*, 66–7.
39. E.g., Hamor, *A True Discourse*, ii.237.
40. Quinn (ed.), *The Roanoke Voyages*, i.337–8.
41. Quinn et al. (eds), *New American World*, iii.371.
42. Krapp, *The English Language in America*, i.173.
43. *New English Canaan*, 112.
44. *The Journal of John Winthrop*, 299.
45. See Calloway (ed.), *The World Turned Upside Down*, 1–19.
46. Quinn et al. (eds), *New American World*, iii.476.
47. See Francis Magnel's observations in Barbour, *The Jamestown Voyages*, i.154. On *truchements*, see Fisher, *Champlain's Dream*, 496, and Sayre *Les sauvages américains*, 7. The latter suggests that "the English more often kidnapped Indians in the hope that they could learn English and then promote their captors' interests among their tribe" (24).
48. Barbour (ed.), *The Complete Works of Captain John Smith*, ii.258–60.
49. *A True Discourse of the Late Voyages of Discouerie*, 12.
50. Seyer (ed.), *Memoirs Historical and Topographical*, ii.247.
51. Quinn et al. (eds), *New American World*, iv.216–18.
52. Dodding states that he showed Calichoughe's corpse to the woman (Egnock or Ignorth), in order to convince her that the English did not practice either human sacrifice or cannibalism. Egnock's indifference convinces Dodding and others that the woman had regarded Calichoughe "with an astonishing degree of contempt." Four days after Calichoughe's burial on November

8, 1577 she was buried, dead from unspecified causes and leaving no record of ever having spoken English. The child died a short time later.

53. See, for example, Quinn et al. (eds), *New American World*, iii.371; Barbour (ed.), *The Complete Works of Captain John Smith*, ii.447; and Bradford, *Of Plymouth Plantation*, 79–81.

54. See further Greenblatt, *Marvelous Possessions*, 86–118.

55. Quinn et al. (eds), *New American World*, iii.351.

56. *New English Canaan*, 104.

57. *New Englands Prospect*, 92.

58. Barbour (ed.), *The Jamestown Voyages*, i.104.

59. See Wright, "Medieval Mixed-Language Business" and "Macaronic Writing in a London Archive, 1380–1480."

60. V.ii.265–6. See OED, s.v., 'broken', sense 13.d.

61. *A Relation or Journal of the Beginning and Proceedings of the English Plantation*, 32.

62. *A Voyage into New England*, 22.

63. *A Key into the Language of America*, A7r.

64. Axtell, "Babel of Tongues," 36.

65. Quinn (ed.) *The Roanoke Voyages*, ii.569–60; Hakluyt, *Principall Navigations*, 506. Also see Strachey, *The Historie of Travaile*, 12.

66. Mullaney, *The Place of the Stage*, 163; Lewis and Clark, *The Journals of Lewis and Clark*, 54. Identification of Welsh-descended Indians continues to be something of a cottage industry.

CHAPTER EIGHT

1. Throughout this chapter I use 'South Seas,' 'Oceania,' and 'South Pacific' interchangeably to embrace Melanesia, Micronesia, and Polynesia. When referring to one of these regions in particular, I use the conventional designations, though I recognize that these are the subject of continuing debate and reassessment.

2. Salmond, *Aphrodite's Island*, 41–2.

3. Walker, *Ka Whawhai Tonu Matou*, 80–1, and Campbell, *A History of the Pacific Islands*, 152–4.

4. Beaglehole (ed.), *The Journals of Captain James Cook*, iii.1306–8.

5. *Observations*, 244.

6. Beaglehole (ed.), *The Journals of Captain James Cook*, i.169. Another Tahitian, Hitihiti, served as an interpreter for much of Cook's second voyage.

7. Lovett, *The History of the London Missionary Society*, i.120–1, 161.

8. *Typee*, 81.
9. *Typee*, 142.
10. *Before the Wind*, 25.
11. *The Discovery of Tahiti*, 119.
12. Beaglehole (ed.), *The Journals of Captain James Cook*, iii.1103.
13. *Journal of the Right Hon. Joseph Banks*, 59. Several years before John Byron, who captained the British ship Dolphin on one of the first pan-Pacific voyages of exploration, likewise had judged the Patagonians' speech to be something less than a language: "Their language appeared to us to be nothing more than a confused jargon, without any mixture of the Spanish or Portugueze, the only European tongues of which it was possible for them to obtain any knowledge; and with which it is probable it would have been mixed, had they any immediate intercourse with the Spaniards or Portugueze of South America" (*A Voyage round the World*, 47).
14. *The Voyage of the Beagle*, 414.
15. *Hawaii*, 349.
16. *An Account of the Natives*, i.xxvii.
17. *Observations*, 250.
18. *New Zealand and Its Aborigines*, 99.
19. *Hawaii*, 347.
20. *Journal of the Right Hon. Joseph Banks*, 164.
21. *Typee*, xiv, 126.
22. Beaglehole (ed.), *The Journals of Captain James Cook*, i.286–7, 425; iii.1253–4 and 1231–5, 817; Foster, *Observations*, 389–400.
23. *A Residence of Twenty-One Years*, 153.
24. *A Narrative of Missionary Enterprises*, 527, 529.
25. *An Account of the Natives*, ii.xxviii–xxx. The grammar and dictionary begin at ii.353.
26. Quoted in Lovett, *The History of the London Missionary Society*, i.185.
27. *Journal of the Right Hon. Joseph Banks*, 164.
28. *A Grammar and Vocabulary*, n.p. In fact, such grammatical paradigms could be forced on English with just as poor a fit. Priestley's *Rudiments* (14–21), for instance, offers similarly static conjugations of English verbs.
29. *Typee*, 225.
30. *Observations*, 184–90, 249–50.
31. *Hawaii*, 66.
32. *A Narrative of Missionary Enterprises*, x–xi.
33. *History of the Hawaiian Islands*, 40.
34. *A Residence of Twenty-One Years*, 101–2.

35. *Journal of a Residence in the Sandwich Islands*, 110–1.
36. Lovett, *The History of the London Missionary Society*, i.266; Robertson, *The Discovery of Tahiti*, 193.
37. Lovett, *The History of the London Missionary Society*, ii.528; Ellis, *Polynesian Researches*, 262–3.
38. *A View of the Present State of Ireland*, 67.
39. Campbell, *A History of the Pacific Islands*, 64.
40. Quoted in Lovett, *The History of the London Missionary Society*, i.135; Darwin, *The Voyage of the Beagle*, 405.
41. *Six Months in Hawaii*, 231.
42. Thomas and Eves (eds), *Bad Colonists*, 64, and Melville, *Typee*, 139.
43. *A Narrative of Missionary Enterprises*, 453.
44. *Polynesian Researches*, 72.
45. *New Zealand and Its Aborigines*, 99–100.
46. *Nineteen Years in Polynesia*, 359.
47. *History of the Hawaiian Islands*, 105.
48. *A Residence of Twenty-One Years*, 103.
49. *Voyages made in the years 1788 and 1789*, i.193.
50. *Journal of the Right Hon. Joseph Banks*, 407.
51. Ross and Moverley, *The Pitcairnese Language*; and Siegel, *The Emergence of Pidgin and Creole Languages*.
52. See further Chaudenson, *Creolization of Language and Culture*; and Mufwene, *The Ecology of Language Evolution*.
53. "the people of New-brittain speak a very different Language from those of New-Holland. Now should it be found that the Natives of New-Britain and those of New Guiney have had one Origin and speake the same Language, it will follow of Course that the New-Hollanders are a different people from both" (Beaglehole (ed.), *The Journals of Captain James Cook*, i.411). Cook uses a similar phrase to distinguish among the aboriginal residents of New Holland (Australia): "it is very probable that they are a different people and speake a different Language" (i.398).
54. "The Society's Work," 87–8.
55. Belich, *Replenishing the Earth*, 4.
56. On the development of British identity see further Colley's landmark *Britons*.
57. On diglossia in medieval England, see further Machan, *English in the Middle Ages*, 71–110.

CHAPTER NINE

1. *A Vocabulary*, 9.
2. See Simpson, *The Politics of American English*; Kramer, *Imagining Language in America*; and Howe, *Language and Political Meaning in Revolutionary America*.
3. *Dissertations on the English Language*, 36.
4. Quoted in Unger, *Noah Webster*, 96.
5. See further Baron, *Grammar and Good Taste*.
6. Quoted in Reece, *The Origins of the American High School*, 38.
7. *The American Spelling Book*, 55; and *An American Dictionary of the English Language*, s.v. 'love' (n.) and 'patriotism' (n.).
8. *McGuffey's Second Eclectic Reader*, 28; and *McGuffey's Fifth Eclectic Reader*, 101.
9. Cubberley, *Readings in Public Education in the United States*, 313. Emphasis in the original.
10. Quoted in Spring, *The American School*, 83. See further Cmiel, *Democratic Eloquence*.
11. The ironic twist of this initiative is that as a female-dominated profession, elementary and secondary education is also a low-paying profession, relative to others, and having been typed as female, one less likely to attract males.
12. Coleman, *American Indian Children at School*, 44; and Adams, *Education for Extinction*, 26–7. Private and mission schools dedicated to the education of Indians also persisted throughout the period, and their enrollments considerably amplified enrollments in federal schools. In 1900, for example, enrollment in private as well as federal boarding schools exceeded 26,000. See Reyhner and Eder, *American Indian Education*, 151. Also see Mitchell, *Raising Freedom's Child*. On Dartmouth, see Calloway, *The Indian History of An American Institution*. A good overview of Carlisle in particular can be found in Witmer, *The Indian Industrial School*.
13. Quoted in Prucha (ed.), *Americanizing the American Indians*, 196.
14. *Battlefield and Classroom*, 284–5.
15. Prucha (ed.), *Americanizing the American Indians*, 233.
16. Prucha (ed.), *Americanizing the American Indians*, 14.
17. The founder of Hampton was Samuel Chapman, the son of a missionary in Hawaii. Pratt and he remained close throughout their lives, and a small number of Indians continued to enroll in Hampton even after Carlisle opened. See Robinson, "Indian Education at Hampton Institute."
18. Prucha (ed.), *Americanizing the American Indians*, 251.

19. *Battlefield and Classroom*, 268. A good, balanced discussion of the complex achievements of Carlisle can be found in Pfister, *Individuality Incorporated*, 31–95. The educational treatment of American Indians has many parallels with the education of non-Anglophone indigenes in Ireland, Scotland, Wales, Australia, and New Zealand. See the discussion of Coleman, *American Indians, the Irish, and Government Schooling.*
20. "Miss Alice Fletcher on Indian Names."
21. "What's in a Name." Though published in one of the Carlisle newspapers, this address initially was delivered before the St. Louis Indian Teachers' Institute.
22. Prucha (ed.), *Americanizing the American Indians*, 198.
23. Prucha (ed.), *Americanizing the American Indians*, 213.
24. Prucha (ed.), *Americanizing the American Indians*, 203.
25. Prucha (ed.), *Americanizing the American Indians*, 203.
26. Works like the *Synopsis of Course Study and Directions, Information concerning the United States Industrial School at Carlisle, Course of Study for The Indian Schools of the United States,* and the various Carlisle catalogues and reports of the Commission of Indian Affairs detail a well-planned, step-by-step progression for all of the conventional disciplines. How much of this structure was put into practice is of course difficult to say.
27. *My People the Sioux*, 146.
28. *Battlefield and Classroom*, 155.
29. *Information concerning the United States Industrial School*, 54–5.
30. Adams, *Education for Extinction*, 136–42; and Robinson, "Indian Education at Hampton Institute." Birch's *Methods of Teaching English* also used the objective method. Pedagogy taken from deaf education is mentioned early on, but it's not clear that Carlisle used it for very long. See "Home Items" and "Beginnings, Methods and Progress."
31. "Literary Society Details."
32. Francis La Flesche specifies that the boarding school he attended used a McGuffey reader, while Charles Eastman notes only that he received "a little English primer." See La Flesche, *The Middle Five*, x; and Eastman, *From the Deep Woods*, 44.
33. "Beginnings, Methods and Progress," and *Annual Report of Commissioner of Indian Affairs*, 236–7.
34. *From the Deep Woods*, 46. For discussion of pedagogical methods in the instruction of Indians, see Spack, *America's Second Tongue*, 45–76.
35. *Synopsis of Course of Study and Directions.*

36. *Methods of Teaching English*, 7.
37. *Battlefield and Classroom*, 222.
38. *Battlefield and Classroom*, 121.
39. *From the Deep Woods*, 49, 58, 57, 66.
40. Trennert, *The Phoenix Indian School*, 60–1.
41. Vučković, *Voices from Haskell*, 179.
42. *Methods of Teaching English*, 7.
43. "My Dear Friend."
44. "Letter."
45. *Adventures in the Apache Country*, 390.
46. *Battlefield and Classroom*, 180, 187.
47. *The Middle Five*, 76, xviii. In fact, La Flesche reveals his education and rhetorical sophistication by, for the most part, using utterly conventional non-standard expressions like 'ain't' and even, improbably, 'old boy.'
48. Quoted in Adams, *Education for Extinction*, 142. The various Carlisle newspapers contain many letters and articles with sentences like these: "This morning I can not glad William and Max and Oliver and Pollock and Sarah all go ont I can not glad this morning me I say Oliver Good-bye," and "Dear Miss Semple you letter do you like sweet apple yes, Im like sweet apple has good to eat and do you like sour apple?" Authorship of student writing is sometimes in doubt, since Pratt, although he did publish works under his own name, also could well have published institutionally supportive pieces that he attributed to students and former students. Particularly in the earliest student newspapers, however, the writing is sometimes so garbled as to seem credibly the production of new learners—unless, that is, one regards Pratt as so Machiavellian as intentionally to mangle his own prose.
49. Quoted in Pfister, *Individuality Incorporated*, 89. See further Hoxie, *A Final Promise*.
50. By 1911, 5,351 students had attended the school since it opened its doors; 583 of these graduated. See "Carlisle Commencement" and Adams, *Education for Extinction*, 290.
51. *Battlefield and Classroom*, 209.
52. *My People the Sioux*, 167.
53. *Battlefield and Classroom*, 55.
54. "Carlisle Indian School" and Lomawaima, *They Called It Prairie Light*, 15.
55. Vučković, *Voices from Haskell*, 73, 89–90.
56. Coleman, *American Indian Children at School*, 155, and Vučković, *Voices from Haskell*, 84–5. On the subsequent history and present

character of the English used by Native American, see Leap, *American Indian English.*

57. "True Friendship," written in quatrains of octosyllabic lines, and "Iniskin or the Buffalo Rock."
58. "Education." See further Pfister, *Individuality Incorporated,* 69–71.
59. Goodburn, "Literary Practices at the Genoa Industrial School."
60. *The Middle Five,* xvi–xviii.
61. *My People the Sioux,* 129, 239, 189.
62. E.g., Spack, *America's Second Tongue;* and Cheyfitz, *The Poetics of Imperialism.*
63. Pratt, *Battlefield and Classroom,* 215–6.
64. "Carlisle Commencement."
65. *Catalogue and Synopsis of Courses,* 56.
66. *Information concerning the United States Industrial School at Carlisle,* 55, and "Spelling Words."
67. *My People the Sioux,* 147. See further Pfister, *Individuality Incorporated,* 55–6.
68. Riney, *The Rapid City Indian School,* 78.
69. Quoted in Adams, *Education for Extinction,* 23; emphasis in the original.
70. Trennert, *The Phoenix Indian School,* 65–6.
71. *My People the Sioux,* 187.
72. "How a Little Sioux Boy."
73. Vučković, *Voices from Haskell,* 215.
74. *My People the Sioux,* 155.
75. *My People the Sioux,* 256.

CHAPTER TEN

1. Wheeler, "Fight to Disarm His Life's Work, Henry Ford Vows."
2. Gibson and Lennon, "Historical Census Statistics."
3. Spring, *American Education,* 239.
4. Spring, *American Education,* 239.
5. Berrol, *Immigrants at School,* 43–4.
6. Gibson and Lennon, "Historical Census Statistics"; and Siegel, Martin, and Bruno, "Language Use and Linguistic Isolation," 1.
7. On the population of North American Indians, which fell from perhaps a 5.5 million pre-Columban high to as low as 237,000 in 1900, see Shoemaker, *American Indian Population Recovery in the Twentieth Century.*

8. Hooker, *Life in the Shadows of the Crystal Palace*, 46, and Mason, "'Americans First'," 193.

9. Meyer, *The Five Dollar Day*, 2.

10. *The New Immigration*, 160, 297.

11. Korman, *Industrialization, Immigrants, and Americanizers*, 42–6.

12. Quoted in Korman, *Industrialization, Immigrants, and Americanizers*, 153.

13. Mirel, *Patriotic Pluralism*.

14. *A Study of American Intelligence*, 197, 205, 210. In the years to come, it's important to acknowledge, at least Brigham would repudiate much of his early argument.

15. Quoted in Spring, *The American School*, 113.

16. Quoted in Berrol, *Immigrants at School*, 223.

17. Quoted in Meyer, *The Five Dollar Day*, 78.

18. Hooker, *Life in the Shadows*, 85, and Babson, *Working Detroit*, 25.

19. Roberts, *The New Immigration*, 78–85.

20. Roberts, "The Y.M.C.A. Teaching Foreign-Speaking Men," 22

21. Mirel, *Patriotic Pluralism*, 68–76.

22. Mason, "'Americans First'," and Lape, "The English First Movement in Detroit." For the coordination of this movement, see Mirel, *Patriotic Pluralism*, 76–8. On Americanization and English education in industries, see Korman, "Americanization at the Factory Gate."

23. *Reading and Language Lessons*, 3.

24. Price, *The Direct Method of Teaching English*, and O'Brien, *English for Foreigners*.

25. *English for Coming Americans*, 6, 28, 30.

26. *The New Immigration*, 4, 140, 286.

27. "The Y.M.C.A. Teaching Foreign-Speaking Men," 19, 20.

28. Mason, "'Americans First'," 200.

29. "The Y.M.C.A. Teaching Foreign-Speaking Men," 21, 22.

30. Battistella, *Do You Make These Mistakes in English?*

31. Quoted in Meyer, *The Five Dollar Day*, 16.

32. Taylor's most influential books were *Shop Management* and *The Principles of Scientific Management*, which post-date Ford's introduction of the assembly line. So far as I can tell, Ford did not explicitly espouse Taylorism, though many of his management activities were certainly consistent with it.

33. "Automobile Trade Notes."

34. "Educational Statistics Home Plant."

35. "Ford 'Original Americans'," and Witmer, *The Indian Industrial School*, 78. An additional 60 former Carlisle students were hired by

Ford to work at the Hog Island shipyard (near Philadelphia) during the First World War (Pfister, *Individuality Incorporated*, 94).

36. Quoted from an unidentified newspaper article in *Five Dollar Day (1909–1919)*, folder 1.

37. Quoted in Meyer, *The Five Dollar Day*, 126.

38. "The Ford Idea in Education," 910.

39. "The Ford Idea in Education," 914.

40. "The So-Called Profit Sharing System in the Ford Plant," 302. As described in several memos in the Ford archives, the system evolved over time, including the lowering of the third group's age to 21 and the formalizing of the status of female workers.

41. "The Ford Idea in Education," 916.

42. "The Ford Idea in Education," 912.

43. "Assimilation through Education," 407.

44. *Helpful Hints and Advice*, 32.

45. Quoted from an unidentified newspaper article in *Five Dollar Day (1909–1919)*, folder 1.

46. "Editorial" and "Assimilation through Education," 407.

47. "Editorial" and *Factory Facts from Ford* (1917), 54.

48. "Better Workmen and Citizens," 315–17, and *Factory Facts from Ford* (1917), 55.

49. There are extant photographs of both classroom situations, though those of long tables arrayed before chalkboards and set up on the lawn outside the Crystal Palace may well be staged. One account written shortly after the school closed implies that workers were paid for the 90-minute sessions, but Ford documents consistently describe the classes as taking place before or after the work day. See "Ford and Labor," 3.

50. Hooker, *Life in the Shadows*, 116–7.

51. "The Ford Idea in Education," 915.

52. "Industrial Teachers," 117.

53. "Assimilation through Education," 410; *Factory Facts from Ford* (1917), 55; *Factory Facts from Ford* (1915), 51.

54. "Better Workmen and Citizens," 316. It is perhaps because Ford relied on these ephemeral sheets rather than textbooks that apparently no teaching materials survive, though Rev. Marquis's later decision to destroy many of the materials associated with the Educational Department may be a factor as well.

55. Bushnell, *The Truth about Henry Ford*, 214.

56. *Factory Facts from Ford* (1915), 53; "Assimilation through Education," 410.

57. "Assimilation through Education," 410.

58. "A Brief Account," and Nevins and Hill, *Ford*, i.358.
59. *Factory Facts from Ford* (1917), 55.
60. Korman, *Industrialization, Immigrants, and Americans*, 143, 160, 162, 186.
61. Quoted in Babson, *Working Detroit*, 35.
62. Korman, *Industrialization, Immigrants, and Americanizers*, 145.
63. Korman, "Americanization at the Factory Gate," 243.
64. "A Motto Wrought into Education"; "The Making of Americans"; "From Codfish to Motor Cars"; De Witt, "Industrial Teachers," 119; Lippmann, *Public Opinion*, 86–7.
65. "Program for Second Annual Americanization Day," and "Better Workmen and Citizens," 319.
66. *Factory Facts from Ford* (1917), 55.
67. "A Motto Wrought into Education," 407.
68. *Factory Facts from Ford* (1920), 53; "Better Workmen and Citizens," 319.
69. "The Ford 'American Club'."
70. E.g., "Assimilation through Education," and "Give Men a Chance—Not Charity."
71. Nevins and Hill, *Ford*, ii.340–1. Since most of the records of the Ford Sociological Department have been lost, exact enrollment figures are unavailable.
72. "Better Workmen and Citizens," 318.
73. Mason, "'Americans First'," 196.
74. "Assimilation through Education," 410.
75. "The Ford Idea in Education," 911–12.
76. Ford, *My Life and Work*, 111.
77. Meyer, *The Five Dollar Day*, 161.
78. "Educational Statistics Home Plant," and *Factory Facts from Ford* (1920), 55.
79. "The So-Called Profit Sharing System," 307.
80. "Testimonials." This and several other testimonials are designated as translations from another language. Also see Nevins and Hill, *Ford*, i.559–60.
81. *Factory Facts from Ford* (1915), 51.
82. "The So-Called Profit Sharing System," 305–6.
83. "Profit Sharing in the United States," 106.
84. Quoted from a Company letter of April 29, 1914 to the manager of the Cincinnati plant in *Five Dollar Day (1909–1919)*, folder 2.
85. Hooker, *Life in the Shadows*, 87.
86. Nevins and Hill, *Ford*, i.553, and Hooker, *Life in the Shadows*, 86.
87. Mason, "'Americans First'," 196.

88. Ford, *My Life and Work,* 77.
89. Batchelor, *Henry Ford;* Bryan, *Beyond the Model T;* Baldwin, *Henry Ford and the Jews;* Grandin, *Fordlandia.*
90. Grandin, *Fordlandia,* 252–3. In his 1919 libel suit, Ford devoted part of his testimony to trying to evade and qualify his earlier judgment of history. See Butterfield, "Henry Ford, The Wayside Inn, and the Problem of 'History is Bunk'."

CHAPTER ELEVEN

1. Reynolds, *In Command of History,* 143–4.
2. Quoted in Read, "British Recognition of American Speech in the Eighteenth Century," 39. On the barbarism of colonial English, also see Read, "Milestones in the Branching of British and American English."
3. Quoted in Bailey, *Images of English,* 129.
4. *Greater Britain,* i.318.
5. Quoted in Summerfield, "Patriotism and Empire," 29–30. Also see Richards, *Imperialism and Music,* 334.
6. Bridges, "The Society's Work," 87–8.
7. "About Us."
8. Quoted in Williamson, "The Doctrinal Politics of Stanley Baldwin," 199.
9. *Essays in Appreciation,* 300–1.
10. Quoted in Gilbert, *Churchill,* 89.
11. Quoted in Addison, "Winston Churchill's Concept of 'The English-Speaking Peoples'," 105.
12. Quoted in Toye, *Churchill's Empire,* 136.
13. Quoted in Addison, "Winston Churchill's Concept of 'The English-Speaking Peoples'," 106. Also see Churchill, "If Lee Had Not Won the Battle of Gettysburg." Churchill's puzzling negative arises because, perhaps not intellectually challenged enough by the notion of imaginary history, he imagines that Lee *had* won and then traces what followed therefrom, allowing the reader to realize what the South's loss had cost the English-speaking peoples and the world.
14. *The Idea of History,* 97.
15. *History of the English-Speaking Peoples,* i.viii.
16. *History of the English-Speaking Peoples,* iv.263.
17. The one exception is an account of German unification (iv.267–82), which Churchill intrudes without explanation or explicit

connection to the English-speaking peoples. Here again, I think, the presence of the chapter and its title—"The Rise of Germany"— reflect the political immediacy of the 1930s.

18. Kennedy, *A Bibliography of Writings on the English Language*, 404–5. Also see Gneuss, *English Language Scholarship*, 66.

19. *The Second World War*, i.ix.

20. Quoted in Toye, *Churchill's Empire*, 195.

21. *Blood, Toil, Tears and Sweat*, 165.

22. *Blood, Toil, Tears and Sweat*, 175, 195, 224.

23. *The Second World War*, v.124.

24. *Blood, Toil, Tears and Sweat*, 297, 301.

25. Boyle (ed.), *The Churchill-Eisenhower Correspondence*, 167.

26. Quoted in Toye, *Churchill's Empire*, 203.

27. *Blood, Toil, Tears and Sweat*, 177, 178.

28. Quoted in Morgan and Evans, *The Battle for Britain*, 15.

29. Chandler et al. (eds), *The Papers of Dwight David Eisenhower*, iii.1913.

30. Quoted in Toye, *Churchill's Empire*, 195.

31. See Addison, "Winston Churchill's Concept of 'The English-Speaking Peoples'." Toye has described Churchill's English-speaking peoples as "a seemingly racialized vision in which the Britons of the 'White Dominions' and America were linked as part of a broader global community with a common interest in defending freedom" (*Churchill's Empire*, 190). This much is true. But it's also true that the concept did allow Churchill to rally the Empire to withstand (with the considerable assistance of the Soviet Union and the United States) an overwhelming enemy and that the colonies as well as the dominions not only supported the concept but, as I argue at the close of this chapter, had their own autonomy hastened by it—which, of course, was not anything Churchill foresaw or desired.

32. *History of the English-Speaking Peoples*, ii.152.

33. For a concise statement of this policy see "Foreign Publicity."

34. See Edwards, *Berlin Calling*; Keen, *Treason on the Airwaves*; and Bergmeier and Lotz, *Hitler's Airwaves*, 45–121.

35. On Pound see Bergmeier and Lotz, *Hitler's Airwaves*, 73–9; also see Conolly, *Bernard Shaw and the BBC*, 106–14.

36. Crook, *International Radio Journalism*, 82.

37. Quoted in Bergmeier and Lotz, *Hitler's Airwaves*, 298.

38. Cole, *Lord Haw-Haw—and William Joyce*, and Martland, *Lord Haw Haw: The English Voice of Nazi Germany*.

39. Howe, *The Hunt for 'Tokyo Rose'*, 5.

40. Quoted in Close, *Tokyo Rose / An American Patriot*, 41–2.

41. Quoted in Cole, *Lord Haw-Haw*, 129.

42. Braverman, *To Hasten the Homecoming*, 78, and Close, *Tokyo Rose / An American Patriot*, 142–3.

43. Quoted in Braverman, *To Hasten the Homecoming*, 77.

44. Quoted in Cole, *Lord Haw-Haw*, 115, 132–4.

45. Cole, *Lord Haw-Haw*, 115; Martland, *Lord Haw Haw*, 42.

46. Quoted in Braverman, *To Hasten the Homecoming*, 86.

47. In 1942, when the audience at a London theater recognized Eisenhower's presence and began to call for a speech, he observed with self-deprecation, "It's nice to be back in a country where I can *almost* speak the language" (quoted in Ambrose, *Eisenhower*, 205).

48. Quoted in Gilbert, *Churchill*, 504.

49. "Remarks to the Advertising War Council Project."

50. Quoted in Gilbert, *Churchill*, 837.

51. Beevor, *D-Day*, 410.

52. "Food Conference," 3, 4.

53. *List of Publications for Training*, 240–2.

54. See Braverman, *To Hasten the Homecoming*, 82–4; Calder, *The People's War*, 358; and Stenton, *Radio London and Resistance in Occupied Europe*, 50–61.

55. "Declaration regarding the Defeat of Germany," and "Instrument of Surrender of Japanese Forces."

56. See further Chapman, *The British at War*, and McLaughlin and Parry, *We'll Always Have the Movies*, esp. 138–48.

57. For the former view, see Morgan and Evans, *The Battle for Britain*. For the latter, see Rose, *Which People's War?*, and Calder, *The People's War*.

58. Churchill made the remark in a speech to the Conservative Party conference on 15 March 1945 (*Victory* (ed. Eade), 75).

59. Fischer, *A History of the Pacific Islands*, 172.

60. Smyth, "Britain's African Colonies and British Propaganda," and Thompson, "The Language of Imperialism and the Meanings of Empire." This divided treatment of the "other" may be characteristic of colonialism. See Loomba, *Colonialism—Postcolonialism*, 173 and, more generally, Webster, *Englishness and Empire*, esp. 92–118, and Young, *The Idea of English Ethnicity*.

61. "Political Situation in the Union of South Africa," 2–3.

62. Belich, *Replenishing the Earth*, 456–78.

63. Reynolds, *In Command*, 45.

64. Wa Thiong'o, *Decolonising the Mind*, xiv; Mazrui, *English in Africa after the Cold War*, 54; Kachru, *The Other Tongue*.

65. McLaughlin and Parry, *We'll Always Have the Movies*, 27.
66. Boyle (ed.), *The Churchill-Eisenhower Correspondence*, 178.
67. Wiles et al., *English for the Armed Forces*, 2.
68. The popular humorist Park Kendall, for example, relates his confusion over the fact that in the United States 'bison' means 'buffalo' but down "in Australia a bison is what they wash there [sic] hands and face in" (*Still in the Draft*, n.p.).
69. It's important to note as well that not all Britons shared Churchill's enthusiasm for the English-speaking peoples. In his memoirs, for example, Field-Marshall Montgomery concentrates on military tactics and strategy and never engages the idea of a kinship based on language. In fact, he makes his resentment and dissatisfaction with the United States (and Eisenhower in particular) especially clear. See Montgomery, *The Memoirs of Field-Marshall the Viscount Montgomery of Alamein*.
70. Nicholas, *The Echo of War*, 239. Also see Asa Briggs, *The History of Broadcasting in the United Kingdom*.
71. Moore, *Speaking Our Language*, 139–40.
72. *Jungle Warfare*, 58.
73. Soames (ed.), *Speaking for Themselves*, 476.
74. Chandler et al. (eds), *The Papers of Dwight David Eisenhower*, ii.928 and i.503.
75. Chandler et al. (eds), *The Papers of Dwight David Eisenhower*, iv.2326.
76. Chandler et al. (eds), *The Papers of Dwight David Eisenhower*, ii.1271.
77. *A Short Guide to New Zealand*, 34–9.
78. Such war-time second-language manuals include Gettins, *Some Military Conversations*; Fergusson, *Essential French Military Terms*; and Von Aldenbruck, *Servicemen's Language Guide*.
79. *British Military Terminology*, 1.
80. *British Military Terminology*, 83.
81. *British Military Terminology*, 84, 85.
82. *British Military Terminology*, 85.
83. *Basic English and Its Uses*, 22.
84. "Report of Committee on Basic English," 1.
85. "Report of Committee on Basic English," 2.
86. "Report of Committee on Basic English," 3.
87. "Report of Committee on Basic English," 3.
88. Rose, *Which People's War?*, 11. The touchstone of modern discussions of nationhood remains Anderson, *Imagined Communities*.

89. "Study of the Organization of the European Theater of Operations," 32–3. Also see "Use of Personnel Other Than U.S. Military," 4.
90. Reynolds et al. (eds), *Allies at War*, xx. The line is often attributed to President John Kennedy at the 1963 ceremony making Churchill an honorary American citizen, and he did say it there. But he got it by reading Murrow's introduction to a recording of Churchill's wartime speeches. See Clarke, *Ask Not*, 68.

CHAPTER TWELVE

1. "Salman Kahn's Surgery in US Successful"; "Three Youths Arrested"; "Lawyer Regrets Lying." All quotations are taken from editions released on September 1, 2011.
2. For a book that does just this, see Mair, *Twentieth-Century English*.
3. Moro, *The Boundaries of Babel*.
4. *Aspects of the Theory of Syntax*, 3.
5. Such structural approaches, that is, fail to account for their own construction. As Newmeyer observes, there is "no theory-independent way to talk about possibility and impossibility in language" (*Possible and Probable Languages*, 3).
6. See further Townend, *Language and History in Viking Age England*.
7. Wright, "Medieval Mixed-Language Business Discourse," 382. I have expanded all abbreviations.
8. Machan, "When English Became Latin," and Mufwene, "Some Offspring of Colonial English are Creole."
9. The radioactive element technetium, for instance, is so unstable in nature that virtually all of it has been manufactured in laboratories. See Kean, *The Disappearing Spoon*, 138–40.
10. *Making the Social World*.
11. Searle, I should note, well might disagree with my analysis. He sees language as the foundation of all other institutions and not itself the product of declarations (see pp. 61–89 in particular). In so doing, though, I think he understandably treats language as a philosopher of language would—as an abstraction and not something particular (like English) that itself can be open to argument. By the same token, what I am here arguing about English in no way challenges what Searle says about language's role in fashioning social reality.
12. *Complete Poetry and Collected Prose*, 1165.
13. *Complete Poetry and Collected Prose*, 410.
14. *Complete Poetry and Collected Prose*, 25.

15. *The English Language in America*, i.275.
16. *The American Language*, 96.
17. "Minstrel of America." Sandberg used the phrase while giving a speech on Abraham Lincoln before a special joint session of Congress.
18. See, for example, Lighter's "Slang," Pederson's "Dialects," Schneider's "English in North America," and Finegan's, "English in North America."
19. In this sense, English might be likened to what is sometimes called a meme, or a self-replicating behavior that transfers ideas across a culture.
20. Both figure prominently in Lerer's *Inventing English*.
21. Parry, *The Trophies of Time*, and Vine, *In Defiance of Time*.
22. *Dissertations on the English Language*, 22–3.
23. *A Handbook of Phonetics*, 196.
24. *The Last Lingua Franca*, xix. For modern anxiety about the spread of English, see Phillipson, *Linguistic Imperialism* and *English-Only Europe?*; Pennycook, *The Cultural Politics of English as an International Language*; and Mair (ed.), *The Politics of English as a World Language*.
25. "Language Use in the United States: 2007."

Bibliography

Abley, Mark, *The Prodigal Tongue: Dispatches from the Future of English* (Boston, MA: Houghton Mifflin, 2008).

"About Us," English-Speaking Union, <http://www.esu.org/about-us>.

"A Brief Account of the Educational Work of the Ford Motor Company," *Ford Form 2697*, December 1916.

Adams, David Wallace, *Education for Extinction: American Indians and the Boarding School Experience, 1875–1928* (Lawrence, KS: University Press of Kansas, 1995).

Addison, Paul, "Winston Churchill's Concept of 'The English-Speaking Peoples'," in Attila Pók (ed.), *The Fabric of Modern Europe: Studies in Social and Diplomatic History* (Nottingham: Astra Press, 1999), 103–17.

Ælfric of Eynsham, *Lives of Saints, Being a Set of Sermons on Saints' Days Formerly Observed by the English Church*, ed. Walter W. Skeat, EETS 76, 82, 94, 114 (London: N. Trübner, 1881–1900).

Ælfric of Eynsham, *Grammatik und Glossar: Text und Varianten*, ed. Julius Zupitza (1880; rpt. Berlin: Max Niehans, 1966).

Algeo, John, "What is a Briticism?," in A. N. Doane et al. (eds), *Old English and New: Studies in Language and Linguistics in Honor of Frederic G. Cassidy* (New York: Garland, 1992), 287–304.

Algeo, John, "British and American Biases in English Dictionaries," in Braj B. Kachru and Henry Kahane (eds), *Cultures, Ideologies, and the Dictionary: Studies in Honor of Ladislav Zgusta* (Tübingen: Max Niemeyer Verlag, 1995), 205–12.

Algeo, John, "Vocabulary," in Suzanne Romaine (ed.), *The Cambridge History of the English Language*, iv, *1776–1997* (Cambridge: Cambridge University Press, 1999), 57–91.

Algeo, John (ed.), *The Cambridge History of the English Language*, vi, *English in North America* (Cambridge: Cambridge University Press, 2001).

Algeo, John, "External Factors," in Algeo (ed.), *English in North America*, 1–58.

Allan, Keith and Kate Burridge, *Forbidden Words: Taboo and Censoring of Language* (Cambridge: Cambridge University Press, 2006).

Allsopp, Jeanette, "Dictionaries of Caribbean English," in Cowie (ed.), *The Oxford History of English Lexicography*, i.353–77.

Alston, R. C., *English Grammars Written in English and English Grammars Written in Latin by Native Speakers* (Leeds: E. J. Arnold, 1965).

Alter, Stephen G., *Darwinism and the Linguistic Image: Language, Race, and Natural Theology in the Nineteenth Century* (Baltimore, MD: Johns Hopkins University Press, 1999).

Ambrose, Stephen E., *Eisenhower: Soldier and President* (New York: Simon and Schuster, 1990).

"A Motto Wrought into Education," *Ford Times*, April 1916, 407–9.

Anderson, Benedict, *Imagined Communities: Reflections on the Origin and Spread of Nationalism*, rev. edn (London: Verson, 1991).

A New English Dictionary on Historical Principles, 10 vols, 20 parts, ed. James A. H. Murray et al. (Oxford: Clarendon Press, 1888–1928).

Annual Report of Commissioner of Indian Affairs (Washington, D.C.: Bureau of Indian Affairs, 1907).

A Relation or Journal of the Beginning and Proceedings of the English Plantation Setled at Plimoth in New England (London: John Bellamie, 1622).

"Arizona Constitution," <http://www.azleg.gov/Constitution.asp>.

Ascham, Roger, *The Scholemaster, or Plaine and Perfite Way of Teachyng Children, to Vnderstand, Write, and Speake, the Latin Tong* (London: John Daye, 1570).

A Short Guide to New Zealand (Washington, D.C.: War and Navy Departments, 1943).

"Assimilation through Education: What the Ford English School Is Doing to Help the Foreign-born Ford Employee," *Ford Times*, June 1915, 406–11.

A Survey of Education in Hawaii, Made under the Direction of the Commissioner of Education (Washington, D.C.: Government Printing Office, 1920).

"Automobile Trade Notes," *New York Times*, November 15, 1914, VIII, 6, col. 3.

Axtell, James, "Babel of Tongues: Communicating with the Indians in Eastern North America," in Edward G. Gray and Norman Fiering (eds), *The Language Encounter in the Americas, 1492–1800: A Collection of Essays* (New York: Berghahn Books, 2000), 15–60.

Babbitt, E. H., "College Words and Phrases," *Dialect Notes*, 2 (1900), 3–70.

Babson, Steve, *Working Detroit: The Making of a Union Town* (Detroit, MI: Wayne State University Press, 1986).

Bacci, Massimo Livi, *The Population of Europe: A History* (Oxford: Blackwell, 2000).

Bailey, Richard W., "The English Language in Canada," in Bailey and Manfred Görlach (eds), *English as a World Language* (Ann Arbor, MI: University of Michigan Press, 1982), 134–76.

Bailey, Richard W., *Images of English: A Cultural History of the Language* (Ann Arbor, MI: University of Michigan Press, 1991).

Bailey, Richard W., "American English Abroad," in Algeo (ed.), *English in North America*, 456–96.

Baldwin, Neil, *Henry Ford and the Jews: The Mass Production of Hate* (New York: Public Affairs, 2001).

Banks, Joseph, *Journal of the Right Hon. Joseph Banks*, ed. Joseph D. Hooker (London: Macmillan, 1896).

Barbour, Philip L. (ed.), *The Jamestown Voyages under the First Charter, 1606–1609*, Hakluyt Society 136, 137 (London: Cambridge University Press, 1969).

Barbour, Philip L. (ed.), *The Complete Works of Captain John Smith (1580–1631)*, 3 vols (Chapel Hill, NC: University of North Carolina Press, 1986).

Barfield, Owen, *History in English Words* (New York: George H. Doran, 1926).

Baron, Dennis E., *Grammar and Good Taste: Reforming the American Language* (New Haven, CT: Yale University Press, 1982).

Batchelor, Ray, *Henry Ford: Mass Production, Modernism, and Design* (Manchester: Manchester University Press, 1994).

Battistella, Edwin L., *Bad Language: Are Some Words Better Than Others?* (Oxford: Oxford University Press, 2005).

Battistella, Edwin L., *Do You Make These Mistakes in English? The Story of Sherwin Cody's Famous Language School* (Oxford: Oxford University Press, 2009).

Bauer, Laurie, *Watching English Change: An Introduction to the Study of Linguistic Change in Standard Englishes of the Twentieth Century* (London: Longman, 1994).

Bauer, Laurie, "Competition in English Word Formation," in Ans van Kemenade and Bettelou Los (eds), *The Handbook of the History of English* (Malden, MA: Blackwell, 2006), 177–98.

Baugh, Albert C. and Thomas Cable, *A History of the English Language*, 5th edn (Upper Saddle River, NJ: Prentice Hall, 2001).

Beaglehole, J. C. (ed.), *The Journals of Captain James Cook on His Voyages of Discovery*, 4 vols (Cambridge: Cambridge University Press, 1955–1974).

Bede, The Venerable, *The Old English Version of Bede's Ecclesiastical History of the English People*, ed. Thomas Miller, EETS nos 95, 96, 110, 111 (London: N. Trübner, 1890–98).

Bede, The Venerable, *Historiam Ecclesiasticam Gentis Anglorum*, ed. Charles Plummer (1896; rpt. Oxford: Clarendon Press, 1975).

Beevor, Anthony, *D-Day: The Battle for Normandy* (New York: Viking, 2009).

"Beginnings, Methods and Progress," *Eadle Keatah Toh*, vol. 1, no. 5, August 1880.

Belich, James, *Replenishing the Earth: The Settler Revolution and the Rise of the Anglo-World, 1783–1939* (Oxford: Oxford University Press, 2009).

Benham, Manette K. P. and Ronald H. Heck, *Culture and Education Policy in Hawai'i: The Silencing of Native Voices* (Mahwah, NJ: Lawrence Erlbaum, 1998).

Beowulf and the Fight at Finnsburg, ed. Fr. Klaeber, 3d edn (Boston, MA: Heath, 1950).

Bergmeier Horst J. P. and Rainer E. Lotz, *Hitler's Airwaves: The Inside Story of Nazi Radio Broadcasting and Propaganda Swing* (New Haven, CT: Yale University Press, 1997).

Berrol, Selma Cantor, *Immigrants at School: New York City, 1898–1914* (New York: Arno Press, 1978).

Best, George, *A True Discourse of the Late Voyages of Discouerie* (London: Henry Bynnyman, 1578).

"Better Workmen and Citizens," *Ford Times*, February 1917, 315–9.

Biller, Peter, *The Measure of Multitude: Population in Medieval Thought* (Oxford: Oxford University Press, 2000).

Bingham, Hiram, *A Residence of Twenty-One Years in the Sandwich Islands*, 3rd edn (Canandaigua, NY: H. D. Goodwin, 1855).

Birch, C. E., *Methods of Teaching English*, 2nd edn (Lawrence, KS: Haskell Institute, 1914).

Bird, Isabella, *Six Months in Hawaii* (1875; rpt. London: KPI, 1986).

Blake, N. F., *Caxton and His World* (London: Andre Deutsch, 1969).

Blank, Paula, *Broken English: Dialects and the Politics of Language in Renaissance Writings* (New York: Routledge, 1996).

Blank, Paula, "The Babel of Renaissance English," in Lynda Mugglestone (ed.), *The Oxford History of English*, 212–39.

Bosworth, Joseph, *The Origin of the English, Germanic and Scandinavian Languages and Nations* (London: Longman, 1848).

Boyle, Peter G. (ed.), *The Churchill-Eisenhower Correspondence, 1953–1955* (Chapel Hill, NC: University of North Carolina Press, 1990).

Bradford, William, *Of Plymouth Plantation, 1620–1647*, ed. Samuel Eliot Morison (New York: Alfred A. Knopf, 1952).

Bradley, Henry, *The Making of English* (London: Macmillan, 1904).

Braverman, Jordan, *To Hasten the Homecoming: How Americans Fought World War II through the Media* (Lanham, MD: Madison Books, 1996).

Brewer, Charlotte, *Treasure-House of the Language: The Living OED* (New Haven, CT: Yale University Press, 2007).

Brewer, Charlotte, "The Use of Literary Quotations in the *Oxford English Dictionary*," *Review of English Studies*, 61 (2010), 93–125.

Bridenbaugh, Carl, *Jamestown, 1544–1699* (New York: Oxford University Press, 1980).

Bridges, Robert, "The Society's Work" (Society for Pure English, tract XXI, 1925), in W. F. Bolton and David Crystal (eds), *The English Language*, 2 vols, ii, *Essays by Linguists and Men of letters, 1858–1964* (Cambridge: Cambridge University Press, 1969), 86–99.

Briggs, Asa, *The History of Broadcasting in the United Kingdom*, 5 vols (London: Oxford University Press, 1961–1965), iii, *The War of Words*.

Brigham, Carl C., *A Study of American Intelligence* (Princeton, NJ: Princeton University Press, 1923).

British Military Terminology, Military Intelligence Service (Washington, D.C.: War Department, May 15, 1943), U.S. Army Heritage & Education Center.

Brown, William, *New Zealand and Its Aborigines: Being an Account of the Aborigines, Trade, and Resources of the Colony* (London: Smith Elder, 1845).

Browne, J. Ross, *Adventures in the Apache Country* (New York: Harper & Brothers, 1869).

Brut: Edited from British Museums ms. Cotton Caligula A. IX and British Museum ms. Cotton Otho C. XIII, ed. G. L. Brook and R. F. Leslie, EETS nos 250, 277 (London: Oxford University Press, 1963, 1978).

Bryan, Ford R., *Beyond the Model T: The Other Ventures of Henry Ford* (Detroit, MI: Wayne State University Press, 1990).

Bullokar, John, *An English Expositor, Teaching the Interpretation of the Hardest Words Vsed in Our Language* (London: John Legatt, 1616).

Bullokar, William, *The Amendment of Orthographie for English Speech* (1580; rpt. Amsterdam: De Capo Press, 1968).

Bullokar, William, *Pamphlet for Grammar* (London: Edmund Bollifant, 1586).

Burchfield, Robert, *Unlocking the English Language* (London: Faber and Faber, 1989).

Burridge, Kate, *Blooming English: Observations on the Roots, Cultivation and Hybrids of the English Language* (Cambridge: Cambridge University Press, 2004).

Burridge, Kate, *Weeds in the Garden of Words: Further Observations on the Tangled History of the English Language* (Cambridge: Cambridge University Press, 2005).

Bushnell, Sarah T., "Give Men a Chance – Not Charity." *National Magazine* 49 (1920), 155–8.

Bushnell, Sarah T., *The Truth about Henry Ford* (Chicago, IL: The Reilly & Lee Co., 1922).

Butterfield, Ardis, *The Familiar Enemy: Chaucer, Language and Nation in the Hundred Years War* (Oxford: Oxford University Press, 2009).

Butterfield, Jeremy, *Damp Squid: The English Language Laid Bare* (Oxford: Oxford University Press, 2008).

Butterfield, Robert, "Henry Ford, The Wayside Inn, and the Problem of 'History is Bunk'," in John C. Wood and Michael C. Wood (eds), *Henry Ford: Critical Evaluations in Business and Management*, 2 vols (London: Routledge, 2003), i.113–25.

Byron, John, *A Voyage round the World in His Majesty's Ship the Dolphin*, 2nd edn (London: J. Newbery and F. Newbery, 1767).

Cable, Thomas, "History of the History of the English Language: How Has the Subject Been Studied?," in Haruko Momma and Michael Matto (eds), *A Companion to the History of the English Language* (Malden, MA: Blackwell, 2008), 11–17.

Calder, Angus, *The People's War, Britain, 1939–1945* (New York: Pantheon, 1969).

Calloway, Colin G. (ed.), *The World Turned Upside Down: Indian Voices from Early America* (Boston, MA: St Martin's, 1994).

Calloway, Colin G., *The Indian History of An American Institution: Native Americans and Dartmouth* (Hanover, NH: Dartmouth College Press, 2010).

Camden, William, *Remains concerning Britain* (1605; rpt. Yorkshire: EP Publishing Limited, 1974).

Cameron, Deborah, *Verbal Hygiene* (London: Routledge, 1995).

Campbell, I. C., *A History of the Pacific Islands* (Berkeley, CA: University of California Press, 1989).

Carew, Richard, "The Excellency of the English Tongue," in Camden, *Remains*, 42–51.

"Carlisle Commencement '11," PI 6-1, Box 12, Cumberland County Historical Society.

"Carlisle Indian School: Seventy-Five Different Languages Spoken by the Students," *New York Times*, March 17, 1912, section 7, X13.

Cassidy, Frederic G. and Joan Houston Hall (eds), *Dictionary of American Regional English*, 5 vols (Cambridge, MA: Belknap Press of Harvard University Press, 1985–2012).

Cassidy, Frederic G. and Joan Houston Hall, "Americanisms," in Algeo (ed.), *English in North America*, 184–218.

Cassidy, Frederic G. and Richard N. Ringler (eds), *Bright's Old English Grammar & Reader*, 3rd edn (New York: Holt, Rinehart and Winston, 1971).

Catalogue and Synopsis of Courses (Carlisle, PA: Carlisle Indian Press, 1915).

Cawdry, Robert, *A Table Alphabeticall: Conteyning and Teaching the True Writing, and Vnderstanding of Hard Vsuall English Wordes* (London: Roberts, 1604).

Chambers, J. K., "'Lawless and Vulgar Innovations': Victorian Views of Canadian English," in Sandra Clarke (ed.), *Focus on Canada* (Amsterdam: John Benjamins, 1993), 1–26.

Chambers, R. W. and Marjorie Daunt (eds), *A Book of London English 1384–1425* (Oxford: Clarendon Press, 1931).

Chambers, William and Robert Chambers, *History of the English Language and Literature* (London: W. and R. Chambers, 1861).

Chancellor, William E., *Reading and Language Lessons for Evening Schools* (New York: American Book Company, 1904).

Chandler, Alfred D. Jr. et al. (eds), *The Papers of Dwight David Eisenhower*, 21 vols (Baltimore, MD: The Johns Hopkins Press, 1970–2001).

Chapman, James, *The British at War: Cinema, State and Propaganda, 1939–1945* (London: I. B. Tauris, 1998).

Chaucer, Geoffrey, *The Riverside Chaucer*, ed. Larry D. Benson, 3rd edn (Boston, MA: Houghton Mifflin, 1987).

Chaudenson, Robert, *Creolization of Language and Culture*, rev. in collaboration with Salikoko S. Mufwene, trans. Sheri Pargman et al. (London: Routledge, 2001).

Cheyfitz, Eric, *The Poetics of Imperialism: Translation and Colonization from The Tempest to Tarzan* (New York: Oxford University Press, 1991).

Chiswick, Barry R. and Paul W. Miller, "Language Skills and Earnings among Legalized Aliens," *Journal of Population Economics*, 12 (1999), 63–89.

Chomsky, Noam, *Aspects of the Theory of Syntax* (Cambridge, MA: MIT Press, 1965).

Churchill, Sir Winston, "If Lee Had Not Won the Battle of Gettysburg," in J. C. Squire (ed.), *If It Had Happened Otherwise: Lapses into Imaginary History* (London: Longmans, 1931), 175–96.

Churchill, Sir Winston, *Victory: War Speeches by the Right Hon Winston S. Churchill O.M., C.H., M.P.*, ed. Charles Eade (London: Cassell, 1946).

Churchill, Sir Winston, *The Second World War*, 6 vols (Boston, MA: Houghton Mifflin, 1948–1953).

Churchill, Sir Winston, *A History of the English-Speaking Peoples*, 4 vols (New York: Dodd, Mead, 1956–58).

Churchill, Sir Winston, *Blood, Toil, Tears and Sweat: The Great Speeches*, ed. David Cannadine (London: Penguin, 2007).

Clark, Herbert H., *Arenas of Language Use* (Chicago, IL: University of Chicago Press, 1992).

Clark, Herbert H., *Using Language* (Cambridge: Cambridge University Press, 1996).

Clarke, Thurston, *Ask Not: The Inauguration of John F. Kennedy and the Speech that Changed America* (New York: Holt, 2010).

Cleland, James, *Hērō-paideia, or The Institution of a Young Noble Man* (London: Joseph Barnes, 1607).

Close, Frederick P., *Tokyo Rose / An American Patriot: A Dual Biography* (Lanham, MD: Scarecrow Press, 2010).

Cmiel, Kenneth, *Democratic Eloquence: The Fight over Popular Speech in Nineteenth-Century America* (New York: William Morrow, 1990).

Cole, J. A., *Lord Haw-Haw – and William Joyce: The Full Story* (London: Faber and Faber, 1964).

Coleman, Julie, *A History of Cant and Slang Dictionaries*, ii, *1785–1858* (Oxford: Oxford University Press, 2004).

Coleman, Julie, *The Life of Slang* (Oxford: Oxford University Press, 2012).

Coleman, Michael C., *American Indian Children at School, 1850–1930* (Jackson, MS: University Press of Mississippi, 1993).

Coleman, Michael C., *American Indians, the Irish, and Government Schooling: A Comparative Study* (Lincoln, NE: University of Nebraska Press, 2007).

Colley, Linda, *Britons: Forging The Nation, 1707–1837* (New Haven, CT: Yale University Press, 1992).

Collingwood, R. G., *The Idea of History* (Oxford: Clarendon Press, 1946).

Conolly, L. W., *Bernard Shaw and the BBC* (Toronto: University of Toronto Press, 2009).

Considine, John, *Dictionaries in Early Modern Europe: Lexicography and the Making of Heritage* (Cambridge: Cambridge University Press, 2008).

Considine, John, "Literary Classics in *OED* Quotation Evidence," *Review of English Studies*, 60 (2009), 620–38.

Cook, Emily S., "What's in a Name," *The Arrow*, September 22, 1904, vol. 1., no. 5.

Course of Study for The Indian Schools of the United States, Industrial and Literary (Washington, D.C.: Government Printing Office, 1901).

Cowie, A. P. (ed.), *The Oxford History of English Lexicography*, 2 vols (Oxford: Clarendon Press, 2009).

Craik, George L., *A Manual of English Literature and of the History of the English Language from the Norman Conquest*, 2 vols (Leipzig: Tauchnitz, 1874).

Crook, Tim, *International Radio Journalism: History, Theory and Practice* (London: Routledge, 1998).

Crosfield, Thomas, *The Diary of Thomas Crosfield*, ed. Frederick S. Boas (London: Oxford University Press, 1935).

Crotch, W. J. B. (ed.), *The Prologues and Epilogues of William Caxton*, EETS os 176 (1928; rpt. New York: Burt Franklin, 1971).

Crouse, Karen, "Mastering the Language Game: Tutors Help L.P.G.A. Golfers Understand One Another Better," *New York Times*, October 14, 2010, B12, B14.

Crowley, Tony, *The Politics of Discourse: The Standard Language Question in British Cultural Debates* (Basingstoke: Macmillan, 1989).

Crowley, Tony (ed.), *Proper English? Readings in Language, History and Cultural Identity* (London: Routledge, 1991).

Crowley, Tony, *Standard English and the Politics of Language*, 2nd edn (Houndmills: Palgrave Macmillan, 2003).

Crystal, David, *The Cambridge Encyclopedia of the English Language*, 2nd edn (Cambridge: Cambridge University Press, 2003).

Crystal, David, *The Stories of English* (Woodstock, NY: Overlook, 2004).

Crystal, David, "English Worldwide," in Hogg and Denison (eds), *A History of the English Language*, 420–39.

Cubberley, Ellwood P., *Readings in Public Education in the United States: A Collection of Sources and Readings to Illustrate the History of Educational Practice and Progress in the United States* (Boston, MA: Houghton Mifflin, 1934).

Cursor Mundi, ed. Richard Morris, EETS nos 57, 59, 62, 66, 68, 99, 101 (London: Trübner, 1874–93).

Darwin, Charles, *The Origin of Species and The Descent of Man* (New York: The Modern Library, 1936).

Darwin, Charles, *The Voyage of the Beagle*, intro. Leonard Engel (Garden City, NY: Doubleday, 1962).

Dávila, Alberto et al., "Accent Penalties and the Earnings of Mexican-Americans," *Social Science Quarterly*, 74 (1993), 902–16.

Dearborn, Benjamin, *The Columbian Grammar: or, An Essay for Reducing a Grammatical Knowledge of the English Language to a Degree of Simplicity* (Boston, MA: Samuel Hall, 1795).

"Declaration regarding the Defeat of Germany and the Assumption of Supreme Authority by Allied Powers," June 5, 1945, The Avalon Project, <http://avalon.law.yale.edu/wwii/ger01.asp>.

De Klerk, Vivian (ed.), *Focus on South Africa* (Amsterdam: John Benjamins, 1996).

De Klerk, Vivian, *Corpus Linguistics and World Englishes: An Analysis of Xhosa English* (London: Continuum, 2006).

De Witt, Clinton C., "Industrial Teachers," in *Proceedings: Americanization Conference* (Washington, D.C.: Government Printing Office, 1919), 114–19.

Dickens, Charles, *Bleak House*, ed. Norman Page (Harmondsworth: Penguin, 1975).

Dilke, Charles Wentworth, *Greater Britain: A Record of Travel in English-Speaking Countries during 1866 and 1867*, 2 vols (London: Macmillan, 1868).

Dood, Philip, *The Reverend Guppy's Aquarium: Encounters with Heroes of the English Language, from the Earl of Sandwich to Joseph P. Frisbie* (London: Random House, 2007).

Dorman, Larry, "L.P.G.A. Sees Use of English as a Facilitator for Better Business Deals," *New York Times*, August 31, 2008, Sports 5.

Durkin, Philip, *The Oxford Guide to Etymology* (Oxford: Oxford University Press, 2009).

Earle, John, *The Philology of the English Tongue* (Oxford: Clarendon Press, 1892).

Eastman, Charles A., *From the Deep Woods to Civilization: Chapters in the Autobiography of an Indian* (1916; Lincoln, NE: University of Nebraska Press, 1977).

Eburne, Richard, *A Plaine Path-Way to Plantations* (London: G.P., 1624).

Echard, Siân, *Printing the Middle Ages* (Philadelphia, PA: University of Pennsylvania Press, 2008).

"Editorial," *Ford Times*, December 1916, 195.

Edmond, Rod, *Representing the South Pacific: Colonial Discourse from Cook to Gauguin* (Cambridge: Cambridge University Press, 1997).

"Education," *School News*, vol. 1, no. 4, September 1880.

"Educational Statistics Home Plant," typescript (January 27, 1917), Nevins and Hill Research, Box 27, acc. 572, Benson Ford Research Center.

Edwards, John Carver, *Berlin Calling: American Broadcasters in Service to the Third Reich* (New York: Praeger, 1991).

Edwards, Philip (ed.), *Last Voyages: Cavendish, Hudson, Raleigh: The Original Narratives* (Oxford: Clarendon Press, 1988).

Ellis, William, *Polynesian Researches, during a Residence of Nearly Six Years in the South Sea Islands*, 2 vols (London: Fisher, Son, and Jackson, 1829).

Emerson, Oliver Farrar, *The History of the English Language* (London: Macmillan, 1894).

Emmett, Boris, "Profit Sharing in the United States," *Bulletin of the United States Bureau of Labor Statistics*, 208 (1917).

"English Language Unity Act of 2009," U.S. English, <http://www.us-english.org/view/575>.

Errington, Joseph, *Linguistics in a Colonial World: A Story of Language, Meaning, and Power* (Malden, MA: Blackwell, 2008).

Factory Facts from Ford, 2nd edn (Detroit, MI: Ford Motor Company, 1915).

Factory Facts from Ford, 3rd edn (Detroit, MI: Ford Motor Company, 1917).

Factory Facts from Ford, 4th edn (Detroit, MI: Ford Motor Company, 1920).

Fergusson, B. E., *Essential French Military Terms: English-French* (Aldershot: Gale & Polden, 1942).

Ferreiro, J. A., *Everyday English for Hawaii's Children* (Wailuku, HI: Maui Publishing Co., n.d.).

Filppula, Markku et al., *English and Celtic in Contact* (New York: Routledge, 2008).

Finegan, Edward, "English in North America," in Hogg and Denison (eds), *A History of the English Language*, 384–419.

Fischer, Steven Roger, *A History of the Pacific Islands* (Houndsmills: Palgrave, 2002).

Fisher, David Hackett, *Champlain's Dream* (New York: Simon & Schuster, 2008).

Five Dollar Day (1909–1919), 2 folders (December 1909 – February 1914, and March 1914 – July 1919), Benson Ford Research Center.

Fjalldal, Magnús, "How Valid Is the Anglo-Scandinavian Passage in *Gunnlaug's Saga* as Historical Evidence?" *Neophilologus*, 77 (1993), 601–9.

Fletcher, Alice, "Miss Alice Fletcher on Indian Names," *The Arrow*, September 8, 1904, vol. 1., no. 3.

"Food Conference: Memorandum by the Secretary of State for Foreign Affairs," War Cabinet, June 28, 1943, National Archives.

Foote, Peter and Randolph Quirk (eds), *Gunnlaugssaga Ormstungu* (London: Viking Society for Northern Research, 1953).

"Ford and Labor," *Pipp's Weekly* 4 (August 25, 1923), 1–3.

Ford, Henry, *My Life and Work* (Garden City, NY: Doubleday, 1922).

"Ford 'Original Americans'," *Ford Times*, February 1916, 305.

"Foreign Publicity: A Memorandum by the Secretary of State for Foreign Affairs," War Cabinet, July 10, 1939, National Archives.

Foster, Johann Reinhold, *Observations Made during a Voyage round the World*, ed. Nicholas Thomas et al. (1778; Honolulu: University of Hawaii Press, 1996).

Fowler, H. W. and F. G. Fowler, *The King's English*, 2nd edn (Oxford: Clarendon Press, 1919).

Fowler, William C., *The English Language in Its Elements and Forms, with a History of Its Origin and Development*, rev. edn (New York: Harper and Brothers, 1855).

Franklin, Wayne, *Discoverers, Explorers, Settlers: The Diligent Writers of Early America* (Chicago, IL: University of Chicago Press, 1979).

Free, John, *An Essay Towards an History of the English Tongue* (London: W. Sandby, 1749).

Freedman, Paul, "Rural Society," in Michael Jones (ed.), *The New Cambridge Medieval History*, vi, *c.1300–c.1415* (Cambridge: Cambridge University Press, 2000), 82–101.

"From Codfish to Motor Cars," *Ford Times*, August 1915, 29–31.

Fuller, Mary C., *Voyages in Print: English Travel in America, 1576–1624* (Cambridge: Cambridge University Press, 1995).

Garg, Anu, *The Dord, the Diglot, and an Avocado or Two: The Hidden Lives and Strange Origins of Words* (New York: Plume, 2007).

Garner, Bryan A, "Shakespeare's Latinate Neologisms," in Vivian Salmon and Edwina Burness (eds), *A Reader in the Language of Shakespearean Drama: Essays* (Amsterdam: John Benjamins, 1987), 207–28.

Gettins, J. H., *Some Military Conversations and Official Communications in French*, 4th edn (Aldershot: Gale & Polden, 1944).

Gibson, Campbell J. and Emily Lennon, "Historical Census Statistics on the Foreign-born Population of the United States: 1850–1990," US Census Bureau, <http://www.census.gov/population/www/documentation/twps0029/twps0029.html>.

Gil, Alexander, *Logonomia Anglica* (1621; rpt. Menston: Scolar Press, 1968).

Gilbert, Martin, *Churchill: A Life* (New York: Holt, 1991).

Gildas, *The Ruin of Britain and Other Works*, ed. and trans. Michael Winterbottom (London: Philmore, 1978).

"Glossary of Terms," South Carolina Education Oversight Committee, <http://www.eoc.sc.gov/Pages/index.aspx>.

Gneuss, Helmut, *English Language Scholarship: A Survey and Bibliography from the Beginnings to the End of the Nineteenth Century* (Binghamton, NY: Medieval and Renaissance Texts and Studies, 1996).

Goodburn, Amy, "Literary Practices at the Genoa Industrial School," *Great Plains Quarterly*, 19 (1999), 35–52.

Gordon, Elizabeth et al., *New Zealand English: Its Origins and Evolution* (Cambridge: Cambridge University Press, 2004).

Görlach, Manfred, *Explorations in English Historical Linguistics* (Heidelberg: Carl Winter, 2002).

Gough, Daniel, "Black English in South Africa," in de Klerk (ed.), *Focus on South Africa*, 53–77.

Grandin, Greg, *Fordlandia: The Rise and Fall of Henry Ford's Forgotten Jungle City* (New York: Metropolitan Books, 2009).

Greenblatt, Stephen, *Marvelous Possessions: The Wonder of the New World* (Oxford: Clarendon, 1991).

Grigg, David B., *Population Growth and Agrarian Change: An Historical Perspective* (Cambridge: Cambridge University Press, 1980).

Gunson, Niel, *Messengers of Grace: Evangelical Missionaries in the South Seas, 1797–1860* (Melbourne: Oxford University Press, 1978).

Hakluyt, Richard, *The Principall Navigations, Voiages, and Discoveries of the English Nation*, 2 vols. (1589; rpt. London: Cambridge University Press, 1965).

Hamilton, Derrick et al., "Measuring the Wage Costs of Limited English: Issues with Using Interviewer Versus Self-Reports in Determining Latino Wages," *Hispanic Journal of Behavioral Sciences*, 30 (2008), 257–79.

Hamor, Ralph, *A True Discourse of the Present Estate of Virginia* (London: John Beale, 1615).

Hansen, Harry (ed.), *The World Almanac and Book of Facts for 1950* (New York: New York World-Telegram, 1950).

Harley, Heidi, *English Words: A Linguistic Introduction* (Malden, MA: Blackwell, 2006).

Harrison, Matthew, *The Rise, Progress and Present Structure of the English Language*, 3rd edn (Philadelphia, PA: E. C. and J. Biddle, 1861).

Hart, John, *An Orthographie* (1569; rpt. Menston: Scolar Press, 1969).

Helpful Hints and Advice to Employes [sic]: To Help them Grasp the Opportunities which are Presented to them by the Ford Profit-sharing Plan (Detroit, MI: Ford Motor Company, 1915).

Henry, H., *The Poor Letter H: Its Use and Abuse* (London: Effingham Wilson, 1859).

Herbert, Christopher, *Culture and Anomie: Ethnographic Imagination in the Nineteenth Century* (Chicago: University of Chicago Press, 1991).

Hickes, George, *Institutiones Grammaticæ Anglo-Saxonicæ et Moeso-Gothicæ* (Oxford: Sheldon Theatre, 1689).

Hoad, Terry, "Preliminaries: Before English," in Mugglestone (ed.), *The Oxford History of English*, 7–31.

Hogg, Richard and David Denison (eds), *A History of the English Language* (Cambridge: Cambridge University Press, 2006).

Holborow, Marnie, *The Politics of English: A Marxist View of Language* (London: Sage, 1999).

Holinshed, Ralph, *The First and Second Volumes of Chronicles* (London: Henry Denham, 1587).

"Home Items," *Eadle Keatah Toh*, vol. 1, no. 1, January 1880.

Honey, John, *Does Accent Matter? The Pygmalion Factor* (London: Faber and Faber, 1989).

Honey, John, *Language Is Power: The Story of Standard English and Its Enemies* (London: Faber and Faber, 1997).

Hooker, Clarence, *Life in the Shadows of the Crystal Palace, 1910–1927: Ford Workers in the Model T Era* (Bowling Green, OH: Bowling Green State University Popular Press, 1997).

Hopkins, Manley, *Hawaii: The Past, Present, and Future of Its Island-Kingdom* (London: Longman, 1862).

Horace, *Epistles, Book II and Epistle to the Pisones (Ars Poetica)*, ed. Njall Rudd (Cambridge: Cambridge University Press, 1989).

Hosada, Megumi and Eugene Stone-Romero, "Effects of Foreign Accents on Employment-Related Decisions," *Journal of Managerial Psychology*, 25 (2010), 113–32.

"How a Little Sioux Boy, 13 Years Old, Feels about Talking English," *School News*, vol. 2, no. 7, December 1881.

Howe, John, *Language and Political Meaning in Revolutionary America* (Amherst, MA: University of Massachusetts Press, 2004).

Howe, Russell Warren, *The Hunt for 'Tokyo Rose'* (Lanham, MD: Madison Books, 1990).

Hoxie, Frederick E., *A Final Promise: The Campaign to Assimilate the Indians, 1880–1920*, with a new preface (Lincoln, NE: University of Nebraska Press, 2001).

Hudson, Anne (ed.), *Selections from English Wycliffite Writings* (Cambridge: Cambridge University Press, 1978).

Hughes, Geoffrey, *A History of English Words* (Oxford: Blackwell, 2000).

Hulme, Peter, *Colonial Encounters: Europe and the Native Caribbean, 1462–1797* (London: Methuen, 1986).

Hulse, Carl, "'Recovery' is in; 'Stimulus' is so Seven Months Ago," *New York Times*, November 26, 2008, A20.

Information concerning the United States Industrial School at Carlisle, Pennsylvania (Carlisle, PA: Carlisle Indian School, 1908).

"Iniskin or the Buffalo Rock," PI 6-1, Box 12, Cumberland County Historical Society.

"Instrument of Surrender of Japanese Forces under the Command or Control of the Supreme Commander," September 2, 1945, The Avalon Project, <http://avalon.law.yale.edu/wwii/j3.asp>.

"International Poll Finds Americans Twice as Frustrated with Bad English than with Technical Incompetence of Contact Center Agents; Foreign Accents Most Significant Contact Center Frustration among U.S. Respondents," *Business Wire*, May 1, 2006, <http://0-search.proquest.com.libus.csd.mu.edu/docview/445237266/1344C70D22C7D7A1343/1?accountid=100>.

Jarves, James Jackson, *History of the Hawaiian Islands*, 4th edn (1843; rpt. Honolulu, HI: Henry M. Whitney, 1872).

Jespersen, Otto, *Growth and Structure of the English Language*, 9th edn (Oxford: Blackwell, 1946).

Johnson, Dr Samuel, *A Dictionary of the English Language*, 2 vols (London: Strahan, 1755).

Jones, Hugh, *An Accidence to the English Tongue* (London: John Clarke, 1724).

Jones, Richard Foster, *The Triumph of English* (Stanford, CA: Stanford University Press, 1953).

Jonson, Ben, *The English Grammar* (1640; rpt. Menston: Scolar Press, 1972).

Jungle Warfare, FM 72–20 (Washington, D.C.: October 27, 1944), U.S. Army Heritage & Education Center.

Kachru, Braj B., *The Other Tongue: English Across Cultures*, 2nd edn (Urbana, IL: University of Illinois Press, 1992).

Kachru, Braj B. et al. (eds), *The Handbook of World Englishes* (Malden, MA: Blackwell, 2006).

Kacirk, Jeffrey, *The Word Museum: The Most Remarkable English Words Ever Forgotten* (New York: Touchstone, 2000).

Kahn, Charles H., *The Art and Thought of Heraclitus: An Edition of the Fragments with Translation and Commentary* (Cambridge: Cambridge University Press, 1979).

Kaluza, Max, *Historische Grammatik der Englischen Sprache*, 2 vols (Berlin: Emil Felber, 1900).

Katamba, Francis, *English Words: Structure, History, Usage*, 2nd edn (London: Routledge, 2005).

Kean, Sam, *The Disappearing Spoon, and Other True Tales of Madness, Love, and the History of the World from the Periodic Table of the Elements* (New York: Little Brown, 2010).

Keen, Judith, *Treason on the Airwaves: Three Allied Broadcasters on Axis Radio during World War II* (Westport, CT: Praeger, 2009).

Kelman, James, *How Late It Was, How Late* (London: Secker and Warburg, 1994).

Kendall, Park, *Still in the Draft* (New York: M. S. Mill Co., 1942).

Kendall, Thomas and Samuel Lee, *A Grammar and Vocabulary of the Language of New Zealand* (London: R. Watts, 1820).

Kennedy, Arthur G., *A Bibliography of Writings on the English Language: From the Beginning of Printing to the End of 1922* (1927; rpt. New York: Hafner, 1961).

Korman, Gerd, *Industrialization, Immigrants, and Americanizers: The View from Milwaukee, 1866–1921* (Madison, WI: State Historical Society of Wisconsin, 1967).

Korman, Gerd, "Americanization at the Factory Gate," in John C. Wood and Michael C. Wood (eds), *Henry Ford: Critical Evaluations in Business and Management*, 2 vols (London: Routledge, 2003), i.223–51.

Kramer, Michael P., *Imagining Language in America: From the Revolution to the Civil War* (Princeton, NJ: Princeton University Press, 1992).

Krapp, George Philip, *Modern English: Its Growth and Present Use* (New York: Charles Scribner's Sons, 1909).

Krapp, George Philip, *The English Language in America*, 2 vols (New York: The Century Co., 1925).

Kron, Josh, "For Rwandan Students, Ethnic Tensions Lurk," *New York Times*, May 17, 2010, A9.

Lacey, Marc, "Arizona Candidate Challenged over Level of English Skills," *New York Times*, January 26, 2012, A11, A18.

La Flesche, Francis, *The Middle Five: Indian Schoolboys of the Omaha Tribe*, foreword David A Baerreis (1900; rpt. Lincoln, NE: University of Nebraska Press, 1978).

Landau, Sidney I., "Major American Dictionaries," in Cowie (ed.), *The Oxford History of English Lexicography*, i.182–229.

"Language Use in the United States: 2007," US Census Bureau, <http://www.census.gov/hhes/socdemo/language/data/acs/ACS-12.pdf>.

Lape, Esther Everett, "The English First Movement in Detroit," *The Immigrants in America Review*, 1 (1915), 46–50.

Lass, Roger W., "Where Do Extraterritorial Englishes Come from? Dialect, Input, and Recodification in Transported Englishes," in Sylvia Adamson et al. (eds), *Papers form the 5th International Conference in English Historical Linguistics* (Amsterdam: John Benjamins, 1990), 245–80.

Lass, Roger W., *Historical Linguistics and Language Change* (Cambridge: Cambridge University Press, 1997).

Lass, Roger W., "Language Periodization and the Concept 'Middle'," in Irma Taavitsainen et al. (eds), *Placing Middle English in Context: Selected Papers from the Second Middle English Conference* (Berlin: Mouton de Gruyter, 2000), 7–41.

"Lawyer Regrets Lying against Police Chief," *The Guardian* (Nigeria), September 1, 2011, <http://odili.net/news/source/2011/sep/1/6.html>.

Leap, William L., *American Indian English* (Salt Lake City, UT: University of Utah Press, 1993).

Lee, John R., "The So-Called Profit Sharing System in the Ford Plant," *Annals of the American Academy of Political and Social Science*, 65 (1916), 297–310.

Leech, Geoffrey et al., *Word Frequencies in Written and Spoken English* (Harlow: Longman, 2001).

Leonard, Sterling, *The Doctrine of Correctness in English Usage, 1700–1800* (Madison, WI: University of Wisconsin Press, 1929).

Lerer, Seth, *Inventing English: A Portable History of the Language* (New York: Columbia University Press, 2007).

Levett, Christopher, *A Voyage into New England* (London: William Jones, 1624).

Lewin, Tamar, "Foreign Students Take More Seats on Campus, and Pay the Freight," *New York Times*, February 5, 2012, A1, A21.

Lewis, C. S., *Studies in Words*, 2nd edn (Cambridge: Cambridge University Press, 1967).

Lewis, Meriwether and William Clark, *The Journals of Lewis and Clark* (Whitefish, MT: Kessinger Publishing, 2004).

Lewis, M. Paul (ed.) *Ethnologue: Languages of the World* (Dallas, TX: SIL, 2009).

Lighter, Jonathon E., "Slang" in Algeo (ed.), *English in North America*, 219–52.

Lippi-Green, Rosina, *English with an Accent: Language, Ideology, and Discrimination in the United States*, 2nd edn (London: Routledge, 2012).

Lippmann, Walter, *Public Opinion* (New York: Harcourt, Brace, 1922).

List of Publications for Training, FM-21-6 (Washington, D.C.: War Department, February 1, 1944), U.S. Army Heritage & Education Center.

"Literary Society Details," *The Arrow*, January 12, 1905, vol. 1, no. 20.

Lomawaima, K. Tsianina, *They Called It Prairie Light: The Story of Chilocco Indian School* (Lincoln, NE: University of Nebraska Press, 1994).

Loomba, Ania, *Colonialism – Postcolonialism* (London: Routledge, 1998).

Lounsbury, Thomas R., *History of the English Language*, rev. edn (New York: Henry Holt, 1894).

Lovett, Richard, *The History of the London Missionary Society 1795–1895*, 2 vols (London: Henry Frowde, 1899).

Luick, Karl, *Historische Grammatik der Englischen Sprache* (1914–40; rpt. Cambridge, MA: Harvard University Press, 1964).

Lyell, Charles, *The Geological Evidences of the Antiquity of Man* (London: John Murray, 1863).

Machan, Tim William, "*forlynen*: A Ghost Word Rematerializes," *Notes and Queries*, 31 (1984), 22–4.

Machan, Tim William, "Kynaston's *Troilus*, Textual Criticism, and the Renaissance Reading of Chaucer," *Exemplaria*, 5 (1993), 161–83.

Machan, Tim William, *English in the Middle Ages* (Oxford: Oxford University Press, 2003).

Machan, Tim William, *Language Anxiety: Conflict and Change in the History of English* (Oxford: Oxford University Press, 2009).

Machan, Tim William, "French, English, and the Late Medieval Linguistic Repertoire," in Jocelyn Wogan-Browne et al. (ed.), *Language and Culture in Medieval Britain: The French of England c.1100–c.1500* (York: York Medieval Press, 2009), 363–72.

Machan, Tim William, "When English Became Latin," in Brian Cummings and James Simpson (eds), *Cultural Reformations: Medieval and Renaissance in Literary History* (Oxford University Press, 2010), 247–63.

Machan, Tim William, "Chaucer and the History of English," *Speculum*, 87 (2012), 147–75.

Machan, Tim William and Charles T. Scott (eds), *English in Its Social Contexts: Essays in Historical Sociolinguistics* (New York: Oxford University Press, 1992).

Mackay, Charles, *The Lost Beauties of the English Language: An Appeal to Authors, Poets, Clergymen, and Public Speakers* (New York: J. W. Bouton, 1874).

Mair, Christian (ed.), *The Politics of English as a World Language: New Horizons in Postcolonial Cultural Studies* (Amsterdam: Rodopi, 2003).

Mair, Christian, *Twentieth-Century English: History, Variation, and Standardization* (Cambridge: Cambridge University Press, 2006).

Makoni, Sinfree et al. (eds), *Black Linguistics: Language, Society and Politics in Africa and the Americas* (London: Routledge, 2003).

Mallet, Max et al., "The Most Annoying, Pretentious and Useless Business Jargon," *Forbes*, January 26, 2012, <http://www.forbes.com/sites/groupthink/2012/01/26/the-most-annoying-pretentious-and-useless-business-jargon/>.

Marquis, Rev. Samuel S., "The Ford Idea in Education," in National Education Association of the United States, *Addresses and Proceedings of the Fifty-Fourth Annual Meeting*, 54 (Ann Arbor, MI: NEA, 1916), 910–17.

Marsh, George, *Lectures on the English Language*, edited with additional lectures and notes by William Smith (London: Murray, 1872).

Marshall, Jonathan, *Language Change and Sociolinguistics: Rethinking Social Networks* (New York: Palgrave Macmillan, 2004).

Martin, John, *An Account of the Natives of the Tonga Islands*, 2nd edn, 2 vols (London: John Murray, 1818).

Martland, Peter, *Lord Haw Haw: The English Voice of Nazi Germany* (Kew: The National Archives, 2003).

Mason, Gregory, "'Americans First': How the People of Detroit Are Making Americans of the Foreigners in the City," *The Outlook*, 114 (1916), 193–201.

Matthews, David, *The Invention of Middle English: An Anthology of Primary Sources* (Turnhout: Brepols, 2000).

May, Stephen, *Language and Minority Rights: Ethnicity, Nationalism and the Politics of Language* (London: Longman, 2001).

Mazrui, Alamin M., *English in Africa after the Cold War* (Clevedon: Multilingual Matters, 2004).

McCrum, Robert, *Globlish: How English Became the World's Language* (New York: W. W. Norton, 2010).

McEnery, Tony, *Swearing in English: Bad Language, Purity and Power from 1586 to the Present* (London: Routledge, 2006).

McGuffey, William, *McGuffey's Second Eclectic Reader*, rev. edn (New York: American Book Company, 1879).

McGuffey, William, *McGuffey's Fifth Eclectic Reader*, rev. edn (New York: American Book Company, 1879).

McKean, Erin, *Totally Weird and Wonderful Words* (Oxford: Oxford University Press, 2006).

McLaughlin, Robert L. and Sally E. Parry, *We'll Always Have the Movies: American Cinema during World War II* (Lexington, KY: University of Kentucky Press, 2006).

McWhorter, John H., *Doing Our Own Thing: The Degradation of Language and Music and Why We Should, Like, Care* (New York: Gotham Books, 2003).

McWhorter, John H., *Language Interrupted: Signs of Non-native Acquisition in Standard Language Grammars* (Oxford: Oxford University Press, 2007).

Meares, John, *Voyages made in the Years 1788 and 1789, from China to the N.W. Coast of America*, 2 vols (London: J. Walter, 1791).

Melville, Herman, *Typee, a Peep at Polynesian Life*, ed. Harrison Hayford et al. (Evanston, IL., Northwestern University Press, 1968).

Mencken, H. L., *The American Language: An Inquiry into the Development of English in the United States*, 4th edn (New York: Alfred A. Knopf, 1936).

Mesthrie, Rajend and Rakesh M. Bhatt, *World Englishes: The Study of New Linguistic Varieties* (Cambridge: Cambridge University Press, 2008).

Meyer III, Stephen, *The Five Dollar Day: Labor, Management, and Social Control in the Ford Motor Company, 1908–1921* (Albany, NY: State University of New York Press, 1981).

Michael, Ian, *The Teaching of English: From the Sixteenth Century to 1870* (Cambridge: Cambridge University Press, 1987).

Milroy, James, "The Consequences of Standardisation in Descriptive Linguistics," in Tony Bex and Richard J. Watts (eds), *Standard English: The Widening Debate* (London: Routledge, 1999), 16–39.

Milroy, James, "The Legitimate Language: Giving a History to English," in Watts and Trudgill (eds), *Alternative Histories of English*, 7–25.

Milroy, James and Lesley Milroy, *Authority in Language: Investigating Standard English*, 3rd edn (London: Routledge, 1999).

Milton, John, *Complete Poems and Major Prose*, ed. Merritt Y. Hughes (New York: Odyssey, 1957).

"Minstrel of America," *New York Times*, February 13, 1959, 21.

Mirel, Jeffrey E., *Patriotic Pluralism: Americanization, Education, and European Immigrants* (Cambridge, MA: Harvard University Press, 2010).

Mitchell, Mary Niall, *Raising Freedom's Child: Black Children and Visions of the Future after Slavery* (New York: New York University Press, 2008).

Mojsin, Lisa, *Mastering the American Accent* (Haupauge, NY: Barron's Educational Series, 2009).

Montgomery, Bernard Law, *The Memoirs of Field-Marshall the Viscount Montgomery of Alamein* (Cleveland, OH: World Publishing, 1958).

Moore, Bruce, *Speaking Our Language: The Story of Australian English* (Melbourne: Oxford University Press, 2008).

Morgan, David and Mary Evans, *The Battle for Britain: Citizenship and Ideology in the Second World War* (London: Routledge, 1993).

Morley, Joan, "Perspectives on English for Academic Purposes," in James E. Alatis (ed.), *Linguistics and Language Pedagogy: The State of the Art* (Washington, D.C.: Georgetown University Press, 1991), 143–66.

Moro, Andrea, *The Boundaries of Babel: The Brain and the Enigma of Impossible Languages*, trans. Ivano Caponigro and Daniel B. Kane (Cambridge, MA: MIT Press, 2008).

Morton, Herbert C., *The Story of 'Webster's Third': Philip Gove's Controversial Dictionary and Its Critics* (Cambridge: Cambridge University Press, 1994).

Morton, Thomas, *New English Canaan or New Canaan* (Amsterdam: Jacob Stam, 1637).

Mufwene, Salikoko S., "African-American English," in Algeo (ed.), *English in North America*, 291–324.

Mufwene, Salikoko S., *The Ecology of Language Evolution* (Cambridge: Cambridge University Press, 2001).

Mufwene, Salikoko S., "Some Offspring of Colonial English are Creole," in Markku Filppula et al. (eds), *Vernacular Universals and Language Contacts: Evidence from Varieties of English and Beyond* (New York: Routledge, 2009), 280–303.

Mugglestone, Lynda, *'Talking Proper': The Rise of Accent as Social Symbol*, 2nd edn (Oxford: Oxford University Press, 2003).

Mugglestone, Lynda, *Lost for Words: The Hidden History of the Oxford English Dictionary* (New Haven, CT: Yale University Press, 2005).

Mugglestone, Lynda, "English in the Nineteenth Century," in Mugglestone (ed.), *The Oxford History of English*, 274–304.

Mugglestone, Lynda (ed.), *The Oxford History of English* (Oxford: Oxford University Press, 2006).

Mugglestone, Lynda, "The Oxford English Dictionary," in Cowie (ed.), *The Oxford History of English Lexicography*, i.230–59.

Mühlhäusler, Peter, *Pidgin & Creole Linguistics* (Oxford: Blackwell, 1986).

Mulcaster, Richard, *The First Part of the Elementarie* (1582; rpt. Menston: Scolar Press, 1970).

Mullaney, Steven, *The Place of the Stage: License, Play, and Power in Renaissance England* (Chicago, IL: University of Chicago Press, 1988).

Mummert, Roger, "Sounds Like Home," *New York Times*, June 20, 2008, D7.

Murray, Sir James A. H., "Ninth Annual Address of the President to the Philological Society," *Transactions of the Philological Society*, 1880, 117–55.

Nevalainen, Terttu and Helena Raumolin-Brunberg, *Historical Sociolinguistics: Language Change in Tudor and Stewart England* (London: Longman, 2003).

Nevins, Allan and Frank Ernest Hill, *Ford: The Times, the Man, the Company*, 3 vols (New York: Scribner, 1954–63).

Newmeyer, Frederick J., *Possible and Probable Languages: A Generative Perspective on Linguistic Typology* (Oxford: Oxford University Press, 2005).

Nicholas, Siân, *The Echo of War: Home Front Propaganda and the Wartime BBC, 1939–1945* (Manchester: Manchester University Press, 1996).

Norton, David, *A History of the English Bible as Literature* (Cambridge: Cambridge University Press, 2000).

Novick, Peter, *That Noble Dream: The 'Objectivity Question' and the American Historical Profession* (Cambridge: Cambridge University Press, 1988).

O'Brien, Sara R., *English for Foreigners* (Boston, MA: Houghton Mifflin, 1909).

Of Arthour and Merlin, ed. O. D. Macrae-Gibson, EETS nos 268 and 269 (London: Oxford University Press, 1973, 1979).

Ogden, Charles K., *Basic English: A General Introduction with Rules and Grammar* (London: Kegan Paul, 1930).

Oglivie, Sarah, "Rethinking Burchfield and World Englishes," *International Journal of Lexicography*, 21 (2008), 23–59.

Oliphant, T. L. Kington, *The Sources of Standard English* (London: Macmillan, 1873).

Oliver, Harry, *March Hares and Monkeys' Uncles* (London: Metro Publishing, 2005).

Orwell, George, "Politics and the English Language," in John E. Joseph (ed.), *Language and Politics*, 4 vols (London: Routledge, 2010), iv.129–39.

Osselton, N. E., "The Early Development of the English Monolingual Dictionary (Seventeenth and Early Eighteenth Centuries)," in Cowie (ed.), *The Oxford History of English Lexicography*, i.131–54.

Ostler, Nicholas, *The Last Lingua Franca: English until the Return of Babel* (New York: Walker Publishing, 2010).

Ostler, Rosemarie, *Dewdroppers, Waldos, and Slackers: A Decade-by-decade Guide to the Vanishing Vocabulary of the Twentieth Century* (Oxford: Oxford University Press, 2003).

"Overseas Applicants," Harrow School, <http://www.harrowschool.org.uk/1721/admissions/how-to-apply-to-harrow/overseas-applicants/>.

Oxford English Dictionary, <http://www.oed.com/>.

Paris, Matthew, *Chronica Majora*, 7 vols, Rolls Series 57 (London: Longman, 1872–83).

Parry, Graham, *The Trophies of Time: English Antiquarians of the Seventeenth Century* (Oxford: Oxford University Press, 1995).

Payack, Paul J. J., *A Million Words and Counting: How Global English Is Rewriting the World* (New York: Citadel Press, 2008).

Pederson, Lee, "Dialects," in Algeo (ed.), *English in North America*, 253–90.

Pennycook, Alastair, *The Cultural Politics of English as an International Language* (London: Longman, 1994).

Perry, Theresa and Lisa Delpit (eds), *The Real Ebonics Debate: Power, Language, and the Education of African-American Children* (Boston, MA: Beacon Press, 1998).

Peyton, V. J., *The History of the English Language* (1771; rpt. Menston: Scolar Press, 1970).

Pfister, Joel, *Individuality Incorporated: Indians and the Multicultural Modern* (Durham, NC: Duke University Press, 2004).

Phillipson, Robert, *Linguistic Imperialism* (Oxford: Oxford University Press, 1992).

Phillipson, Robert, *English-Only Europe? Challenging Language Policy* (London: Routledge, 2003).

Pickering, John, *A Vocabulary, or Collection of Words and Phrases* (Boston, MA: Cummings and Hillard, 1816).

Pinker, Stephen, *The Stuff of Thought: Language as a Window into Human Nature* (New York: Viking, 2007).

Poe, Edgar Allan, *The Collected Tales and Poems of Edgar Allan Poe* (New York: Modern Library, 1992).

"Political Situation in the Union of South Africa: Memorandum by the Secretary of State for Dominion Affairs," War Cabinet, November 19, 1942, National Archives.

Poplack, Shana et al., "'Deformed in the Dialects': An Alternative History of Non-Standard English," in Watts and Trudgill (eds), *Alternative Histories of English*, 87–110.

"Popular Baby Names for 2012," babycenter, <http://www.babycenter.com/popularBabyNames.htm?year=2012>.

Porter, Samuel, "Letter," *Eadle Keatah Toh*, vol., no. 1, January 1880.

Pratt, Richard Henry, *Battlefield and Classroom: Four Decades with the American Indian, 1867–1904*, ed. Robert M. Utley (New Haven, CT: Yale University Press, 1964).

Price, Isaac, *The Direct Method of Teaching English to Foreigners* (New York: Frank D. Beattys and Co., 1913).

Priestley, Joseph, *Rudiments of English Grammar: Adapted to the Use of Schools* (London: R. Griffiths, 1761).

"Program for Second Annual Americanization Day," July 4, 1916, "Vertical File, Ford English School," Benson Ford Research Center.

"Pronunciation Workshop," <http://pronunciationworkshop.com>.

Prucha, Francis Paul (ed.), *Americanizing the American Indians: Writings by the 'Friends of the Indian', 1880–1900* (Cambridge, MA: Harvard University Press, 1973).

Puttenham, George, *The Arte of English Poesie* (1589; rpt. Menston: Scolar Press, 1968).

Quinion, Michael, *Gallimaufry: A Hodgepodge of our Vanishing Vocabulary* (Oxford: Oxford University Press, 2006).

Quinn, David B. (ed.), *The Voyages and Colonising Enterprises of Sir Humphrey Gilbert*, Hakluyt Society 83, 84 (London: Hakluyt Society, 1940).

Quinn, David B. (ed.), *The Roanoke Voyages, 1584–1590*, Hakluyt Society 104, 105 (London: Hakluyt Society, 1955).

Quinn, David B. with the assistance of Alison M. Quinn and Susan Hillier (eds), *New American World: A Documentary History of North America to 1612*, 5 vols (New York: Arno Press, 1979).

Quirk, Randolph, "Language Variety: Nature and Art," in R. B. Noss (ed.), *Varieties of English in Southeast Asia* (Singapore: Singapore University Press, 1983), 3–19.

Quirk, Randolph, "Language Varieties and Standard Language," *English Today: The International Review of the English Language*, 21 (1990), 3–10.

Quirk, Randolph et al., *Comprehensive Grammar of the English Language* (London: Routledge, 1985).

Rastell, John. *Exposiciones terminorum legum Anglorum* (London: Rastell, 1523).

Ravitch, Diane, *The Language Police: How Pressure Groups Restrict What Students Learn* (New York: Alfred A. Knopf, 2003).

Read, Allen Walker, "Milestones in the Branching of British and American English," in *Milestones in the History of English in America*, ed. Richard W. Bailey, 3–21.

Read, Allen Walker, "British Recognition of American Speech in the Eighteenth Century," in *Milestones in the History of English in America*, ed. Richard W. Bailey, 37–54.

Read, Allen Walker, *Milestones in the History of English in America*, ed. Richard W. Bailey (Durham, NC: Duke University Press, 2002).

Read, David, *New World, Known World: Shaping Knowledge in Early Anglo-American Writing* (Columbia, MO: University of Missouri Press, 2005).

Reece, William J., *The Origins of the American High School* (New Haven, CT: Yale University Press, 1995).

"Report of Committee on Basic English," The War Cabinet, December 6, 1943, National Archives.

"Resolution on the Students' Rights to Their Own Language," National Council of the Teachers of Education, <http://www.ncte.org/positions/statements/righttoownlanguage>.

Reyhner, Jon and Jeanne Eder, *American Indian Education: A History* (Norman, OK: University of Oklahoma Press, 2004).

Reynolds, David, *In Command of History: Churchill Fighting and Writing the Second World War* (London: Allen Lane, 2004).

Reynolds, David et al. (eds), *Allies at War: The Soviet, British, and American Experience, 1939–1945* (New York: St Martin's, 1994).

Richards, I. A., *Basic English and Its Uses* (London: Kegan Paul, 1943).

Richards, Jeffrey, *Imperialism and Music, 1876–1953* (Manchester: Manchester University Press, 2001).

Richler, Howard, *A Bawdy Language: How a Second-Rate Language Slept Its Way to the Top* (Toronto: Stoddart, 1999).

Ricks, Christopher, *Essays in Appreciation* (Oxford: Clarendon Press, 1996).

Riney, Scott, *The Rapid City Indian School, 1898–1933* (Norman, OK: University of Oklahoma Press, 1999).

Roberts, Peter, *English for Coming Americans: A Rational System for Teaching English to Foreigners* (New York: YMCA, 1909).

Roberts, Peter, *The New Immigration: A Study of the Industrial and Social Life of Southeastern Europeans in America* (New York: Macmillan, 1912).

Roberts, Peter, "The Y.M.C.A. Teaching Foreign-Speaking Men," *The Immigrants in America Review*, 1 (1915), 18–23.

Roberts, Sam, "Unlearning to Tawk Like a New Yorker," *New York Times*, November 21, 2010, A29.

Robertson, George, *The Discovery of Tahiti*, ed. Hugh Carrington (1948; rpt. Nendlen: Kraus, 1967).

Robinson, William H., "Indian Education at Hampton Institute," in Schall (ed.), *Stony the Road*, 1–33.

Roosevelt, Franrklin D., "Remarks to the Advertising War Council Conference," March 8, 1944, The American Presidency Project, <http://www.presidency.ucsb.edu/ws/index.php?pid=16498&st=&st1=#axzz1iceN5cWo>.

Rose, Sonya O., *Which People's War? National Identity and Citizenship in Britain, 1939–1945* (Oxford: Oxford University Press, 2003).

Ross, Alan S. C. and A. W. Moverley, *The Pitcairnese Language* (London: Andre Deutsch, 1964).

"Salmon Kahn's Surgery in US Successful," *The Times of India*, September 1, 2011, <http://articles.timesofindia.indiatimes.com/2011-09-01/news-interviews/29953417_1_trigeminal-neuralgia-salman-khan-surgery>.

Salmon, Vivian, "Thomas Harriot (1560–1621) and the English Origins of Algonkian Linguistics," *Historiographia Linguistica*, 19 (1992), 25–56.

Salmond, Anne, *Aphrodite's Island: The European Discovery of Tahiti* (Berkeley, CA: University of California Press, 2010).

Sayre, Gordon, *Les sauvages américains: Representations of Native Americans in French and English Colonial Literature* (Chapel Hill, NC: University of North Carolina Press, 1997).

Schall, Keith L. (ed.), *Stony the Road: Chapters in the History of Hampton Institute* (Charlottesville, VA: University Press of Virginia, 1977).

Schildkraut, Deborah J., *Press 'One' for English: Language Policy, Public Opinion, and American Identity* (Princeton, NJ: Princeton University Press, 2005).

Schmid, Hans-Jörg, "New Words in the Mind: Concept-Formation and Entrenchment of Neologisms," *Anglia*, 126 (2008), 1–36.

Schneider, Edgar W., "English in North America," in Kachru et al. (eds), *The Handbook of World Englishes*, 58–73.

Schneider, Edgar W., *Postcolonial English: Varieties around the World* (Cambridge: Cambridge University Press, 2007).

Schütz, Albert J., *The Voices of Eden: A History of Hawaiian Language Studies* (Honolulu, HI: University of Hawaii Press, 1994).

Searle, John R., *Making the Social World: The Structure of Human Civilization* (Oxford: Oxford University Press, 2010).

Seyer, Samuel (ed.), *Memoirs Historical and Topographical of Bristol and It's [sic] Neighbourhood*, 2 vols (Bristol: John Matthew Gutch, 1821, 1823).

Sheridan, Thomas A., *Course of Lectures on Elocution* (1762; rpt. Menston: Scolar Press, 1968).

Shoemaker, Nancy, *American Indian Population Recovery in the Twentieth Century* (Albuquerque, NM: University of New Mexico Press, 1999).

Siegel, Jeff, *The Emergence of Pidgin and Creole Languages* (Oxford: Oxford University Press, 2008).

Siegel, Paul, Elizabeth Martin, and Rosalind Bruno, "Language Use and Linguistic Isolation: Historical Data and Methodological Issues," US Census Bureau, February 12, 2001, <http://www.census.gov/hhes/socdemo/language/data/census/li-final.pdf>.

Simonson, Douglas et al., *Pidgin to da Max* (Honolulu, HI: BessPress, 2005).

Simpson, David, *The Politics of American English, 1776–1850* (New York: Oxford University Press, 1986).

Skeat, W. W., "Report upon 'Ghost-Words,' or Words which Have No Real Existence," *Transactions of the Philological Society*, 2 (1885–7), 350–74.

Skene, John, *De Verborum significatione: The Exposition of the Termes and Difficill [sic] Words, Conteined in the Foure Buikes of Regiam Majestatem* (Edinburgh: Robert Waldegrave, 1597).

Sledd, James and Wilma R. Ebbitt (eds), *Dictionaries and THAT Dictionary: A Casebook on the Aims of Lexicographers and the Targets of Reviewers* (Chicago, IL: Scott, Foresman, 1962).

Smith, Thomas, *De recta & emendata linguæ Anglicæ scriptione, dialogus* (Paris: Robert Stephan, 1568).

Smitherman, Geneva, *Word from the Mother: Language and African Americans* (New York: Routledge, 2006).

Smyth, Rosaleen, "Britain's African Colonies and British Propaganda during the Second World War," *Journal of Imperial and Commonwealth History*, 14 (1985), 65–82.

Soames, Mary (ed.), *Speaking for Themselves: The Personal Letters of Winston and Clementine Churchill* (New York: Doubleday, 1998).

Spack, Ruth, *America's Second Tongue: American Indian Education and the Ownership of English, 1860–1900* (Lincoln, NE: University of Nebraska Press, 2002).

"Spelling Words," PI 3-6 through PI 4-6-12, Box 8, Cumberland County Historical Society.

Spenser, Edmund, *A View of the Present State of Ireland*, ed. W. L. Renwick (Oxford: Clarendon Press, 1970).

Sprat, Thomas, *The History of the Royal Society of London, for the Improving of Natural Knowledge* (1667; rpt. London: Samuel Chapman, 1722).

Spring, Joel H., *American Education: An Introduction to Social and Political Aspects*, 3rd edn (New York: Longman, 1985).

Spring, Joel H., *The American School, 1642–2000*, 5th edn (Boston, MA: McGraw-Hill, 2001).

Standing Bear, Luther, *My People the Sioux*, ed. E. A. Brininstool (1928; rpt. Lincoln, NE: University of Nebraska Press, 1975).

Starnes, DeWitt T. and Gertrude E. Noyes, *The English Dictionary from Cawdrey to Johnson, 1604–1755* (Chapel Hill, NC: University of North Carolina Press, 1946).

Stenton, Michael, *Radio London and Resistance in Occupied Europe: British Political Warfare 1939–1943* (Oxford: Oxford University Press, 2000).

Stewart, C. S., *Journal of a Residence in the Sandwich Islands during the Years 1823, 1824, and 1825*, 3rd edn (London, H. Fisher, 1830).

Stockwell, Robert and Donka Minkova, *English Words: History and Structure* (Cambridge: Cambridge University Press, 2001).

Strachey, William, *The Historie of Travaile into Virginia Britania*, ed. Louis B. Wright and Virginia Freund, Hakluyt Society 103 (London: Hakluyt Society, 1953).

Strachey, William, *For the Colony in Virginea Britannia: Lawes Divine, Morall and Martiall*, ed. David H. Flaherty (Charlottesville, VA: University Press of Virginia, 1969).

Stubbs, William (ed.), *Select Charters and Other Illustrations of English Constitutional History from the Earliest Times to the Reign of Edward the First*, 9th edn, ed. H. W. C. Davis (Oxford: Clarendon Press, 1913).

"Study of the Organization of the European Theater of Operations," Report 2, The General Board, United States Forces, European Theater (1945), U. S. Army Heritage & Education Center.

Summerfield, Penny, "Patriotism and Empire: Music-Hall Entertainment, 1870–1914," in *Imperialism and Popular Culture*, ed. John M. MacKenzie (Manchester: Manchester University Press, 1986), 17–48.

Sweet, Henry, *A Handbook of Phonetics* (Oxford: Clarendon Press, 1877).

Sweet, Henry, *A Short Historical English Grammar* (Oxford: Clarendon Press, 1892).

Synopsis of Course of Study and Directions (Carlisle, PA: United States Indian School, n.d.).

Taylor, Frederick, *Shop Management* (New York: Harper, 1911).

Taylor, Frederick, *The Principles of Scientific Management* (New York: Harper, 1911).

"Testimonials," acc. 1098, Profit-Sharing Plan Testimonials, Benson Ford Research Center.

"The Elementary and Secondary Education Act," <http://www2.ed.gov/policy/elsec/leg/esea02/index.html>.

"The Ford 'American Club'," *Ford Times*, June 1916, 524.

"The Making of Americans," *Ford Times*, November 1916, 151–2.

"The Varieties of English Speech," *The Quarterly Review*, 207 (1907), 86–109.

Thomas, Nicholas and Richard Eves (eds), *Bad Colonists: The South Seas Letters of Vernon Lee Walker & Louis Becke* (Durham, NC: Duke University Press, 1999).

Thompson, Andrew S., "The Language of Imperialism and the Meanings of Empire: Imperial Discourse in British Politics, 1895–1914," *The Journal of British Studies*, 36 (1997): 147–77.

"Three Youths Arrested for Loansharking Activities," *Straits Times* (Singapore), September 1, 2011, <http://www.straitstimes.com/BreakingNews/Singapore/Story/STIStory_708349.html>.

Tieken-Boone van Ostade, Ingrid, *The Bishop's Grammar: Robert Lowth and the Rise of Prescriptivism in English* (Oxford: Oxford University Press, 2011).

Titlestad, Peter, "English, the Constitution and South Africa's Language Future," in de Klerk (ed.), *Focus on South Africa*, 163–73.

Toller, T. N., *Outlines of the History of the English Language* (London: Macmillan, 1900).

Tooke, John Horne, *Epea pteroenta. Or, the diversions of Purley*, 2nd edn, 2 vols (London: J. Johnson's, 1798–1805).

Toon, Thomas E., "The Social and Political Contexts of Language Change in Anglo-Saxon England," in Machan and Scott (eds), *English in Its Social Contexts*, 28–46.

Townend, Matthew, *Language and History in Viking Age England: Linguistic Relations between Speakers of Old Norse and Old English* (Turnhout: Brepols, 2002).

Toye, Richard, *Churchill's Empire: The World that Made Him and the World He Made* (London: Macmillan, 2010).

Trench, Richard Chenevix, "On Some Deficiencies in Our English Dictionaries," *Transactions of the Philological Society* (1857), 1–70.

Trench, Richard Chenevix, *English Past and Present*, 13th edn (London: Macmillan, 1886).

Trennert, Jr., Robert A., *The Phoenix Indian School: Forced Assimilation in Arizona, 1891–1935* (Norman, OK: University of Oklahoma Press, 1988).

"True Friendship," *The Arrow*, September 8, 1904, vol. 1, no. 3, 1.

Truss, Lynne, *Eats, Shoots & Leaves: The Zero Tolerance Approach to Punctuation* (New York: Gotham, 2004).

Tsait-kope-Ta, Paul C., "My Dear Friend," *Eadle Keahtah Toh*, vol. 1, no. 2, April 1880.

Turner, George, *Nineteen Years in Polynesia: Missionary Life, Travels, and Researches in the Islands of the Pacific* (London: John Snow, 1861).

Twain, Mark, *Adventures of Huckleberry Finn*, ed. Susan K. Harris (Boston, MA: Houghton Mifflin, 2000).

Tyng, Charles, *Before the Wind: The Memoir of an American Sea Captain, 1808–1833*, ed. Susan Fels (New York: Viking, 1999).

Unger, Harlow Giles, *Noah Webster: The Life and Times of an American Patriot* (New York: John Wiley, 1998).

"U.S. Citizenship and Immigration Services," <http://www.uscis.gov/portal/site/uscis>.

Use of Personnel Other Than U.S. Military, Report 11, Office of the Theater Chief Quartermaster (November 1, 1945), U.S. Army Heritage & Education Center.

Usk, Thomas, *Testament of Love*, in W. W. Skeat (ed.), *Complete Works of Geoffrey Chaucer*, vii, *Chaucerian and Other Pieces* (Oxford: Oxford University Press, 1897).

Verstegan, Richard, *A Restitution of Decayed Intelligence* (1605; rpt. Ilkley: Scolar Press, 1976).

Vine, Angus, *In Defiance of Time: Antiquarian Writing in Early Modern England* (Oxford: Oxford University Press, 2010).

Von Aldenbruck, E. Wayne et al., *Servicemen's Language Guide: 8 Foreign Languages Made Easy* (Binghamton, NY: Literary Guide, 1944).

Vorlat, Emma, *The Development of English Grammatical Theory, 1586–1737: With Special Reference to the Theory of Parts of Speech* (Leuven: University Press, 1975).

Vučković, Myriam, *Voices from Haskell: Indian Students between Two Worlds, 1884–1928* (Lawrence, KS: University of Kansas Press, 2008).

Walker, Ranginui, *Ka Whawhai Tonu Matou: Struggle without End* (Auckland: Penguin, 1990).

Wallis, John, *Grammatica Linguæ Anglicanæ* (Oxford: Lichfield, 1653).

Wa Thiong'o, Ngũgĩ, *Decolonising the Mind: The Politics of Language in African Literature* (London: James Currey, 1986).

Watts, Richard, *Language Myths and the History of English* (Oxford: Oxford University Press, 2011).

Watts, Richard and Peter Trudgill (eds), *Alternative Histories of English* (London: Routledge, 2002).

Webster, Noah, *Dissertations on the English Language* (1789; rpt. Menston: Scolar Press, 1967).

Webster, Noah, *An American Dictionary of the English Language*, 2 vols (New York: S. Converse, 1828).

Webster, Noah, *The American Spelling Book* (1831; rpt. New York: Columbia University Press, 1962).

Webster, Wendy, *Englishness and Empire, 1939–1965* (Oxford: Oxford University Press, 2005).

Webster's Ninth New Collegiate Dictionary (Springfield, MA: Merriam-Webster, 1988).

Welsford, Henry, *On the Origins and Ramifications of the English Language* (London: Longman, 1845).

Wheeler, Charles N., "Fight to Disarm His Life's Work, Henry Ford Vows," *Chicago Tribune*, May 25, 1916, 10.

Whitman, Walt, *Complete Poetry and Collected Prose* (New York: Viking, 1982).

Wierzbicka, Anna, *Experience, Evidence, and Sense: The Hidden Cultural Legacy of English* (Oxford: Oxford University Press, 2010).

Wiles, A. G. D. et al., with a Foreword by Charles P. Summerall, *English for the Armed Forces: Writing, Speaking, Reading*, 2nd edn (New York: Harper, 1943).

Williams, John, *A Narrative of Missionary Enterprises in the South Sea Islands* (London: John Snow, 1837).

Williams, Joseph M. "'O! When Degree is Shak'd': Sixteenth-Century Anticipations of Some Modern Attitudes toward Usage," in Machan and Scott (eds), *English in Its Social Contexts*, 69–101.

Williams, Roger, *A Key into the Language of America* (1643; rpt. Bedford, MA: Applewood Books, 1997).

Williamson Philip, "The Doctrinal Politics of Stanley Baldwin," in Michael Bentley (ed.), *Public and Private Doctrine: Essays in British History Presented to Maurice Cowling* (Cambridge: Cambridge University Press, 1993), 181–208.

Willinsky, John, *Empire of Words: The Reign of the OED* (Princeton, NJ: Princeton University Press, 1994).

Wilson, Thomas, *The Arte of Rhetorique, for the Vse of Al Suche as are Studious of Eloquence* (London: Richard Grafton, 1553).

Winslow, Edward, *Good Newes from New-England* (London: I. D., 1624).

Winthrop, John, *The Journal of John Winthrop, 1630–1649*, ed. Richard S. Dunn and Laetitia Yeandle (Cambridge, MA: Belknap, 1996).

Wist, Benjamin O., *A Century of Public Education in Hawaii* (Honolulu, HI: Hawaii Educational Review, 1940).

Witmer, Linda F., *The Indian Industrial School: Carlisle, Pennsylvania, 1879–1918* (Carlisle, PA: Cumberland County Historical Society, 1993).

Wogan-Browne, Jocelyn et al. (eds), *The Idea of the Vernacular: An Anthology of Middle English Literary Theory, 1280–1520* (University Park, PA: The Pennsylvania State University Press, 1999).

Wood, William, *New Englands Prospect* (London: Thomas Cotes, 1634).

Woodbine, George E., "The Language of English Law," *Speculum*, 18 (1943), 395–436.

Wright, Joseph (ed.), *The English Dialect Dictionary*, 6 vols (London: H. Frowde, 1898–1905).

Wright, Joseph, *The English Dialect Grammar* (Oxford: Oxford University Press, 1905).

Wright, Laura, "Macaronic Writing in a London Archive, 1380–1480," in Matti Rissanen et al. (eds), *History of Englishes: New Methods and Interpretations in Historical Linguistics* (Berlin: Mouton de Gruyter, 1992), 762–70.

Wright, Laura, "Medieval Mixed-Language Business Discourse and the Rise of Standard English," in Janne Skaffari et al. (ed.), *Opening Windows on Texts and Discourses of the Past* (Amsterdam: John Benjamins, 2005), 381–99.

Wyld, H. C., *A History of Modern Colloquial English*, 3rd edn (Oxford: Blackwell, 1936).

Young, Robert J. C., *The Idea of English Ethnicity* (Malden, MA: Blackwell, 2008).

Zandvoort, R. W., *Wartime English: Materials for a Linguistic History of World War II* (Groningen: J. B. Wolters, 1957).

Zernike, Kate, "Veterans Fight to Reclaim the Name 'Swift Boat,'" *New York Times*, June 30, 2008, A1, A15.

Zipf, G. K., "The Meaning-Frequency Relationship of Words," *Journal of General Psychology*, 33 (1945), 251–56.

Index